OVERPROMISING AND UNDERPERFORMING?

Understanding and Evaluating New Intergovernmental Accountability Regimes

Public reporting has been used experimentally in federal-provincial relations since the mid-1990s as an accountability mechanism to promote policy effectiveness, intergovernmental cooperation, and democratic legitimacy. Our understanding of how well it is working, however, remains limited to very specific policy sectors – even though this information is essential to policymakers in Canada and beyond. *Overpromising and Underperforming?* offers a deeper analysis of the use of new accountability mechanisms, paying particular attention to areas in which federal spending power is used.

This is the first volume to specifically analyse the accountability features of Canadian intergovernmental agreements and to do so systematically across policy sectors. Drawing on the experiences of other federal systems and multilevel governance structures, the contributors investigate how public reporting has been used in various policy fields and the impact it has had on policymaking and intergovernmental relations.

PETER GRAEFE is an associate professor in the Department of Political Science at McMaster University.

JULIE M. SIMMONS is an assistant professor in the Department of Political Science at the University of Guelph.

LINDA A. WHITE is an associate professor in the Department of Political Science and the School of Public Policy and Governance at the University of Toronto.

IPAC
The Institute of
Public Administration of Canada

IAPC
L'Institut d'administration
publique du Canada

**The Institute of Public Administration of Canada Series
in Public Management and Governance**

Editor: Patrice Dutil

This series is sponsored by the Institute of Public Administration of Canada as part of its commitment to encourage research on issues in Canadian public administration, public sector management, and public policy. It also seeks to foster wider knowledge and understanding among practitioners, academics, and the general public.

For a list of books published in the series, see page 341.

Overpromising and Underperforming?

Understanding and Evaluating New Intergovernmental Accountability Regimes

EDITED BY PETER GRAEFE,
JULIE M. SIMMONS,
AND LINDA A. WHITE

IPAC
The Institute of
Public Administration of Canada

IAPC
L'Institut d'administration
publique du Canada

UNIVERSITY OF TORONTO PRESS
Toronto Buffalo London

© University of Toronto Press 2013
Toronto Buffalo London
www.utppublishing.com
Printed in Canada

ISBN 978-1-4426-4521-9 (cloth)
ISBN 978-1-4426-1334-8 (paper)

Printed on acid-free, 100% post-consumer recycled paper with vegetable-based inks.

Library and Archives Canada Cataloguing in Publication

Overpromising and underperforming? : understanding and evaluating
new intergovernmental accountability regimes / edited by Peter Graefe,
Julie M. Simmons, and Linda A. White.

(IPAC (Institute of Public Administration of Canada series in public
management and governance))
Includes bibliographical references and index.
ISBN 978-1-4426-4521-9 (bound). – ISBN 978-1-4426-1334-8 (pbk.)

1. Government accountability – Canada. 2. Intergovernmental cooperation – Canada
– Evaluation. 3. Administrative agencies – Canada – Evaluation. I. Graefe, Peter
II. Simmons, Julie M., 1974– III. White, Linda A. (Linda Ann), 1967– IV. Series:
Institute of Public Administration of Canada series in public management and
governance

JL65.O94 2013   352.3'50971   C2012-905075-X

This book has been published with the help of a grant from the Canadian Federation
for the Humanities and Social Sciences, through the Awards to Scholarly Publications
Program, using funds provided by the Social Sciences and Humanities Research
Council of Canada.

University of Toronto Press acknowledges the financial assistance to its publishing
program of the Canada Council for the Arts and the Ontario Arts Council.

University of Toronto Press acknowledges the financial support of the Government of
Canada through the Canada Book Fund for its publishing activities.

Contents

Part Four: Conclusion

Foreword

We live in the age of accountability: Never before have demands for detailed reports of government and business policy and actions been so often articulated. It must be recognized that states in most parts of the world have made giant strides over the past few decades in revealing what they are doing and how they are spending money. Those demands have led, in this country, to easily accessed records of who prime ministers, premiers and mayors, and most senior executives meet so that lobbyists can be tracked. Their expense accounts for travel and hospitality are made easily accessible on a quarterly basis. The freedom of information acts are invoked every day to access details on internal communications. Parliament has equipped itself with a wide variety of agents who inspect myriad aspects of the work of government, ranging from its financial accounts to how well it protects the individual privacy of citizens. Governments have adopted new processes to allow employees to 'blow the whistle' and report wrongdoing without fearing that this gesture will impair their careers, but that gesture has not been very effective. The media, hungry for revelations about errors in government, continue to be the addresses for plain brown envelopes filled with convincing evidence of malfeasance. The Internet, no less, has become a forum to reveal secret documents. Transparency International has created an index on how accountable governments are, and as I write this, Canada ranks tenth in the world. This is a good result, but not a great one. Governments still appear opaque in some areas. In sum, it is impossible not to recognize that, either through its actions or through those of others, the state in Canada is more accountable than ever.

And yet students of government can still claim that governments in this country are not kept sufficiently accountable for their actions. Their cry is a modern echo of those who protested the Quebec Act of 1774, or of those who complained two hundred years ago that the government structures created in 1791 were not compatible with emerging ideas of democracy and that only governments that were 'responsible,' or accountable, could be legitimate. They have a kinship with the fathers of confederation and with every brand of reformist that has helped shape the modern state.

Accountability is indeed the holy grail of democratic government, and it can never be too perfect. Canada has gone further in experimenting with methods and institutions that should help governments account to each other and to their citizens on how monies transferred from one order to the other are actually spent. This book does pioneer work in exploring the nature of these mechanisms and in exploring the degrees to which these new instruments of accountability actually work.

What makes this book so interesting for me is that it stands at the intersections of the processes that make Canadian governance complex. It tracks the problems of accountability, particularly the ability of governments to compel other jurisdictions to provide the 'full story' of how they spent the funds entrusted to them. The sovereignty of provinces in areas of exclusive jurisdiction has made it practically impossible for the federal government to coerce the subnational order to provide a full accounting. Federalism, indeed, is critical to this Gordian knot, and this book sheds a new light on the practices that have been adopted, abandoned, and piloted to make governments more accountable. The story of the New Public Management is also perceived in these stories: the notion that government works best by pushing administration 'down and out,' or to the levels closest to the population, decentralized as it may be. The final frontier is public reporting: the notion that governments can be held accountable by means of the new Internet technologies now made available to Canadians.

There is bold thinking, and even bolder dreaming, in the idea that information made available to the public will compel governments to spend money where it was committed. It assumes a great deal in the idea that Canadians will find benefit in this new data 'dashboard.' That quasi Athenian optimism may one day be reached, but more realistically, it launches a challenge to those who have the time, expertise, and ability to respond to these reports and thus keep governments accountable on how they use scarce resources. Among 'those,' I join the editors and contributors of this fine book in the hope that the person reading these words will also dedicate time and effort to keeping governments accountable.

Patrice Dutil
Ryerson University
Editor, IPAC Series in Public Management
and Governance
Labour Day, 2012

Acknowledgments

The idea for this project arose – as many good ideas do – from a panel at the Canadian Political Science Association annual meeting in Vancouver in June 2008. Several of the contributors to this volume presented papers on the success or failure of intergovernmental accountability agreements in specific policy areas. It seemed worthwhile to bring scholars working on these issues together to discuss them more expansively and to see whether the experience with public reporting in particular was similar across all policy areas where it was being utilized. Thanks to the generous support of the Social Sciences and Humanities Research Council of Canada (SSHRC) Workshop Grant program, and the Institute of Public Administration of Canada's Study Team program, we assembled a fabulous group of scholars and practitioners to present and discuss their work at the School of Public Policy and Governance at the University of Toronto. This included the contributors whose work appear in this volume, as well as Matthew Mendelsohn, director of the Mowat Centre for Policy Innovation, School of Public Policy and Governance, University of Toronto; and Reto Steiner, an assistant professor at the Center of Competence for Public Management, University of Bern, and member of the Upper House of the Swiss Parliament for the canton of Bern.

We would like to extend our thanks especially to Leslie Seidle (senior research associate, Institute of Research on Public Policy; senior policy advisor, Forum of Federations), Josée Bergeron (advisor, Secretariat on Canadian Intergovernmental Affairs, Government of Quebec), Mel Cappe (president, Institute for Research on Public Policy, and professor, School of Public Policy and Governance, University of Toronto), Caryl Arundel (public policy / management consultant and member, Board of Directors, Canadian Urban Institute), Thomas Hueglin (professor,

Political Science, Wilfrid Laurier University), and Richard Simeon (professor, Department of Political Science, University of Toronto) who acted as discussants and provided excellent comments and feedback to the workshop participants.

We also want to thank Petra Jory, the events planner extraordinaire at the School of Public Policy and Governance, and MPP students Cristina Di Cerbo and Daniel Oettl, who helped organize and run the SSHRC workshop. We especially thank our research assistant, Pratima Arapakota, who did a marvellous job in copy editing and assembling the draft manuscript. Pratima, Cristina, and Daniel represent the next generation of public policy practitioners and it is to that community, as well as the scholarly community, that we dedicate this volume.

Daniel Quinlan, the acquisitions editor for Political Science and Law at the University of Toronto Press, was an enthusiastic and unflagging supporter of this project from the beginning, and he expertly assisted us in transforming the workshop papers into an edited book. We would also like to thank Wendy Feldman, the director of research at IPAC, and the many forums IPAC provides to discuss work within the broader policy community, including the IPAC national conference. It is our hope that practitioners and policy scholars will find this work useful.

We deeply appreciate the support and assistance of the staff in the Political Science Departments at McMaster University, University of Guelph, and the University of Toronto through all phases of this project. This manuscript is being published with the financial assistance of the Awards to Scholarly Publications Program of the Canadian Federation for the Humanities and Social Sciences and the IPAC Study Grant, without which volumes on Canada, and Canadian public policy and public administration, would struggle.

We also want to thank the three anonymous reviewers of the manuscript for their helpful and detailed comments for improving the volume, as well as for the inspirational humour in the comment that 'to the extent a book about Canadian federalism can be something to look forward to reading, this may be that book.'

Peter Graefe
Julie M. Simmons
Linda A. White

Glossary of Acronyms

AG	auditor general
AMO	Association of Municipalities Ontario
ATA	Alberta Teachers' Association
AYP	adequate yearly progress
BCP	Building Canada Plan
CAP	Canada Assistance Plan
CCAAC	Child Care Advocacy Association of Canada
CCAF-FCVI	Canadian Comprehensive Auditing Foundation / La Fondation canadienne pour la vérification intégrée
CCTB	Canada Child Tax Benefit
CEA	Canadian Education Association
CESC	Canadian Education Statistics Council
CETA	Comprehensive Economic and Trade Agreement
CHA	Canada Health Act
CHST	Canada Health and Social Transfer
CIHI	Canadian Institute for Health Information
CMEC	Council of Ministers of Education, Canada
CST	Canada Social Transfer
CTB	Child Tax Benefit
CUPE	Canadian Union of Public Employees
DEA	Dominion Education Association
DFAIT	Department of Foreign Affairs and International Trade
DG	Directorate General
EAPD	Employability Agreement for Persons with Disabilities
ECD	early childhood development
ECDA	Early Childhood Development Agreement
ECDLC	Early Childhood Development, Learning & Care

EES	European Employment Strategy
EI	Employment Insurance
ELCC	Early Learning and Child Care
EMCO	Employment Committee
ESEA	Elementary and Secondary Education Act
EU	European Union
FCM	Federation of Canadian Municipalities
FMC	First Ministers' Conference
FPT	Federal-Provincial-Territorial
GATT	General Agreement on Tariffs and Trade
GDP	gross domestic product
GST	Goods and Services Tax
HELP	Human Early Learning Partnership
HRDC	Human Resources Development Canada
HRSDC	Human Resources and Skills Development Canada
IASA	Improving America's Schools Act
IMF	International Monetary Fund
IO	international organizations
LMA	Labour Market Agreement
LMAPD	Labour Market Agreement for Persons with Disabilities
LMDA	Labour Market Development Agreement
MAMROT	Ministry of Municipal Affairs, Regions and Land Occupancy
MTC	Making the Connections project
NA	National Assembly
NAFTA	North American Free Trade Agreement
NAP	National Action Plan(s)
NCB	National Child Benefit
NCLB	No Child Left Behind Act
NDP	New Democratic Party
NPM	New Public Management
OAG	Office of the Auditor General
OECD	Organization for Economic Cooperation and Development
OMC	Open Method of Coordination
OMN	Omnibus Agreement
PCAP	Pan-Canadian Assessment Program
PIRC	Performance Indicator Reporting Committee
PISA	Programme for International Student Assessment
PSAB	Public Sector Accounting Board

PT	provincial-territorial
QUAD	quality, universal, affordable, developmental
SAIP	Student Achievement Indicators Program
SOFIL	Société de financement des infrastructures locales du Québec
SUFA	Social Union Framework Agreement
TBS	Treasury Board Secretariat
TIOW	Targeted Initiative for Older Worker
UNESCO	United Nations Educational, Scientific and Cultural Organization
VRDP	Vocational Rehabilitation of Disabled Persons
WIS	Working Income Supplement
WTO	World Trade Organization

List of Tables

PART ONE

Establishing Benchmarks

1 Introduction: Accountability and Governance

PETER GRAEFE, JULIE M. SIMMONS,
AND LINDA A. WHITE

The headline in the *Globe and Mail* could not have been more devastating: 'Funds for Medical Machines Buys Lawn Tractors' (Priest 2002). According to this and other newspaper reports, a portion of the New Brunswick government's $24.5 million share of monies that the federal government earmarked in the early 2000s for hospital diagnostic equipment was spent on a number of equipment purchases that fell outside of the 'medical equipment' category, such as lawnmowers and floor scrubbers. Although the New Brunswick government defended the hospital purchases as necessary for the operation of hospitals in the province, in the media stories that followed, many observers – including the head of the Commission on the Future of Health Care in Canada, Roy Romanow – stated categorically that provincial governments should account strictly for how they spend federal transfers for health care (Laghi 2002). And, in fact, the federal and provincial governments agreed in 2004 to more performance reporting on health-care spending (see Patrick Fafard's chapter 2 in this volume). But eight years later, the auditor general would publicly complain that the lack of monitoring of how provinces spent $25.4 billion in federal health transfers meant 'we don't know if we're getting good value for money,' leading the Canadian Medical Association president to demand that 'improving accountability should be a precondition for future cash transfers' (Picard 2010).

Much further from the media spotlight, and more recently, a citizens organization in Hamilton used the planning and reporting requirements of the federal Gas Tax Fund to point out that funds that were initially intended to support 'environmentally sustainable municipal infrastructure projects' had, in the case of Hamilton, largely been spent on roads. While the existence of public reports allowed citizens to question city priorities, the lack of clear, binding, and detailed federal program requirements led a local councillor to argue that the program had evolved into 'basically whatever you want' (Citizens at City Hall 2010). Where could citizens who supported the announced goals of the program turn for accountability? They could hold their elected officials to account in future elections, but was the fault mostly that of road-crazy local councillors, or of federal and provincial parliamentarians who had agreed that funds for environmental sustainability could be used for 'whatever you want'?

Public reporting as a means to hold provincial governments to account for federal transfer spending has become increasingly popular since the late 1990s, and commitments to public reporting have been made in a number of federal-provincial-territorial agreements covering a vast swath of policy areas. Yet, after over a decade of experimentation with this new form of accountability in Canadian federal-provincial relations, little sustained scholarly reflection on that experience has emerged. We do not understand how – and indeed if – these accountability mechanisms are working to promote policy effectiveness or whether they provide adequate benchmarks to ensure that tax dollars are spent in the most efficient manner. Similarly, how these accountability arrangements affect intergovernmental relations has not been assessed: do they make for more cooperative or conflict-ridden encounters? Finally, do these arrangements affect the public's involvement in and awareness of the policy process?

This edited volume fills this scholarly lacuna and contributes to a greater understanding of the use of accountability mechanisms within federal systems. These accountability questions are especially crucial to scholars of federalism. In federal systems, an important aspect of public administration involves the planning and delivery of policies across orders of government. When one order of government is funding a program and another is delivering it, or when decisions taken by one order of government affect the legal authority of another order, accountability concerns suggest the need to develop institutions and practices to ensure that governments coordinate their efforts, fulfil their substantive obligations, and account for their expenditures – or, in the absence of a will to coordinate, to disentangle their efforts. Scholars must also look beyond institutional mechanisms to consider the effects of accountability measures and processes on proximate issues, such as policymaking processes in general, decision-making transparency, and the public's right to know. Finally, all institutional mechanisms demand normative reflection, as they are bound to serve certain conceptions of the political good rather than others. Beyond their effectiveness in policymaking and beyond their legitimacy with stakeholders and the broader public, they privilege particular mixes of democracy and federalism. Therefore, there is a need to consider how the institutions and practices crafted to manage questions of administration relate to broader values.

It is from this vantage point that we seek to understand the public policy agreements since 1996. Following the 1995 budget and its significant cuts to federal cash transfers to provinces for health, education, and social services, the form of federal-provincial agreements changed. While some academic observers portrayed the 1995 budget as the end of 'social Canada,' by 1996–8 the federal government was concluding agreements with the provinces for social policy renewal initiatives in child benefits, labour market policy, and policies for persons with disabilities. Nevertheless, these new agreements differed from older ones in how they approached the issue of accountability. Whereas earlier policy agreements required direct provincial reporting to the federal government on the use of federal money and made the federal contribution conditional on fulfilling specified program commitments, the post-1995 agreements were more open-ended and less binding. They involved provinces in developing annual plans and annual reports to be distributed to the public, but the reporting relationship was explicitly not from one order of government to another.

The new accountability regime is therefore quite different from traditional hierarchical accountability arrangements and does not rely on government-to-government relationships so much as the government–citizen relationship and, by extension, the ability of citizens to hold governments to account at the ballot box. Having such a reporting relationship was important, given that, at the time, the extent to which provincial governments could or should be accountable to the federal government came under question. Over a decade later, however, there has been little sustained evaluation of this regime, either of how it has been implemented into policy agreements in different social policy sectors, or how it has worked in practice.

This lack of evaluation may stem in part from the 'high politics' focus of much work on Canadian federalism, and the interest in actors' performance (that is, 'whose ox got gored') in any given agreement (for example, did the provinces or the federal government get the upper hand in the 1999 Social Union Framework Agreement (SUFA) or the 2004 Health Accord?). But even where more policy-driven scholars have delved into the nitty-gritty of this new accountability regime as part of their study of specific issue areas, there has been little comparative analysis in Canada of how it is similar or different across issue areas or across time. For instance, while a preliminary survey of various social policy areas notes the emergence of this regime in all of them (Graefe 2006), it does not systematically disentangle generic features from the specific features of particular policy areas. Similarly, while studies of particular policies, such as Friendly and White's (2008) analysis of child care, demonstrate significant changes in the conduct and form of intergovernmental relations since the mid-1990s, they lack the comparative scope to determine whether those changes apply across policy areas in Canada. Instead, the scholarly literature in Canada addresses a number of disparate questions: How effective have the new reporting measures been in ensuring accountability (Anderson and Findlay 2007; Kershaw 2006)? Have the new reporting measures spurred learning and the sharing of best practices (Graefe and Levesque 2006; Saint-Martin 2004)? Have the new reporting measures allowed the federal government to shape provincial policy choices (Boismenu and Graefe 2004; Day and Brodsky 2007)? Is the new accountability regime consistent with normative principles of democratic accountability (B. Cameron 2007) or federalism (Boismenu 2006; Noël 2003)?

This volume seeks to bring together many of those who have been working in this area around a common set of questions and concerns. While the particular factors that led to this new form of accountability are unique to Canada, the need for intergovernmental cooperation and intergovernmental accountability are not unique. This volume's first objective, therefore, is to explore these questions through comparative reflection within Canada by leading scholars on accountability and governance across a number of policy areas, and through reflection by scholars of accountability regimes in other federal and multi-level political systems – the United States and the European Union. The chapters in this volume examine variation in the use of intergovernmental accountability mechanisms, drawing on the experiences across a number of policy sectors both within Canada and abroad. Contributors to this volume evaluate these accountability mechanisms using empirical and normative criteria such as effectiveness, intergovernmental cooperation, policy learning, and democratic legitimacy. A number of contributors also reflect on alternative accountability arrangements, such as benchmarking and the use of the Office of the Auditor General (OAG) and other accounting officers.

In mapping all the areas and perspectives together, the volume reveals the broader processes of constructing accountability regimes and clarifies which elements are common across the policy fields and jurisdictions and which ones remain idiosyncratic. It also addresses the question of whether there is a temporal dynamic. In other words, is there evidence that the forms of accountability and reporting are changing, and is there evidence that some of the initial differences between policy fields are narrowing as experience with the new regime favours the development of some generic approaches?

A second objective of this volume is to consider the proximate effects of this accountability regime at the federal-provincial interface along two policy-related dimensions. The new mechanisms arise out of federal-provincial negotiations, but they in turn shape the conduct of policymaking, and their impact here needs to be more fully elucidated, now that they have been in place for some time. Part of the promise of reporting as a form of accountability was that it might enable the sharing of information and best practices, and thus allow for enhanced policy-learning between jurisdictions (Saint Martin 2004). Another purported benefit was that reporting to the public would empower citizens to demand high-quality programs that delivered results (for a discussion, see Phillips 2003). After over a decade of experimenting with such mechanisms, this volume asks if there are lessons to be learned across policy areas on the ability of these new mechanisms to promote inter-provincial bureaucratic policy learning, or to empower citizens in policymaking. Have any lessons been learned to improve mechanisms of learning and participation? In other words, how have these agreements performed and how effective have they been?

Beyond trying to map these agreements and assess their proximate effects, the third objective of this volume is to encourage normative reflection about how this new regime lines up with principles of federalism and democracy. Examining the linkage of the new institutional mechanisms and their proximate effects with larger values and principles opens space for a dialogue about how these mechanisms could be reinforced to better realize certain values, or configured differently in order to satisfy a different set of principles.

While the scope of this volume is large, it does not encompass all policy sectors. Attention in this volume is placed particularly on government programs where the federal government transfers money to provincial governments to fund programs and services, in return for provincial commitments to report to the public on both how they disposed of the funds and with what results. The choice to look at these agreements means the volume analyses those areas of intergovernmental relations where the spending power looms large, including health care, child care, children's benefits, education, labour market training, and infrastructure funding, and not more regulatory areas such as the environment or the financial sector. Similarly, a volume of this size cannot engage in comparative analysis of the intergovernmental accountability mechanisms in place across all federal systems in the Organization for Economic Cooperation and Development (OECD).[1] Instead, we draw on two key intergovernmental accountability regimes – the federal No Child Left Behind educational provisions in the United States, and the Open Method of Coordination (OMC) mechanisms in the European Union (EU) – to explore whether lessons can be learned from those experiences. We comment further on the comparative lessons drawn in the concluding chapter in this volume.

The Concept of Accountability

Accountability – that is, the requirement that governments be answerable for their responsibilities and conduct – has assumed an important place in discussions of modern governance. Even well outside the corridors of politics, folk-punk troubadour Billy Bragg has suggested 'No power without accountability' as a mantra for re-democratizing political and economic decision-making. There are accountability relationships at myriad levels in government. Klassen and Wood in their chapter in this volume distinguish between administrative, political, and democratic moments in accountability relationships. Traditionally, accountability relationships are perceived between administrators in the permanent executive and their administrative superiors, their political 'masters,' and the public. Administrators and elected officials also have a duty to uphold the rule of law and professional norms and institutions. The political executive in turn needs to account to the legislature on its activities to implement initiatives. And, ultimately, citizens require the ability to hold their governments to account to ensure state activities are in accordance with societal demands and expectations.

Accountability continues to give rise to a voluminous literature in public administration, for several reasons. First, as public administration has embraced the contracting out of services or the development of arm's-length agencies, determining who is ultimately responsible for the use of public authority and funds (and problems in that use) is difficult. Second, as the size of government has grown, the traditional bargain of ministerial responsibility has broken down, or at least is being redefined. Scandals such as the one related to the federal government's sponsorship program have given rise to debates about whether accountability relationships need to be restructured in order to better reflect current realities (Commission of Inquiry 2006; Jarvis 2009; Savoie 2006).

Sperling (2009, 8) writes that accountability really comprises two aspects: answerability and enforcement: 'First, public officials are obliged to provide information about their actions, and to explain and justify publicly the decisions on which their actions are based.' Second, 'powerholders who have violated their public duties are subject to sanctions such as impeachment or elections ending their term in office.' Ebrahim and Weisband (2007, 5) thus argue that accountability comprises four core components:

- Transparency – collecting information and making it available and accessible for public scrutiny
- Answerability or Justification – providing clear reasoning for actions and decisions, including those not adopted, so that they may reasonably be questioned
- Compliance – monitoring and evaluation of procedures and outcomes, combined with transparency in reporting those findings
- Enforcement or Sanctions – imposing sanctions for shortfalls in compliance, justification, or transparency

Ebrahim and Weisband (2007, 5) go on to state, 'Because each of these components builds on the others (with transparency being necessary for compliance, and enforcement depending on all), accountability relies on the presence of all four. But for numerous observers, what underlies the power of accountability mechanisms is enforceability.' Control, however, needs to be balanced by another factor: legitimacy. In other words, without legitimacy, control is not possible. As Sperling (2009, 10) argues, 'Technically, it is only when both the principals and the agents acknowledge their relationship that accountability can be said to exist.' If a government does not ascribe to the logic of a principal-agent relationship, it will feel less pressure to be answerable to citizens or another level of government.

This classical understanding of accountability nevertheless misses more instrumental dimensions to accountability when applied to relationships between formally autonomous or independent actors, such as in federal systems. One way to think systematically about accountability in a federal system is to use the tools of rational choice institutionalism. Studies of federalism in Canada have tended to neglect incorporating game theoretic observations explicitly into their analyses, with some exceptions (e.g., Brander 1985; James 1999; Sproule-Jones 1993).[2] Certainly, federalism and constitutional scholars have been aware of the game theoretic dynamics at play and often work deductively on the basis of imputing preferences for governments and analysing how these preferences produce particular outcomes when filtered through institutional rules. We find it useful to incorporate these rational choice frameworks into our introductory discussion of accountability, because understanding these dynamics as instrumental and incentive-based may help practitioners design better accountability mechanisms – to move from competitive to cooperative games while retaining some modicum of accounting for actions.

As Ebrahim and Weisband (2007, 4) point out, the problem with accountability in a federal system is that it connotes at its core a *principal-agent relationship* that consists of a lead actor (or principal) who sets goals and then employs agents to accomplish them. As Brown (1983, 634) observes, 'Accountability requires a "locus of authority," a centre of definitive power and responsibility.' A federal system of government, however, provides for two loci of authority, 'and neither one is able to authoritatively coerce the other.'

When it comes to demanding accountability for the allocation of federal expenditures on pan-Canadian priorities, the federal government in Canada has little substantive jurisdiction over social policy outside of unemployment insurance and pensions. It has instead used its spending power to extract compliance from provincial governments in other social policy areas such as health care and social assistance. Typically, the federal government offers to pay a share of provincial expenditures on a given program, provided that the program is consistent with specific standards set by the federal government. That is, the federal government tries to 'hire' agents (that is, provinces) to deliver services in order to promote a particular policy agenda. The 'agents,' in return, get paid in provincial transfers and/or tax points.

The spending power is controversial, because it involves the federal government setting policy priorities in areas of provincial jurisdiction. While provinces could always refuse the federal offer, to do so would have the effect of provincial citizens paying federal taxes in support of a program available only to people in other provinces. Since 1965, the federal government has permitted provincial governments to opt out, with fiscal compensation, of some federal-provincial shared-cost programs, provided provincial governments establish a program comparable to the federal one. Under such circumstances, provinces are still 'hired agents,' as the federal government remains the architect of the broad contours of provincial policies. Quebec, the only province to routinely make use of this provision, has argued that compensation is frequently insufficient to mount a provincial program (Banting, 1988; Telford 2003). Given that the federal spending power amounts to 'a deal that you can't refuse,' provinces·may accept its use but try to subvert some of the hierarchy implicit within it.

One dynamic that arises out of attempting to establish such a principal-agent accountability relationship through the use of the federal spending power is a *collective action problem*. As with all principal-agent relationships, it is not easy for the principal and agents (that is, the provinces) to cooperate, despite the prospect of mutual gain. Moe (2005, 216) argues, 'The agent has interests of his own ... that give him incentives not to do what is best for the principal. He also has an informational advantage that makes such shirking possible ... As a result, the principal has reason to distrust his agent.' Moe (216) argues, 'The way around the [collective action] problem is for the principal to devise an efficient set of rules, incentive structures, and monitoring mechanisms that – by mitigating the information asymmetry and bringing the agent's interests into alignment with the principal's – represents a mutually beneficial arrangement to which both parties can credibly commit, and is either self-enforcing or enforceable by a third party such as the courts.'

The challenge is designing just such rules and incentive structures to recreate a form of principal-agent accountability, especially where avoiding it is a first-order preference for some or all of the purported 'agents' (such as the provinces). Thus, the very act of demanding an account can create hierarchical relationships between actors where there are no formal hierarchies. This can occur in several ways. For instance, the very act of demanding certain forms of accounting can alter the behaviour, ideas, and identity of the reporting party. The fact of having to report on a particular indicator can lead to policy goal displacement with attention turned exclusively to that dimension at the expense of broader objectives. Another consequence is mission creep – the expansion of an initiative beyond the initial goals. The requirement to prepare reports may also lead to a reassignment of resources to the task, and potentially to changes in expertise valued in an organization or department. This concern is the classic critique of accountability provisions tied to funding for non-profit organizations: the organizations come to hire specialists and to focus on reporting at the expense of the representational and mobilization activities that were at the heart of their original creation (e.g., Taylor 2003).

Another form of hierarchy arises from a move from process-based accountability to results-based accountability. If actors are held accountable, not on the basis of acting within the bounds of particular programs or agreements but on their capacity to meet certain goals, the actor receiving accounts is potentially able to steer activities towards certain ends or objectives. In American foreign aid policy, for instance, some have looked to the Bush administration's Millennium Challenge Account, which required states to provide data on indicators related to sixteen criteria of good governance, as a form of 'imperialism,' pushing developing countries to adopt American understandings of what constitutes good political, social, and economic governance (e.g., Mawdsley 2007; Soederberg 2004). The Open Method of Coordination in the European Union has likewise drawn attention for its use of benchmarking, results reporting, and peer review, and the capacity of such forms of accountability to steer divergent national welfare models towards a 'European' social policy model (Jaccobson 2004; Zeitlin 2005). This may lead to domestic political accountability, should citizens and interest groups make use of the information provided or turn the consultative stages of the process into windows of policy influence. While this is a weak form of 'accountability,' in that member states simply commit to reporting and peer review, it is in this less heroic sense that we can observe how even a soft form of accountability through reporting can rework relationships in multilevel governance.

These dynamics may explain why scholars portray the institutional rules of the game in federal systems as promoting not just collective action problems but also *joint decision-making traps*. As Scharpf (2006, 848) points out, decentralized bargaining models that presume negotiations between self-interested actors can achieve the same outcome as those imposed by a (benevolent and omniscient) dictator, so long as one can transform self-interested bargaining into solidaristic problem-solving – 'either by a procedural separation of co-operative problem-solving from distributive bargaining or by a solidaristic transformation of preferences' (849). Agreements that are 'welfare improving' can occur in voluntary negotiation systems, because 'all participants must prefer the outcome to the status quo,' or else 'the liberty of individual action will continue to prevail if negotiations should fail' (848). A problem arises, though, in compulsory as opposed to voluntary negotiation systems, 'where certain purposes can be realized only through agreement': 'the veto of one or a few governments' is 'likely to generate sub-optimal policy outcomes – resulting either in blockages or inefficient lowest-denominator compromises.' (848). When accountability can be used instrumentally to influence the choices of other actors, a series of political questions can be raised about the normative justifications of such power, but also more prosaically about how the actors themselves negotiate and navigate those power relations. These aspects of hierarchy are obviously of interest in federal systems, since federalism as a normative principle calls in part to the values of non-hierarchy and non-subordination in relationships between federated entities.

The Canadian Experience of Intergovernmental Accountability

As many scholars have observed about the exercise of power in Canada, even though the two orders of government are constitutionally sovereign and there is no hierarchy or subordination so long as the two orders of government exercise jurisdictional authority within their own watertight compartments, 'hierarchy has never been lacking in Canadian federalism' (Simeon and Nugent 2008, 92). The shift to an accountability system built around public reporting in Canada in fact reflects a partial relaxation of hierarchy in intergovernmental accountability relationships, at least in comparison to the instruments used previously. One obviously needs to be careful with nuances here, and with distinctions between the formal structuring of accountability arrangements and the ongoing implementation and monitoring of those arrangements. We see some merit to arguments that accountability mechanisms have never been that strong in Canada in the first place (Graefe 2006, 3) and that the conditions that were or are in place, such as in the Canada Health Act, have been ruled not justiciable (Choudhry 1996) and thus only politically enforceable. In many instances, the federal government has chosen not to enforce rules (see, for example, Flood and Thomas 2010; Graefe 2006, 4). As Biggs (1996, 12) argues, observing the case of the Canada Assistance Plan, 'For its part, the federal government has not used its leverage to insist on a national information strategy' for CAP program spending, so there was little way to determine 'program effectiveness and the impact of policy and program changes' (11). In sum, the current regime based on reporting should not be compared with a mythical past of frictionless hierarchical accountability. But this story of the politics of non-enforcement risks presenting an overly flat history, as federal-provincial conflict has produced softer forms of accountability arrangements. The present arrangements have characteristic ways of working that differ from earlier ones, and these are brought out by historical comparisons with earlier arrangements.

As Barbara Cameron illustrates in chapter 12, the post-war pattern in areas where the federal government transferred money to the provinces to deliver specific social policies (what Keith Banting [1997] refers to as 'shared cost federalism') was to create fairly hierarchical accountability arrangements between the federal and provincial governments to ensure the accountability of the political executive to Parliament. In the period after the Second World War, an important segment of the Canadian welfare state (social assistance and social services, hospital and physician insurance, post-secondary education) was built with conditional federal grants. Often referred to as the 'federal spending power,' these grants usually took the form of the federal reimbursement of a share of eligible provincial expenditures. The grants were 'conditional' in the sense that provinces sent their accounts to the relevant federal department, which would then verify whether they fit within the program parameters agreed upon, and reimburse only those in conformity. As Cameron (2007) has indicated, these agreements had a firm statutory basis at both the federal and provincial level, such that this accountability, while providing the central government with substantial hierarchical leverage with the provinces, could be justified in ensuring that the federal department could provide comprehensive accounting to Parliament on the use of federal financial resources.

Provincial governments resented these arrangements, both for the bureaucratic bother of preparing accounts and then haggling over them with the federal department, and more broadly for enabling the federal government to set the parameters of public policy in areas of provincial jurisdiction, in the process upsetting provincial priorities, plans, and programs (Smiley 1962). With the growing power of provincial governments, both in building bureaucratic capacity and in developing nationalist (Quebec) and regionalist (the West, Newfoundland) identities that challenged a pan-Canadian sense of the national community, shared-cost federalism proved less legitimate as a means to group provincial policies within a shared pan-Canadian agenda. By the 1980s, the federal government no longer attempted to structure accountability around matching federal and provincial statutes and the sending of provincial accounts to Ottawa. With the 1984 Canada Health Act, Canada entered a period of 'political accountability,' again to use Cameron's characterization, where the federal executive was determined not to transfer health funds to provinces that did not comply with the conditions set out in the federal statute.

The greater unilateralism in this formula made its use much more contingent on political readings of power, and on the willingness to have public arguments with provinces over what constituted compliance with the Act and what sanctions were appropriate for non-compliance. Given that the federal government was stealthily reducing its share of health funding over the 1980s and early 1990s through partial indexation, its legitimacy to demand provincial compliance was diminished. The coup de grâce occurred with the 1995 federal budget. In that budget, the federal government eliminated the CAP, bundling transfer payments for health and social assistance into the Canada Health and Social Transfer (CHST) and drastically cutting the size of overall transfers. Recognizing that cuts to federal transfers meant less legitimacy of federal oversight, the federal government revoked all conditions for receipt of social assistance transfers, save for the prohibition on residency requirements. It did, however, maintain the Canada Health Act. In one fell swoop, then, the forms of accountability elaborated over the preceding forty years were suddenly exhausted: the biggest program on the administrative model, the CAP, was gone, while the political accountability of the CHA lacked legitimacy in the eyes of most academic observers. After all, how could the federal government withhold money to provinces in violation of the CHA when it had just cut the transfer by a third, and when the remaining cash transfer to the provinces was eventually scheduled to run to zero, given how the health transfer was calculated at the time (Courchene 1995).

The question of how one could imagine a legitimate and workable form of accountability in the post-1995 period, especially where the federal government lacked the money to 'purchase' much provincial answerability with the spending power, was answered by the 1999 Social Union Framework Agreement between the federal government and the governments of all provinces except Quebec. Most contemporary academics and practitioners treat the SUFA a bit dismissively as a stepping stone in a longer process of bringing the federal and provincial governments into a more productive dialogue after the recriminations about unilateral deficit shifting of the early and mid-1990s, rather than as an enduring framework for managing federal-provincial relations. For our purposes, though, the SUFA is highly significant, as it sets out the governments' thinking, at that period, about accountability, and the language and vision laid out in SUFA is very similar to what is found in the sectoral social policy agreements of the late 1990s and early 2000s. The agreement contained language that demands 'transparency and accountability' to constituents, which, it is argued, strengthens the social union. In this context, each government agreed to 'monitor and measure outcomes of its social programs and report regularly to its constituents on the performance of these programs,' as well as to share information and best practices and participate in developing joint indicators. They also agreed to 'use third parties, as appropriate, to assist in assessing progress on social priorities' (Government of Canada and Governments of the Provinces and Territories 1999).

Nevertheless, these new agreements differed from older ones in how they approached the issue of accountability (see Phillips 2003). Whereas earlier social policy agreements required direct provincial reporting to the federal government on the use of federal money and made the federal contribution conditional on fulfilling specified program commitments, the post-1995 agreements were more open-ended and less binding. In some cases, provinces had to provide proposed annual plans to the federal government, although these were often 'for information purposes only.' Provinces no longer were bound to report to the federal government, but instead were committed to providing annual reports to the public on their use of federal monies, and for their success in meeting certain mutually determined indicators. The new accountability regime does not rely on government-to-government relationships so much as the government–citizen relationship, and by extension the ability of citizens to hold governments to account at the ballot box (Cameron 2007). Certainly, the elements of Ebrahim and Weisbrod's definition of accountability were all here: *transparency* in annual reports, *answerability* in annual plans, *compliance* in monitoring and reporting on progress on stated goals, and *enforcement* in being held to account by citizens. But in the absence of much legitimacy for a hierarchical role for the federal government, there were a number of weak connections between the elements, as the chapters of this collection indicate. Most notably there is the heroic linkage between the first three elements and the ability of citizens to sanction a government through elections, but also in the weakness of institutions to ensure *answerability* in terms of participating in setting plans or in discussing reported outcomes.

While this story of declining federal hierarchical authority followed by attempts to rebuild a form of legitimate federal social policy leadership sets the context for the adoption of public reporting, it does not explain why this particular instrument was chosen. It is generally accepted in the Canadian literature that this emphasis on reporting is evidence of the influence of New Public Management thinking. This point was made originally by Susan Phillips (2003; see also Saint-Martin 2004), who emphasized how public reporting fit well with the managerial thinking then in vogue in the federal public service. At a broad level, reporting is consonant with the idea of moving the attention of public administration from process (e.g., whether the provinces spend money in conformity with the relevant intergovernmental agreement) to results and outcomes for 'clients' (e.g., what services the provinces provided with the money, and with what effects for users). It also fit with a citizen-as-consumer-driven public service, as presumably reporting to citizens would enable the latter to make informed choices and thereby push governments to be more responsive to shortcomings. In a blunt form, the comparison of provincial outcomes could lead to interprovincial 'beauty contests' whereby citizens in an underperforming province could shame their government and ultimately put electoral pressure on it. In a more sophisticated form, citizens and bureaucrats could observe the best practices of high-performing provinces and seek to mimic or adapt them.

A final element of the New Public Management thinking was the individualization of state–society relationships. While a number of intergovernmental agreements mention 'stakeholders' and see their engagement as leading to better policy outcomes, the headline language is one of reporting to 'Canadians.' This again is in keeping with the de-legitimization of intermediary organizations such as interest groups that characterized the federal bureaucracy during this period (Laforest and Phillips 2007).[3] The linkage was also noted and taken up soon after by Alain Noël (2003) to provide a normative critique of the federalist shortcomings of such an approach: the hierarchy implied in 'steering rather than rowing,' and of seeing provinces as service delivery agents to be managed by an outcomes-oriented federal framework, sat poorly with federal values of autonomy and non-subordination.

However, just as the concept of New Public Management needs to be treated with caution, given divergent understandings of what practices and ideas it contains, so too must claims that the new regime is largely

NPM-inspired. There are at least two caveats here. The first is to recognize that performance measurement and evidence-based policy, while brought into the New Public Management movement, have existed for some time. For instance, as Jennifer Wallner's chapter 11 on education makes clear, the measurement and tracking of student results has a long pedigree in that field. Similarly, Patrick Fafard's chapter 2 indicates that the push to evidence-based policy in health care had a momentum of its own that could be reduced only abusively to a New Public Management outlook.

 A second and more substantial point is raised in Paul Manna's chapter 10 about performance reporting in American education. He observes that if performance reporting is to work as a tool to spur learning and the adoption of best practices, it needs to be driven by clear targets and outcomes. Yet in the area he studies, the actual reporting regime was much more eloquent in setting out process expectations, but left the states to set their own measures of what constituted acceptable progress.[4] This insight is useful for thinking about the Canadian case too. If we look at the various agreements that contain reporting requirements, they are striking in their absence of clearly defined goals to be achieved. While broad objectives are enunciated, there is nowhere a clear enunciation of concrete outcomes or performances that are expected. Patrick Fafard's chapter 2 on health agreements and Julie M. Simmons's chapter 3 on the National Child Benefit, for instance, both make the case that the agreements lack the clear definitions of expected outcomes that might really structure and channel provincial behaviour.

Finally, as federal, provincial, and municipal governments have become increasingly intertwined in the design and delivery of programs and services in Canada, scholarly investigation has also turned to whether and how Canadian citizens exercise their role in the classical equation of accountability (e.g., Anderson 2008; Cutler 2008). Cutler and Mendelsohn (2005) observe that Canadians – regardless of their personal level of knowledge and expertise, or the policy issue – find it difficult to trace whether provincial or federal elected executives are responsible for various policy developments. Retrospective voting – a assumption of the democratic dimension of the classical understanding of accountability – is less likely when voters are confused about which government is responsible, or if they blame both orders of government for the state of health care, economic, or environmental policy, for example (Cutler 2004). In such a context, public reporting is a thin reed for promoting accountability, be it provincial accountability for the use of federal monies, or the broader accountability of both governments to citizens in implementing promises related to social rights.

Exploring a More Robust (and Realistic) Conceptualization of Accountability

Public reporting in the absence of any specific reporting requirements can really be seen as the softest form of accountability, reflecting the inability of Canadian intergovernmental bargaining to effect a 'solidaristic transformation of preferences' in the direction of strong central leadership. Governments report on their actions, but in the absence of specific reporting requirements, enforcement is not possible.

The legitimacy challenge that hierarchical models of intergovernmental accountability raise suggests that we need to move away from understanding intergovernmental accountability in hierarchical terms. Sperling (2009, 9–10) points out that democracy comprises two forms of accountability: vertical accountability of governments to citizens – which in turn requires certain conditions such as freedom of speech and information, the right to vote, and so on – and horizontal accountability of government institutional checks on each other's power. While the former can be seen as a principal-agent relationship and is fundamental to democracy, the latter relationship of governments to each other need not be premised on a principal-agent model.

In fact, drawing on Grant and Keohane (2005), one can conceptualize accountability relationships on a continuum from hierarchical to non-hierarchical.

Command-and-Control Mechanisms Enforced by the Courts

Under a command-and-control view of accountability, the federal government uses its coercive power to tie agents' (in this case, the provinces') hands. This has traditionally been conceived of as conditionality in federal transfers, with the threat to withdraw funds in the case of noncompliance (Mendelson 2003). As discussed above, the federal government has found it difficult to carry through with the withdrawal of funds, given the defunding of social and health services.

Thus, one way to ensure enforceability would be for both levels of government to agree to cede enforcement authority to a third party, who would then have the legal authority to enforce agreements. As Moe (2005, 216) argues, rules, monitoring mechanisms, and so on can be 'either self-enforcing or enforceable by a third party such as the courts.' Governments could agree to make intergovernmental agreements justiciable, in the same way that federal and provincial governments agreed in 1982 to make human rights violations justiciable under the Charter of Rights and Freedoms. In this case, intergovernmental principal-agent dynamics are absent; answerability instead is to the courts, which also maintains enforcement authority. This approach might be greeted with scepticism in Canada following the 1991 Canada Assistance Plan judgment from the Supreme Court, which adopted a classic view of Parliamentary supremacy to dismiss provincial complaints that the federal government unilaterally changed the terms of an intergovernmental agreement. However, as Poirier (2004) notes, the degree to which intergovernmental agreements are binding in a justiciable sense depends greatly on how they are written, so the Canada Assistance Plan case should not be seen as closing this door. It remains that the relatively flimsy intergovernmental agreements being dealt with in this volume, dubbed by some as 'agreements by press release' are far from such a mutually binding legal text.

Incentive-Compatible Instruments

There has not been much appetite in Canada to draw up intergovernmental agreements as constitutional documents with justiciable terms. Rather, the preferred method since the mid-1990s has been the use of 'performance partnerships.' These are agreements 'in which partners discuss how to combine resources from both players to achieve a specified end-state. The end-state is expected to be measurable in order for a partnership to be successful' (Radin 2000, 148). Such partnerships require some form of fiscal accountability, such as public reports, with specific criteria for measurement and auditing. One can see these kinds of performance partnerships emerge in the United States as agreements between federal officials and state or local agents. One example Radin (2000, 148) gives is between the U.S. Environmental Protection Agency and American states. And certainly there are numerous forces leading toward more monitoring and accounting for results in the form of New Public Management. At the EU level, supranational institutions perform that monitoring and enforcement, although there is evidence that member states do not always comply with EU level directives and regulations (e.g., Borzel et al. 2010).

One could argue that all intergovernmental agreements are premised on some sort of social contract theory, that is, an acceptance of certain standards or rules, with the realization that, while participants 'may lose on particular decisions, they expect to be better off than they would be outside the framework' (Moe 2005, 219). Thus, participants accept some kind of governance structure – as Moe explains them, 'relational contracts in which actors agree to procedures that allow them to adjudicate disputes, adjust to new developments, and otherwise ensure that their original agreement is maintained over time in a changing environment.' Because of the voluntary nature of contracts, participants 'can walk away if they believe they are not better off' (219). One example that Radin (2000) gives is negotiated performance measures, in which actors establish mutually agreed upon measures in order to evaluate spending outcomes, with waivers in order to allow some actors to establish their own approach to a problem.

Such relational contracts perform well in resolving disputes, but they may build in such loose accountability requirements that they have no teeth. As many of the chapters in this volume reveal, 'performance partnerships' with public reporting have proven to be exceedingly weak accountability tools. It would seem at minimum that effective intergovernmental governance requires some ability to enforce decisions. How can we achieve that without enforcing principal-agent dynamics?

The focus needs to be on increasing benefits of cooperation through selective incentives. For example, in Switzerland, cantons that report deficiencies in compliance are rewarded with extra funding. In other words, there is no penalty for revealing non-compliance; just the opposite (Steiner 2008).

Accountability to the Population through Legislatures

Democracy in the modern era is '"a system of governance in which rulers are held accountable for their actions in the public realm by citizens, acting indirectly through the competitions and cooperation of their representatives"' (Sperling 2009, 8, quoting Schmitter and Karl 1991). A number of scholars (e.g., Simeon and D. Cameron 2002, 292) have proposed allowing citizens to scrutinize intergovernmental agreements through their representatives. Intergovernmental agreements would either be submitted to the federal Parliament and provincial legislatures for approval or require approval directly via citizen referenda.

Thus, governments would be accountable to their own populations through representatives who would be empowered to scrutinize compliance with agreements. The trick is, of course, the drafting of agreements as legislation, which governments have been reluctant to do in an era of 'intergovernmental agreement by press release.' As Barbara Cameron argues in this volume, the very weak statutory basis of recent agreements is a significant stumbling block to achieving the basic forms of accountability at the heart of responsible government and needs to be revisited in any attempt to craft a new system of accountabilities.

Accountability to Designated Third Parties

Another kind of accountability arrangement involves contracting out scrutiny to neutral third parties, which are adequately resourced to scrutinize compliance and report on non-compliance (Biggs 1996, 36). Tammy Findlay's chapter 4 documents just such an arrangement with the federal Human Resources and Skills Development Ministry funding the Child Care Advocacy Association of Canada to scrutinize provincial spending on early childhood education and care. One can see these kinds of reporting relationships established in independent, arm's-length bodies such as the Canadian Human Rights Commission or the Auditor General, as documented in Julie M. Simmons and Amy Nugent's chapter 13, or perhaps sector 'councils' such as the Health Council of Canada, whose membership is drawn from provincial governments and the health-care-delivery sector, as documented in Patrick Fafard's chapter 2. Two weaknesses of this form of accountability are, first, the adequacy of enforcement powers, beyond shaming that the publicizing of results can elicit; and second, monitoring of the third party. As Sperling (2009, 15) points out, 'When democratic states transfer (or "outsource") formerly public functions and services to the private sector, citizens largely relinquish their powers of oversight.'

International Surveillance

Grace Skogstad's chapter 9 points out that forces of accountability are moving beyond the state itself to, for example, international organizations (IOs) such as the International Monetary Fund (IMF) and World Bank, international courts, and so on, and private actors such as military contractors (see also Sperling 2009). Thus, 'not only are national governments supposed to be accountable to their populations,' but they are also 'expected to demonstrate their responsiveness to transnational governance institutions, to exhibit accountability "upward"' (7). The surveillance function performed by multilateral and international organizations is generally regarded as a 'softer' form of enforcement, unless, of course, the IO involved has some kind of enforcement power. But even this 'soft' power of naming and shaming can be effective. Sperling (2009, 6) writes, 'State leaders – depending on the relative power of their state in the global system – have in some cases become more responsive to multinational corporations or other transnational entities than to their putative domestic constituents.' In other words, effective accountability can become de-territorialized or detached from traditional state forms. But it works only if governments care what the world thinks of them.

These alternative accountabilities encourage us to dream big; we return to this theme in the conclusion. Raising them here has two benefits in reading the contributions to this volume. First, it maintains a constant reminder of the ways that accountability could be organized, and thus counterposes what exists (as described in the cases in this volume) with what might exist. At the same time, the case studies also raise questions about the feasibility or normative interest of many of these suggestions, raising the difficult question of 'where to go from here' that we wrestle with in the conclusion.

NOTES

1 In the OECD, there are federal arrangements also in Austria, Australia, Belgium (since 1993), Germany, and Switzerland. As well, some countries have established quasi-federal arrangements such as in Spain and the United Kingdom (Pierson 1995).
2 Game theoretic conceptualizations of intergovernmental dynamics are implicit in some of the literature on multilevel governance, such as Simeon's (1971) magisterial *Federal-Provincial Diplomacy*, which examines decentralized domestic federal-provincial bargaining during the 1970s as two-level games, a concept later popularized in Putnam's (1988) work.
3 Indeed, at the workshop where papers in this volume were first presented, the question of the legitimacy of interest groups using the public reports remained contentious, both for the presenters and for the practitioners who served as discussants.

4 Recognizing the limitations of such variable standards, U.S. governors and
  state school chiefs developed a set of national education standards (the
  Common Core) that more than half of U.S. states have since adopted (see
  Manna chapter 10 in this volume). While that Common Core of standards
  was developed before the announcement of new federal monies totalling
  $4.35 billion under the Race to the Top program, many states have signed
  on to those standards in order to improve their chances of winning a Race
  to the Top grant (Manna, this volume; see also Lewin 2010).

REFERENCES

Anderson, Cameron D. 2008. 'Economic Voting, Multilevel Governance
    and Information in Canada.' *Canadian Journal of Political Science* 41 (2):
    329–54.
Anderson, Lynell, and Tammy Findlay. 2007. *Making the Connections: Using
    Public Reporting to Track Progress on Child Care Services in Canada.* Ottawa:
    Child Care Advocacy Association of Canada.
Banting, Keith G. 1988. 'Federalism, Social Reform and the Spending Power.'
    Canadian Public Policy 14:S81–S92.
– 1997. 'The Past Speaks to the Future: Lessons from the Postwar Social
    Union.' In *Canada: The State of the Federation 1997 – Non-Constitutional
    Change,* edited by Harvey Lazar, 39–69. Kingston: Institute of Intergovern-
    mental Relations.
Biggs, Margaret. 1996. *Building Blocks for Canada's New Social Union.* CPRN
    Working Paper no. F/02. Ottawa: Canadian Policy Research Networks.
Boismenu, Gérard. 2006. 'Les nouveaux visages de vieux démons: les défis
    posés au fédéralisme par la restructuration de la protection sociale au
    Canada.' *Lien social et politiques* 56:7–71.
Boismenu, Gérard, and Peter Graefe. 2004. 'The New Federal Toolbelt:
    Rebuilding Social Policy Leadership.' *Canadian Public Policy* 30 (1): 71–89.
Borzel, Tanja, Tobias Hofmann, Diana Panke, and Carina Sprungk. 2010.
    'Obstinate and Inefficient: Why Member States Do Not Comply with
    European Law.' *Comparative Political Studies* 43 (11): 1363–90.
Brander, James A. 1985. 'Economic Policy Formation in a Federal State: A
    Game Theoretic Approach.' In *Intergovernmental Relations,* edited by Richard
    Simeon, 33–69. Toronto: University of Toronto Press.
Brown, M. Paul. 1983. 'Responsiveness versus Accountability in Collaborative
    Federalism: The Canadian Experience.' *Canadian Public Administration*
    26 (3): 629–39.

Cameron, Barbara. 2007. 'Accounting for Rights and Money in the Canadian Social Union.' In *Poverty: Rights, Social Citizenship, Legal Activism*, edited by Margot Young, Susan B. Boyd, Gwen Brodsky, and Shelagh Day, 162–80. Vancouver: University of British Columbia Press.

Choudhry, Sujit. 1996. 'The Enforcement of the Canada Health Act.' *McGill Law Journal* 41 (2): 461–508.

Citizens at City Hall. 2010. 'Environment Fund Used for Roads and City Hall.' http://www.hamiltoncatch.org/view_article.php?id=690.

Commission of Inquiry into the Sponsorship Scandal and Advertising Activities. 2006. *Restoring Accountability*. Ottawa: The Commission.

Courchene, Thomas J. 1995. *Redistributing Money and Power: A Guide to the Canada Health and Social Transfer*. Toronto: C.D. Howe Institute.

Cutler, Fred. 2004. 'Government Responsibility and Electoral Accountability in Federations.' *Publius* 34 (2): 19–38.

– 2008. 'Whodunnit? Voters and Responsibility in Canadian Federalism.' *Canadian Journal of Political Science* 41 (3): 627–54.

Cutler, Fred, and Matthew Mendelsohn. 2005. 'Unnatural Loyalties or Native Collaborationists? The Governance and Citizens of Canadian Federalism.' In *Insiders and Outsiders: Alan Cairns and the Reshaping of Canadian Citizenship*, edited by Gerlad Kernerman and Phillip Resnick, 71–89. Vancouver: University of British Columbia Press.

Day, Shelagh, and Gwen Brodsky. 2007. *Women and the Canadian Social Transfer: Securing the Social Union*. Ottawa: Status of Women Canada.

Ebrahim, Alnoor, and Edward Weisband, eds. 2007. *Global Accountabilities: Participation, Pluralism and Public Ethics*. New York: Cambridge University Press.

Flood, Colleen M., and Bryan Thomas. 2010. 'Blurring the Public/Private Divide: The Canadian Chapter.' *European Journal of Health Law* 17:1–22.

Friendly, Martha, and Linda A. White. 2008. 'From Multilateralism to Bilateralism to Unilateralism in Three Short Years: Child Care in Canadian Federalism 2003–2006.' In *Canadian Federalism: Performance, Effectiveness and Legitimacy*, 2nd ed., edited by Grace Skogstad and Herman Bakvis, 182–204. Toronto: Oxford University Press.

Government of Canada and Governments of the Provinces and Territories. 1999. 'A Framework to Improve the Social Union for Canadians,' 4 Feb. http://www.scics.gc.ca/english/conferences.asp?a=viewdocument&id=638.

Graefe, Peter. 2006. 'Federalism and Social Policy: Evaluating Recent Federal-Provincial Agreements.' *Canadian Review of Social Policy* 57: 1–15.

Graefe, Peter, and Mario Levesque. 2006. 'La nouvelle gouvernance fédérale et les politiques sociales au Canada: leçons des ententes en matière de l'intégration en emploi des personnes ayant des handicaps.' *Lien social et politiques* 56:75–88.

Grant, Ruth W., and Robert O. Keohane. 2005. 'Accountability and Abuses of Power in World Politics.' *American Political Science Review* 99 (1): 29–43.

Jaccobson, Kerstin. 2004. 'Soft Regulation and the Subtle Transformation of States: The Case of EU Employment Policy.' *Journal of European Social Policy* 14 (4): 355–70.

James, Patrick. 1999. 'The Chain Store Paradox and Constitutional Politics in Canada.' *Journal of Theoretical Politics* 11 (1): 5–36.

Jarvis, Mark D. 2009. 'The Adoption of the Accounting Officer System in Canada: Changing Relationships?' *Canadian Public Administration* 52 (4): 525–48.

Kershaw, Paul. 2006. 'Weather-Vane Federalism: Reconsidering Federal Social Policy Leadership.' *Canadian Public Administration* 49 (1): 196–219.

Laforest, Rachel, and Susan Phillips. 2007. 'Citizen Engagement: Rewiring the Policy Process.' In *Critical Policy Studies*, edited by Michael Orsini and Miriam Smith, 67–90. Vancouver: University of British Columbia Press.

Laghi, Brian. 2002. 'Make Sure Cash Used for Health: Romanow Health Act Should Include New Principle on Provincial Accountability, Ottawa Told.' *Globe and Mail*, 9 Nov.

Lewin, Tamar. 2010. 'Many States Adopt National Standards for Their Schools.' *New York Times*, 21 July.

Mawdsley, Emma. 2007. 'The Millennium Challenge Account: Neo-liberalism, Poverty and Security.' *Review of International Political Economy* 14 (3): 487–509.

Mendelson, Michael. 2003. 'Accountability Versus Conditionality: The Future of the Canada Social Transfer.' Ottawa: Caledon Institute of Social Policy.

Moe, Terry M. 2005. 'Power and Political Institutions.' *Perspectives on Politics* 3 (2): 215–33.

Noël, Alain. 2003. 'Without Quebec: Collaborative Federalism with a Footnote?' In *Forging the Canadian Social Union: SUFA and Beyond*, edited by Sarah Fortin, Alain Noël and France St-Hilaire. Montreal: IRPP.

Phillips, Susan. 2003. 'SUFA and Citizen Engagement.' In *Forging the Canadian Social Union: SUFA and Beyond*, edited by Sarah Fortin, Alain Noël and France St-Hilaire. Montreal: IRPP.

Picard, André. 2010. 'Health Care System's Value Can't Be Measured, Auditor-General Says.' *Globe and Mail*, 24 Aug. http://www.theglobeandmail.com/news/politics/health-care-systems-value-cant-be-measured-auditor-general-says/article1684077/.

Pierson, Paul. 1995. 'Fragmented Welfare States: Federal Institutions and the Development of Social Policy.' *Governance* 8 (4): 449–78.

Poirier, Johanne. 2004. 'Intergovernmental Agreements in Canada: At the Crossroads between Law and Politics.' In *Canada: The State of the Federation 2002*, edited by J. Peter Meekison, Hamish Telford, and Harvey Lazar, 425–62. Kingston: Institute of Intergovernmental Relations.

Priest, Lisa. 2002. 'Fund for Medical Machines Buys Lawn Tractors.' *Globe and Mail*, 4 Apr.

Putnam, Robert D. 1988. 'Diplomacy and Domestic Politics: The Logic of Two-Level Games.' *International Organization* 42 (3): 427–60.

Radin, Beryl A. 2000. 'Intergovernmental Relationships and the Federal Performance Movement.' 2000. *Publius* 30 (1–2): 143–58.

Saint-Martin, Denis. 2004. *Coordinating Interdependence: Governance and Social Policy Redesign in Britain, the European Union and Canada*. Research Report F41. Ottawa: Canadian Policy Research Networks.

Savoie, Donald J. 2006. 'The Canadian Public Service Has a Personality.' *Canadian Public Administration* 49 (3): 261–81.

Scharpf, Fritz W. 1988. 'The Joint-Decision Trap: Lessons from German Federalism and European Integration.' *Public Administration* 66:239–78.

– 2006. 'The Joint-Decision Trap Revisited.' *Journal of Common Market Studies* 44 (4): 845–64.

Schmitter, Philippe, and Terry Lynn Karl. 1991. 'What Democracy Is ... and Is Not.' *Journal of Democracy* 2 (3): 75–88.

Simeon, Richard. 1971. *Federal-Provincial Diplomacy: The Making of Recent Policy in Canada*. Toronto: University of Toronto Press.

Simeon, Richard, and David Cameron. 2002. 'Intergovernmental Relations and Democracy: An Oxymoron If There Ever Was One?' In *Canadian Federalism: Performance, Effectiveness, and Legitimacy*, edited by Herman Bakvis and Grace Skogstad, 278–95. Toronto: Oxford University Press.

Simeon, Richard, and Amy Nugent. 2008. 'Parliamentary Canada and Intergovernmental Canada: Exploring the Tensions.' In *Canadian Federalism: Performance, Effectiveness, and Legitimacy*. 2nd ed., edited by Herman Bakvis and Grace Skogstad, 89–111. Toronto: Oxford University Press.

Smiley, Donald. 1962. 'The Rowell-Sirois Report, Provincial Autonomy, and Post-War Canadian Federalism.' *Canadian Journal of Economics and Political Science* 28 (1): 54–69.

Soederberg, Susanne. 2004. 'American Empire and "Excluded States": The Millennium Challenge Account and the Shift to Pre-emptive Development.' *Third World Quarterly* 25 (2): 279–302.

Sperling, Valerie. 2009. *Altered States: The Globalization of Accountability*. New York: Cambridge University Press.

Sproule-Jones, Mark. 1993. *Governments at Work: Canadian Parliamentary Federalism and Its Public Policy Effects*. Toronto: University of Toronto Press.

Steiner, Reto. 2008. 'Benchmarking in Swiss Public Administration.' Paper presented at the Workshop of the Federal Ministry of the Interior and the Forum of the Federations, 15 Feb. http://www.forumfed.org/libdocs/DEIntGov2008/Benchmarking-Switzerland-Overview.pdf.

Taylor, Marilyn. 2003. *Public Policy in the Community*. London: Palgrave.

Telford, Hamish. 2003. 'The Federal Spending Power in Canada: Nation Building or Nation Destroying?' *Publius* 33 (1): 23–44.

Zeitlin, Jonathan. 2005. 'The Open Method of Coordination in Action: Theoretical Promise, Empirical Realities, Reform Strategy.' In *The Open Method of Coordination in Action: The European Employment and Social Inclusion Strategies*, edited by Phillipe Pochet and Jonathan Zeitlin, 447–504. Brussels: P.I.E. Peter Lang.

PART TWO

Emerging Accountability?
Structures: Canadian Case Studies

2 Intergovernmental Accountability and Health Care: Reflections on the Recent Canadian Experience[1]

PATRICK FAFARD

During the past twenty years, the federal, provincial, and territorial governments have attempted to encourage Canadians to hold them accountable in new and different ways for the operations of health-care service-delivery systems. There has been a considerable effort to expand and improve the information available to Canadians as voters, as taxpayers, and, to a lesser extent, as patients. Some of this effort involves individual citizens and their provincial or territorial governments acting independently. Thus, for example, as part of a broader strategy of public accountability, the Government of Alberta has vastly expanded the amount of information that is publicly available on the operations of the health-care system (Baker et al. 1998; Thomas 2004). Similarly, the Government of Ontario, in the redesign of the Ontario health-care delivery system, has emphasized the role of the Ministry of Health and Long-Term Care less as an organization that delivers health-care services and more as one that ensures that high-quality services get delivered in a timely way (Ontario, MOHLTC 2004; Veillard et al. 2010).

However, accountability has also become central to the intergovernmental relationship that is so critical to health care in Canada. Because of the large costs associated with a publicly funded heath-care system and the implicit transfer from the relatively healthy and wealthy to the relatively less healthy and less wealthy, the Government of Canada plays a critical role in redistributing wealth via the tax system and a large, complex set of intergovernmental transfers. The trend over the past decade has been to supplement (but not to replace) the weak command-and-control approach that is central to the Canada Health Act with a system of public accountability based on clear pan-Canadian indicators of health system performance and public access to information about health outcomes and costs (Boychuk 2007). In addition to efforts by provincial and territorial governments to make themselves more accountable for health care, by means of its spending power, the Government of Canada has sought to introduce an additional performance-reporting regime with a view to exercising policy leadership in health care. Beginning in the late 1990s and culminating in the 2004 'health deal for a generation,' the Government of Canada expanded its own commitment to performance reporting to the realm of intergovernmental fiscal transfers with a view to using such reporting to gently 'steer' provinces in a certain direction (Graefe 2008; Simmons 2009).

Does a pan-Canada performance-reporting regime enhance accountability of governments and further encourage change? Can the federal government exercise policy leadership in health-care services delivery by means of a combination of lightly conditional transfers and a performance-reporting regime that is focused on wait times? In an effort to begin to answer these questions, this chapter first offers a description of the successive intergovernmental agreements between 1999 and 2004 that incrementally raised the level of federal funding for health care and linked the increased transfers to a regime of health-system performance measures. Second, this chapter assesses these new accountability arrangements and offers at least a partial explanation for the fact that the performance management and accountability regime applied to Canadian health-care federalism was largely a failure.

The Evolution of Performance Reporting in Health-Related Intergovernmental Relations

As noted in the introduction to this volume, performance reporting, both as a management tool and as a means of enhancing accountability, has been common in Canada and other federations for a number of years. Thus, it is perhaps not surprising that performance measurement was introduced into the practice of Canadian intergovernmental relations.

In the case of health-care transfers, a move to performance reporting is even less surprising for at least three reasons. First, there is the strong push for better measurement within the health-care system generally as part of the calls for 'evidence-based medicine' or 'evidence-based decision-making' in medicine, which very soon became a push for evidence-based health care more generally (Dopson and Fitzgerald 2005).

Second, as the pressure mounted on the Government of Canada to reverse the cuts it made to transfers to provincial governments in the mid-1990s, some began to argue that when federal transfers for health care were increased, provinces should be asked to report on what they were doing with these funds. In particular, Monique Bégin, a former minister of national health and welfare under former prime minister Pierre Trudeau, was calling for 'a report card for the health care system' (Gray 1998). The idea of more reporting on what was being done in the health-care system was also linked to the idea of 'national standards' for health care. This idea can be traced back to the Charlottetown Accord and also took hold in the late 1990s and eventually became part of the work of the Provincial-Territorial Ministerial Council on Social Policy Reform and Renewal as well as federal government proposals for a 'Health Accord' (Peach and Warriner 2007).

Finally, the federal, provincial, and territorial governments developed their commitment to reporting to the public on health care in the context of a perceived crisis in the Canadian health-care system. As spending on health-care delivery dipped in the mid-to late 1990s, the quantity and quality of services declined, or at least did not grow as quickly. Tight health-care budgets meant that any available slack in the system was removed and the underlying inefficiencies of the delivery system were revealed. Performance reporting was an attempt to counter the view that health services delivery in Canada was inexorably in decline.

The 1999 Exchange of Letters

The bold experiment in linking performance reporting to intergovernmental health transfers began with a 1999 exchange of letters between governments that linked increases in federal funding, not to a formal 'report card' as such, but to a more general commitment of enhanced information and accountability. For their part, in a January 1999 letter, premiers made the easy commitment to use any new federal funds made available through the Canada Health and Social Transfer (CHST) for core health services. They further committed to make information about the health-care system available to Canadians. In a subsequent letter to the premiers, Prime Minister Jean Chrétien linked increased health-care funding with federal goals of accountability and mobility (Peach and Warriner 2007). Having achieved modest gains on the accountability front, the Government of Canada began to incrementally increase health-care transfers. The 1999 federal budget included a one-time $3.5 billion CHST supplement for health care and increased the floor of federal cash transfers under the CHST by a further $2.5 billion above and beyond earlier incremental increases (Lazar, St-Hilaire, and Tremblay 2004).

However, at this early stage, governments were nowhere near a full-blown performance-reporting regime. Rather, in the context of a loose commitment to pan-Canadian standards, the provinces agreed to the need for enhanced information to being more accountable for the dollars they spent on health care. Again, for most provinces this was a relatively easy commitment to make. It happened at a time when they were planning (e.g., Saskatchewan) or had already implemented (e.g., Alberta) a government-wide performance-measurement regime (Thomas 2004, 12–13; Yeates 2000). Moreover, most provinces were looking to know more as well as explain more about the use of public funds spent on health services delivery.

First Ministers' 2000 Health Communiqué

Within months of the exchange of letters and the 1999 federal budget, provincial and territorial governments returned to the table and called on the Government of Canada to increase health-care funding in light of projections that federal surpluses were going to rise quite quickly over the next several years (Lazar, St-Hilaire, and Tremblay 2004). The federal government once again signalled that it was willing to entertain increased funding for health care as long as it was associated with enhanced public reporting on the performance of the health-care system. To oversimplify a complex process, the Government of Canada announced new funding for provinces for health care, specifically $21.1 billion over five years (Lazar, St-Hilaire, and Tremblay 2004). The increase in funding was linked to an intergovernmental agreement reached at the end of the First Ministers' Conference in Ottawa on 11 September 2000 (Canadian Intergovernmental Conference Secretariat 2000). This agreement is styled as a strategic plan for the health-care system and outlines a vision, principles, and an action plan. Ottawa and the provinces committed themselves to reform in critical areas including primary health care, supply of health services personnel, home care and continuing care, and pharmaceuticals management. In effect, first ministers endorsed the ongoing work plan of ministers of health.

Perhaps even more significantly, the communiqué described a commitment to reporting to Canadians, arguing, 'Clear public reporting, with appropriate, independent, third party verification will enhance the performance of health services' (Canadian Intergovernmental Conference

Secretariat 2000). The communiqué describes an ambitious and broad approach to performance reporting. Fourteen indicators are divided into three topic areas: health status (e.g., life expectancy, infant mortality), health outcomes (e.g., change in life expectancy, improved quality of life), and the quality of service (e.g., waiting times for key diagnostic and treatment services, adequacy of public health surveillance).

To make it possible for governments to begin reporting in 2002, the deputy ministers of health subsequently created a Performance Indicator Reporting Committee (PIRC) to coordinate efforts in attaining compa-rable reporting in the fourteen selected indicators (Ontario, MOHLT n.d.). The PIRC then divided the fourteen performance indicators into sixty-seven specific measures. In September 2002, in a remarkable dem-onstration of intergovernmental collaboration, the federal, provincial, and territorial governments released reports with data on most, if not all of the sixty-seven indicators, including rates of disease, lifestyle choices, wait times, and outcomes (Health Council 2005). Not all provinces were able or willing to report on all sixty-seven indicators, sometimes simply because the data were not available.

The release of the reports attracted little public and media attention. While unfortunate, this is not surprising, given the complexity of the documents, the overarching intergovernmental wrangling about the health-care transfers, and the fact that no single jurisdiction was demon-strably a winner or a loser. Moreover, the release of these health services performance reports was also eclipsed by the release, a few weeks later, of the *Report of the Standing Senate Committee on Social Affairs, Science and Technology* led by Senator Michael Kirby and the *Report of the Commission on the Future of Health Care in Canada* led by former Saskatchewan premier Roy Romanow.

2003 Accord on Health-Care Renewal

In the fall of 2002, Roy Romanow released his report on the future of the Canadian health-care system and called on the Government of Canada to increase transfers to the provinces for health (Canada, Royal Com-mission on the Future of Health Care in Canada 2002). However, the report also sought to link this reinvestment to a change agenda, hence Mr Romanow's admonition that Ottawa should 'buy change' (Perkel 2003) and the principle that Canadians have a right to a process or a forum that allows them to assess the effectiveness of health-care ser-vices. This principle led Mr Romanow to recommend the creation of a

Health Council of Canada, which, he argued, would supplement the existing dysfunctional and remote intergovernmental relations and provide 'national' leadership. As he saw it, the first task of the council would be to establish a national performance review framework that would result in 'annual reports to the public and governments that are widely distributed, discussed and debated across the country' (Canada, Royal Commission on the Future of Health Care in Canada 2002, 53). However, while this framework and these reports would include a range of data on health status, health outcomes, and service delivery, the Health Council envisaged by Romanow would also report on 'results achieved by intergovernmental structures, agencies and organizations' and 'issues in dispute among governments and how they are resolved' (53).

In essence, the Romanow Report linked increased fiscal transfers to provinces to increased transparency and accountability by means of a broad-based, extensive performance-reporting regime. To that extent, he endorsed the status quo approach of governments reporting on a large number of quite diverse indicators and the reporting role of the Canadian Institute for Health Information (CIHI). However, he was implicitly critical of the existing regime and sought to enhance it by giving a new, somewhat arm's-length Health Council the role of issuing the performance reports and otherwise encouraging and animating the pan-Canadian debate and discussion that he expected the reports to engender.

In short order, in February 2003 first ministers signed an accord on health-care renewal, worth $34.8 billion over five years. The cornerstone of the accord was the establishment of a special Health Reform Fund worth $16 billion over five years, which was aimed at primary health care, home-based care, and catastrophic coverage for drugs. As was true in the 2000 accord, they promised action in a wide range of areas, including patient safety, health human resources, technology assessment, innovation and research, and healthy living (Canadian Intergovernmental Conference Secretariat 2003). However, they also returned to the theme of accountability and adopted a performance-reporting regime designed to accomplish a number of linked objectives.

First, in order to address the perception that the Canadian health-care system was in crisis, first ministers agreed that 'enhanced accountability to Canadians and improved performance reporting are essential to reassuring Canadians that reforms are occurring' and that 'Canadians are entitled to better and more fully comparable information on the timeliness and quality of health care services.' Second, in order to advance a reform agenda, the 2003 accord retains and extends the broad-based reporting regime initially set out in 2000 (and endorsed in the Romanow Report) and goes on to promise additional comparable indicators to be developed by health ministers.

The accord includes a three-page annex in which first ministers not only direct their health ministers to work out additional indicators but also sets out in considerable detail what they want done. While some of the indicators are drawn from the 2000 accord, many are new. Some are very general (e.g., degree of technology utilization based on evidence) and others are very specific (e.g., 'readmissions for selected conditions including AMI, pneumonia, congestive heart failure'). As was true in 2000, first ministers abandoned the very general language that is traditionally used in such documents (and gives governments some flexibility), and instead opted for very specific wording. However, some indicators are not particularly relevant or, at least, particularly flattering to specific jurisdictions. Moreover, even though several jurisdictions were unable to report in September 2002 on some of the indicators agreed to in 2000, the 2003 First Ministers' Conference (FMC) communiqué adds to the reporting obligations.

Whether and to what extent the performance reporting anticipated in the agreement enhances accountability to ordinary citizens is less clear. Somebody or something is required to explain to laypeople the significance of, to take one example, the percentage of the population 'routinely receiving needed care from a multi-disciplinary primary health care organization or team' (one of the indicators adopted in the 2003 communiqué). This is one reason the 2003 FMC communiqué also announced the creation of a Health Council. Similar to (but in critical respects different from) the Health Council envisaged in the Romanow Report, the council agreed to by first ministers in 2003 was created to 'monitor and make annual public reports on the implementation of the Accord, particularly its accountability and transparency provisions.' Health ministers were tasked with setting up the council within three months, with the caveat that it was to work with Quebec's existing Council on Health and Welfare.[2] This caveat was a precursor to subsequent intergovernmental wrangling over the composition and mandate of the council and the eventual decision by Alberta and Quebec not to join.

2004: A Ten-Year Plan to Strengthen Health Care

In December 2003, Paul Martin succeeded Jean Chrétien as leader of the Liberal Party of Canada and prime minister. Like his predecessor, Prime

Minister Martin understood that it was good politics for the Government of Canada to be seen to be an active player in health care. As a former finance minister, Martin also understood the medium-term imperative of health-care reform as a way to limit the rate of growth of health care. Of course, the Government of Canada was also under continuing pressure to increase transfers to provinces and address what had come to be known as the 'vertical fiscal imbalance,' an argument that there was a structural imbalance between federal and provincial revenues and expenditures, to the detriment of the latter. The very existence of such an imbalance, or, assuming it was real, its size and extent, were hotly debated inside and between governments and among scholars (Lazar, St-Hilaire, and Tremblay 2004). Nevertheless, 'fiscal imbalance' was a phrase that argued for yet another round of increases in federal transfers to provinces, particularly as long as there was a gap between the current projections for federal health transfers and those recommended by the Romanow Commission (the 'Romanow gap').

Once again, the Government of Canada was unwilling to increase transfers absent a strong commitment by provincial governments to systemic change. Romanow's admonition to 'buy change' still echoed loudly, at least within the Government of Canada. At first glance, the most important element was the announcement that the Government of Canada would commit $41 billion over ten years in support of the action plan. This put the CHST on firm upward track (with an escalator of 6 per cent per year) and closed the Romanow gap. However, by 2004, the Government of Canada, and indeed several provincial governments, was increasingly concerned with one particular aspect of health care reform: wait times. Thus, when first ministers met in September 2004 and agreed to a '10-Year Plan to Strengthen Health Care,' their agreement focused extensively on reducing wait times but in a very particular way. To bolster provincial efforts, the 2004 agreement included a promise by Ottawa to invest $4.5 billion over the next six years, beginning in 2004–5, on a Wait Times Reduction Fund with an emphasis on five priority areas: joint replacement, cardiac care, cancer, cataracts, and diagnostic imaging.

First ministers also agreed to supplement and focus the health-care delivery system performance-measurement regime. The 2004 agreement included a commitment to an extensive set of comparable performance 'indicators' by 31 December 2005.[3] First ministers also promised evidence-based 'benchmarks' for access to care for cancer and heart conditions, as well as diagnostic imaging procedures, joint replacements, and sight restoration. The agreement also provided for later multi-year 'targets' to achieve these benchmarks. Each jurisdiction promised to report to 'its' citizens by 31 December 2005, and the Canadian Institute for Health Information (CIHI) was mandated to report on progress on wait times across jurisdictions. Interestingly, the Health Council was also tasked to prepare an annual report on the health status of Canadians, health outcomes, and the progress of elements set out in the communiqué.

Three things stand out in the 2004 agreement. First, a new set of performance indicators related specifically to surgical and diagnostic wait times was added to the broad set of indicators established in 2000. Second, there remains a mishmash of 'indicators,' 'targets,' and 'benchmarks' suggesting confusion over the nature and goals of the performance management regime. Third, following on its decision not to participate in the work of the Health Council, the Government of Quebec secured a partial opt-out of the 2004 agreement. In a separate communiqué, the Governments of Canada and Quebec explicitly endorsed a degree of asymmetrical federalism, acknowledged Quebec's 'desire to exercise its own responsibilities with respect to planning, organizing and managing health services within its territory,' and asserted that the 2004 agreement should be interpreted in a way that made clear that Quebec had its own wait-times reduction plan. This was an explicit acknowledgment that while all governments might agree that reducing wait times is a priority, there might well be disagreements about how, and when, and in what ways.

The Conservative Government: From a Wait Times 'Guarantee' to Relative Silence

Less than a year after the September 2004 agreement, which many thought would put a damper on the intense political wrangling over health care, the Supreme Court of Canada rendered its decision in *Chaoulli v. Québec*.[4] In this decision the Court ruled that the Quebec Health Insurance Act and the Hospital Insurance Act prohibition of private medical insurance violated the Quebec Charter of Human Rights and Freedoms. In a four to three decision, the Court found the acts violated Quebeckers' rights to life and security of person under the Quebec Charter. While the legal impact of the decision was relatively modest – the Government of Quebec was able to amend its legislative framework to accommodate the decision – the symbolic and political impact was considerable. While most Canadians remained blissfully unaware of either the judgment or the debates about it (Boychuk 2007), the decision did underline for the federal and provincial governments the fact that if patients were asked to wait too long, the matter could end up before the courts, with unpredictable outcomes. The judgment thus breathed new life into the debate about wait times in Canadian health care.

The response of both the Liberal minority government of Paul Martin and the opposition Conservatives was to begin to talk not just about indicators, benchmarks, or even targets, but to introduce the idea of a wait times 'guarantee.' Thus, the 2006 federal election, coming just six months after the Chaoulli decision, featured a debate between the two major parties on the best way of guaranteeing Canadians that they would receive timely health-care services (Boychuk 2007). For their part, the Conservatives promised that all Canadians would receive treatment within clinically acceptable wait times or they would be eligible to receive treatment in another jurisdiction, whether in another province, the United States, or perhaps private for-profit providers operating outside the publicly funded system (Boychuk).

The second Conservative budget in March 2007 allocated $612 million to help accelerate implementation of patient wait times guarantees. This set the stage for a vague announcement in April 2007 that Ottawa had signed agreements with all provinces and territories to implement the guarantee. However, except for Ontario, none of the provinces was clear about how someone might invoke the guarantee of service within the prescribed wait time. This led the Health Council of Canada to observe that it was not clear how a guarantee was, in practical terms, different from a benchmark or a target and to ask what options individuals would have if their waits were longer than guaranteed (Health Council 2007, 19). The answer to this question may never be revealed. The spring of 2007 may have marked the end of the pan-Canadian public discussion of wait times and indeed of the broader question of measuring the overall performance of health-care service delivery. There was but a brief discussion of wait times in the fall election in 2008, and the federal government has said almost nothing about wait times since then and seems to avoid commenting on health-care delivery by provinces. In fact, in an interview with *ABC News* in August 2009, when asked about wait times, the prime minister avoided responding directly and instead said, 'I don't lecture the provinces publicly on how they should be running their health care systems' (Tapper 2009). That said, the Conservative government led by Prime Minister Stephen Harper continues to make references to some form of accountability for health-care transfers, albeit in a muted way.

For example, the 2004 intergovernmental agreement on health transfers expires in 2014 and in the months leading up to the 2011 federal election the skirmishing began on what should be included in a new agreement. During the election the Conservative Party made a public commitment to continue with a health-care fiscal transfer and have it grow at 6 per cent per year (albeit for an unspecified number of years). However, this commitment was linked to a still very general concern about accountability. Thus in the Speech from the Throne in June 2011 the government committed itself to 'working with the provinces and territories to ensure that the health care system is sustainable and that there is accountability for results' (Canada, Governor General 2011, 8).

However, the prospect of intergovernmental collaboration leading to further refinements to an accountability and performance indicator regime for health care in Canada dimmed considerably in the fall of 2011. At the annual meeting of ministers of finance, the Government of Canada announced that increases in the Canada Health Transfer would continue at six per cent annually until 2017, then slow to match the increase in the nominal gross domestic product until 2024 (Ibbitson 2011). However, the announcement contained no references to accountability, or to health reform. Rather than link the CHT increase to a broader health reform package negotiated with provincial and territorial governments, the federal government chose to proceed quite unexpectedly and unilaterally. The announcement caught provinces by surprise, set the terms of the debate over health funding, and effectively weakened the ability of provincial governments to influence the terms of the federal government for health care. However, the substance and form of the announcement also created significant intergovernmental tensions (Juneau 2011). The sudden announcement also made that much more difficult for the federal minister to pursue her stated goal of 'efforts to develop comparable measures and performance reporting' (Aglukkaq 2012). Thus, by early 2012 the goal of linking federal government funding for health care to a comprehensive performance reporting system was, if not dead, on life support.

Implications and Lessons

Having described the evolution of the public reporting regime in Canadian health care over the past decade or so I now want to turn to a broader evaluation and consider some of the questions introduced at the outset.

*The Theory and Practice of an Intergovernmental Accountability Regime
for Health Services Delivery*

The Government of Canada made a conscious and deliberate decision
in the late 1990s to link increases in federal government transfers for
health care to a new system of performance measurement. The reasoning behind the change is quite clear. If the federal government wishes to
use its spending power to elicit change in the delivery of health services,
it needs to link new and existing transfers for health to a set of targets
that have been jointly agreed upon. Specifically, the model requires:

- a transparent accounting by all governments who deliver or are
  responsible for the delivery of health-care services;
- that performance measures be jointly established with provincial and
  territorial governments; and
- that compliance with the new reporting regime be subject to review
  and comment by a third-party agency in order to help citizens make
  sense of the numbers.

In practice, implementation of this new regime proved to be more
difficult than anticipated – so much so that the experiment, while interesting, should be deemed a failure. If performance data are to be used
as a tool of accountability or even as a management tool, the governments whose performance is being measured have to be engaged in
a dialogue and committed to comparing themselves to others. This
engagement and commitment do not currently exist and lead Canadians
back to the reality that accountability is largely a 'within province' affair,
and then only on the basis of incomplete data (Health Council 2007).
There are several reasons for this.

First, while all provincial and territorial governments were willing to
embrace a system of performance measurement for health-care delivery
(in fact several had already instituted such systems), they were not
equally willing to embrace the same system and report on the same
basis. So, while all governments – federal, provincial, and territorial – do
occasionally issue performance reports based on the same indicators,
compliance has been uneven. Moreover, even though all provincial and
territorial governments agree that better public information on health
services delivery is a good thing and are willing to report progress (or a
lack thereof) on reducing surgical and diagnostic wait times, they are not
equally willing to be subject to oversight by the same third-party agency

– the Health Council of Canada (although in early 2012 Alberta did join). Thus, at the outset Quebec and Alberta opted not to join the Health Council in the first place. Their objection was rooted in an unwillingness to be subject to review by a body that they did not appoint or at least that could not be relied upon to understand the particular realities of health services delivery in each province. More fundamentally, Quebec rejected the premise of a pan-Canadian health-care performance-reporting regime where each province would be evaluated, directly or indirectly, on the basis of a common set of performance measures and subject to a common third-party review and comment. In other words, the governments of Quebec and Alberta subscribed to the view that, precisely because health care is largely a matter of provincial jurisdiction, they wanted to be accountable each to their own electorate. This is less a disagreement on how to manage and run the health-care system and much more a disagreement on the nature of the federation.

Second, while the theory was that all jurisdictions should report on a common set of performance indicators, establishing these indicators proved to be much more difficult and complex than anticipated. As outlined above, successive meetings of first ministers endorsed a confusing mix of numbers that in fact are meant to measure and evaluate quite different things. This is not surprising. As Harty (2008, 228) has observed, 'Often, the set of performance indicators and data presented in performance reports includes a haphazard set of information that intertwines indicators of outputs, workload data, internal process indicators, and even at times in input indicators.' In the case of Canadian health services delivery, at different times first ministers mandated the collection and reporting of indicators that mixed, on the one hand, data useful to health system managers and designed to allow for improved performance (e.g., 'number of diagnostic professionals to operate equipment'), and on the other hand data designed to enhance accountability to the public (e.g., percentage of the population having a regular family doctor). In general, performance measurement models have two distinct purposes: (1) enhanced accountability to stakeholders (in this case, voters and taxpayers), and (2) managerial improvement (Denhardt and Aristigueta 2008). In this case, those two purposes were combined to produce a confusing mix of indicators that did little to enhance accountability to the general public.

Third, the decision to link increased federal transfers for health care to a performance-measurement and accountability regime reflects the particular set of political realities of the late 1990s and early 2000s.[5]

Faced with the need to inject significant amounts of new money into the health-care system, the Government of Canada hoped to link new funding to a reasonably high-profile change agenda. Health care was a top-of-mind issue for Canadians, and both orders of government were interested in being able to show signs of positive change and improvement. Moreover, the decision to embrace a performance-reporting regime in the late 1990s reflected the tenor of the times in the health sector and public sector management more generally. The OECD had recently embraced performance measurement for the health sector (OECD 2002), and federal and provincial public servants were still working through the implementation of a range of reforms associated with the New Public Management revolution of the 1990s. However, as public concern about the health-care system abated, or at least was overtaken by concerns about the environment and the economy (and the revelations of fraud and corruption captured by the catchphrase 'the sponsorship scandal'), the interest and enthusiasm of both orders of government for health-care performance reporting dwindled.

Fourth, the model upon which the performance-management regime was built assumes that an independent third party would not only ensure that the individual health-system performance reports released by governments were rolled up into a single report but also provide comment and context for the data being released by governments. While the Government of Canada could have been the party to issue reports on the implementation of health care accords, the Health Council was created to avoid any suggestion that provincial and territorial governments were reporting and accountable to the Government of Canada. In fact, along with the Wait Time Alliance, both the Health Council of Canada and the Canadian Institute for Health Information (CIHI) took on the job of reporting on wait times in Canada and rolling up provincial and territorial data on progress to reduce wait times.

The Wait Time Alliance for Timely Access to Health Care is a physician-dominated group associated with the Canadian Medical Association. Faced with the apparent inability of governments to agree on clinically justifiable benchmarks for wait times for diagnostic and surgical care, medical organizations banded together to try to influence the debate and issue their own assessment of progress in implementing the 2004 accord. Over time, the Wait Time Alliance has broadened its focus beyond the initial five priority areas and, to some extent, serves as an alternative to the Health Council in providing third-party oversight of the performance-reporting regime (Health Council of Canada 2011).

The Health Council and CIHI are, to borrow Marchildon's naming convention, 'intergovernmental organizations,' linked to both orders of government (Marchildon 2005). In the case of the Health Council, direction is provided by a board whose chair is a consensus nomination by the federal, provincial, and territorial ministers of health. The other twenty-six board members are named by the participating jurisdictions, half as direct representatives of participating governments and the other half selected by ministers of health as representatives of the general public or as health system experts. In the case of CIHI, it is funded by both Health Canada and provincial and territorial ministries of health. Its fifteen-member Board of Directors is a mix of senior officials from ministries of health, senior executives from health-services delivery organizations, and the chief statistician of Canada.

There are, however, several important differences between the Health Council and CIHI. For example, while CIHI was created in 1994 to serve as a neutral purveyor of statistical information about the health-care system, the Health Council was created in 2003 as an integral part of the performance-reporting regime for health care. Another difference is that the role of CIHI is limited to simply providing data with a modest amount of interpretation or context. Thus, CIHI issues annual reports on the evolution of wait times in Canada. Health system experts are the main consumers of CIHI data, including data on wait times. Moreover, CIHI does not have a formal role of reporting on the implementation of the 2003 and 2004 health accords; this is the responsibility of the Health Council of Canada. And, at least to some extent, the council has reported faithfully on the implementation of the agreements, often, however, lamenting the lack of complete and comparable information. More importantly perhaps, in the absence of comprehensive performance information from provinces, the council has not been able to fulfil its role as an independent arbiter of the performance-reporting regime created by intergovernmental agreement. The council is not nearly as influential as anticipated by some and could be interpreted as merely a health policy think tank generously funded by government, with privileged access to provincial and federal ministers of health. Rather than focus solely on reporting on how individual jurisdictions were complying with the accord, in recent years the council has become a vehicle to showcase and disseminate information about innovation and best practices in the Canadian health-care system.

Finally, the eventual collapse of the performance-management regime may be the result of confusion about what it means to make government more 'accountable' to citizens. Accountability is an elusive concept, all the more so when the focus is a highly complex public and private enterprise like health care. On a positive note, as is true in other policy sectors examined in this volume, health care is an area where governments made a determined effort to construct a non-hierarchical accountability regime. However, Quebec, and for a time Alberta as well, remained aloof from the process, arguing that the accountability regime was insufficiently non-hierarchical or, as I argue below, it was based on accountability of a single health-care system to a single public.

In conceptual terms, this early commitment to performance reporting was essentially a commitment to greater transparency, the first of the four core components of accountability suggested by Ebrahim and Weisband (2007) and discussed in the introductory chapter. Later iterations of the accountability regime moved from transparency to two of the other components: a degree of answerability/justification and a modicum of compliance reporting by the Health Council of Canada and civil society organizations – notably the Wait Time Alliance.

The theory is that enhanced performance reporting will allow citizens to more effectively hold governments to account for the success, and especially the lack thereof, of the health-care system. Yet there is little evidence that voters, as much as they say that health care is a priority, vote on the basis of their policy preferences or experience with the health-care system. Nor do voters vote retrospectively or use their vote to punish governments that have not performed well – at least when there are two orders of government with some responsibility for the policy area (Anderson 2008; Cutler 2004; Cutler and Mendelsohn 2005). Moreover, the inherent complexity of wait times as an issue makes it difficult to attribute blame or give credit. The problem is compounded if the performance-reporting regime is based on a large number of indicators where the outcomes for each are hard to attribute solely or even primarily to the provincial government. Thus, it is not surprising that neither parliamentarians, provincial legislators, nor the media, much less the general public are actually willing and able to make much use of the performance data that are released (Canada, Office of the Auditor General of Canada 2005; McDavid and Huse 2011; Thomas 2004).

Implications for Intergovernmental Relations

As suggested at the outset of this chapter, the recent Canadian experience with performance reporting in health care is part of a larger story of a shift in Canadian intergovernmental relations towards a model of federal leadership on performance measurement as a tool for ensuring greater accountability leading to policy change but also a more subtle form of federal policy leadership (Simmons 2009). Note, however, that in this formulation there are two objectives: accountability and program improvement by means of federal leadership. These dual objectives are common in performance-reporting regimes (Scheirer 2000). A pan-Canadian system of performance indicators is meant to allow for provincial comparisons that should permit voters to hold provincial governments more accountable, presumably by punishing them at election time. There is also an objective of federal leadership. The process of establishing the pan-Canadian performance-reporting regime gives the federal government influence over the health-care system – influence that is exercised indirectly when voters and interest groups seek to hold provincial governments accountable, rather than directly, as is the case with penalties to offending provinces pursuant to the terms of the Canada Health Act. Alternatively, subtle federal leadership is achieved as a result of the fact that, in the presence of comparable indicators, provinces begin to emulate each other (Simmons 2009).

Simmons (2009) correctly observes that the effectiveness of such a strategy will vary by policy sector. She goes on to postulate, 'If there are areas of policy where a national vision of community is desired to infuse provinces' design and delivery of policies and programs, the public reporting model offers a more partnership-oriented practice of federalism as compared to the highly conditional grants of the postwar era' (8). This poses the question of whether there is a national vision of community for health care. There are several reasons to suggest there is not.

First, it is not clear that all Canadians want a national vision of community to inform health care. While the Canadian commitment to a publicly funded health-care system is ostensibly a singular part of Canadian identity, it is more likely that it is a singular part of Canadian efforts to distinguish the country from the United States. This matters because some Canadians do not wish to aggressively distinguish themselves from the United States and do not need or want to rally around a pan-Canadian vision of health care. Alternatively, some Canadians, notably Québécois, have other ways of distinguishing themselves from the United States and similarly do not need to make medicare a central part of their identity. In any case, 'a health system different from that of the United States' does not require a particularly complex or robust pan-Canadian vision.

Second, as has often been observed, there is not a single Canadian health-care system; there are several, suggesting a relatively weak commitment to a single vision for health care. Over the past forty years, provincial governments have developed distinctive health-care regimes. For example, there are significant differences between provinces in the structure and management of the health-care system (e.g., regionalization), the size and scope of the basket of publicly insured services (e.g., pharmacare, home care), and the roles and responsibilities of different health professions (e.g., nurse practitioners, pharmacists). More importantly, individual provincial governments are held accountable for the health-care system in each province, regardless of how similar it is to – or different it is from – other provinces and territories.

Third, following Banting and Boadway (2004, 36), a national vision based on a common social citizenship means that 'stripped to its essentials, social citizenship implies that a sick baby at one end of the country is entitled to medical care on the same terms and conditions as a sick baby at the other end of the country.' Simmons (2009) correctly observes that different conceptions of Canada as a sharing community and of the roles of the federal and provincial governments lead to different versions of what matters for a sick baby. Thus, she argues that the performance-reporting regime for Canadian health care developed between 1999 and 2004 is one that privileges, not 'the same terms and conditions' as suggested by common social citizenship, but rather, whether 'the parents of a sick baby determine whether they would have received similar medical care in a different province' (Simmons 2009, 4). Yet in the real world of parents and sick babies, and indeed for most government services, the core question is not usually about the terms and conditions of care, or whether care is similar to or different from that of other provinces. Rather, the core question is whether the health-care system can help my sick baby. Whether and to what extent the means by which the sickness is addressed is the same as or different from that in another province matters relatively little, as long as the health of the baby is assured. While some may be concerned about the overall terms and conditions under which health care is delivered, beyond some basic general principles (e.g., a tax-funded single-payer system), most citizens are more concerned that the health-care delivery system is there for them when they need it. Stated a bit more generally, patients and citizens in a given province ultimately evaluate a health-care system not by comparing it to the system in other provinces, but by coming to some conclusion about whether the system works for them. Stated more broadly still, informed observers may decry the lack of uniformity in home care, palliative care, or pharmaceutical care from one province to the next and call for 'national' – that is to say, pan-Canadian – standards, but citizens are more likely to ignore the health-care system until they need it, and when they do, be focused on getting what they need, hopefully paid for by 'the government,' with little or no reference to what is happening in other provinces. That said, some Canadians, operating with a more organic conception of both federalism and government services, are also willing to forego enhanced service delivery, and one therefore assumes comparable service delivery, in favour of preserving and reflecting local preferences (Fafard, Rocher, and Côté 2009, 2010).

From Accountability to Marketing

So if, as is argued here, the performance-reporting regime grafted onto federal health-care transfers is a failure, in hindsight why did the federal, provincial, and territorial governments invest so much time and energy into the process? The hypothesis that I suggest here can be summarized in one word: *marketing*.

Performance reports as a marketing tool are nothing new. They are very common in the private sector, where companies incorporate performance measures into how they market their particular good or service. In the case of automobiles, for example, reliability ratings by magazines, performance ratings by rating agencies, and safety and fuel-economy ratings by governments have all become common fare in print, radio, television, and now Internet advertising by the major automobile manufacturers (Shaker and Basem 2010). The general idea appears to be to use performance indicators to tell a story about how reliable, well-performing, safe, and efficient an automobile is in order to influence consumer choice. Specifically, once a third-party agency (e.g., *Consumer Reports* magazine) compares and contrasts the products of firms in a given sector, those firms that do well then use the ratings in their marketing campaigns. In other words, performance reports are not only or even primarily about being accountable, they are about messaging and marketing.

It would appear that public sector managers are able to emulate their private sector counterparts and take whatever performance data they have to tell a positive story about government in general and health-care delivery in particular. Since the early 2000s, the federal and provincial governments have strategically used new health-care performance data to convey the fact that the publicly funded health-care system is not crumbling, that wait times for surgery and key diagnostic procedures are, in fact, being reduced, and that the Canadian health-care system is getting better. Moreover, the reports of the Health Council of Canada have become a part of that effort.

However, not all governments are equally committed to telling a 'good news' story about the Canadian health-care system or at least telling the story in the same way. Several provinces are experimenting with changes to health-care service delivery that call on private clinics to play a greater role in delivery and diagnostic and surgical procedures. Here the message is not that the publicly funded and publicly delivered health-care system is getting better. Instead the message is that service delivery can be improved if governments make greater use of private providers.

However, to the extent that performance data are about marketing, it may not matter whether jurisdictions report using the same indicators at the same time. As a way of increasing public confidence in the health-care system, what matters is the simple message that wait times are getting shorter, even if there is considerable variation among surgical or diagnostic procedures or among different jurisdictions. Seen as a marketing exercise, the Canadian experiment with pan-Canadian performance reporting was a modest success.

Conclusion

Notwithstanding its considerable flaws, both in general terms and with respect to health care, performance reporting is here to stay (Adair et al. 2006a, 2006b; Radin 2006; Thomas 2004). But performance reporting, as such, is by no means a guarantee of accountability to citizens. At best, performance reports such as those that were grafted onto Canadian health-care transfers over the past decade are a support to accountability. In effect, performance information 'supports an operational accountability relationship, it does not itself guarantee accountability, and an exchange of performance information is not itself an accountability relationship' (Brown, Porcellato, and Barnsley 2006, 74). Moreover, the overview of the marriage of performance reporting with intergovernmental health transfers presented in this chapter is an unhappy one.

Over a period of less than eight years, the federal, provincial, and territorial governments experimented with a dizzying array of indicators, benchmarks, and even guarantees. At some points, the performance reporting was intentionally very broad; in other cases, health system performance was to be captured by a much narrower set of numbers that focused on how long patients waited for selected surgeries and diagnostic tests. However, by 2007 the performance-reporting regime was in decline.

The failure to implement a stable system of performance reporting linked to federal health-care transfers is the result of a number of factors. First, provincial and territorial governments were not all equally willing to embrace the same pan-Canadian system of health-care performance reporting. Second, devising a set of health-care-related performance measures that was simultaneously robust, measurable, and compelling proved to be more difficult than anticipated. Third, the decision to tie federal transfers to a performance-measurement scheme reflected an underlying set of political and ideational conditions that did not last. Fourth, the regime was predicated on a third-party evaluation of the health-system performance indicators, but the Health Council of Canada never did establish itself in this role, in part because some provinces never agreed to participate, and in part because several provincial governments simply lost interest in reporting. Fifth, the collapse of the performance regime reflects that citizens are not able to make much sense of the reams of data that the regime generates, even with the interpretative role of the Health Council.

Most importantly, the experiment failed because it was predicated on the existence of a shared Canadian embrace of a single health-care system. As I attempted to demonstrate in the latter part of this chapter, there are in fact several Canadian health-care systems, and accountability remains focused on provincial and territorial governments and those who actually deliver health-care services. It is difficult to imagine a single performance-indicator regime supporting what are, of necessity, several distinct and individually complex accountability relationships.

NOTES

1 I would like to acknowledge the assistance of Jennifer Linehan, who was enormously helpful in working out many of the details of the successive intergovernmental agreements referenced in this paper. I would also like to thank Leslie Seidle, Peter Oliver, John Wright, and the editors of this volume for helpful comments on an earlier draft of this chapter. All remaining errors of fact and interpretation remain, of course, my responsibility.

2 The Health Council of Canada held its first meeting in January 2004.
3 Benchmarks were announced in December 2005 for cancer, hip fracture, hip and knee replacements, and cataract and cardiac bypass surgery.
4 *Chaoulli v. Quebec (Attorney General)*, [2005] SCC 35 (June, 2005).
5 I am indebted to Leslie Seidle for emphasizing this point in his comments on an earlier draft of this paper.

REFERENCES

Adair, C.E., E. Simpson, A.L. Casebeer, J.M. Birdsell, K.A. Hayden, and S. Lewis. 2006a."Performance Measurement in Healthcare: Part I – Concepts and Trends from a State of the Science Review.' *Healthcare Policy* 1 (4): 85–104.
– 2006b. 'Performance Measurement in Healthcare: Part II – State of the Science Findings by Stage of the Performance Measurement Process.' *Healthcare Policy* 2 (1): 56–78.
Aglukkaq, Leona. 2012. 'Feds Committed to Maintaining Basic Tenets of Universal, Publicly-Funded Health Care.' *Hill Times Online.* 6 February. http://www.hilltimes.com/policy-briefing/2012/02/06/feds-committed-to-maintaining-basic-tenets-of-universal-publicly-funded/29457.
Anderson, Cameron D. 2008. 'Economic Voting, Multilevel Governance and Information in Canada.' *Canadian Journal of Political Science* 41 (2): 329–54.
Baker, G. Ross, N. Brooks, G. Anderson, A. Brown, I. McKillop, M. Murray, and G. Pink. 1998. 'Healthcare Performance Measurement in Canada: Who's Doing What?' *Healthcare Quarterly* 2 (2): 22–26.
Banting, Keith, and Robin Boadway. 2004. 'Defining the Sharing Community: The Federal Role in Health Care.' In *Money, Politics and Health Care*, edited by Harvey Lazar and France St-Hilaire, 1–77. Montreal and Kingston: Institute for Research on Public Policy and Queen's University, Institute of intergovernmental Relations.
Boychuk, Gerard. 2007. 'How Ottawa Gambles: Rolling the Dice in Health Care Reform.' In *How Ottawa Spends 2005–2006: Managing the Minority*, edited by G. Bruce Doern, 41–58. Kingston and Montreal: McGill-Queen's University Press.
Brown, Adalsteinn, Christina Porcellato, and Jan Barnsley. 2006. 'Accountability: Unpacking the Suitcase.' *Healthcare Quarterly* 9 (3): 72–5.
Canada. Governor General. 2011. Here for All Canadians: Stability, Prosperity, Security; Speech from the Throne, June 3, 2011. Ottawa: Government of Canada.

Canada. Office of the Auditor General of Canada. 2005. *2005 April Report of the Auditor General of Canada*. Ottawa: Office of the Auditor General of Canada.

Canada. Royal Commission on the Future of Health Care in Canada. 2002. *Building on Values: The Future of Health Care in Canada*. Ottawa: Royal Commission on the Future of Health Care.

Canadian Intergovernmental Conference Secretariat. 2000. 'First Ministers' Meeting Communiqué on Health.' http://www.scics.gc.ca/english/conferences.asp?a=viewdocument&id=1144.

– 2003. '2003 First Ministers' Accord on Health Care Renewal.' http://hc-sc.gc.ca/hcs-sss/delivery-prestation/fptcollab/2003accord/index-eng.php.

Cutler, Fred. 2004. 'Government Responsibility and Electoral Accountability in Federations.' *Publius* 34 (2): 19–38.

Cutler, Fred, and Michael Mendelsohn. 2005. 'Unnatural Loyalties or Native Collaborationists? The Governance and Citizens of Canadian Federalism.' In *Insiders and Outsiders: Alan Cairns and the Reshaping of Canadian Citizenship*, edited by Gerald Kernerman and Phillip Resnick, 71–89. Vancouver: University of British Columbia Press.

Denhardt, Kathryn G., and Maria P. Aristigueta. 2008. 'Performance Management Systems: Providing Accountability and Challenging Collaboration.' In *Performance Information in the Public Sector: How It Is Used*, edited by Wouter Van Dooren and Steven Van de Walle, 106–22. New York: Palgrave Macmillan.

Dopson, Sue, and Louise Fitzgerald, eds. 2005. *Knowledge to Action? Evidence-Based Health Care in Context*. Oxford: Oxford University Press.

Fafard, Patrick, François Rocher, and Catherine Côté. 2009. 'Citizens, Clients and Federalism: A Critical Appraisal of Integrated Service Delivery in Canada.' *Canadian Public Administration* 52 (4): 549–68.

– 2010. 'The Presence (or Lack Thereof) of a Federal Culture in Canada: The Views of Canadians.' *Regional and Federal Studies* 20 (1): 19–43.

Graefe, Peter. 2008. 'The Spending Power and Federal Social Policy Leadership: A Prospective View.' *IRPP Policy Matters* 9 (3): 54–106.

Gray, Charlotte. 1998. 'A Rock in a Hard Place.' *Canadian Medical Association Journal* 159 (8): 991–3.

Harty, Harry. 2008. 'Epilogue: The Many Faces of Use.' In *Performance Information in the Public Sector: How It Is Used*, edited by Wouter Van Dooren and Steven Van de Walle, 227–40. New York: Palgrave Macmillan.

Health Council of Canada. 2005. *Health Care Renewal in Canada: Accelerating Change – Annual Report to Canadians 2004*. Toronto: Health Council of Canada.

– 2007. *Health Care Renewal in Canada: Measuring Up?* Toronto: Health Council of Canada.

– 2011. *Progress Report 2011: Health Care Renewal in Canada.* Toronto: Health Council of Canada.

Ibbitson, John. 2011. 'By Attaching No Strings, Flaherty Binds Irate Provinces to Health Plan.' *Globe and Mail*, 20 December. http://www.theglobeandmail.com/news/politics/john-ibbitson/by-attaching-no-strings-flaherty-binds-irate-provinces-to-health-plan/article2277435/. Retrieved April 12, 2011.

Juneau, André. 2011. 'Unilateral Pronouncements Won't Help Us All Get Along'. *Globe and Mail*, 21 December 21. http://www.theglobeandmail.com/news/opinions/opinion/unilateral-pronouncements-wont-help-us-all-get-along/article2278575/.

Lazar, Harvey, France St-Hilaire, and Jean-François Tremblay. 2004. 'Vertical Fiscal Imbalance: Myth or Reality?' In *Money, Politics, and Health Care: Reconstructing the Federal-Provincial Partnership*, edited by Harvey Lazar, and France St-Hilaire, 135–87. Kingston: Institute of Intergovernmental Relations, Queen's University.

Marchildon, G. 2005. *Health Systems in Transition: Canada.* Copenhagen: WHO Regional Office for Europe on Behalf of the European Observatory on Health Systems and Policies.

McDavid, James, and Irene Huse. 2011. Legislator Uses of Public Performance Reports: Findings from a Five-Year Study.' *American Journal of Evaluation* 33 (1): 7–25.

Ontario. Ministry of Health and Long-Term Care (MOHLTC). 2004. 'Ontario's Health Transformation Plan: Purpose and Progress.' Speech by George Smitherman, minister of health. http://www.health.gov.on.ca/english/media/speeches/archives/sp_04/sp_090904.html.

– n.d. 'Ontario's Health System Performance Report.' http://www.health.gov.on.ca/english/public/pub/ministry_reports/pirc_02/pirc_02.html. Retrieved August 13, 2009.

Organisation for Economic Co-operation and Development (OECD). 2002. *Measuring Up: Improving Health System Performance in OECD Countries.* Paris: Organisation for Economic Co-operation and Development.

Peach, Ian, and William Warriner. 2007. *Canadian Social Policy Renewal, 1994–2000.* Halifax: Fernwood.

Perkel, Colin. 2003. 'No New Health-care Bureaucracy, but Public Accountability Key, Romanow Says.' Canadian Press, 3 Feb.

Radin, Beryl A. 2006. *Challenging the Performance Movement: Accountability, Complexity, and Democratic Values.* Washington, DC: Georgetown University Press.

Scheirer, Mary Ann. 2000. 'Getting More "Bang" for Your Performance Measures "Buck."' *Evaluation* 21 (2): 139–49.

Shaker, T.I., and Y.A. Basem. 2010. 'Relationship Marketing and Organizational Performance Indicators.' *European Journal of Social Sciences* 12 (4): 545–57.

Simmons, Julie M. 2009. 'Federalism and Accountabilities in the Social Arena.' *Optimum Online* 39 (2). http://www.optimumonline.ca/article.phtml? id=334.

Tapper, Jake. 2009. 'Interview with Canadian PM Stephen Harper, 8/10/09.' *ABC News.* 10 Aug. http://abcnews.go.com/blogs/politics/2009/08/interview-with-canadian-pm-stephen-harper-81009/.

Thomas, Paul G. 2004. *Performance Measurement, Reporting and Accountability: Recent Trends and Future Directions.* Regina: Saskatchewan Institute of Public Policy.

Veillard, Jeremy, Tai Huynh, Sten Ardal, Sowmya Kadandale, Niek S. Klazinga, and Adalsteinn D. Brown. 2010. 'Making Health System Performance Measurement Useful to Policy Makers: Aligning Strategies, Measurement and Local Health System Accountability in Ontario.' *HealthCare Policy* 5 (3): 49–65.

Yeates, Neil. 2000. 'Performance Management and Accountability in Saskatchewan.' *Public Sector Management* 10 (2): 20–1.

3 The National Child Benefit: Collective Accountability through Public Reporting

JULIE M. SIMMONS

The accountability regime of the National Child Benefit (NCB) is a particularly intriguing case of the new generation of intergovernmental agreements, for several reasons. First, as the product of relatively co-operative intergovernmental negotiations, it allows us to explore the implications of public reporting when both orders of government are enthusiastic about the process, and without the presence of considerable ongoing federal-provincial conflict. Second, unlike in the other cases presented in this volume, where governments report individually to the public, in this case the federal and provincial governments collectively agreed to jointly publish a single annual report and to be held collectively accountable. Third, unlike some other intergovernmental agreements emphasizing public reporting, governments have annually met their commitments to make public certain data. Fourth, as the NCB has been in place longer than most of the agreements considered in this volume, it offers an opportunity to probe whether public reporting has resulted in policy learning or transfer across jurisdictions, and whether there has been convergence or a sustained pattern of diversity in the nature of provincial programs and services, absent more traditional conditions on federal transfers. Fifth, the longevity of the NCB reporting process allows us to probe the link between public reporting and policy evaluation. The latter often is a secondary stated goal of governments in the new generation of accountability agreements.

This chapter has three aims. The first is to identify the nature of the accountability regime associated with the NCB. The second considers the regime in practice. The chapter then offers some observations about the utility of public reporting as a form of accountability, based on this case. Unlike several other cases in this volume that are characterized by intergovernmental wrangling and lack of information sharing, governments have demonstrated considerable dedication to transparent annual public reporting on federal and provincial financial commitments to the NCB, the programs and services these commitments fund, and the results these programs and services are achieving. Nevertheless, like in traditional forms of accountability, it is easier to envision in theory than to put into practice. Public reporting remains confusing and vague, and thus it does not meet its potential as a way for non-governmental actors to hold governments to account for the programs they introduce or the results those programs achieve. The vague nature is owing, however, not to government attempts to obscure their activities from other governments, but to the amorphous nature of the NCB itself, and the pitfalls inherent in performance measurement.

The Anatomy of the National Child Benefit and Evolution of Federal-Provincial Fiscal Arrangements

The NCB is a joint creation of the federal and provincial governments, established in 1997, and in operation the year following.[1] The federal component is the National Child Benefit Supplement (NCB Supplement) to the federal Canada Child Tax Benefit (CCTB), which takes the form of monthly income-tested (as opposed to means-tested) payments to low-income families.[2] A variety of provincial initiatives benefiting children in low-income families represent the provincial component of the NCB. The provincial initiatives must be 'consistent' with the goals of the NCB agreed to by both federal and provincial social services ministers: to reduce the depth of child poverty, promote attachment to the labour market, and reduce overlap and duplication of federal and provincial programs (Federal, Provincial and Territorial Ministers Responsible for Social Services 1999).

There have been federal income supports for families with children in various forms since 1918, when the Child Tax Exemption was first introduced (Federal, Provincial and Territorial Ministers Responsible for Social Services 2001). In 1993 the federal government melded the Family Allowance (initially universal in 1945, then targeted after 1973) and the income-tested refundable child tax credit (introduced in 1978) into a single (non-universal) Child Tax Benefit (CTB). The CTB included a Working Income Supplement (WIS) for working poor families. The CTB was replaced by the CCTB, and the NCB Supplement replaced the WIS. The NCB Supplement reaches a larger number of families than the WIS, as it is not just for the working poor but also for those receiving provincial social assistance.

The evolution of federal-provincial funding arrangements for present-day provincial components of the NCB is less easily traced. Provincial income support (social assistance) for needy individuals as well as a variety of welfare child and youth welfare services were, from 1966 to 1995, cost-shared between the federal and provincial governments under the Canada Assistance Plan (CAP) (see Hobson and St-Hilaire 2000). CAP's conditions precluded provinces from introducing a residency requirement and professionalized the provision of programs, ensuring that access to programs was not ad hoc but rather according to specific criteria. In the case of social assistance, the criterion was *need*, as defined by each province (see Boychuk 1998). When CAP was replaced by the more 'lightly conditioned' (Lazar 2005, 13) 1995 Canada Health and Social Transfer (CHST), provinces had even greater discretion over the design of social assistance and other programs and services benefiting poor children.[3] Since the CHST was a block grant for post-secondary education, health care, social assistance, and social services, provinces also had greater discretion over the amount of funding devoted to the kinds of provincial programs and services that today form the provincial component of the NCB.

However, because of the significant reduction in the value of transfers from the federal government to the provinces under the CHST, the provinces had far fewer dollars to maintain existing programs, let alone introduce new ones. When in 2003 the CHST was divided into the Canada Health Transfer and the Canada Social Transfer (CST), federal funding was slightly more targeted, though no more conditional. Funding for social assistance and other programs and services benefiting low-income families was no longer combined with health-care funding, but still in the same envelope as post-secondary education. The CST is also the vehicle through which the federal government provided funds to provinces in relation to the Early Childhood Development Agreement (2000) and the Early Learning and Child Care Agreement (2003). The NCB exists in addition to the CST. Provinces can introduce, as part of their component of the NCB, programs and services like those funded under the CST.

A departure from the 'hierarchy of governments' approach implied in the conditional CAP, the NCB is a partnership between the two orders of government. In an effort to disentangle provincial design of social policy from federal financing, provincial components of the NCB are funded (in part or in whole) not through a transfer of funds from the federal government to the provinces (as in the case of the CHST and CST), but by provincial government 'recovery' of the income of social assistance recipients by a value equivalent to the NCB Supplement.[4] The idea at the outset was for provinces to decrease payments for social assistance recipients by one dollar for every dollar parents received through the NCB Supplement, until the value of the NCB Supplement exceeded the value of provincial funding for children under social assistance. At that time, any additional increases to the NCB Supplement would be passed on to social assistance families. Given the breadth of the NCB goals that provinces must work within when designing their NCB initiatives, one might conclude that the federal strings or conditions attached to provincial actions are both loose and thin. However, it would be inappropriate to even consider these goals as conditions in the traditional sense; they are not imposed on provinces by the federal government, nor does any funding actually flow directly from one government to another, nor is the federal NCB Supplement conditional upon the introduction of any provincial programs and services. These attributes set the NCB apart from other agreements examined in this volume. Further, there is no piece of legislation outlining the contours of the NCB. It was initially announced in the federal Speech from the Throne in the fall of 1997, and several pamphlets co-authored by all social services ministers also explain how the NCB works.

The accountability requirements of governments are found in the NCB Governance and Accountability Framework, agreed to by all ministers of social services in 1998 (National Child Benefit 1998). Because money does not flow directly from the federal government to provinces, the accountability regime associated with the NCB is also unlike that of any other examined in this volume. In a sense, families on social assistance are the conduits for exchange. This design has been the subject of considerable criticism because of the perception that families receiving social assistance are penalized and / or are not better off (Freiler and Cerny 1998; McKeen 2001; National Council of Welfare 1998; Patterson, Levasseur, and Teplova 2004). Nevertheless, of importance to this discussion, the social assistance payments recovered by provinces are 'provincial dollars' and thus the provinces are not accountable *to the federal government* for how these funds are spent. While each participating government is committed to 'mak[ing] provisions for the level of information sharing [across governments] … required for program management and implementation as well as for program evaluation,' the Governance and Accountability Framework 'emphasize[s] processes that focus on the accountability to the public for program effectiveness and that minimize administrative reporting' (National Child Benefit 1998). Social services ministers are committed to reporting annually on the performance of the program, and the emphasis of the single report is to be on program outcomes (as opposed to inputs or outputs). The report is to 'include data on Government of Canada investments made in the Canada Child Tax Benefit and beneficiaries; provincial/territorial reinvestments and any incremental investments, and beneficiaries; and results and outcomes achieved.' Finally, as part of the participating governments' 'commitment to continual improvement,' the Accountability Framework opens the door for involvement of non-governmental actors. It states that 'evaluation, feedback from stakeholders and the public, and flexibility to adjust the national child benefit over time are important characteristics of the initiative' (National Child Benefit 1988).

The commitment of federal and provincial governments to establishing meaningful measures to gauge the impact of the NCB is considerable. Focusing on reporting results to the public as the primary form of accountability is particularly appealing in this case, because the specific inter-jurisdictional aspects of the NCB belie traditional forms of accountability (i.e., each individual government to its legislature). Even the auditor general puzzled over this conundrum, asking, in his review of the National Child Benefit, 'How should the Auditor General, in fulfilling his obligations to Parliament, look at programs that are not fully federal?' (Auditor General of Canada 1999). Ultimately, social services ministers have committed to a reporting format where all participating governments are equally responsible for reporting on the *results* of the NCB.

The Accountability Regime in Practice: Inputs and Outputs

Each participating government has, since 1998, been remarkably forthcoming with data, investing considerable resources into meeting the reporting commitments. Since 1998, governments have jointly produced an annual report, usually about ninety pages in length, that explains how the NCB works, and details the growth of the NCB Supplement over time, and the amount of funds reinvested and invested by each province into programs that benefit low-income families (inputs). The report also identifies the overall percentage of provincial programs which fall into seven categories: provincial child benefits and earned income supplements; child/day care; supplementary health benefits; early childhood services and children at risk; youth initiatives; First Nations; and other programs, benefits, and services (outputs).[5] Finally, the reports attempt to measure outcomes, detailing 'indicators' of whether the NCB achieves its overall goals of workforce attachment and reducing the depth of poverty.

The auditor general's 1999 report on the NCB acknowledges that 'data do not have to be perfect but they should be as good as possible' (Auditor General of Canada 1999). By many accounts, provincial and federal officials have worked cooperatively to ensure that data are as good as possible. In the early years of the NCB, the technical working group of federal, provincial, and territorial officials worked in a surprisingly cooperative manner to tackle the complex task of sharing federal and provincial data, particularly those regarding family incomes, to deliver the federal and provincial components of the NCB. Identifying how much each provincial government may reinvest in a given year is not a straightforward task, because aggregate data on incomes of families in a province are from the year previous. Nevertheless, the federal and provincial governments agreed to a system whereby the annual NCB Reports present both actual and estimated expenditures for provinces. Unfortunately, and perhaps not entirely because of these complexities, there has always been a lag between the information in the reports and the year of their publication. For example, in 2010 the latest available report was 2007, which was published in 2009, and provides actual expenditures for 2004–5 and 2005–6, but estimates for 2006–7 and 2007–8 (Federal, Provincial and Territorial Ministers Responsible for Social Services 2009, 13). No additional annual reports have been issued since 2009.

For an outsider, however, judging whether the data are 'as good as possible' is not easy. A hallmark of credible data is whether they can be independently verified by a third party. This is not the case with the NCB, as the reports rely entirely on government self-reporting of activity. The reports indicate that the Canada Revenue Agency is the source of federal government data, but how the provincial government data on NCB programs are compiled is unclear. It appears that governments assume that the information provided by other governments is accurate.

Further, when provinces report their NCB initiatives, they combine the value of funds allocated to 'reinvestments' and 'investments.' Reinvestment funds are 'social assistance / child benefit savings and, in some jurisdictions, Children's Special Allowance recoveries' (Federal,

Provincial and Territorial Ministers Responsible for Social Services 2009, 49) – in other words, provincial money made available by reducing funds flowing to social assistance recipients. Investment funds are 'additional funds that some jurisdictions devote to the NCB, over and above the reinvestment amounts' (49). As a result of combining reinvestment and investment funds, it is impossible to identify what programs each jurisdiction has chosen to fund with the money that would otherwise have been used for social assistance, had the federal NCB Supplement not been in place.

At the same time, because investments are defined as 'additional funds' rather than simply 'funds' devoted to the NCB initiative, the reports do not capture all of the programs or all of the funds provinces have set aside for programs that satisfy or work towards the goals of the NCB initiative – only those programs or funds that are new in any given year. The template for provincial reporting allows provinces to report the monetary value of their combined 'investments and reinvestments,' which fall into seven categories mentioned above: provincial child benefits and earned income supplements; child/day care; supplementary health benefits; early childhood services and children at risk; youth initiatives; First Nations; and other programs, benefits, and services. It does not capture the full monetary commitment or all of the programs a province might have in place that fall under any one category. Accordingly, the reports not only make it difficult to track distinctions across provinces regarding the nature of reinvestments, but also do not provide a complete picture of all of a province's programs that fall into any one of the seven categories, let alone all of a province's programs that are oriented towards reducing the depth of poverty and promoting workforce attachment. In practical terms, in an annual progress report, a province reports only the value of *new* money allocated to child / day care and / or the value of reinvested money supporting child / day care. The province would not report the overall value of funds allocated to child / day care. Thus the reader does not have an accurate understanding of the overall size of a province's investment in child / day care from these reports.

To complicate matters further, in the 2007 report, Manitoba explicitly counted as 'additional funds' devoted to the NCB initiative some or all (it is unclear) of the federal funds transferred to provinces through the 2003 Multilateral Framework on Early Learning and 2000 Early Childhood Development Agreement (Federal, Provincial and Territorial Ministers Responsible for Social Services 2009, 68). The other provinces did not explicitly include or exclude this funding, so it is not clear whether it is included in their data or not.

Finally, each NCB annual progress report indicates the actual or estimated expenditures on NCB investments in each province over a four-year period, demonstrating whether a province has increased or decreased spending in any one category. However, comparison across provinces is made difficult because data are aggregate, rather than per capita, and there is no adjustment for inflation. As a result, any comparison of programs in the same province over time is not as accurate as it could be, and accurate interprovincial comparison is elusive. Each annual progress report also includes data dating back to 1997 on the growth of the NCB Supplement – the federal component of the NCB. However, again there is no adjustment for inflation. For the lay reader, the NCB Supplement therefore appears to have increased in value to a greater extent than it has in real terms for low-income families.

A sceptic might be inclined to conclude that governments are deliberately creating a muddy picture to avoid de facto reporting from one order of government to the other. However, without exception, interviews with provincial government officials involved with the National Child Benefit in all but one jurisdiction (PEI) revealed a remarkable level of respect for all other jurisdictions involved in the NCB. This is particularly noteworthy because prior to the development of the NCB, social services ministers had actually ceased to meet in a federal-provincial forum because of the acrimony of federal-provincial relations (Simmons 2005). More accurately, many of the complications identified above are owing to the nature of the NCB initiative itself. The Governance and Accountability Framework states that the NCB 'will see provincial and territorial governments reinvesting social assistance funds made available by the Government of Canada's investment [in the NCB Supplement]' and 'will see provinces and territories exploring whether incremental funds can be devoted to the provincial/territorial component of the National Child Benefit, fiscal resources permitting' (National Child Benefot 1998). It is thus not surprising that the provinces do not separate these two aspects of the provincial components in the annual report.

Policy Learning: Comparing Inputs and Outputs across Jurisdictions

One of the theoretical benefits of public reporting is that governments can learn from the practices reported in other jurisdictions, testing the reasonableness of their own policies, adjusting them to emulate 'best practices,' to remain in the 'middle of the pack,' or ensure that they are similar to those of their immediate neighbours (Allard 2004; Freeman 1985). Harrison (2006, 14) offers that provincial governments will be sensitive to ideas, in the form of 'examples set by other jurisdictions, not because they fear that others' actions will undermine the efficacy of their own but because other jurisdictions offer examples of how to satisfy voters' preferences, or alternatively, benchmarks against which voters will evaluate them.' Another theoretical benefit of public reporting is that non-governmental agencies, opposition parties, or individuals can use reported data to pressure governments to modify their policies, singling out 'laggards.' There is certainly some evidence of convergence in the provincial components of the NCB. Over time, a majority of provinces have established a provincial income-tested child benefit (as opposed to a needs-tested benefit) as their key NCB initiative. The exceptions are Prince Edward Island, New Brunswick, and Alberta. The primary initiative in PEI is a Healthy Child Allowance for families on social assistance to provide for participation in sport recreation and / or cultural activities, while the primary initiative in New Brunswick is a program that aims to 'identify best practices for discipline in the school system when positive environment alone is not enough' (Federal, Provincial and Territorial Ministers Responsible for Social Services 2008, 56). Alberta has adopted an Alberta Child Health Benefit, which provides children in families with limited incomes (not just those on social assistance) with health services outside the Alberta Health Care Insurance. Interestingly, provinces have created provincial child benefits at different stages since 1997, with Ontario and Manitoba doing so most recently in 2008. This suggests that the presence or absence of policy learning across provinces may be evaluated best over the long term.

For social policy advocates the most contentious issue pertaining to the NCB has been whether provinces 'claw back' all or part of the value of the National Child Benefit Supplement from families on social assistance. If provinces do choose to do so, then the poorest children do not benefit from a rise in family incomes brought about by the NCB Supplement. Only New Brunswick has always 'flowed through' the entirety of the value of the NCB Supplement to families receiving social assistance, going against the overall thrust of the NCB. However, at various times since 1997 each of the provinces has 'flowed through' some aspect of the value of the NCB Supplement. More recently this is evident because the value of the NCB Supplement has grown to exceed the proportion of funds some provinces set aside for the children component of social assistance or for their provincial child benefit. In other words, these provincial systems are reaching maturity. In other cases, however, provinces including Nova Scotia, Newfoundland and Labrador, and Manitoba chose to pass along some aspect of the NCB Supplement – usually annual increases – to social assistance recipients before the provincial system reached maturity.

What role has public reporting played in these provincial policy patterns? In terms of government-to-government learning, the role is minimal. Provincial officials reported that they understood the reports to be a mechanism for accountability or for providing 'evidence.' However, they variously described the audience for the reports as 'the public,' 'the feds,' and 'the odd reporter or maybe a few researchers.' The reports were also described as 'painful,' 'after the fact,' and 'not a very productive exercise.'

Some provincial officials were of the view that each jurisdiction developed its initiatives independent of the others. However, the more commonly offered perspective was that there was considerable cross-pollination, as provincial officials 'were interested in keeping pace with developments in other provinces – the extent and types of reinvestments that they were making.' In the words of one official, 'This [was] breaking new ground and we wanted a comfort level around it. We wanted to be moving in a direction that was sound and reaching the right population' (interviews with public servants). Most officials flagged the officials' committees and informal communication as key sources of timely information exchange, rather than the reports themselves, supporting evidence of the role of intergovernmental institutions in fostering communication found in Canada (Papillion and Simeon 2004; Simmons 2004) and other federations (e.g., Beyle 1988; Davis 1998). Officials described these meetings as fostering 'openness and trust,' where information could be gathered about 'best practices' and 'lessons learned' in other jurisdictions. Officials in both Nova Scotia and in Manitoba specifically mentioned aspects of the Saskatchewan model as informing their own. In sum, the formal reporting was described as 'part of the process but not the ingredient for successes' as 'much of this is relationship based' (interviews with public servants). It may be, however, that the obligation to report led to more meetings of the working group and occasions for information exchange than might otherwise have existed.

In terms of use by non-governmental actors, there is some evidence that social policy organizations used the data in the reports to inform the media of differences across jurisdictions, who, in turn report on these differences, particularly on the 'clawback.' For example, each year the National Council on Welfare engages in a benchmarking exercise, calculating welfare incomes in each province, taking into account funds received by parents through the National Child Benefit initiative. A thorough review of provincial newspaper coverage of the NCB across Canada in the last ten years reveals that the Council of Welfare reports have received media attention. In the early days of the NCB, Newfoundland and Labrador adopted the New Brunswick model, 'flowing through' the full value of the NCB Supplement to social assistance recipients.[6] When justifying the 'flow-through' approach in the Newfound and Labrador legislature, the minister of human resources and employment noted she 'felt compelled to respond,' to the province's ranking in the 1998 National Council on Welfare study on welfare incomes.[7] Newspaper reports have also been critical of the NCB and annually report on the National Council of Welfare Reports. For example, one article initially characterized the NCB as 'thin gruel laden with hyperbole' (Brag 1998). Reporting six years later, Beauchesne (2004) argued that 'the clawback is why welfare incomes for families have decreased in most cases since Ottawa introduced the benefit.' But this newspaper coverage and the National Council of Welfare reports have not had traction with the broader public or most governments in an era where government 'hand-ups' are preferred to government 'handouts,' particularly where welfare recipients are concerned.

The limited impact of these studies is likely due to a mix of factors. First, in most provinces that have clawed – or are clawing – back, provincial child benefits are combined with the federal child tax benefit into one monthly payment, so there is no actual change in the value of the lump sum when the National Child Benefit Supplement increases, and a provincial child benefit is decreased by the same amount each year. With no change in the value of their payment, many recipients would not appreciate the federal-provincial quid pro quo of income adjustment that takes place each time the federal government has raised the value of the NCB Supplement. Second, in the NCB era, the population as a whole has not been sympathetic to the idea of enhancing the economic well-being of those receiving social assistance. In this context, promoting workforce attachment – one of the main goals of the NCB – has broad appeal, and there is relatively little fear of 'voter punishment.' Third, once the NCB was firmly established, provinces experiencing any degree of pressure to change their reinvestment/investment strategy again could look to other provinces to rationalize proceeding with the status quo. One provincial official argued, 'It wasn't easy to stay the course,' but, following the election of a new government that had promised to examine the issue of the clawback, 'by then there was enough information in the system by way of what was happening in other provinces, there were sufficient numbers of jurisdictions that had stayed the course throughout the painful transition period' (interviews with public servants). As a result, the new government chose not to end the clawback.

Perhaps one of the more significant reasons more organizations and/or individuals have not utilized the reports is that they are very difficult to navigate. As stated in a National Council of Welfare Annual Report, 'The system of federal and provincial child benefit programs has become incomprehensible to most people. This, coupled with the interaction between child benefits and welfare programs, has made what was already a tangled safety net almost impossible to understand' (National Council of Welfare 2008). As the reports combine investments and reinvestments, explaining whether a provincial government is 'adjusting' social assistance or its provincial child benefit is left to a multitude of footnotes throughout the NCB progress reports. It appears that governments adopted this approach to reporting in an effort to capture variances across provinces, but also to ensure each government presents information in a similar manner. In the words of one official, 'The actual nuances from province to province are probably as varied as the people, and that's the difficulty with those national reports. It would be very difficult to use a standard national template to reflect the different nuances and ins and outs of every jurisdiction. That's one of the challenges in those national reporting regimes. It's challenging to work within the template and still create an accurate report' (interview with public servant). Unfortunately, it's also challenging to read and interpret the reports.

Measuring Outcomes: Aggregate Evaluation

As the NCB is over a decade old, it is possible to consider how 'evaluation, feedback from stakeholders and the public, and flexibility to adjust the national child benefit over time' (National Child Benefit 1998) – important characteristics of the initiative, according to the NCB Governance and Accountability Framework – are working in practice. In short, the NCB *results*-reporting process has come up against a major challenge inherent in performance measurement: the tendency to focus on what is readily measurable, rather than what is intended to be measured (Carroll and Dewar 2002; Thomas 2007).

Since 2001, each of the annual reports includes two chapters focusing on results: one centres on 'general outcome indictors,' re-named 'societal indicators' in later reports; the other on 'the direct impact of the National Child Benefit Initiative.' With reference to the first objective of the NCB initiative (to reduce the depth of child poverty), the reports utilize three different measures of low income – post-tax Low-Income-Cut-Offs, the Low Income Measure, and the Market Basket Measure – and track the following 'societal indicators' from 1984 onwards: the incidence, duration, and depth of low income among families with children.[8] With reference to the second objective of the NCB initiative (to promote workforce attachment), the reports track two additional 'societal indicators': the percentage of low-income families in which the parents had paid employment, and changes to social assistance caseloads over time. However, the reports acknowledge that these measures indicate changes to the overall economic well-being of low-income families with children over time, not the extent to which the NCB is responsible for these changes.

In an effort to more accurately gauge the 'direct impact' of the NCB initiative, five of the last six annual reports have included a simulation comparing the differences in low-income indicators under two different benefit structures: the NCB Supplement and provincial / territorial re-investments, and investments in income benefits under the National Child Benefit to the benefit structure in place before the NCB was introduced. The three low-income indicators are:

- the number and incidence of children as well as families with children living in low income;
- the average change in disposable income that families with children saw in a given year, given the value of NCB income supports; and
- the change in the depth of income, or the low-income gap (the aggregate amount of income that low-income families would need to reach a predetermined low-income line).

The reports acknowledge that this approach captures only the *income benefit* aspects of the NCB. However, this is a major shortcoming, because so much of the NCB initiative does not take the form of an income benefit. In the last *Annual Progress Report*, income benefits in the form of provincial child benefits and earned supplements were estimated to be just 10 per cent of NCB reinvestments and investments in 2007–8 (Federal, Provincial and Territorial Ministers Responsible for Social Services 2009, 14). This approach does not attempt to measure the impact of the vast majority of provincial investments and reinvestments, which take the form of child / day care, supplementary health benefits, early childhood services and children at risk services, youth initiatives, First Nations, and other NCB benefits and programs.[9]

Concluding Observations

Given the unrealistic nature of a return to either watertight compartments of constitutional responsibility or traditional conditional federal-provincial arrangements, the NCB accountability framework represents a bold experiment to embrace the 'chameleon quality' (Sinclair 1995, 219) of accountability. Introducing a new way in which accountability might be experienced, it redefines the 'principals' as the public and 'agents' as governments in the intergovernmental accountability relationship. Federalism adds ambiguity to accountability (Simmons 2009). The NCB Accountability Framework is an attempt to both embrace federal principles of partnership and non-subordination, and achieve collective accountability. Its operation thus far allows us to reach certain conclusions about public reporting as a form of accountability. Whereas traditional analysis of intergovernmental relations has suggested that trust and cooperation among intergovernmental officials is synonymous with secrecy (Breton 1996), this case demonstrates that cooperation can in fact be associated with relative transparency. Yet while information for annual reports has been forthcoming, there is no question that the data provided in the annual progress reports on the NCB make inter-jurisdictional comparison of inputs and outputs difficult.

Based on this case alone, it would not be prudent to dismiss public reporting as an appropriate way to achieve accountability for *outputs* when new social policy programs have as many inter-jurisdictional aspects as the NCB. Rather, it is the particular attributes of the NCB that obstruct citizens' ability to use the reports to hold governments to account. Where provincial investments and reinvestments link up with other provincial programs is an accounting abstraction that renders elusive credible, auditable information. There is still promise that public reporting can serve as a way to benchmark policy outputs across jurisdictions in other cases.

This case indicates the dominance of closed-door intergovernmental relations among officials rather than transparent public reporting as the driver of inter-jurisdictional policy learning. In terms of vitalizing civil society, the impact of public reporting is inconclusive. There is little evidence of advocacy organizations, outside of the National Council of Welfare, utilizing the reports to pressure one government or another, and where there is such evidence, it seems to have had limited effect on government policy direction. However, it is difficult to gauge whether this is owing to the complexity of the reports, and/or because the message of active advocacy organizations does not resonate with the general public and thus sitting governments. It may be that with less dense public reporting, and with a different policy issue, there would be greater uptake by civil society organizations and governments more attentive to the campaigns of these organizations.

Using public reporting to achieve accountability for *outcomes* is more difficult. Despite its institutionalization within the public sector, accountability for results is routinely bedevilled by the analytical challenge of isolating a program's effects from other environmental factors (Thomas 2007). This challenge is magnified in this case, again because of the multifaceted nature of the NCB itself. Governments have yet to accurately isolate the impact of income supports, let alone that of the many programs benefiting children that also comprise the NCB initiative. This case also sheds light on the utility of public reporting as a way to hold *all* partners to account for outcomes, rather than simply individual partners for the outcomes of their specific program(s). Collective accountability offers a way to sidestep the intergovernmental wrangling that seems to manifest when one government reports to the other, or when governments de facto report to each other via public reports. But collective accountability through results reporting hinges on the ability to accurately simultaneously isolate the impact of the initiatives of thirteen different governments as a whole – an unrealistic enterprise in this case, and likely in many. We still lack an effective way to jointly hold governments responsible, even when intergovernmental conflict is at a minimum. Perhaps the way forward for future intergovernmental joint initiatives is to think outside the public reporting box.

NOTES

1   While the Government of Quebec has stated that it agrees with the basic principles of the National Child Benefit, it does not take part in the

initiative. All references to provincial governments throughout this chapter do not include Quebec.

2 For families with an income of $20,921 or less, the NCB Supplement was initially valued at $605 for families with one child, an additional $405 for families with two, and an additional $330 for each additional child. Families, in the case of a two-child family, earning up to $25,921 received a reduced amount (Federal, Provincial and Territorial Ministers Responsible for Social Services 1999). For the year 2010–11, for families with an annual net income of $23,855 or less, the NCB Supplement was valued at $2118 for the first child, $1873 for the second child, and $1782 for each additional child (Canada Revenue Agency 2011).

3 Social assistance no longer had to be based on need, and provinces could introduce work requirements. See Graefe (2006).

4 The term *recovery* is used in the NCB progress reports. However, other terms used in the reports to refer to the same action are *offset, adjustment*, and *reinvestment*. The term most frequently used by critics of the NCB arrangement is *clawback*, though this term is never found in government publications. This study primarily uses the term *adjustment* but does from time to time use the other terms mentioned here. One term that government documents use to describe the opposite of *adjustment* is *flow-through.*

5 Over time the names of these categories have changed slightly.

6 In 1999/2000 this province restructured its income support program entirely, removing children from social assistance and introducing the income-tested Newfoundland and Labrador Child Benefit (Federal, Provincial and Territorial Ministers Responsible for Social Services 2008, 11).

7 The minister stated that the National Council on Welfare statistics show that 'in 1996, 72 percent of single parent families in the province lived below the poverty line – the highest rate of all the provinces.'

8 Post-tax LICOs is the primary measure used in the reports and is defined as 'the income level at which a family spends 20 percentage points more of its income on basic needs (including food, shelter and clothing) relative to the average family.' The Low Income Measure considers a family to be low income if 'its income, adjusted for family size, is less than half the median income.' The Market Basket Measure is based on the actual cost of food, clothing, shelter, transportation, and other necessary goods and services' and, unlike the other two measures, takes into account geographical differences in these living costs. Michael Mendelson (2005) identifies the implications of each of these measures as a barometer of poverty and argues that without an actual poverty line, it is not possible to accurately determine the value of an adequate child benefit.

9 Social services ministers also commissioned a Synthesis Report, which
   brings together evidence from no fewer than twenty technical reports
   (Federal, Provincial and Territorial Ministers Responsible for Social Services
   2005a). The contours of this report are too many to discuss here. Suffice to
   say, this report demonstrates the unrealistic nature of attempting to isolate
   the impact of a program as multifaceted as the NCB initiative, as it focuses
   on income supports only.

REFERENCES

Allard, Scott W. 2004. 'Competitive Pressures and the Emergence of Mothers'
   Aid Programs in the United States.' *Policy Studies Journal* 32 (4): 521–44.

Auditor General of Canada. 1999. *Report of the Auditor General of Canada,
   Chapter 6, Human Resources Development Canada – Accountability for Shared
   Social Programs*. April. Ottawa: Queen's Printer.

Beauchesne, Eric. 2004. 'Advisory Group Calls Cuts "Cruel and Punitive."'
   Regina Leader Post, 8 July.

Beyle, Thad L. 1988. 'The Governor as Innovator in the Federal System.'
   Publius 18 (3): 131–52.

Boychuk, Gerard W. 1998. *Patchworks of Purpose*. Montreal and Kingston:
   McGill-Queen's University Press.

Brag, Robert. 1998. 'Child-Benefit Plan Offers Thin Gruel Laden with
   Hyperbole.' *Calgary Herald*, 23 July.

Breton, Albert. 1996. *Competitive Governments: An Economic Theory of Politics
   and Public Finance*. Cambridge: Cambridge University Press.

Canada Revenue Agency. 2011. 'Canada Child Benefits Including Related
   Federal, Provincial and Territorial Programs for the Period July 2011 to June
   2012.' http://www.cra-arc.gc.ca/E/pub/tg/t4114/t4114-11e.pdf.

Carroll, Barbara Wake, and David I. Dewar. 2002. 'Performance Management.'
   In *Handbook of Canadian Public Administration*, edited by Christopher Dunn,
   413–29. Toronto: Oxford University Press.

Davis, Glyn. 1998. 'Carving Out Policy Space for State Government in a
   Federation: The Role of Coordination.' *Publius* 28 (4): 147–64.

Federal, Provincial and Territorial Ministers Responsible for Social Services.
   1999. *The National Child Benefit Progress Report: 1999*. Ottawa: Minister of
   Public Works and Government Services Canada.

– 2001. *The National Child Benefit Progress Report 2000*. Ottawa: Her Majesty
   the Queen in Right of Canada.

– 2002. *The National Child Benefit Progress Report: 2001*. Ottawa: Her Majesty
   the Queen in Right of Canada.

– 2003. *The National Child Benefit Progress Report: 2002*. Ottawa: Her Majesty the Queen in Right of Canada.
– 2004. *The National Child Benefit Progress Report: 2003*. Ottawa: Her Majesty the Queen in Right of Canada.
– 2005a. *Evaluation of the National Child Benefit Initiative: Synthesis Report*, February. Ottawa: Minister of Public Works and Government Services Canada.
– 2005b. *The National Child Benefit Progress Report: 2004*. Ottawa: Her Majesty the Queen in Right of Canada.
– 2007. *The National Child Benefit Progress Report: 2005*. Ottawa: Her Majesty the Queen in Right of Canada.
– 2008. *The National Child Benefit Progress Report 2006*. Ottawa: Her Majesty the Queen in Right of Canada.
– 2009. *The National Child Benefit Progress Report 2007*. Ottawa: Her Majesty the Queen in Right of Canada.
Freeman, Patricia K. 1985. 'Interstate Communication among State Legislators regarding Energy Policy Innovation.' *Publius* 15 (4): 99–111.
Freiler, Christa, and Judy Cerny. 1998. *Benefiting Canada's Children: Perspectives on Gender and Social Responsibility*. Ottawa: Status of Women Canada.
Graefe, Peter. 2006. 'State Restructuring, Social Assistance and Canadian Intergovernmental Relations: Same Scales, New Tune.' *Studies in Political Economy* 78:93–117.
Harrison, Kathryn. 2006. 'Provincial Interdependence: Concepts and Theories.' In *Racing to the Bottom? Provincial Interdependence in the Canadian Federation*, edited by Kathryn Harrison. Vancouver: UBC Press.
Hobson, Paul A.R., and France St-Hilaire. 2000. 'The Evolution of Federal-Provincial Fiscal Arrangements: Putting Humpty Together Again.' In *Canada: The State of the Federation 1999/2000 toward a New Mission Statement for Canadian Fiscal Federalism*, edited by Harvey Lazar, 159–88. Montreal and Kingston: McGill-Queen's University Press.
Lazar, Harvey. 2005. 'Trust in Intergovernmental Fiscal Relations.' In *Canadian Fiscal Arrangements: What Works, What Might Work Better*, edited by Harvey Lazar, 3–36. Montreal and Kingston: McGill-Queen's University Press.
McKeen, Wendy. 2001. 'Shifting Policy and Politics of Federal Child Benefits in Canada.' *Social Politics* (Summer): 186–90.
Mendelson, Michael. 2005. *Measuring Child Benefits: Measuring Child Poverty*. Ottawa: Caledon Institute of Social Policy.
National Child Benefit. 1998. *The National Child Benefit NCB Governance and Accountability Framework*, March. http://www.nationalchildbenefit.ca/eng/98/account.shtml.
National Council of Welfare. 1998. *Child Benefits: Kids Are Still Hungry*. Ottawa: Minister of Public Works and Government Services Canada.

– 2008. *National Council of Welfare Reports: Welfare Incomes 2006–2007*, vol. 128. Ottawa: Her Majesty the Queen in Right of Canada.

Office of the Auditor General of Canada. 1999. *1999 April Report of the Auditor General of Canada – April 1999*. http://www.oag-bvg.gc.ca/internet/English/parl_oag_199904_e_1140.html.

Papillion, Martin, and Richard Simeon. 2004. 'The Weakest Link? First Ministers Conferences in Canadian Intergovernmental Relations.' In *Canada: The State of the Federation 2002: Reconsidering the Institutions of Canada Federalism*, edited by J. Peter Meekison, Hamish Telford, and Harvey Lazar, 113–40. Montreal and Kingston: McGill-Queen's University Press.

Paterson, Stephanie, Karine Levasseur, and Tatyana Teplova. 2004. 'I Spy with my Little Eye … Canada's National Child Benefit.' In *How Ottawa Spends 2004–2005: Mandate Change in the Paul Martin Era*, edited by G. Bruce Doern, 131–500. Montreal and Kingston: McGill-Queen's University Press.

Simmons, Julie M. 2004. 'Securing the Threads of Cooperation in the Tapestry of Intergovernmental Relations: Does the Institutionalization of Ministerial Conferences Matter?' In *Canada: The State of the Federation 2002: Reconsidering the Institutions of Canada Federalism*, edited by J. Peter Meekison, Hamish Telford, and Harvey Lazar, 285–311. Montreal and Kingston: McGill-Queen's University Press.

– 2009. 'Federalism and Accountabilities in the Social Arena.' *Optimum Online: The Journal of Public Sector Management* 39:1–10.

Sinclair, Amanda. 1995. 'The Chameleon of Accountability: Forms and Discourses.' *Accounting, Organizations and Society* 20 (2/3): 219–37.

Thomas, Paul G. 2007. 'Why Is Performance-Based Accountability So Popular in Theory and Difficult in Practice?' Paper presented to the World Summit on Public Governance: Improving the Performance of the Public Sector, Taipei City, 1–3 May.

4 Democratizing Intergovernmental Accountability Regimes: Community Engagement and Public Reporting in Early Learning and Child Care in Canada[1]

TAMMY FINDLAY

This book evaluates new accountability mechanisms on the basis of policy effectiveness, intergovernmental cooperation, and democratic legitimacy. While touching on all three, democratic legitimacy is the primary focus of this chapter, specifically the space for citizen participation in monitoring public expenditures. Notions of 'accountability' and 'citizen engagement' are now ubiquitous in public policy, and federalism is no exception. Canada's 1999 Social Union Framework Agreement (SUFA) emphasizes 'collaborative' federalism, public reporting, and the involvement of third parties in the social policy process (SUFA 1999). In this way, there has been some shift in emphasis toward less hierarchical forms of 'societal accountability' in multilevel governance, discussed in the introduction. This chapter will assess the extent to which 'new' accountability mechanisms effectively integrate community[2] engagement. It draws from experiences with a community capacity-building project by the Child Care Advocacy Association of Canada (CCAAC) and analyses the public reporting regime associated with the three federal-provincial-territorial (FPT) agreements on early learning and child care. The chapter maintains that, despite real challenges, public reporting can be a valuable element in democratizing intergovernmental relations. However, it will require a full commitment to supporting community participation. And even with significant citizen engagement, the new accountability regime, which relies entirely on public reporting, cannot replace the historical practices of legislated standards, audited information, and reporting to legislatures.

This argument will unfold in five parts. It will first provide a description of the current accountability regime for Early Learning and Child Care (ELCC), in which public reporting takes a prominent place. Second, through the case study of the CCAAC's Making the Connections project (MTC), it will discuss some of the central obstacles to citizen engagement in FPT reporting. Continuing to reflect on MTC, the third section will explore some of the democratic potential that public reporting represents. The resources and supports needed to maximize this potential are then considered in the fourth part. The chapter concludes by locating public reporting as *one* important component within a wider accountability regime in social policy.

Early Learning and Child Care: The New Accountability Regime

As elaborated in other chapters in this volume (see Cameron, chapter 12, for instance), a substantial shift in approach to social policy and FPT relations has occurred in Canada, involving a movement away from a regime based on conditionality and cost-sharing toward a New Public Management (NPM)–inspired paradigm spelled out in the SUFA. This can be seen clearly in ELCC policy.

Accountability and Early Learning and Child Care

This chapter takes the definition of accountability outlined in the introduction as the starting point: accountability is understood to entail both *answerability* and *enforcement*. Answerability must exist within governments (such as between the executive and the legislature), across governments, and especially between governments and their citizens. Enforcement ensures that should there be a lapse or failure in these relationships, there is some consequence.

As with other policy areas in this collection, accountability in ELCC involves responsibilities of one level of government to another, as well as the responsibilities those governments have to their citizens. Over time, these relationships have been transformed on both fronts. In the past, the accountability mechanism in ELCC policy was through the Canada Assistance Plan (CAP), which placed federal conditions on financial transfers to the provinces and cost sharing (Cameron 2007; Friendly and White 2008). The CAP regime certainly was not perfect. For instance, it problematically defined child care[3] as a welfare policy, and the CAP has been criticized for its heavy-handed federal oversight of the provinces (Boismenu and Graefe 2004; Cameron). Despite these weaknesses, CAP provided guarantees of social citizenship rights and the procedural right to appeal (Cameron), which have since been greatly weakened. By the mid-1970s, there was a shift in fiscal federalism, and an accompanying loosening of accountability for federal transfers (Boismenu and Graefe) and social rights, coinciding with broader state retrenchment.

As mentioned in the introduction, changing approaches to public policy – notably under neoliberalism and NPM – have been increasingly influential in the realm of federalism. Susan Phillips (2001) wonders whether citizens are emerging as the 'third force of federalism,' and Kershaw (2006) notes that citizens are now expected 'to fill the void by serving as policy watchdogs who will hold all levels of government to account.' Within this context, the intra- and intergovernmental relationships have been written out of accountability, leaving a greatly circumscribed government–citizen relationship, where public reporting has become the central accountability mechanism for child-care policy and funding in Canada.

The FPT Agreements on Early Learning and Child Care

Over the last decade, spurred by the human capital and child-focused policy of the social investment state, three agreements among federal, provincial, and territorial (FPT) governments resulted in new federal transfers to provinces and territories to advance ELCC services and supports. In 2000, the Early Childhood Development Agreement (ECDA) was introduced to channel $2.2 billion into four areas: healthy pregnancy, infancy, and birth; parenting and family supports; early childhood development, learning, and care; and community supports. In response to criticisms from the policy community that child care was stalled (and in some cases, deteriorating) under the ECDA, in 2003 the Multilateral Agreement on Early Learning and Child Care (Multilateral Agreement) emerged to specifically direct $1.05 billion federal dollars to improving access to affordable, quality, provincially and territorially regulated ELCC programs and services. As will be shown later, this is a significant difference between the ECDA and the Multilateral Agreement. Finally, with a minority Liberal government in place, in 2005 the Bilateral Agreements-in-Principle on ELCC (Bilateral Agreements) committed $5 billion over five years towards a national child-care system, working in cooperation with provinces and territories and building on the Multilateral Agreement. The Bilateral Agreements differed across the provinces in their enthusiasm for direct public funding, universality, and non-profit expansion, but there were common commitments to public investment in regulated ELCC that meet the QUAD principles (quality, universally inclusive, accessible, developmental), and considerably more dollars on the table (Anderson and Findlay 2005c; Cool 2007). The Bilateral Agreements were cancelled in 2006 by the Harper Conservative government.

These FPT agreements represent political rather than legal commitments. Federal transfers under both the ECDA and Multilateral Agreement (and the $250 million annual federal transfer for child-care spaces confirmed in the 2007 federal budget) currently flow annually to provinces and territories through the Canada Social Transfer (CST), which does not have program-specific spending conditions attached to it. Therefore, questions have been raised in a range of circles from the community (Bascombe 2001; Anderson 2004; National Children's Alliance 2001) to the auditor general of Canada (Canada, Auditor General of Canada 1999, 2002), about accountability for federal transfers. Without legal agreements or spending conditions in place (i.e., enforcement), the agreements involve commitments by FPT governments to produce annual public reports that describe each government's priorities, investments, and progress, and rely on citizens to review these public reports and provide feedback to governments.

The accountability principle underlying public reporting is straightforward: governments must demonstrate to citizens that they did what they said they were going to do. As part of the ECDA, governments signed on to a 'Shared Framework for Reporting on Progress in Improving and Expanding Early Childhood Development (ECD) Programs and Services.' Governments established shared principles: a respect for the diversity of jurisdictions, a pledge to improve reporting over time, and an agreement to consult with third parties on indicators and progress 'as appropriate.' Their annual reports were also to acknowledge the federal contribution; report on *changes* in expenditures from the previous year; report on investments in the four ECD areas; describe the programs, including their objectives, target population, program description, department(s) responsible, and delivery agent(s); and report on program indicators, including expenditures, availability, accessibility, affordability, and quality (Early Child Development 2004a, 2004c).

Under the Multilateral Agreement, governments made specific performance and reporting commitments from 2002/3 onwards related to ELCC. They agreed to provide public reports with descriptive and expenditure information on all ELCC programs and services, as well as indicators of availability, affordability, and quality (Early Child Development 2004b). Governments promised 'to further invest in provincially/territorially regulated early learning and child care programs for children under six,' and to 'use the federal transfers to improve access to affordable, quality early learning and child care programs and services.' FPT governments were to publicly report 'descriptive and expenditure information on all ELCC programs and services; indicators of availability, such as number of spaces in ELCC settings broken down by age of children and type of setting; indicators of affordability, such as number of children receiving subsidies, income and social eligibility for fee subsidies, and maximum subsidy by age of child; and indicators of quality, such as training requirements, child/caregiver ratios and group size, where available' (Early Child Development 2004b).

Getting provincial consensus for a third ELCC agreement was a difficult and lengthy process for Social Development Minister Ken Dryden and Paul Martin's minority government. In the end, each province signed a separate agreement-in-principle with the federal government. It seems that the key points of contention were related to ideological resistance to regulated child care from Alberta and New Brunswick; funding concerns from smaller jurisdictions such as PEI and the territories; and Quebec's traditional opposition to federal conditions (CUPE 2009; Friendly and White 2008). There is little indication that public reporting figured prominently in this federal-provincial conflict, but it does appear that in some jurisdictions more so than in others, there was greater sensitivity about how the reporting would be used. For instance, to dampen enthusiasm for interprovincial comparisons, Alberta, British Columbia, New Brunswick, and PEI resurrected the language from previous FPT agreements that 'the purpose of public reporting is to be accountable to their publics, not to each other' (Anderson and Findlay 2007; Early Childhood Development 2004c).

In the now defunct Bilateral Agreements, each provincial government (except Quebec) agreed to annual public reporting, as well as an additional and noteworthy accountability measure: the production of action plans spelling out how the funds transferred from the federal government would be spent over five years (2005/6–2009/10). Upon the development of an action plan, provinces were to enter into a five-year funding agreement with the federal government. Before the collapse of the Martin Liberal minority government, two provinces – Manitoba and Ontario – had done so. Quebec also signed a Bilateral Funding Agreement but was not required to submit an action plan (Anderson and Findlay 2005; Canada, HRSDC 2005; Friendly and White 2008).

In all three ELCC agreements, public reporting serves as the primary accountability mechanism. However, unlike in the ECDA and the Multilateral Agreement, in which governments were to report on common indicators, in the Bilateral Agreements there were notable variations. The most crucial difference (and clearly an ideological one) is that only Manitoba and Saskatchewan included language specifying that investments would be made strictly in non-profit services. And whereas all provinces would report on availability, affordability, quality, and availability, only Manitoba would report on *changes* over time, and only some provinces would report on fees and French and other language services (Anderson and Findlay 2007; HRSDC 2005). As a consequence, the shift from a Multilateral to Bilateral Agreements allowed for divergence not only in ELCC policy,[4] but also in accountability. In terms of the impact on policy outcomes, as will be seen, one of the most critical changes in the accountability regime occurred between the ECDA and the Multilateral Agreement. The latter became much more directive, and when child care was a *required* focus of investment, this had a positive impact on policy outcomes.

Because the first two ELCC agreements have yielded most of the public reporting, they were the main focus of the community-based review discussed here. In these agreements, governments made two main commitments: (1) to *provide clear reporting* so that the public can track progress, and (2) to *improve* and *expand* ECD programs for Canadian families, including child-care services (Early Childhood Development 2004a, 2004b). The CCAAC project asked whether either commitment had been adequately met.

Child-Care Policy: Making the Connections[5]

Child Care Policy: Making the Connections (MTC) is a project of the Child Care Advocacy Association of Canada (CCAAC), a pan-Canadian, non-profit, membership-based organization dedicated to promoting quality, inclusive, publicly funded, non-profit child care that is accessible to all. The objective of the MTC project was to support the public in understanding the implications of child-care policy and investments under FPT agreements, as laid out in the public reporting. The project's mandate covered child-care policy and funding developments (outside of Quebec) under FPT agreements for a three-year period, beginning in November 2004, and the project was funded by the federal Social Development Partnerships Program. I was the senior researcher on the project.

MTC analysed five years of reporting for thirteen jurisdictions and the result was a common framework for analysis of public reporting to confirm whether the FPT Agreement commitments were met, and whether child-care services were improving as a result. Annual expenditures were tracked using a simplified investment chart (see the template in table 4.1), which was used in presentations, discussions, and meetings with communities and governments over the course of the project.

All figures in the investment charts were taken directly from the public reports. They were totalled and summarized so the public could track the changes in investments from the baseline year (2000/1) to 2005/6. Blank areas in the chart indicated that the information was not available, or was not clear, consistent, and/or comparable. The total investment in ECD programs, including child-care services, was divided into two components – the federal transfers and the resulting provincial contribution – to support the public in understanding which investments were funded through federal transfers and/or provincial contributions. Federal transfers not yet invested in ECD, including child-care services, were also identified.

Tracking Public Reporting: The Basic Challenges

MTC measured performance on the basis of governments' own performance commitments in the FPT agreements, as well as guidelines for clear reporting of the Public Sector Accounting Board (PSAB).[6] On balance, MTC concluded that progress could not be tracked clearly using public reports. Reporting was difficult to access, it lacked timeliness, clarity, accuracy, comparability, utility, comprehensiveness, and in some cases, it was quite biased.

In terms of access, the annual reporting relies almost exclusively on the Internet, and even if one has regular Internet access, reports are not always easy to find. The links from the main federal ECD/ELCC website to several provincial/territorial (PT) sites are not kept current and do not always lead directly to the PT reports – they may lead only to the relevant ministry, so additional searching is often needed. Some reports, or the links to them, have been removed either temporarily or permanently. Once reports are found, many are quite long, and PDF files take time to download, especially those with a lot of pictures. In community meetings of the MTC project, rural participants expressed concerns about accessing reports with dial-up service. Such reports can also be costly for parents and caregivers to print. In addition, community members frequently told us that they do not have the time to read reports that are

Table 4.1 Summary of annual reporting on Early Childhood Development, Learning & Care (ECDLC) activities (template)

	Total baseline funding year 0 00/01	← Annual Investment Increase (Decrease) →					Total year 5 funding 05/06	Total change over baseline
		Year 1 01/02	Year 2 02/03	Year 3 03/04	Year 4 04/05	Year 5 05/06		
ECD – Early Learning & Child Care Services								
ECD – Income supports to families								
ECD – All other programs & services								
Total investment – All ECD programs								
Less: Total federal transfers								
Provincial contribution to ECDLC programs (or federal transfers not yet invested in ECDLC)								

fifty pages and longer. Furthermore, many reports are not released on a timely basis, are not dated, or are not clearly dated. Under the ECDA, reports are to be published in September each year, and under the Multilateral Agreement, in November (Early Childhood Development 2004b, 2004c). Few governments have consistently achieved this goal. For instance, the federal government's 2004/5 and 2005/6 combined report was released in August 2007.[7]

The ECDA/Multilateral Agreement reporting does not always meet PSAB standards of clarity, comprehensiveness, and comparability. As a result, project staff spent over thirty hours analysing some governments' reporting, trying to extract both financial and non-financial information that was not clearly and consistently presented and summarized in a way that was comparable from year to year. Out of respect for citizens' time constraints, public reporting should be as straightforward as possible. A 2006 study of the Canadian Comprehensive Auditing Foundation (CCAF-FCVI) found that clarity and usability of public performance reports was a widespread concern, and this was also reflected during MTC through feedback from parents, child-care workers, and academics who viewed the FPT reports as too long, confusing, and difficult to understand.

Some provinces do not provide complete baseline ECD and / or child-care expenditure information, or do so inconsistently. Without a baseline, overall progress and use of federal transfers cannot be tracked and confirmed. While federal transfers are generally acknowledged in the report text, they are seldom clearly reflected in the financial reporting section. In some reports there was a mismatch between the information in the text of the report and that in the financial section of the same report, or between information from previous years.

Reporting templates vary considerably across governments. The agreements allow for diverse approaches, supporting provincial and territorial autonomy, but fundamental differences across reporting practices make it much more difficult for the public to track the progress on child-care investments in some jurisdictions than in others, resulting in a lack of procedural equality across the country. Some jurisdictions (for example, the federal government) do not consistently total the financial information, so the public is unable to easily see and compare trends in total investments.

Public reporting could help to address public cynicism about FPT relations, by bringing greater transparency (one of the central elements of answerability outlined in the introduction) to public policies such as child care. However, MTC found in communities a lack of interest and trust in public reporting, largely due to problems in data presentation and credibility, all of which are permissible under the FPT agreements. Both the ECDA and Multilateral Agreement permit governments to report only on their chosen 'priorities' (Early Childhood Development 2004a, 2004b). As a result, some reporting appears to be skewed in favour of good news, providing no explanation of apparent reductions in funding and / or service. A study by the CCAF-FCVI (2006), a national, non-profit organization focused on public sector governance, management, and accountability research, found that legislators, citizens, NGOs, and the media believe that performance reports read like public relations tools and lack sincerity. So when expenditure reductions are not explained, the trustworthiness of public performance reporting – already a widely recognized concern – is further diminished. In the long run, such public suspicion serves the ends of conservative and public choice notions of government failure, and robs communities of their enthusiasm for engagement.

The federal government's 2004 / 5 and 2005 / 6 combined public report provides an interesting example. On the one hand, it clearly and comparably includes all programs from previous years, even those that have been discontinued, and generally includes an explanation for any expenditure reductions. On the other hand, it does not include any information on the terminated Bilateral Agreements, which were introduced by the previous Liberal government and transferred $700 million to provinces and territories in 2004 / 5 and 2005 / 6 combined.[8] This omission appears to place partisan politics ahead of public accountability.

Another challenge can be seen in the way public reporting falls short in elucidating intergovernmental relationships for citizens. In the Multilateral Agreement, governments agreed to 'publicly recognize and explain the respective roles and contributions of governments to this initiative' (Early Childhood Development 2004b). The idea is that in a federal system, citizens have a right to know which government has supported which programs and services and to what extent. But the reporting does not always make the distinctions clear, and in some cases, actually obscures it even further. While federal transfers are generally acknowledged in the report text, they are seldom plainly reflected in the financial reporting section – the summary piece most likely to be used by busy communities.

These reporting gaps are especially frustrating because incomplete reporting information and problematic choices in performance indicators makes it nearly impossible to confirm whether governments have made substantive progress in ELCC. It appears that in certain jurisdictions there were some improvements in income supports, such as federal maternity and parental benefits and targeted programs for lower- and modest-income families in several provinces, quality and affordability of existing child-care spaces, inclusion of children with special needs, and expanded access through new spaces, but this cannot be verified in the reporting. Overall, MTC found that the records of FPT governments in meeting both their reporting and performance requirements were spotty, raising questions about accountability from the perspective of both answerability and enforcement.[9] And it should be stressed that these are rather limited accountability standards that governments have set for themselves, in comparison to what communities seek.

Citizen Engagement in Public Reporting

MTC was based on the idea that public reporting can be a vital tool of accountability, but there are several challenges for truly engaging citizens in the process, beyond some of the basic obstacles of time and knowledge. The FPT agreements specifically note that governments are reporting to their publics, and not to each other (Early Childhood Development 2004a, 2004b, 2004c). The only accountability mechanism for investments in child-care services is through public monitoring and pressure, which places a lot of responsibility on communities. It appears that citizen engagement is serving as a replacement for, rather than a supplement to, the state's responsibility for accountability.

Neither individual citizens nor most community organizations have the time and resources to undertake a review comparable to MTC. While this project has supported some capacity-building, the reality is that communities do not have the resources to actively participate in this kind of citizen engagement, even if they are invited to. It is not practical for citizens to track the public reporting on their own, so it raises questions about the heavy reliance on this approach as *the* accountability mechanism when parents and community groups are already time-strapped and over-burdened. In Kershaw's (2006) early assessment of the CCAAC experiment he raised the issue of downloading and privatizing the responsibility for accountability onto child-care advocacy organizations, the majority of which are staffed and run by (often unpaid) women. Democracy takes time, and time is gendered.

The MTC project relied on only 1.5 paid staff and the volunteer work of the people committed to child care at the CCAAC and in provinces and territories who, on their own time, found ways to engage in policy discussions. MTC faced very practical constraints, including the inability of citizens to attend community meetings due to working schedules and other time limitations. These challenges are endemic to a female-dominated advocacy movement, as well as a feminized child-care labour force whose working hours and family responsibilities make participatory governance difficult.

Public reporting in its current manifestation also redefines the role of community knowledge in the policy process in ways that further advance NPM values. Organizations are not only being steered away from advocacy toward service provision, but also toward increasingly technical auditing activities. Communities, therefore, are reoriented toward reactive rather than proactive action. Taylor (2003, 123) highlights this diversionary thrust, noting, 'Partnership workers and community representatives spend their time explaining the external world to the community rather than driving community perspectives into programme design and planning.' In Canada, Laforest and Orsini (2005) have also shown that the growing emphasis on 'evidence-based policy making and monitoring' is undermining the representational function of voluntary organizations by distancing them from the community.

Furthermore, Phillips (2001, 20) wonders whether there is community capacity for this shift in responsibility: 'The main implication of the SUFA accountability provisions is to place the onus on citizens, unrealistically in my opinion, to review outcomes, assess their meaning, compare them across provinces and take political action to achieve better results. In effect, it makes social scientists of us all. This is unrealistic not because citizens are apathetic or not up to the task. Outcome measurement is a complex task and public debate about it requires access to relevant data and technical information, the ability to assess the quality of measurement as well as institutional venues for debate on the adequacy and policy implications of the data.' The public reporting regime asks communities to apply their knowledge in new ways, with very different political implications.

There are certainly limitations to public reporting as an accountability mechanism. But the answer is not to return to top-down, 'eleven white men in suits-style' executive federalism. Bakvis and Skogstad (2002a) note that, too often, Canadian intergovernmental relations have eschewed democratic participation in favour of competition between governments. As one strategy, public reporting has the potential to alter the democratic landscape of federalism.

MTC and Community Capacity-Building

Simeon and Cameron (2002) trace concern over the democratic character of federalism to Donald Smiley, who took issue with executive federalism's secrecy, its lack of citizen participation, and its weak accountability. They identify the Meech Lake Accord as the height of Canadian impatience with executive federalism and note that after Meech, the Charlottetown Accord, and the Calgary Declaration, there were brief experiments in the 1990s with popular engagement in intergovernmental relations. Even though governments promised new space for 'citizen engagement,' by the time SUFA emerged, FPT negotiations settled back into old patterns of executive federalism (Cameron 2004; Simeon and Cameron 2002). Public reporting has been raised as one alternative to top-down, closed-door intergovernmental relations, and the MTC experience shows that it is possible that public reporting could play a role in democratizing federalism.

The MTC project was a unique popular education experiment to build community capacity for understanding public reporting. The ultimate goal was to advance public knowledge of child-care policy and investments under the FPT agreements in order to facilitate advocacy. It involved broad-based consultation with parents and communities, service providers, FPT governments, researchers, and academics across Canada. The Steering Committee, consisting of regional and pan-Canadian sectoral representatives of the CCAAC's Council of Child Care Advocates, acted as a liaison between FPT groups and governments and provided information sharing, input, advice, and feedback. A Reference Group also served a technical or peer review function, bringing a range of expertise on child-care policy analysis and financing, intergovernmental relations, and community and citizen engagement. Throughout the course of MTC, community networks and partnerships were developed and enhanced.

The early stages of the project work involved an initial assessment of the public reports and sharing some of the observed weaknesses in meetings with governments and communities. These meetings helped to establish a dialogue with governments about their public reporting and investments and to gauge the level of public familiarity with the reporting. It was clear that the FPT Agreements were not widely understood and, in particular, that the federal transfers to provinces and territories were not highly visible to communities. This led to the development of a series of fact sheets to increase public awareness and understanding of the FPT Agreements and federal transfers (Anderson and Findlay 2005a, 2005b, 2005c, 2005d). The fact sheets started by explaining what the MTC project was about, then proceeded to outline each of the FPT Agreements, compare the Agreements to CCAAC goals, and finally to explore the use of action plans as an accountability mechanism. These fact sheets were aimed at improving the answerability and enforcement of child-care policy under these agreements.

Two other tools followed from the fact sheets. These resources were intended to support communities, but also to address the apparent lack of understanding among governments about effective child-care policy and investments, as observed in public reporting and in meetings. Therefore, a Child Care Planning Checklist was created to assist communities and governments in working together to develop a comprehensive child-care plan. The Child Care System Implementation Model was also introduced to facilitate discussion about the policy and funding approaches that are most likely to improve access to quality, affordable child-care services. In March 2006 there was a national forum, which provided an opportunity to discuss these project materials in detail. The final step was the MTC report (Anderson and Findlay 2007), released in November 2007, containing the detailed analyses of public reporting related to child-care services. In several ways, MTC opened up new opportunities for citizen engagement in the FPT process and provided insight into the development of ELCC policy.

MTC showed that public reporting can offer some opportunities to bring new voices into the FPT process. For instance, the project invited communities to think about the respective roles of the levels of government in child care, and this community capacity-building work seemed to influence political strategies. When the federal Conservative government cancelled the Bilateral Agreements, advocates in many provinces developed quite sophisticated responses. They participated in the national Code Blue for Child Care campaign to restore the agreements, while warning their provincial governments that they will be expected to move ahead on ELCC with or without federal participation, encouraging their provincial leaders to join them in demanding that the federal government live up to its obligations. The MTC tools and meetings provided a foundation for this dual-pronged approach. In her presentation to the Nova Scotia House of Assembly Committee on Community Services about the province's Early Learning & Child Care Plan, Margo Kirk, executive director of the University Children's Centre in Halifax, also drew from the MTC report to make arguments about accountability and transparency in the use of public funds for child care (Nova Scotia 2008).

The MTC dialogues across the provinces not only contributed to better community understanding, they also educated governments about effective ELCC policy. Meetings with provincial officials, especially when presenting the Child Care System Implementation Model, were quite revealing. For example, some government officials automatically associated child-care subsidies with affordability and accessibility of services, without consideration of their relationship to parent fees, or the reality that subsidies are a continuation of Canada's problematic welfare policy approach to child care. The level of knowledge in government on what is required to achieve quality, affordable, accessible ELCC was surprisingly low, and officials would benefit greatly from tapping into child-care community expertise.

Research has shown that citizen engagement can produce better public policy by providing fresh knowledge (Phillips 2001). Even in the relatively limited MTC experiment, community participation generated valuable insight about federalism and child-care policy. Much federalism literature is spent promoting provincial flexibility, or respect for 'distinctive provincial needs and tastes' (Bavkis and Skogstad 2008b, 136), but the MTC experience raises the question of whose 'needs and tastes' – governments' or citizens'? One interesting lesson taken from the project is that provincial diversity is often overstated and ideologically motivated. Through cross-Canada consultations, what was striking was the extraordinary *consistency* in objectives and challenges across communities around three aspects of child care: wages, fees, and spaces. If the policy process around child-care actively involved citizens, the clear policy consensus would be readily evident. Simeon and Cameron (2002, 291–2) stress that 'the presence of third parties, with policy goals, not governmental interests, at the centre of their concern helps to ensure that the intergovernmental politics of turf and blame avoidance does not dominate substantive policy discussion.' It is only by excluding advocates from the discussion that such a divided perspective on child-care policy has emerged in the media and in political discourse.

These findings mesh with Friendly's (2000) conclusions that Canada's child-care policy is driven less by respect for provincial policy diversity than a lack of coherence and political will. Too often, federalism and jurisdictional arguments act as a guise for blocking substantive policy progress and undermine democracy. As Bakvis and Skogstad (2008b) remind us, Canadians are much more interested in policy outcomes than federal principles. Unfortunately, these interests were not reflected in the FPT agreements, especially the Bilateral Agreements, where good (i.e., coordinated, universal) public policy was sacrificed for more provincial flexibility and avoidance of jurisdictional conflict (Friendly and White 2008).

This is not necessarily a product of intergovernmental relations, however. The issue is one of responsiveness of political institutions and accountability to citizens for social rights more generally. Even though the NPM emphasizes partnerships with the voluntary sector and consultations with 'clients,' it is accompanied by public sector downsizing and the reduction of resources to communities. And FPT agreements exist within this wider context that is transforming the relationship between states and citizens and where there is a long history of a (neo) liberal, residual welfare state and gendered social policy (Cameron 2004). Canada's ranking as last among industrialized nations in support for families (especially mothers) with children (Brodie and Bakker 2007; OECD 2006) is not merely a reflection of the complications of multilevel governance. It is related to the balance of social forces and power relations. Therefore, any crisis in legitimacy surrounding federalism (Bakvis and Skogstad 2002b) or democratic deficit in intergovernmental relations cannot be seen in isolation from the broader political system.

Building a Democratic Accountability Regime

Phillips (2001) has pointed out that Canada is behind other jurisdictions in citizen involvement in intergovernmental relations, and in many ways, the MTC project reinforces Bakvis and Skogstad's (2002b, 20) conclusion that 'the increase in collaborative federalism has not been coupled with greater transparency and citizen participation.' Nevertheless, public reporting could provide space for citizens in the FPT process that has been limited thus far.

To be sure, this assumes that basic recommendations about clear, timely, comprehensive reporting must be met,[10] including:

- direct links to reports from the federal ECD website,
- reports available on time and dated,
- printer-friendly and summary reports,
- clear tracking of policy and investment changes from the baseline onward,

- investments clearly totalled, and
- a comparable template across jurisdictions.

These would improve answerability through transparency and are relatively straightforward, requiring only that governments follow existing and recognized reporting guidelines. Beyond this, for citizens to actively participate in public reporting, they need more sweeping change: expertise, resources, access to information, structures for participation, and community and organizational capacity for real engagement (Simmons 2008).

Engaging Citizens Requires Resources

Significant resources are required at FPT government levels to support a comprehensive and genuine approach to citizen engagement. As Phillips (2001) indicates, this requires attention to both the 'how' and 'where' of citizen engagement, and the public funding of advocacy groups. Funding requirements that prohibit advocacy are detrimental to democracy and must be removed. The type of public funding also matters. Under project-based – as opposed to core – funding, community-based organizations like the CCAAC are confined to meeting specific deliverables, with the potential for extensive government direction and possible interference. During the term of the MTC project, for example, funding under the Bilateral Agreements was in place and therefore included in discussions with communities and governments. In addition, some provinces had publicly reported on their investments under these agreements in 2005/6. However, as the process neared the end, Human Resources and Skills Development Canada (HRSDC) insisted that the project report should analyse only the agreements in effect. This directive placed limitations on the scope of the work by taking the politically sensitive Bilateral Agreements largely out of the equation.

Tightly controlled projects could fall into the trap of what Boismenu and Graefe (2004, 77) have called the 'selective cultivation of research themes and expertise,' with governments steering, rather than communities driving the process. This seems to align with the sceptics that Taylor (2003, 220–1) describes, who 'would point to the current hegemony of technocratic cultures – the new managerialism, the audit culture – and the way in which they have reinvented central, top-down control in less visible forms. This, they would argue, has taken politics

out of the public sphere and policy-making.'[11] Because advocacy organizations are negatively affected by these new performance measures,
and they are also vulnerable to funding cuts by government (Phillips
2001), they need core, stable public funding that is independent of
partisan politics.

In the case of MTC, project funding came from the federal government. The question is open as to whether joint funding from FPT governments would have made a difference. Since FPT governments had
already begun their reporting prior to the project, it is unlikely that it
would have affected the quality of data presented. But it is possible that
PT governments would be more open to using the tools developed and
taking up the MTC recommendations if they had been parties to the
community-based review. In ELCC, though, governments said they
would consult with third parties only 'as appropriate' (Early Childhood
Development 2004a), so it differs from the health care case, where both
the federal and provincial governments were more enthusiastic about
third-party monitoring. Even in health care, Fafard's chapter 2 points
to some of the difficulties in getting all provinces to participate in institutions designed to facilitate third-party involvement. Thus, although
FPT cooperation in empowering community is a potentially attractive
prospect, requiring it may simply cement the conditions for executive
federalism to supplant citizen engagement.

Infrastructure is also necessary to facilitate participation (Phillips
2001). Governments must establish mechanisms for a broad range of
citizens (including parents, child-care workers and employers, advocates, researchers, and academics) to be involved. Day and Brodsky
(2007, 91) envision structures to facilitate citizen engagement and public
reporting, suggesting that a 'Canada Social Programs Council could
have appointees chosen by all levels of government ... with expertise in
the area of social programs, social rights, and intergovernmental fiscal
arrangements. They could include persons from non-governmental
organizations representing vulnerable and disadvantaged groups.'

There are existing models of citizen engagement as well, such as
the Council of the Federation's Premiers' Advisory Panel on Fiscal
Imbalance. An application of deliberative democracy, it gathered
ninety-three randomly selected citizens to reflect on the state of fiscal
federalism in Canada (Maxwell, MacKinnon, and Watling 2007). The
participants underlined the continued significance of the federal
spending power, national standards, and a preference for conditional
transfers over tax points (Maxwell, MacKinnon, and Watling). In the

same way, citizens assemblies or councils could be involved in public reporting. Citizen engagement in FPT governance ought to be institutionalized using such methods.

Engagement in What?

With resources and institutional support, citizens can better engage with public reporting, but another lesson from MTC is that it is not enough to bring community in only at the evaluation stage. Participation has to be built in throughout the entire policy process. Otherwise, community members will continue to express frustration at how some government consultations are conducted and the limited impact that these consultations have on resulting child-care policy and funding. This reinforces a point made by Simmons (2008) that superficial involvement will simply increase citizen disillusionment.

Benhabib's conditions for legitimate democratic deliberation emphasize the need for participation to span all stages of the process (cited in Denhardt and Denhardt 2003). MTC is an example of involving third parties in the *final review* of the reporting process. The bulk of its findings concentrate on whether governments met the accountability standards they set for themselves, rather than a sustained critique of the nature or adequacy of the agreements. Consequently, communities were engaged in monitoring compliance with FPT priorities that they had little say in setting in the first place. Communities also have a right to be involved in *developing goals* and *plans*. As Denhardt and Denhardt (133) argue, 'Performance measures ought to be developed based on an open public process,' and Taylor (2003, 124) concurs that communities have to be involved in establishing the criteria for evaluation. At a bare minimum, following the PSAB's recommendation (2007), public reporting should describe the extent to which users were involved in the report and in the selection of performance measures.

PSAB suggests that chosen indicators should focus on the 'few critical aspects of performance.' It is not unrealistic to expect governments to work with communities to determine which indicators are critical to improving access to quality, affordable child-care services, and not select the indicators that suit them politically, as appears to be the case in the FPT agreements. On the basis of FPT objectives, PSAB guidelines, the experience and views of the child-care community, and the research and international evidence, MTC recommended that FPT governments consider critical indicators of performance for child care: training, wages, parent fees, subsidy rates, percentage of children with a regulated child-care space, and percentage of children from various targeted groups (Aboriginal communities, children with disabilities) with access to regulated space.

FPT governments should also develop short- and long-term child-care action plans that reflect community input. There is an abundance of comprehensive, community-driven ELCC action plans for governments to draw from. For Taylor, these sorts of plans have a lot of demo-cratic potential. She believes that 'accountability to a jointly agreed action plan with outcomes defined by local communities and agencies together offers an alternative way forward and a powerful informal mechanism. Developing community-based criteria for success can be a powerful tool for developing common agendas and an understanding of where different people are coming from' (2003, 204). It is noteworthy that in the cancelled Bilateral Agreements, provinces and territories committed to consulting with communities in the development of ELCC action plans. This feasible initiative would have been a true innovation, had the action plans emerged from a stronger foundation than this par-ticular FPT Agreement. On the whole, all three ELCC FPT Agreements would have benefited from a regime that relied on a much more exten-sive array of enforcement-oriented accountability mechanisms, as outlined below.

Putting Public Reporting in Its Place

Much can be done to make the FPT process more participatory. Still, without fundamental transformation of social and economic relations (i.e., social equality, work/life balance), citizens alone cannot monitor public reporting. Nor should they. Citizens are only one piece of the accountability puzzle and are not solely responsible for using public reporting. As the editors argue in the introduction to this volume, accountability inside and between governments still matters.

Defining who is 'the public' is the first step in finding the appropriate place for public reporting. Viewed too narrowly, citizens and community-based organizations become the only public voices, and the media and governments are able to escape their obligations. As the CCAF-FCVI (2006, 11) states, 'Governments should be the primary user of perfor-mance measurement and information,' as this information can 'provide a sound basis for helping the Legislature hold the government to account.' Cameron (2007) further argues that accountability through the principle of responsible government is essential for democratic inter-governmental relations. Governments must develop and implement a defined role for legislators.

Public reporting is not a new concept for governments. What *is* new is the suggestion that public reporting, on its own, provides sufficient accountability. Traditional financial reporting occurs within a comprehensive accountability framework. What we have now is sole reliance on public reporting. Components of a more comprehensive framework are either missing or weaker because the standards related to public reporting are still under development, the FPT Agreements do not have the same force as legislation, and there is no requirement for the public reporting to be presented to the legislature or audited.

The child-care community has long recommended that governments use additional avenues, including reporting to Parliament/Legislatures, auditing, and legislated standards. Such accountability measures existed in the past and are well explored in the federalism literature as necessary in the future. Reporting to legislatures is central to accountability (Day and Brodsky 2007), and Simeon and Cameron (2002) outline a more extensive form of 'legislative federalism,' including reporting on ministerial meetings, creating a standing committee on intergovernmental relations, legislative ratification of major FPT agreements, and opportunities for cross-government meetings of legislators.

Auditing is also crucial for an accountability regime that relies heavily on publicly reported information, and it is consistent with the strong measurement-orientation of contemporary governments. The MTC review neither resembled, nor could it take the place of, an external audit. It did not have the mandate, the authority, or the resources to confirm the accuracy of the information provided by governments in their reports, the reasonableness of the estimates used, or the appropriateness of the methodology employed. Governments had no obligation to respond to its findings.

Child-care advocates continue to see standards enshrined in legislation as vital for ensuring a quality, universal system. Indeed, the MTC analysis highlights the effect of changing accountability mechanisms and affirms the importance of federal leadership on child-care policy and funding. It was clear in the investment shifts between the ECDA and the Multilateral Agreement that dedicated federal transfers specifically for child-care services were central to any progress. Recall that under the ECDA, governments were not required to invest specifically in child-care services. The result was that in several jurisdictions the proportion of total ECD dollars invested in child-care services *decreased* between 2000/1 and 2002/3. It was evident that unless governments are specifically directed to invest in child care, many will focus on what advocates call 'ABC – anything but child care.' This refers to the range of 'boutique' programs that emerged from the ECDA, such as those promoting healthy pregnancy and early childhood. It was not until dedicated transfers through the Multilateral Agreement were in place that the relative decline in child-care services started to level off or reverse. The dedicated federal transfers (i.e., transfers 'with strings attached') helped to focus specific attention to child-care services while promoting and protecting Canada's commitment to comparable social services across jurisdictions.

For child-care advocates, these conditions are certainly preferable to unrestricted transfers to PT governments but do not have the same stability as legislation, as demonstrated in the ease with which the Bilateral Agreements were cancelled. While unfashionable in the present political climate, Day and Brodsky (2007) maintain that national standards and conditions are key to social rights and citizenship and should not be subject to fickle federalism. Even though 'conditionality' is now called 'federal intrusion,' 'federal imposition,' 'central control,' 'federal invasion of provincial jurisdiction,' 'trenching on the sovereignty of the provinces' – phrases that imply that this is a highly illegitimate exercise (11), they insist that 'the federal government's exercise of its spending power is a central mechanism for maintaining Canada's social union and for operationalizing women's human rights. No alternative has presented itself … The subject matter of the social union is not the rights of governments, but the rights of the people whom they serve' (83). Cameron (2007, 175) adds, 'In the Social Union regime, the principle of social citizenship is entirely eclipsed by concerns about jurisdictional matters. It is the powers of government, not the rights of citizens, that are the central focus.' The federal spending power and conditionality continue to be critical for accountability and democratic citizenship.[12]

It might seem contradictory to call for 'bottom-up' citizen engagement alongside 'top-down' national standards, but they are not necessarily at odds.[13] One is actually required for the other to thrive. If citizen engagement allows marginalized voices to be heard in public policy, national standards can help to bring those voices from the margins to the centre. The counterpart to answerability is enforcement. As such, putting public reporting in its proper place means not using it as a replacement for established accountability practices but instead adding another layer of accountability to the mix.

Conclusion

This chapter began by sketching the contours of this ELCC accountability regime and then reflected on the place of communities in it. As a distinctive experiment in citizen engagement, MTC provides a glimpse into the potentially powerful role that the public could play in the policy process, if community capacity-building were truly integral to FPT accountability.

Unfortunately, in ELCC policy, the conditions for substantive citizen involvement are absent, as child-care community input and knowledge is not being used effectively, and time and resources are lacking. Moreover, while it can be a key component of an overarching accountability framework, many are worried about the growing reliance on public reporting as *the* accountability mechanism in the public sector and caution that other imperative elements, such as service and reporting standards and a defined role for legislators, appear to have diminished or disappeared. Democratizing intergovernmental accountability in Canada requires embedding genuine citizen engagement within a broad social citizenship regime where legislated standards, audited information, and reporting to legislatures still have a home.

NOTES

1 Findings from this paper were first published in the CCAAC project report *Child Care Policy: Making the Connections* (2007). Another version of this paper was presented at the Annual Meeting of the Canadian Political Science Association (CPSA), 6 June 2008, with Lynell Anderson and was published in 2010 in *Canadian Public Administration*. I would like to thank Lynell for her support and insight throughout and beyond MTC as well as our co-participants on the CPSA panel, 'Federalism, Accountability and Public Policy,' Barbara Cameron, Peter Graefe, Mario Levesque, Susan Phillips, and Linda A. White for their feedback. I also acknowledge the support of the Human Early Learning Partnership, University of British Columbia, the International Collaboration on Complex Interventions, University of Calgary, and the Mount Saint Vincent University New Scholars

Grant. Feedback from Josée Bergeron, workshop discussant, workshop participants, the editors, Peter Graefe, Julie M. Simmons, and Linda A. White, and anonymous reviewers was greatly appreciated.

2 *Community* refers broadly to those outside of government with an interest in early learning and child care, including parents, child-care workers, advocates, organizations, and researchers.

3 Following the CCAAC, I will use the terms *early learning and child care* and *child care* interchangeably because quality child care includes early learning.

4 For some, this is the greatest advantage of Bilateral agreements over Multilateral ones. Friendly and White (2008) argue that one of the benefits of a bilateral process is that it allows progressive actors to proceed without being stalled by reluctant jurisdictions. For others, the Bilateral Agreements simply reinforce the lack of a coordinated system of ELCC across the country.

5 In Anderson and Findlay (2010), we discuss in much more detail the results of the MTC project and our recommendations for clear public reporting.

6 The PSAB is an independent body that sets accounting standards developed over time through consultation with governments.

7 In his June 2007 comments to the Standing Senate Committee on Social Affairs, Science and Technology, Shawn Tupper, director general, Social Policy, Human Resources and Social Development Canada acknowledged the problem of late reporting but insisted that governments have confirmed their commitment to public reporting (*Proceedings of the Standing Senate Committee* 2007).

8 In fact, even basic information about the Bilateral Agreements is no longer available on the HRSDC website

9 It is ironic that non-governmental organizations are increasingly expected to provide comprehensive reporting, while governments are not living up to the same standard.

10 For more comprehensive recommendations, see Findlay and Anderson (2010).

11 Taylor (2003) identifies three main orientations toward community participation: the optimists, the pessimists, and the pragmatists. She places herself in the third camp.

12 It should be emphasized that this is the case only outside of Quebec.

13 Turgeon and Hjartarson (chapter 7) also note that state-centred and society-centred mechanisms might be complementary.

REFERENCES

Anderson, Lynell. 2004. *BCs Annual Reporting on Early Childhood Development (ECD): Analysis of Impacts on Child Care*. Vancouver: Child Care Advocacy Forum.

Anderson, Lynell and Tammy Findlay. 2005a. 'Fact Sheet #1: Public Funding and Child Care Policy: How Do We "Make the Connection"?' Child Care Advocacy Association of Canada. September. http://www.ccaac.ca/mtc/en/pdf/mtc_factsheet1.pdf.

– 2005b. 'Fact Sheet #2 (Part A): What Are the Federal Provincial Territorial Agreements?' Child Care Advocacy Association of Canada. September. http://www.ccaac.ca/mtc/en/pdf/mtc_factsheet2a.pdf.

– 2005c. 'Fact Sheet #2 (Part B): Will the FPT Agreements Achieve the Child Care Goals?' Child Care Advocacy Association of Canada. November. http://www.ccaac.ca/mtc/en/pdf/mtc_factsheet2b.pdf.

– 2005d. 'Fact Sheet #3: What Are the Action Plans and Who Develops Them?' Child Care Advocacy Association of Canada. September. http://www.ccaac.ca/mtc/en/pdf/mtc_factsheet3.pdf.

– 2007. 'Making the Connections: Using Public Reporting to Track the Progress on Child Care Services in Canada.' Child Care Advocacy Association of Canada (CCAAC). http://www.ccaac.ca/mtc/en/pdf/mtc_finalreport_en.pdf.

– 2010. 'Does Public Reporting Measure Up? Federalism, Accountability and Child Care Policy in Canada.' *Canadian Public Administration* 53 (3): 417–38.

Bakvis, Herman, and Grace Skogstad, eds. 2002a. *Canadian Federalism: Performance, Effectiveness, and Legitimacy*. 1st ed. Toronto: Oxford University Press.

– 2002b. 'Canadian Federalism: Performance, Effectiveness, and Legitimacy.' In Bakvis and Skogstad, *Canadian Federalism*, 1st ed., 3–23.

–, eds. 2008a. *Canadian Federalism: Performance, Effectiveness, and Legitimacy*. 2nd ed. Toronto: Oxford University Press.

– 2008b. 'Canadian Federalism: Performance, Effectiveness, and Legitimacy.' In Bakvis and Skogstad, *Canadian Federalism*, 2nd ed., 3–22.

Bascombe, Dianne. 2001. 'Towards Better Public Policy.' Canadian Child Care Federation. http://www.cccf-fcsge.ca/practice/from%20where%20i%20sit/policy_en.html.

Boismenu, Gérard, and Peter Graefe. 2004. 'The New Federal Tool Belt: Attempts to Rebuild Social Policy Leadership.' *Canadian Public Policy* 30 (1): 71–89.

Brodie, Janine, and Isabella Bakker. 2007. *Canada's Social Policy Regime and Women: An Assessment of the Last Decade.* Ottawa: Status of Women Canada.

Cameron, Barbara. 2004. 'The Social Union, Executive Power and Social Rights.' *Canadian Woman Studies* 23 (3–4): 49–56.

– 2007. 'Accounting for Rights and Money in Canada's Social Union.' In Margot Young, Susan B. Boyd, Gwen Brodsky, and Shelagh Day. *Poverty: Rights, Social Citizenship and Legal Activism,* edited by Margot Young et al., 162–180. Vancouver: UBC Press.

Canada. Auditor General of Canada. 1999. *1999 Report of the Auditor General of Canada.* Ottawa: Office of the Auditor General of Canada.

– 2002. *2002 Report of the Auditor General of Canada.* Ottawa: Office of the Auditor General of Canada.

Canada. Human Resources and Skills Development Canada. 1999. 'A Framework to Improve the Social Union for Canadians: An Agreement between the Government of Canada and the Governments of the Provinces and Territories.' http://www.socialpolicy.ca/52100/m6/su.htm.

Canada. Parliament. 2007. *Proceedings of the Standing Senate Committee on Social Affairs, Science and Technology* 24. http://www.parl.gc.ca/39/1/parlbus/commbus/senate/com-e/soci-e/24mn-e.htm?Language=E&Parl=39&Ses=1&comm_id=47.

CCAF-FCVI Inc. 2006. *Users & Uses: Towards Producing and Using Better Public Performance Reporting: Perspectives and Solutions.* Ottawa: CCAF-FCVI.

CUPE. 2009. 'Public Child Care Profile: New Brunswick.' http://cupe.ca/child-care/brunswick-profile.

Day, Shelagh, and Gwen Brodsky. 2007. *Women and the Social Transfer: Securing the Social Union.* Ottawa: Status of Women Canada.

Denhardt, J.V., and R.B. Denhardt. 2003. *The New Public Service: Serving, Not Steering.* Armonk, NY: M.E. Sharpe.

Early Childhood Development. 2004a. 'First Ministers' Meeting Communiqué on Early Childhood Development.' http://www.scics.gc.ca/english/conferences.asp?a=viewdocument&id=1145.

– 2004b. 'Multilateral Framework Agreement on Early Learning and Child Care.' http://www.ecd-elcc.ca/eng/elcc/elcc_multiframe.shtml.

– 2004c. 'Shared Framework for Reporting on Progress in Improving and Expanding Early Childhood Development (ECD) Programs and Services.' http://www.ecd-elcc.ca/eng/ecd/ecd_sharedframe.shtml.

Friendly, Martha. 2000. *Child Care and Canadian Federalism in the 1990s: Canary in a Coal Mine.* Toronto: Childcare Resource and Research Unit.

Friendly, Martha, and Linda A. White. 2008. 'From Multilateralism to Bilateralism to Unilateralism in Three Short Years: Child Care in Canadian Federalism, 2003–2006.' In Bakvis and Skogstad, *Canadian Federalism*, 2nd ed., 182–204.

Human Resources and Skills Development Canada (HRSDC). 2005. 'Early Learning and Child Care Agreements.' No longer available online.

Kershaw, Paul. 2006. 'Weather-vane Federalism: Reconsidering Federal Social Policy Leadership.' *Canadian Public Administration* 49 (2): 196–219.

Laforest, Rachel, and Michael Orsini. 2005. 'Evidence-Based Engagement in the Voluntary Sector: Lessons from Canada.' *Social Policy & Administration* 39 (5): 481–97.

Maxwell, Judith, Mary Pat MacKinnon, and Judy Watling. 2007. 'Taking Fiscal Federalism to the People.' Canadian Policy Research Networks (CPRN). http://www.cprn.org/documents/47307_en.pdf.

National Children's Alliance. 2001. *Strengthening Capacity Project National Meeting: Summary Report.* http://www.nationalchildrensalliance.com/nca/pubs/2001/march01report.pdf.

Nova Scotia. 2008. 'Early Learning & Child Care Plan.' *Hansard.* Nova Scotia House of Assembly Committee on Community Services, 5 Feb. http://www.gov.ns.ca/legislature/hansard/comm/cs/cs_2008feb05.htm.

Organisation for Economic Cooperation and Development (OECD). 2006. *Starting Strong II: Early Childhood Education and Care.* Paris: OECD Publishing.

Phillips, Susan D. 2001. 'SUFA and Citizen Engagement: Fake or Genuine Masterpiece?' *Policy Matters* 2 (7): 1–36.

Public Sector Accounting Board (PSAB). 2007. 'Public Performance Reporting: Guide to Preparing Public Performance Reports.' http://www.psab-ccsp.ca/other-non-authoritative-guidance/item14604.pdf.

Simeon, Richard, and David Cameron. 2002. 'Intergovernmental Relations and Democracy: An Oxymoron If There Ever Was One?' In Bakvis and Skogstad, *Canadian Federalism*, 1st ed., 278–95.

Simmons, Julie M. 2008. 'Democratizing Executive Federalism: The Role of Non-Governmental Actors in Intergovernmental Agreements.' In Bakvis and Skogstad, *Canadian Federalism*, 2nd ed., 355–79.

Taylor, Marilyn. 2003. *Public Policy in the Community.* New York: Palgrave Macmillan.

5 Evolving Federal-Provincial Accountability Regimes in Active Labour Market Policy

THOMAS R. KLASSEN AND DONNA E. WOOD

Accountability is a system of checks and balances designed to make certain that governments fulfil their obligations and conduct a full accounting of expenditures. These checks and balances ensure that funds are spent for the purpose intended, that there is an audit trail, and that the impact of spending can be measured or reported. Accountability can take different forms and manifest itself in many ways, as discussed in the first chapter of this book. Our interest is in three dimensions of this concept, particularly in the context of a federal system of government: democratic, political, and administrative. These dimensions, as noted in the introductory chapter, capture the major relationships – between citizens, politicians, and administrators – that are at the heart of democratic governance.

Democratic accountability refers to the involvement of citizens in the activities of the state to ensure that initiatives are in accordance with the needs and interests of social groups, stakeholders, or society as a whole. Democratic accountability mechanisms ensure that governments report in a transparent fashion to citizens, and that the activity itself is subject to citizen involvement. Stakeholders, because they command specific knowledge, can evaluate executive behaviour and act as a 'transmission belt' to inform citizens. The democratic dimension of accountability is particularly challenging in complex multilevel governance systems where policies cross jurisdictional boundaries and decisions are often an outcome of elite bargaining.

Political accountability refers to the role of legislatures and the political executive in ensuring that public policy outcomes are effective and efficient, and that they adhere to federal principles. This aspect is particularly salient when one order of government is funding a scheme and another is designing and delivering it.

Lastly, administrative accountability refers to the forms, processes, and procedures for managing particular initiatives. It focuses on the activities undertaken by the permanent executive (in accordance with the established rules and procedures) that are required to implement a particular program or initiative. This is important when two orders of government must cooperate to ensure effective and efficient policy outcomes.

Our conceptualization of accountability fits with that of Luc Turgeon and Josh Hjartarson in their chapter 7 in this volume. They note that intra-state accountability (that is, between autonomous actors and agencies of the state) is especially important in Canada. As thus, administrative accountability – that is, the interaction between the permanent executives of the two levels of government – is central to understanding outcomes. However, as Turgeon and Hjartarson also note, democratic accountability, or in their words 'societal accountability' and political (or electoral) accountability must also be considered.

This chapter uses these three dimensions of accountability to analyse active labour market policy in Canada from the mid-1990s to the present. This policy field has been at the forefront of important developments in accountability regimes in Canada, as activities devolved from the Government of Canada to provincial[1] governments through the transfer of federal funding, assets, and staff (Wood and Klassen 2008b). The Labour Market Development Agreements (LMDAs) – negotiated and implemented since 1996 with all thirteen provincial/territorial jurisdictions – marked a significant departure from previous federal-provincial approaches and accountability regimes in the policy domain. The more recent Labour Market Agreements (LMAs) – negotiated and implemented in 2007 and 2008 – mark a yet further evolution of accountability mechanisms. These agreements were further enhanced in 2009, via an Omnibus agreement, to mitigate the impact of the economic downturn.[2] The dramatic devolution has raised the question, which we address below, as to as to whom provincial governments are (or should be) accountable.

This policy field is unique from those analysed in other chapters in the volume, in three important respects. First is the speed and scale of devolution. Second, there are no established institution(s) that can assess or interpret accountability results. Third, there are a variety of federal-provincial agreements in active labour market policy. Although largely similar from one province to another, each type of agreement has its own accountability framework. The implications of all of these characteristics are evaluated in this chapter.

The first section of the chapter provides a brief account of federal-provincial jurisdiction for the policy domain, explains why governance changed dramatically in the mid-1990s, and outlines how these changes were realized in the form of new federal-provincial bilateral agreements. The second section outlines the key features of the accountability regime that was put in place for the LMDAs in the 1990s and compares this to the more recent developments that have given rise to a new LMA regime that now exists alongside the LMDA one. The third section of the chapter analyses these regimes with regard to the three dimensions of accountability noted above: democratic, political, and administrative. In particular we examine the extent to which the experience with accountability measures in the first regime affected the measures in the more recent regime. Was there any learning in this specific area, and if so, of what sort? The final section explores the implications of our findings for the robustness of Canada's active labour market programs, and for Canadian federalism more generally.

We do not assess accountability regimes for two other important federal-provincial labour market agreements – the Targeted Initiative for Older Workers and the Labour Market Agreement for Persons with Disabilities – as these are analysed in other chapters in this book. As cost-shared or cost-matched funding arrangements, these agreements differ significantly from the LMDA and LMA regimes. The empirical data for this chapter were obtained through a review of federal-provincial agreements, reports, and media releases, supplemented by a review of the accountability and governance literature. We also draw on extensive interviews with federal and provincial officials.

Governance of Labour Market Policy in Canada

Jurisdiction

Labour market adjustment matches demand for labour with the supply of labour. It facilitates worker transitions across the life cycle – from school to work, from unskilled to skilled, from unemployment to employment, from declining firms to new opportunities, from work to retirement – and also supports workers when there are no jobs available.

In theory, this function can be left entirely to the private parties: workers (and their families) and employers. However, historically governments in Canada have played a critical supporting role. Active measures such as vocational training, wage subsidies to employers, job matching services, and other related interventions are designed to improve access to the labour market and jobs, develop employment-related skills, and promote more efficient labour markets. Passive measures such as unemployment insurance and social assistance are designed to mitigate financial hardship for the unemployed by providing income support (OECD 1994).

Labour market policy in Canada consists of a complex set of arrangements that have evolved over time based on constitutional jurisdiction, historical developments, and institutional structures. Of particular importance is the prominent role of provincial governments in nearly all aspects of labour market policy – an atypical arrangement when compared to most other nations (Haddow and Klassen 2006; Noël 2004). Provincial governments have constitutional responsibility for most social programs, including health care, social assistance, education, and training. Ottawa's involvement derives from its responsibility for the economy. In addition, a constitutional amendment in 1940 gave it responsibility for a contributory national unemployment insurance program when, during the Depression, provinces and municipalities found themselves unable to provide adequate relief to the unemployed (Banting 2005).

In the 1950s and 1960s, Ottawa offered financial incentives to provincial governments in order to purchase training for federal Unemployment Insurance claimants. The largely positive federal-provincial working relationship began to deteriorate in the 1960s when Ottawa terminated many cost-sharing arrangements with provinces, instead purchasing training for the unemployed from a variety of providers (Doern 1969; Dupré 1973; Haddow 2003). By the mid-1980s, Ottawa had expanded its own delivery network to 500 field offices across the nation providing Unemployment Insurance as well as other employment services. Ottawa also increased the involvement of business and industry through the establishment of sector councils in the late 1980s, and the Canadian Labour Force Development Board in 1991.

In parallel with these federal activities, the larger and more affluent provinces developed similar employment programs for client groups and industrial sectors felt to be inadequately served by federal programs, or that were identified as provincial priorities. By the mid-1990s, several provinces had established their own extensive and sophisticated local delivery networks that operated, to some extent, in competition with the federal system. Not surprisingly, they also began to aggressively argue that active labour market policy could be more efficient and effective, and duplication eliminated, if decision-making was closer to the local level. In particular, Quebec contended that integration and co-ordination of its social and economic policies was impossible if the federal government controlled the policy domain. The province's nationalist leanings further heightened its desire to take control of as many policy levers as possible (Bakvis and Aucoin 2000; Klassen 2000b).

The Labour Market Development Agreements

In May 1996, in direct response to a 1995 referendum on sovereignty association held by the Quebec provincial government in which nearly half of voters opted for greater sovereignty, through a minister's press release the Chrétien Liberal government committed to withdraw from labour market training and offered to transfer federal Employment Insurance funding, staff, and assets to provincial governments that wished to assume responsibility for active employment measures. The decision was also influenced by OECD discourse emphasizing improved outcomes through decentralization (OECD 2005). The purpose of the Labour Market Development Agreements (LMDAs) was to enable provincial governments to assume an expanded role in the design and delivery of labour market development programs and services, and to acknowledge that labour market training was primarily an area of provincial responsibility.[3]

It took over fourteen years and a change to Conservative leadership under Prime Minister Harper in 2006 for all jurisdictions to finally agree on fully devolved LMDAs.[4] In February 2010, the Yukon Territory was the final jurisdiction to implement a devolved agreement. These indeterminate agreements are authorized through Part II of the 1996 Employment Insurance (EI) legislation, and since 1997/8 have provided $1.95 billion annually from the EI account for the design and delivery of labour market programs across Canada. Overall funding allocations have not changed in over a decade, nor has the formula that distributes these funds between jurisdictions. Funding was initially allocated to jurisdictions through a formula based on a standardized set of objective labour market variables, adjusted in relation to the overall impact of the 1996 EI reforms. In the course of implementing the agreements, approximately two thousand federal positions have been transferred to provincial governments.

As undertakings between executive branches of government, intergovernmental agreements are illustrations of executive federalism – negotiated in secret, behind closed doors by executives, without the involvement of legislators, stakeholders, or citizens. The purpose of the agreements reflects the dominance of executive federalism (as laid out in the purpose statement for Ontario):

> (a) implement, within the scope of Part II of Canada's *EI Act*, new Canada-Ontario arrangements in the area of labour market development that will enable Ontario to assume an expanded role in the design and delivery of labour market development programs in Ontario, to benefit clients,
> (b) provide for cooperative arrangements between Canada and Ontario to reduce overlap and duplication in, and to harmonize and coordinate the delivery of, their respective employment programs and services, and
> (c) provide for the transfer of affected federal employees to Ontario.[5]

Although constitutional realignment in labour market policy had been proposed in the Charlottetown Accord, the defeat of the accord in the 1992 referendum meant that administrative, rather than constitutional, devolution would be pursued. The LMDAs, in effect, acted as a substitute for formal constitutional reform, what Poirier (2001) identifies as 'para-constitutional engineering.' Each agreement was negotiated bilaterally, with the first round of devolved agreements in place in seven jurisdictions by 2000, Ontario in 2005, and the remaining five jurisdictions between 2008 and 2010. There were limited efforts made by the Government of Canada at multilateral negotiation or implementation.

The agreements provided an opportunity for substantive federal-provincial policy coordination – including procedural cooperation through the establishment of bilateral management committees – thereby easing past disagreements on federal-provincial roles and responsibilities (Bakvis 2002). The agreements are indeterminate and are not subject to renewal; however, each agreement contains provisions for either party to give notice of termination. The bilateral agreements are largely similar, with Ottawa controlling how much money is available, setting guidelines on how funds can be used and who can be served. Each agreement has what is referred to as a 'me too' clause to ensure equality of treatment and to reassure those provinces that negotiated the first agreements that preferred treatment obtained through later agreements was also applicable to them. This clause allowed provinces to proceed at their own pace, with the certainty that they would not be disadvantaged for coming later to the negotiation table.

Through the LMDAs provincial governments agree to provide Employment Benefits and Support Measures (EBSMs) similar to those outlined in the EI Act (i.e., targeted wage subsidies, targeted earnings supplements, self-employment assistance, job-creation partnerships, skills development, employment assistance services, labour market partnerships, and research and innovation) to EI clients and reach-back claimants (those that received EI benefits within the past three years or past five years if it was a maternity or parental claim). Employment assistance services – service-needs determination; assessment, selection, and referral; employment counselling services; placement services; labour exchange; and labour mobility assistance – are available to all citizens, not just EI clients. These provisions ensure that all Canadians have access to at least a minimum level of relatively similar employment services across Canada. The agreements also provide the Government of Canada, as the funder for these services, with a continuing role in labour market policy – including the ability to establish priorities in this policy domain – and a way to steer activities to promote national, pan-Canadian interests. Post-devolution Ottawa has retained responsibility for national aspects of labour market development (e.g., labour mobility, labour exchange, and labour market information) as well as supporting sector councils, employers, and selected vulnerable groups (e.g., youth, disabled, and Aboriginal persons).

The Labour Market Agreements and Supplementary Funding

At the urging of provincial governments, the Government of Canada's 2007 budget supplemented the LMDAs with Labour Market Agreements (LMAs) that provide provincial governments with $500 million annually for six years to support skills development for unemployed individuals who are not eligible for EI benefits and employed individuals who are low-skilled. Programs can include, but are not limited to, skills training; on-the-job training and workplace-based skills upgrading; group interventions and job-readiness assistance; financial supports and benefits such as loans, grants, and living allowances; employment counselling and services; and labour market connections such as services to facilitate matching supply and demand and services that promote and enhance labour market efficiency.

Before the significant federal budget cutbacks in the mid-1990s due to deficits and debts, Ottawa had delivered directly a range of labour market programs for designated equity groups – Aboriginal persons, persons with disabilities, members of a visible minority, and women – funded from general tax revenues. After the signing of the first LMDAs, provincial governments argued that limited provincial resources did not permit them to serve those who were most in need of employment supports (that is, non-EI clients) and that the Government of Canada, through its historical involvement in the policy domain, was best positioned to provide the necessary funding. They also argued that federal eligibility restrictions to employment insurance limited client access to LMDA funding.

The purpose of the LMAs is thus to enhance provincial employment and training programming – including an ability to serve groups previously not included in the LMDAs – using federal resources. The agreements specify that the federal funding must be incremental and cannot be used to make up for provincial cutbacks in the same area. The LMAs are funded from the federal Consolidated Revenue Account and are targeted to end in 2014. Unlike the LMDA, where funding was distributed on the basis of historical allocations and labour market variables, LMA funding is distributed between jurisdictions on a per-capita basis.

In response to the economic downturn and the significant increase in the unemployment rate, the 2009 federal budget committed over two years an additional $1 billion to the LMDAs and an additional $500 million to the LMAs targeted to those affected by the economic downturn and those seeking to retrain or upgrade their skills to keep employment. These additional commitments are outlined in Omnibus Amending Agreements to each jurisdiction's LMDA and LMA. In this case, funding is distributed on the basis of the jurisdiction's share of the unemployed.

Funding and Governance of the Policy Domain

Table 5.1 illustrates the federal funding allocations to each jurisdiction through these three agreements in 2009/10. In addition to programming operated under federal-provincial agreements, both orders of government fund and deliver labour market programs themselves for selected target groups (for example, for social assistance recipients, youth, Aboriginal persons, and recent immigrants).

Table 5.1 2009/10 Federal funding agreement allocations to provinces and territories ($ million)

	BC	AB	SK	MB	ON	QC	NS	NB	PEI	NL	NWT	YK	Nun	Total
LMDA*	280.6	104.7	38.5	45.8	538.2	598.4	81.3	92.3	27.2	133.4	3.3	3.7	2.8	1950.0
LMA**	66.0	52.5	15.0	18.3	200.0	116.6	14.1	11.3	2.0	7.6	N/A	N/A	N/A	503.4
OMN***	78.0	50.5	13.5	17.0	313.5	194.5	25.0	21.5	6.5	21.5	N/A	N/A	N/A	741.5
Total	424.6	207.7	67.0	81.1	1051.7	909.5	120.4	125.1	35.7	162.5	3.3	3.7	2.7	3195.0

* From HRSDC, *2009–10 Report on Plans and Priorities*. In addition to these program funds, the LMDAs also pay administrative expenses.

** From HRSDC news releases 28 Feb. 2008 (BC); 2 Sept. 2008 (AB); 22 Feb. 2008 (SK); 11 Apr. 2008 (MB); 21 Feb. 2008 (ON); 30 Apr. 2009 (QC); 13 June 2008 (NS); 29 Feb. 2008 (NB); 5 Sept. 2008 (PEI); 5 Sept. 2008 (NL).

*** From HRSDC news releases 22 May 2009 (all) and 13 Aug. 2009 (NL) OMN – omnibus agreement

All told, when the Targeted Initiative for Older Workers (TIOW) and Labour Market Agreement for Persons with Disabilities (LMAPD) agreements are added to the LMDA, LMA and Omnibus agreement mix, there are almost sixty bilateral federal-provincial agreements in place that govern labour market adjustment in Canada. Each agreement has 'envelope' federal funding allocations, which provinces must track and account for, to ensure that federal funds are spent on initiatives for which they were intended and that there is some mechanism to measure or report on the impact of their spending. Active labour market policy in Canada is indeed a very complex policy domain and one, as we analyse below, for which accountability – democratic, political, and administrative – has been a central concern.

Comparing the Key Features of the LMDA and LMA Accountability Regimes

The LMDAs and LMAs are program-specific transfer agreements that provide provincial governments with federal funding to operate provincial labour market programs under rules and conditions defined by the federal government in keeping with Treasury Board guidelines. Therefore presumably the agreements are all conditional – that is, funding is dependent upon provincial governments fulfilling the terms of the agreements, including reporting to the Government of Canada. However, other than a statement that funding will be withheld if audited statements are not provided, there are no evident sanctions identified if provinces do not fulfil the terms of the agreements.

Table 5.2 illustrates the key features, as well as similarities and differences in the accountability measures of the LMDAs and LMAs as well as the Omnibus agreement. The three dimensions of accountability noted previously – democratic, political, and administrative – are employed to group the key features.

Assessment of the Accountability Regimes

This part of the chapter has two objectives: first, to analyse the regimes according to the three dimensions – political, administrative, and democratic – outlined earlier, and second, to analyse and explain the changes in accountability measures between the first and second regimes (with some reference also to the Omnibus agreement).

Table 5.2 Accountability measures in the LMDAs, LMAs, and Omnibus Agreements

Feature	Labour Market Development Agreement	Labour Market Agreement	Omnibus Agreement
Democratic accountability			
Consultation	There are no requirements for the federal or provincial governments to consult with citizens.	Provinces are to consult with key stakeholders in developing their annual plans. This consultation process is to be described in an annual plan, which is made public.	
Reporting to citizens on plans	There is no requirement for planning documents to be made public.	The annual LMA planning document (that sets targets for services) is to be made public.	
Reporting to citizens on results	The EI Commission (representing the federal government, workers, and employers) releases an *Annual EI Monitoring and Assessment Report.* There is no requirement that provinces report to their constituents.	By 1 October each province reports annually to its citizens on the results of the programs funded through the agreement. At the end of each fiscal year the federal government reports on the aggregate results.	Provinces are expected to include the results attributable to the additional funding in their annual reports.
Political accountability			
Reporting to legislatures	The Government of Canada must table the EI *Annual Monitoring and Assessment Report* in Parliament.	The agreements make no specific mention of a requirement to report to Parliament or provincial legislatures.	The Government of Canada prepares a quarterly report to Parliament.

Feature	Labour Market Development Agreement	Labour Market Agreement	Omnibus Agreement
Administrative accountability			
Planning	Provinces provide an annual plan to Canada three months before the start of the fiscal year.	Provinces provide both an annual plan and a multi-year plan.	Planning for the increased funding is to be reported separately.
Financial reporting	Provinces submit an audited financial statement setting out costs incurred in each EBSM.	Provinces submit an audited financial statement demonstrating program and administrative costs, surplus funds, and the basis of accounting. Funding recipients must demonstrate that federal funding has been used to support program activities that are in addition to, and not substituted for, those supported by normal provincial funding.	There is separate reporting on the additional funding.
Data exchange	The parties agree to exchange information on active EI claimants and other EI clients.	There is no exchange of client specific information, and no personal information is shared between governments.	
Performance indicators	There are three indicators for measuring results of the provincial EBSMs: (1) number of active EI claimants who access provincial benefits and measures, (2) returns to employment of EI clients, with an emphasis on active EI claimants, and (3) savings to the EI Account.	Ten indicators include three beneficiary indicators, two service delivery indicators, and five outcome and impact indicators. Each jurisdiction is to provide Canada with the aggregate information on these indicators no later than five months following the end of each fiscal year. In Quebec, the Emploi-Québec management results indicators are used instead.	

Table 5.2 Accountability measures in the LMDAs, LMAs, and Omnibus Agreements (continued)

Feature	Labour Market Development Agreement	Labour Market Agreement	Omnibus Agreement
Performance targets	Provinces and Canada agree to jointly establish in advance of each fiscal year mutually agreed results targets.	Annual targets for planned activities are included in the annual provincial LMA plan. There is no requirement for mutually agreed targets.	
Dispute resolution	There is no reference to dispute resolution.	A three-stage dispute resolution process is outlined involving dispute avoidance, designated officials, and then ministers.	
Review and evaluation	Early agreements specified the establishment of a joint federal/provincial process to support and oversee evaluations of the provincial programs. Later agreements provided for a joint year two review and evaluations managed and funded by the province, or joint evaluations funded by Canada.	Both parties agree to a joint year two review of the implementation of the agreement. Each province agrees to carry out an evaluation of the impact and effectiveness of the eligible programs and the funding provided. A province can undertake evaluations on its own or jointly with Canada. If joint, Canada will contribute half of the costs.	
Management	Most agreements establish a joint federal-provincial management committee as a forum to resolve issues, discuss annual results targets and annual plans, oversee evaluations, etc. The committee usually meets twice a year or more frequently, and operates on a consensus basis.	Both parties agree to establish a joint committee to oversee the review and evaluations identified, discuss annual plans and reports, and identify ways to better integrate the delivery of programs for Aboriginal peoples.	

To assess accountability regimes, an essential requirement is knowing about the agreements in the first place and the parameters that guide them. The federal-provincial labour market agreements outlined in this chapter were not negotiated as part of a larger political framework or vision developed collaboratively between both orders of government and announced to the public for scrutiny as, for example, the Labour Market Agreement for Persons with Disabilities, or the health or early childhood services accords. The LMDAs were based on a public federal offer made to all jurisdictions, followed by bilateral jurisdiction-by-jurisdiction negotiation behind closed doors without social partner input. The federal LMA offer was announced in the 2007 federal budget. Each agreement was negotiated separately on a bilateral basis and then identified to the public via a separate news release for each jurisdiction posted on the website of the federal minister of human resources and skills development (HRSDC). Until a recent upgrading,[6] there was no single place that provided ready access to all federal-provincial labour market agreements. Although the Forum of Labour Market Ministers was established in 1983 to promote inter-jurisdictional cooperation on a wide variety of labour market issues, it does not maintain a website that consolidates all its activities, and indeed until 2010 ministers had not met since June 2003. Unlike other policy domains such as health,[7] in order to gain an understanding of labour market policy in Canada – and the federal-provincial accountability regimes that underpin it – it is necessary to review news releases, agreements, and evaluation reports issued by the Government of Canada and the thirteen provinces/territories over the past fourteen years.

As shown in table 5.2, the federal-provincial agreements contain few measures related to either democratic or political accountability. The EI Commission (made up of two HRSDC senior officials and two individuals representing workers and employers) is responsible for spending under the LMDAs, and in this case democratic accountability is limited to producing the annual EI *Monitoring and Assessment Report* to Parliament. This report is constructed using data provided by provinces, with a chapter on each jurisdiction that requires provincial review and approval. These reports have been released each year since 1997 but tend to be general and not particularly critical or analytic – indeed the reports caution the reader about making comparisons between jurisdictions. Only the last two years are readily available on the web. The LMDA evaluations required under the agreements specify no timeframes for when evaluations will be completed or released – sixteen years post-devolution, only six summative LMDA evaluations have been made publicly available on HRSDC's website, and no comprehensive Canadian overview has been commissioned or produced.

Under the LMAs, democratic accountability increased substantially, as provinces are required to consult with key stakeholders in developing their plans and to publicly describe this process. The agreements specify that stakeholders include business and labour representatives, community organizations, and representatives of the official language minority communities. Provincial annual plans are posted on the HRSDC website and are easy to access. Federal and provincial governments are also expected annually to report (separately) on the results of their expenditures. The first provincial reports covering 2008/09, 2009/10, and sometimes 2010/11 are available on the HRSDC website. These range from three-page descriptive overviews focused on LMA programming, to copies of entire provincial annual reports for the responsible ministry. In only one report were the indicators outlined in the LMA agreement reported on completely, making it impossible to draw a pan-Canadian picture from the provincial data. The first national report prepared by HRSDC was released in August 2011. It presents a consolidated overview of the client and service delivery indicators, but not the client outcome indicators. Although the report noted, for example, that there was variation between provinces, there was absolutely no attempt to provide information that would allow for analysis of these variations.

The lack of more democratic accountability measures reflects two factors. First, this policy field has historically been an executive driven one in which efforts to increase democracy – particularly the role of key labour market partners – have been dismal failures. The LMDAs were negotiated during a time when many of the ambitious corporatist bodies created at the federal and provincial levels in the late 1980s and early 1990s were viewed by government officials as unable to forge business and labour consensus on labour market adjustment (Klassen 2000b; Sharpe and Haddow 1997). As a consequence, at neither the federal nor provincial level was there motivation to further experiment with increasing the role of stakeholders or citizens more generally. Second, the agreements were negotiated in the absence of political reforms (such as those proposed in the Charlottetown Accord) that sought to increase democratic accountability. Thus, it is not surprising that the agreements reflected the executive-centred model that has been the norm in Canadian intergovernmental relations.

When the LMDA accountability regime was first implemented in the mid-1990s, it was regarded as an important development in ensuring reporting on labour market adjustment interventions to Parliament. However, political accountability is weak under both the LMDAs and the LMAs. Only the LMDA report is tabled in Parliament, and this is at the discretion of the federal minister. There is no requirement for reports to provincial legislators. The quarterly reports to Parliament on economic stimulus spending, of which the Omnibus agreements are a part, represent a significant improvement in political accountability but were precipitated only as a result of opposition party requirements in a minority Parliament.

The LMDAs were negotiated in the context of federal deficits and debts, and a key objective of the accountability regime was to save money to the EI account, while another was to secure provincial agreement. Therefore, when negotiated in 1996, the accountability framework of the LMDAs was designed to ensure that the two orders of government were able to cooperate, or at least interact, with a minimum of friction and in a manner to ensure effective policy outcomes (Klassen 1999). Given both of these objectives, this meant limiting political and democratic accountability, which if extensive would have raised the likelihood of public controversy and debate, diminishing the chance of securing agreement in the first place, especially with Quebec and Alberta. As a result, the vast majority of accountability mechanisms in the three sets of agreements relate to administrative accountability.

As illustrated in table 5.2, the performance measures in the LMDAs are more rudimentary that those in the LMAs. There are only three performance indicators in the LMDAs but ten in the LMAs. As well, the planning process under the LMAs requires multi-year plans as well as the annual ones mandated by the LMDAs. In regard to the management of the agreements, the LMAs include a dispute resolution process and also call for the two orders of government to establish a standing committee. Both agreements call for a review of the implementation of the agreements and evaluations of their impact and effectiveness.

In negotiating the LMAs the federal government insisted on more accountability in both the democratic and administrative elements, but in fact diluted political accountability, in that reports to Parliament are no longer required. Democratic accountability was increased, in that provinces are required to consult stakeholders as part of annual planning and then to make this plan public, along with the results. The federal government has committed to report annually on the aggregate results. The most extensive shift was with regard to administrative accountability, in which the annual planning process was made more detailed, the degree of financial reporting was increased, and a dispute resolution process was outlined. Most significantly, the three performance indicators under the LMDAs (dealing only with client characteristics, program expenditures, and savings to the EI account) were replaced by ten indicators that capture this data in more detail, but also service levels, beneficiaries, and client outcomes. A key change in the transition from the LMDA to the LMA regime is that there is no longer a client data exchange between provincial and federal governments – instead, provinces commit to report on agreed to indicators and targets that they themselves establish, providing considerable provincial flexibility.

The heightened level of administrative accountability under the LMAs was primarily the result of the learning that had occurred over more than a decade under the LMDAs. For example, the reliance on just three performance indicators had been criticized by a number of groups and observers as inadequate. The evaluations of the LMDAs had been undertaken in many jurisdictions by the time the LMAs were negotiated, and these had identified a number of common concerns, such as the short-term nature of the performance measures. For instance, the Quebec evaluation report expressed concern over the lack of measurements related to the quality of employment, particularly in light of that province's desire to increase the social integration of the unemployed (such as by enhancing esteem and self-confidence). The evaluations also highlighted that the LMDAs were incapable of addressing the needs of individuals who were not eligible for services, as they were not EI claimants or reach-back clients. Consequently, the evaluations served as a common base of information and analysis for the negotiation of the LMAs – something that was not available when the LMDAs were initially agreed upon.

In addition, federal and provincial officials had had a decade of experience of managing devolved agreements. The experience in those jurisdictions with early devolved agreements[8] had been surprisingly positive and diminished mistrust in this policy field among officials (Lazar 2002). That the national unemployment rate declined from high levels in the mid 1990s (10.4 per cent in 1994) to record low levels more than a decade later (6.0 per cent in 2007) was also a significant factor in creating positive working relationships between the two orders of government. Given the constructive arrangements that had arisen, the developing capacity of provincial governments, and the considerable latitude that provinces had in the LMDAs, provincial officials were not as opposed, as would have been the case a decade earlier, to more reporting and performance measures, especially if these were largely confined to administrative – rather than democratic or political – accountability.

When the LMDA accountability was first introduced, it was seen as an improvement over the previous ad hoc and decentralized process that Ottawa had put in place with its regional offices, especially in setting consistent measures. And, indeed, Part II of the Employment Insurance Act required the federal government to 'work in concert' with provinces and territories in designing, implementing, and evaluating Employment Benefits and Support Measures. However, with the passage of time, senior officials in Ottawa came to see the measures as overly narrow, while at the same time limiting federal knowledge of provincial program interventions. The data exchange was also seen as unnecessarily complex, especially when provinces adjusted computer systems and could no longer accurately feed the federal reporting system. The solution was to stop the direct exchange of data, increase the number of indicators, and trust that provinces would report accurately, as outlined in the agreements.

A secondary reason for the higher level of administrative accountability in the second-generation agreements was that the federal government was in a stronger, more assertive, and less rushed bargaining position than had been the case in the 1990s (Boismenu and Graefe 2004). Immediately following the Quebec referendum, there was immense political pressure in Ottawa to demonstrative that federalism could respond to the desires of Quebec and to a lesser extent other provinces. As a consequence, for the LMDAs Ottawa adopted a negotiation position from the start that would be acceptable to the provinces most determined to see devolution in the policy field. It is noteworthy that Alberta was the first province to sign a devolved LMDA, with Quebec following shortly thereafter.

With the LMAs there was no political pressure comparable to that of a decade earlier. Indeed, the declining unemployment rates during the period caused active labour market policies to sink even further as a government priority area. Although there were calls for greater democratic accountability in the LMDAs, neither Ottawa nor the provinces were particularly inclined to pursue them very far. For instance, many of the LMDA evaluation reports highlighted the importance of employer, union, and community input into the design and delivery of labour market adjustment programs, especially the need for private sector involvement, given that this is where most of the jobs for clients are found. The requirement in the LMAs for provinces to consult with key stakeholders is sufficiently vague, especially in the absence of institutional arrangements in most provinces, outside of Quebec, to permit a robust voice from labour market partners. This is especially so since the clients served by the LMAs are those without a strong capacity to organize. It is noteworthy that despite significant federal funding to thirty-three national sector councils – industry-led partnership organizations that address skills development – Ottawa has not mandated key connections with provincial governments, which now substantially control the Canadian labour market development system.

In summary, in analysing the shifts between the LMDAs and the LMAs (and most recently the Omnibus agreements) it is obvious that two dimensions of accountability (democratic and administrative) have been enhanced, while one (political) has been diminished. The enhancement has been small in regard to democratic accountability, and more pronounced for administrative accountability. However, the policy domain has become more complex, with three separate accountability regimes under three separate agreements. Clearly there has been learning in this policy field between the mid-1990s and the late 2000s with respect to accountability. Nevertheless, as we discuss in the next section, it remains problematic whether these enhancements translate into more effective labour market adjustment policy.

Implications of the Accountability Regime

The LMDAs, negotiated months after the pivotal Quebec referendum, were the first federal-provincial arrangements negotiated under what was generally understood to be a new era of federal-provincial relations. The accountability mechanisms under them were relatively basic and in some aspects inadequate, and minimized democratic and political accountability. The LMAs negotiated a decade later have addressed some of the shortcomings, although democratic and political accountability remains low.

Intergovernmental agreements require that governments account to each other, but not necessarily that governments increase their reporting and accountability to citizens. The efforts in the Social Union Framework Agreement (SUFA) to shift away from government-to-government reporting to government-to-citizen reporting is somewhat evident in labour market policy, but in the absence of greater transparency has had only limited impact. It is noteworthy that administrative accountability in the agreements is more extensive and in recent years has been strengthened. The agreements may have gotten accountability 'right,' but only as it applies to the permanent executive. In other words, administrative accountability has been the focus of the agreements and has produced a smooth and positive working relationship between the two orders of government (Lazar 2002; Marc 2005). However, as we discuss below, such a relationship, and the accountability features that create and support it, may not necessarily result in robust and effective active labour market policy. For this to occur, political and democratic accountability must be strengthened. We analyse the EI Monitoring and Assessment Reports over the period 1997–2008 to illustrate this shortcoming.

The decline in unemployment rates during this period meant that jurisdictions began to emphasize short-term and inexpensive interventions (job counselling, résumé preparation, etc.) often delivered in a group setting at the expense of longer-term and costly interventions, such as training typically offered on an individual basis. In 1997/8, longer-term interventions accounted for 45.2 per cent of all interventions, while 53.4 per cent of all interventions were short-term (employment assistance services). Ten years later, a dramatic shift had occurred in that longer-term interventions accounted for 18.4 per cent of all interventions, and short-term accounted for 81.5 per cent. Table 5.3 provides a summary of the trend in interventions from 1997 to 2008.

The shift to short-term, less costly interventions has led to more clients being served, but with services that were short-term. However, the annual EI Monitoring and Assessment reports provide little information on the effectiveness of these short-term interventions that have come to dominate the services offered under the LMDAs. The accountability framework of the agreements makes it difficult to determine if the most effective labour market policy is one that favours short-term interventions. The reports provide no analysis that would allow citizens or politicians to act as agents of change. Nor in this policy domain are there mechanisms for all provincial governments and Ottawa to discuss in a multilateral forum how to ensure that active measures are effective (Wood and Klassen 2009). There are not even robust processes for sharing best practices between provincial governments, let alone with contracted service providers from across Canada who are now an integral part of the service delivery network.[9]

Table 5.3 Number of EBSM interventions, participants, and funding allocations 1997 to 2008 under the LMDAs

Intervention	97/98	98/99	99/00	00/01	01/02	02/03	03/04	04/05	05/06	06/07	07/08
Employment Assistance Services	257,732 53.4%	368,304 57.5%	423,798 65.6%	424,387 68.5%	593,437 74.6%	702,361 79.9%	764,323 81.3%	790,906 81.0%	768,253 81.7%	752,047 80.8%	768,034 81.5%
Training	166,150 34.5%	189,456 29.6%	152,916 23.6%	130,601 21.0%	134,358 16.9%	127,815 14.5%	128,518 13.7%	128,721 13.1%	133,092 14.1%	142,386 15.2%	142,782 15.1%
Incentives in the private sector*	30,268 6.3%	56,954 8.9%	40,721 6.3%	40,915 6.8%	41,055 5.2%	38,241 4.4%	36,651 3.9%	33,020 3.3%	31,962 3.4%	30,340 3.2%	26,028 2.8%
Incentives in the public sector**	21,558 4.5%	29,003 4.5%	18,663 2.9%	11,127 1.8%	10,007 1.3%	10,520 1.2%	10,247 1.0%	7,971 0.8%	6,882 0.7%	6,535 0.7%	5,123 0.5%
Other***	6,568 1.4%	6,394 1.0%	9,741 1.5%	12,372 1.9%	16,443 2.0%	– –	– –	17,062 1.7%	– –	– –	– –
Total interventions	482,059	640,788	645,839	619,402	795,300	878,937	939,739	977,680	940,189	931,308	941,967
Total participants	305,000	501,633	481,282	457,839	510,200	637,754	668,000	636,000	627,703	618,202	612,622
Total Part II EBSM expenditures	$2.000b	$2.000b	$1.980b	$1.938b	$2.083b	$1.920b	$1.870b	$1.910b	$1.863b	$1.945b	$1.941b

* Includes direct wage subsidies to employers, financial incentives to workers, and incentives to assist individuals to become self employed
** Includes employment positions created in the public sector (including the broader community/not-for-profit sector) by providing public works or other activities that produce public goods or services
*** In some years Other included pan-Canadian activities
Source: authors' own calculations from the *1997–2008 Annual EI Monitoring and Assessment Reports*, Ottawa: HRSDC

Also, in contrast to some other policy areas, there is no requirement for a matching contribution from provinces, and continued federal funding is not explicitly contingent on provincial performance. This was partially addressed in the LMAs, which have a sunset clause (six years), while the LMDAs remain in force unless either party wishes to terminate the agreement. The availability of federal funding provides an incentive for provinces to seek enhanced federal transfers, instead of improving their own performance and considering the priority of labour market policies in the context of their own spending. Federal-provincial agreements with weak democratic and political accountability requirements provide an opportunity for blame-shifting or avoidance, as citizens are seldom aware of which order of government is really responsible. Blame-shifting was absent when the economy was booming, unemployment was low, and the federal government ran a surplus. These conditions have changed dramatically over the past several years, with both orders of government now running deficits and the federal government anxious to prove that their stimulus funding has resulted in reduced unemployment and up-skilling of the labour force.

Accountability, under the current agreements, is directed primarily at setting priorities and planning requirements while emphasizing particular outcomes, rather than setting strategic goals and imposing conditions on process. The three sets of accounting and reporting requirements currently in use, and the relatively little public disclosure in the active labour market policy field make it gruelling for citizens and stakeholders to hold their governments collectively to account (Graefe and Levesque 2010). National reports are typically insufficiently detailed, and because they are annual they fail to provide the requisite strategic perspective.

In conclusion, the federal-provincial dynamics of this policy field have seen remarkable shifts in a decade-and-a-half. In terms of reducing intergovernmental friction the LMDAs and LMAs have been an undoubted success, largely because of the relatively limited accountability measures in the agreements. These recognize the high degree of intrastate accountability and allow for relationships based on negotiations, rather than establishing overly hierarchical mechanisms. The administrative accountability features of the LMAs are an improvement over those of the LMDAs in that additional data on the outcomes of interventions are collected. With respect to democratic accountability both agreements are weak, although the LMAs make some marginal improvements in ensuring consultation with labour market partners and informing the public of plans and results. The political accountability of both sets of agreements is feeble, reflecting the executive nature of federalism and the nature of the Westminster system. Lastly, as we note, the democratic and political deficiencies are of concern as they point to an inability to forge effective policy in a domain that is critical to Canada's future prosperity.

NOTES

1 When the term *provincial* is used in this chapter, it generally also includes territorial governments.
2 The LMDAs and LMAs can be found at http://www.hrsdc.gc.ca/eng/employment/partnerships/pdlmdanfld.shtml.
3 This was done in conjunction with a major reform to the Unemployment Insurance program, which was re-branded as Employment Insurance (EI). Although active measures could be provincially delivered, federal offices continue to deliver passive Employment Insurance benefits.
4 British Columbia, Nova Scotia, Prince Edward Island, Newfoundland and Labrador, and the Yukon initially signed co-managed agreements where the federal government retained responsibility for program design and delivery.
5 See http://www.hrsdc.gc.ca/eng/employment/partnerships/pdlmdaontario.shtml.
6 See http://www.hrsdc.gc.ca/eng/employment/partnerships/labour_market_development/index.shtml and http://www.hrsdc.gc.ca/eng/employment/partnerships/lma/index.shtml.
7 For example, the Canadian Institute for Health Information (CIHI) provides timely, accurate, and comparable information in order to inform health policies, support the effective delivery of health services, and raise awareness among Canadians of the factors that contribute to good health.
8 Alberta, Manitoba, New Brunswick, Quebec, Saskatchewan, Nunavut, and NWT.
9 For example, in Ontario it is estimated that there are over five thousand service providers funded through the federal-provincial LMDA and LMA agreements (Wood 2010).

REFERENCES

Bakvis, Herman. 2002. 'Checkerboard Federalism? Labour Market Development Policy in Canada.' In *Canadian Federalism: Performance, Effectiveness, and Legitimacy*, edited by Herman Bakvis and Grace Skogstad, 197–219. Toronto: Oxford University Press.

Bakvis, Herman, and Peter Aucoin. 2000. *Negotiating Labour Market Development Agreements*. Canadian Centre for Management Development, Research Report No. 22. Ottawa: CCMD.

Banting, Keith. 2005. 'Canada Nation Building in a Federal Welfare State.' In *Federalism and the Welfare State, New World and European Experiences*, edited by Herbert Obinger, Stephan Leibfried, and Francis G. Castles, 89–137. Cambridge: Cambridge University Press.

Boismenu, Gerard, and Peter Graefe. 2004. 'The New Federal Tool Belt: Attempts to Rebuild Social Policy Leadership.' *Canadian Public Policy* 30 (1): 71–89.

Doern, Bruce. 1969. 'Vocational Training and Manpower Policy: A Case Study in Intergovernmental Liaison.' *Canadian Public Administration* 12 (1): 63–71.

Dupré, Stefan. 1973. *Federalism and Policy Development: The Case of Adult Occupational Training in Ontario*. Toronto: University of Toronto Press.

Graefe, Peter, and Mario Levesque. 2010. 'Impediments to Innovation in the Canadian Social Union: The Case of the Labour Market Agreements for People with Disabilities.' *Canadian Public Policy* 36 (1): 45–62.

Haddow, Rodney. 2003. 'Canadian Federalism and Active Labour Market Policy.' In *New Trends in Canadian Federalism*. 2nd ed., edited by F. Rocher and M.J. Smith, 243–267. Peterborough, ON: Broadview.

Haddow, Rodney, and Thomas Klassen. 2006. *Partisanship, Globalization and Canadian Labour Market Policy: Four Provinces in Comparative Perspective*. Toronto: University of Toronto Press.

Human Resources and Skills Development Canada. various years. *Employment Insurance Monitoring and Assessment Report*. Ottawa: HRSDC.

Klassen, Thomas R. 1999. 'Job Market Training: The Social Union in Practice.' *Policy Options* 20 (10): 40–4.

– 2000a. 'The Federal-Provincial Labour Market Development Agreements: Brave New Model of Collaboration?' In *Federalism, Democracy and Labour Market Policy in Canada*, edited by T. McIntosh, 159–203. Montreal and Kingston: McGill-Queen's University Press.

– 2000b. *Precarious Values: Organizations, Politics and Labour Market Policy in Ontario*. Kingston: Queen's University School of Policy Studies.

Lazar, Harvey. 2002. *Shifting Roles: Active Labour Market Policy in Canada under the Labour Market Development Agreements*. Ottawa: Canadian Policy Research Networks.

Marc, Magali. 2005. 'Federal-Provincial Overlap and Civil Servants: The Case of Occupational Training in Quebec and Ontario.' *Canadian Public Administration* 48 (1): 35–52.

Noël, Alain, ed. 2004. *Federalism and Labour Market Policy: Comparing Different Governance and Employment Strategies*. Montreal and Kingston: McGill-Queen's University Press.

Organisation for Economic Cooperation and Development. 1994. *OECD Jobs Study*. Paris: OECD.

– 2003. *Managing Decentralisation: A New Role for Labour Market Policy*. Paris: OECD.

– 2005. *Integrating Employment, Skills and Economic Development, Conceptual Framework*. Paris: OECD.

Poirier, Johanne. 2001. *The Functions of Intergovernmental Agreements: Post Devolution Concordats in a Comparative Perspective*. London: Constitution Unit, University College London.

Sharpe, Andrew, and Rodney Haddow. 1997. *Social Partnerships for Training: Canada's Experiment with Labour Force Development Boards*. Ottawa: Centre for the Study of Living Standards.

Wood, Donna E. 2010. *Building Flexibility and Accountability into Local Employment Services, Country Report for Canada*. OECD Local Economic and Employment Development (LEED) Working Papers. Paris: OECD. http://www.oecd-ilibrary.org/industry-and-services/building-flexibility-and-accountability-into-local-employment-services_5k9fmrlbh942-en.

Wood, Donna, and Thomas R. Klassen. 2008. 'Intergovernmental Relations Post-Devolution: Active Labour Market Policy in Canada and the United Kingdom 1996–2006.' *Regional and Federal Studies* 18 (4): 331–51.

– 2009. 'Bilateral Federalism and Workforce Development Policy in Canada.' *Canadian Public Administration* 52 (2): 249–70.

6 Accountability in Labour Market Policies for Persons with Disabilities

PETER GRAEFE AND MARIO LEVESQUE[1]

In considering the accountability provisions in intergovernmental agreements, the employability and labour market agreements in the disability sector are potentially interesting for three reasons. First, with the Employability Agreement for Persons with Disabilities (EAPD), signed in 1997, we have one of the earliest social policy agreements adopting the accountability mechanisms around reporting and following the multilateral framework / bilateral agreement model. Second, with the signing of the EAPD's successor agreement, the Labour Market Agreement for Persons with Disabilities (LMAPD) in 2003, the accountability mechanisms were slightly rejigged, providing us with the possibility to consider how and why these mechanisms changed over time. Finally, intergovernmental relations in this sector should rank among the least politicized, as it concerns a relatively small program with little public visibility or electoral salience, and where the low rate of policy success in all countries encourages a fairly pragmatic and incremental style of policy discussion. As such, we might expect federal-provincial conflict and rivalry to be relatively subdued, and the potential for policy learning contained in reporting to be most fully harnessed.

This chapter seeks to describe how accountability has worked in the field of employment programs for persons with disabilities. In the first section, it will describe the evolution of agreements in this sector, with an emphasis on the accountability and reporting requirements found within. The second section will then address how reporting has worked in practice, paying particular attention to intergovernmental conflict on reporting, to government-to-government learning, and to public participation and engagement. The chapter concludes with some brief reflections on normative issues.

To anticipate our conclusions, we find a great deal of conflict that has led to a pro forma process of producing plans and reports that all involved claim to be largely unused by governmental or extra-governmental actors. While it is tempting to blame the reporting regime for this outcome, and by extension either the provincial governments for being too obstinate in protecting constitutional jurisdiction, or the federal government for either refusing to adopt more powerful forms of accountability or for trying to act in an area of provincial jurisdiction, we feel this is too simplistic a response. Given the low political priority of the disability policy file, and the failure of governments at either level to greatly step up their funding of employability supports, it strikes us as odd to make intergovernmental relations the main culprit. Without denying the difficulties of intergovernmental policymaking, our obser-vation of this area reminds us of the adage, 'The smaller the drinking hole, the meaner the animals.'

Context: The Provenance and Content of Recent Agreements

Our interest in this chapter is employment programs for persons with disabilities – a relatively specialized area of intervention, but one that has given rise to federal-provincial bargaining and agreements since the 1950s. This stands in contrast to other parts of the disability policy area where the federal and provincial governments deliver services without much interaction with the other order of government (see Prince 2002). For instance, provinces play a large role in the realm of income support through their social assistance systems. They are also involved in income support and training through workers' compensation. The central gov-ernment likewise has transferred income and delivered services through Canadian Pension Plan disability benefits and Veterans Affairs. More recent central government involvement has taken the form of targeted tax assistance for specific needs and groups as well as the creation of the Opportunities Fund to provide EI-type interventions for people with disabilities who are not EI eligible.

From 1961 to 1997, the Vocational Rehabilitation of Disabled Persons Act (VRDP) regulated federal-provincial interaction in this field. Under its provisions, the provincial and federal governments entered into two- to three-year cost-sharing agreements for programs and services for persons with disabilities. The agreements aimed to help individuals with disabilities seek gainful employment and included such services as support for sheltered workshops and post-secondary education, employment research aid, summer recreation activities, and respite services. These agreements, continually renewed until 1997, were cost-sharing agreements whereby the federal government paid for 50 per cent of the costs of programs offered and administered by the provinces. This was a classic conditional shared-cost program, and like most of the others, it was affected by the central government's restraint policies: along with the Canada Assistance Plan, it went from being an open-ended cost-sharing agreement to being capped at a maximum sum, in the 1994 budget.

While it would be tempting to see federalism as the driver for the creation of the next generation of agreements in this sector, it was at best a proximate cause. Rather, we must realize that many programs came online in the 1950s and grew significantly in the 1970s, yet the depth of the associated expenses was not fully realized at the time (interview with federal government official). In addition, our interviews consistently conveyed the point that both federal and provincial officials were unhappy with the VRDPs, as they remained bound up in an anachronistic understanding of disability. From the *Obstacles Report* in 1981, to the *Report of the Royal Commission on Equality in Employment* in 1984, to the *Equality for All* report in 1985 and the 1992 *Pathway to Integration* report, the ideal of full participation and integration was coming to the fore (Canada, Chambres des Communes 1985; Canada, Commission Royale d'Enquête sur l'Égalité en Matière d'Emploi 1984; Ministres Responsables des Services Sociaux 1998). The 1998 *In Unison* document clearly summarized the change in philosophy: persons with disabilities were no longer clients of programs; rather they were another consumer group and their full participation in all realms of society was imperative (Ministres Responsables des Services Sociaux 1998). Some changes were made to the VRDP in the late 1980s in response to support the mainstreaming of programs, but those involved felt VRDP was not flexible enough to properly adapt to the new philosophy (Prince 2002).

In 1997, the federal and provincial governments negotiated the Multilateral Framework for Employability Assistance for People with Disabilities (EAPD) (Canada 1997) and finalized related bilateral EAPD agreements in 1998. The EAPD was seen as a replacement for the VRDP that better allowed for interventions in the direction of full participation, particularly through developing the employability of persons with disabilities. As part of that shift, the agreement also terminated funding for non-employment-related services such as sheltered workshops and addictions services, albeit with a phase-out period. The EAPD put five-year agreements into place and introduced the new forms of accountability around annual plans and reporting that are interesting, making it one of the first examples of the new accountability (depending on how one views the 1996–8 Labour Market Development Agreements). Another change from the VRDP involved the capping of federal cost sharing at approximately $190 million per year. The EAPD framework was largely reproduced with the 2003 Multilateral Framework for Labour Market Agreements for Persons with Disabilities (LMAPDs) and its bilateral LMAPDs (2004), albeit with some changes around accountability (Canada 2003b). The focus on employability continued, yet the provinces and territories were given increased flexibility in reporting requirements and additional funds for evaluations.

Accountability Features of the EAPD and LMAPD

The multilateral framework (Canada 1997) for the EAPDs made clear that 'the initiative will emphasize annual accountability to consumers and the general public' on the grounds that this would enhance 'program effectiveness, information sharing and the identification of best practices.' Assessment and evaluation mechanisms were also to 'involve persons with disabilities, using either formal structures or advisory groups,' on the grounds that this would ensure efficient allocation of funds and greater goal achievement. The framework set out quantitative and qualitative approaches to reporting that provinces *could* focus on, such as consumer satisfaction, reduction of individual and systemic barriers to participation, pilot projects, and best practices. In terms of measuring results, the governments agreed to a set of indicators largely focused on participant numbers. This included the number of people employed or sustained in employment, the number of people participating in or completing a program (with reasons for unsuccessful completion noted), the number of people served on waiting lists, savings to income-support programs as a result of increased employment earnings, and the number of people who have received supports and have maintained or advanced in their employment. As those we interviewed repeatedly noted, the focus on reporting participant numbers is a poor measure of a program's efficacy, given that little is learned as to how a participant's condition improved.

The two main vehicles for putting these commitments into place were planning and annual reviews. In terms of planning, both federal and provincial governments were to table their plans for mutual review, with provinces expected to 'prepare a multi-year program and expenditure plan for review.' The provinces would then also prepare annual reports on results achieved, which were meant to 'be the basis for making any required adjustments to the multi-year plan.' These reports were incorporated into one national report and made publicly available. This planning and reporting regime was felt to enable a coordinated approach between governments. A third vehicle for translating accountability was the use of program evaluations, in part to balance the quantification of the annual reports with qualitative information. The parties to the agreement agreed to share and make public their findings and to engage in multilateral planning to track evaluations and share information. This process was to also include 'consultation with individuals with disabilities, service providers and other stakeholders.'

The LMAPD's approach to accountability is very similar, announcing that 'public reporting forms the basis of accountability under this framework' and noting that this reflects the commitments made under the Social Union Framework Agreement. As with the EAPD, the forms of accountability are variously defended on the basis of enhancing partnership and cooperation, transparency to the public, the achievement of results, and continual improvement through stakeholder feedback. The agreement contains language on accountability that inflates expectations about it, such as 'governments recognize the important role that accountability plays in an effective, long-term approach towards reaching our shared goal of improving the labour market situation of persons with disabilities' (Canada 2003b).

Under the LMAPD, there are four parts to the accountability framework: annual plans, measurement of results and the release of those results to citizens in report form, program evaluation, and the exchange of information and results. All provinces are required to transmit an annual plan to the federal government, setting out the priority sectors to be addressed, a description of the programs and services to be funded, and an estimate of expenses. Provinces can also set out their reporting and evaluation plans in this document, with the exception of Quebec, which must expressly identify which programs and services will fall within the accountability framework. According to the multilateral framework as well as some bilateral agreements (e.g., Canada-Alberta and Canada-Quebec), these plans are for information purposes only and not to determine which programs are admissible. Our interview respondents were clear that the central government would follow up with a province only where there was a severe problem in the annual plan.

The second aspect – the responsibility to produce reports – has two prongs. First, the provinces committed in the framework to report to citizens on their objectives, to provide descriptions of programs, target groups, and spending on programs and services covered by the bilateral agreements. The reports must include information on indicators, such as the number of people using programs and services and the number of participants completing a program in a given period. They must also include environmental indicators about the labour market experience of persons with disabilities, such as employment rates, wages, and education levels. These details are elaborated in the multilateral framework and are specifically referenced in the bilateral agreements. The second prong of reporting is the commitment to provide a baseline report in 2004, and annual reports on the International Day of Disabled Persons, 3 December of each year. The LMAPD is slightly clearer than the EAPD in how this has to be done, specifying that it be posted on the Internet, and also opens the door to joint communications with common messaging, should provinces opt in.

Turning to program evaluation, the multilateral framework requires provinces to develop evaluation plans concerned either with process or with success in meeting objectives. This angle is most fully developed in the *Framework for Demonstration and Bilateral Evaluations*, which is part of the LMAPD framework, and sets out the procedures for conducting evaluations and reporting the results thereof (Canada 2003a). Demonstration evaluations are fully funded by the federal government, while bilateral ones are cost shared 80:20 by the federal and provincial governments, and provincial ones are shared 50:50. The fourth aspect – the exchange of information and results – is not further elaborated but was probably assumed to flow from the normal working of the first three aspects.

The LMAPD also clearly stipulates that accountability activities 'will be guided by: partnership and cooperation; transparency and commitment to public reporting; a focus on results; commitment to continual improvement based on evaluation and reporting, feedback from stakeholders and the public.' This set of guiding principles is a new wrinkle compared with the EAPD. Indeed, in a naive comparison of the documents, one would say that the LMAPD invests more rhetorical energy into the philosophy of accountability and its expected impacts, and also provides a more detailed set of instructions on what is expected of the parties to the agreement. However, when one digs deeper to look at how accountability has worked in practice, this story of an increasing ambition in and sophistication to reporting is somewhat turned on its head.

Impacts of the New Accountability Regime

In considering the impact of the new accountability regime, we are working from a variety of sources. These include the secondary academic literature on labour market policies for people with disabilities, the annual reports produced by the parties to the agreement, and a series of interviews with provincial and federal officials. In the provincial interviews, we spoke with respondents from five provinces (Alberta, Ontario, New Brunswick, Nova Scotia, and Prince Edward Island). In all cases, we spoke with someone responsible for the intergovernmental relations file, but in some cases we supplemented those interviews with those of program officials or representatives of transversal Premier's Councils responsible for persons with disabilities. While this is not the complete set of provinces, our interviews revealed a good deal of repetition and consensus between provinces and between different functions (intergovernmental, program, transversal), giving us some confidence in their representativeness.

Federal-Provincial Relationships

In the immediate realm of federal-provincial accountability relationships, neither the EAPD nor the LMAPD have worked smoothly. In the case of the EAPD, the approval of program expenditures set out in annual plans by regional HRDC (now Human Resources and Social Development Canada) offices was frustrating and onerous for the provinces, especially when additional (and often extensive) details needed to be furnished. Often, further negotiation and changes were needed before federal approval was given (interviews with officials in all four jurisdictions). The different interpretations given to the EAPD agreements by the regional HRDC offices also did not help matters (interview with Ontario government official). In the words of one federal official, 'HRDC staff [were] constantly in fights with [their] provincial counterparts over eligible expenses.' As a result, the provinces made a point in the LMAPD negotiations that the annual plans be submitted to Ottawa, on the one hand, and be for information purposes only, on the other. This change removed some friction from the relationship but also made the accountability process less dialogical, as the federal government could not say much about provincial plans, provided that they fell within the overall program requirements. Even where provincial plans do not fall comfortably within the requirements, such as with some provinces (e.g., Atlantic) continuing to fund addictions services through the program, the federal government has not exercised its right to refuse funding. Rather, it seems to have recognized the fact that provinces spent significant amounts of money on medical interventions for persons with disabilities and did not want to expend political capital over comparatively 'small' sums of money (interviews with federal government officials.)

Under the EAPD, detailed programmatic reports were also seldom done as the result of difficulties in data collection related to the setting of targets and indicators for programs that had mixed goals (e.g., an employability program might also have independent living or life skills goals). This, coupled with the lack of additional funding for such reporting and a provincial distaste for the production of one national report further ensured that little reporting above the minimum required was done (interviews with Alberta, Ontario, and federal government officials).

The situation has remained the same under the LMAPDs. Some of the required indicators have been simplified (increased emphasis on participation numbers, rather than more detailed per client or per service-provider figures). In addition, provinces now are obliged only to report on numbers 'where possible.' Alberta, in particular, but other provinces as well, fought to have that language inserted into the reporting requirements of the LMAPDs to reflect difficulties in tracking people and services. The reports themselves are also difficult to locate and appear less predictably, now that they are released by individual governments, with New Brunswick's habitually appearing about half a year late.

Methodological issues have also plagued demonstration and federal-provincial bilateral evaluations. The development of accurate measures for outcomes is difficult and time-consuming and may be impossible for complex programs with multiple goals. Indeed, only three provinces (Manitoba, PEI, and Nova Scotia) have undertaken bilateral evaluations, with the federal government underwriting costs. Further complicating matters is the fact that evaluations are data intensive, and the data are difficult to collect in a useable format and in a central repository. In Nova Scotia's case, data were often manually combed from individual client files from field offices scattered across the province within four different provincial ministries. Overcoming such obstacles proved challenging, especially when field offices or branches within the individual ministries were less then forthcoming with information requests for various reasons (e.g., privacy concerns, timelines, workloads) (interviews with Nova Scotia government officials).

The fact that all three evaluations were fully federally funded was of little incentive to the provinces. 'Lead' ministries were selected and charged with representing the province's interests throughout the process. In other words, a significant amount of additional work was typically added to their portfolios without additional remuneration. This gap in funding, coupled with a 'cumbersome' and intensive federally driven evaluation process with 'quite high' expectations and serious methodological issues previously outlined led most provinces to shy away from bilateral evaluations. Even federal officials have admitted that 'they cannot think of anything more onerous in terms of process' (interview with federal government officials). Such processes also greatly increased the time required to perform the evaluations. For instance, Manitoba's evaluation, begun in 2005, was completed in 2008, with the final report released in 2010 (Canada, Human Resources and Skills Development Canada 2010). Similarly, the framework for Nova Scotia's evaluation had been under development since 2004, was finalized in 2008, experienced tendering delays and is expected to be completed in 2013 / 14 (interviews with Nova Scotia government officials; Canada, Treasury Board of Canada Secretariat 2011). In the end, effective evaluations are highly dependent on whether there is an evaluation culture in any given jurisdiction, something which federal officials noted was sorely lacking in most provinces. Evaluation issues aside, political changes have also contributed to the lengthy timelines. This has included several changes in federal government, with the provinces claiming successive federal governments have lacked understanding of the LMAPDs' intent, which has contributed to their slow movement on the file (interviews with provincial government officials). In many ways, it is these disjointed accountability provisions that have limited learning possibilities.

Learning

The new accountability measures have been beside the point in government-to-government learning. The information that funding plans and annual reports contain about interventions that are funded and about outcomes is too general to be of any use to other provinces. For instance, the fact that approximately two-thirds of Albertans with developmental disabilities who participated in employment support programs either obtained or maintained employment in 2008–9 offers little guidance to policymakers and program managers in Ontario or PEI (Alberta 2009, 6).

Even within provinces, the reports are not widely read or circulated, nor are they used in program planning. Some provinces, such as Alberta, use their own LMAPD reports as a 'briefing' for ministers. This is not surprising, given their generality, brevity, and the fact the LMAPD reports represent only a partial picture of what the government does overall for person with disabilities (interview with Alberta government official). If other provincial reports are consulted, it is largely to see how they have documented their results (i.e., report layout) and what results have been reported. One New Brunswick official openly questioned why they should be interested in what other provinces do, given the lack of incentives, for there is 'no more money' to do anything. As for program planning, officials make use of their own *departmental* annual reports, given the significant detail they contain. All provincial officials were clear that the reports are of little value, that they have little to no interest in them, and are doing them as it is 'something they have to do to get funding' (interview with Ontario government official).

Learning thus appears limited, but the learning that does come from the reports is instead a perverse or unintentional form of learning, whereby provincial officials performing intergovernmental relations share information with colleagues in other provinces about their conflicts and disagreements with central government officials. Under the EAPD, for instance, when different regional HRDC offices took different approaches to the annual plans, provincial officials would consult to find ways to work around particular objections. Similarly, under the LMAPDs, the provincial officials we spoke with indicated they were well aware of the tensions between the federal government and New Brunswick surrounding the continued tardiness of the latter's LMAPD annual report disclosure to the public.

This is not to say that there is no information and best-practice sharing between provinces at the program level and in interprovincial working groups. Indeed, interviews with officials indicated that the provinces do watch what the other ones are doing, as well as monitor the international scene for promising practices. Yet even this learning is limited. Governmental reviews of best practices such as that occurred with the EAPD have led to little change, given operational norms and funding levels (Canada, HRSDC 2002). For instance, while nine promising practices were identified for employing persons with disabilities in the 2002

EAPD report, the lack of consideration of the severity of the disability in question has seriously eroded the desired 'client focus' approach, thus undermining attachment to the labour market. Likewise, enhancing client-employee and employer relations largely through educational efforts remains problematic, given ongoing funding limitations (interviews with government officials). So the issue is less that government-to-government learning does not occur, and instead that the reporting mechanisms of the EAPD and LMAPD and funding limitations do virtually nothing to support or further the existing mechanisms.

Public Participation and Engagement

Our research into the EAPD and LMAPD has largely been from the point of view of intergovernmental officials, which gives a limited view of public participation and engagement on these agreements. Our evidence on this front comes largely from interviews with provincial and federal officials, with a scan of the secondary literature to help fill this out. It should also be noted that these agreements are relatively 'small' in a financial sense and deal with a fairly specific set of concerns, albeit ones central to a concept of 'full participation.' As a result, one might expect them to not be front and centre in the demands and strategies of disability advocates, particularly compared to income adequacy and aid in funding supports. Even when engaging with labour market issues, it may be that stakeholder groups are happier to engage with the entire provincial suite of initiatives and not simply those funded under the LMAPD, and so do not look to the annual reports produced under these agreements.

Having said as much, the officials we interviewed were unanimous that the reports were not read much, if at all, by non-governmental stakeholders. While potentially cognizant of the reports, officials noted that they certainly were not brought up in discussions. This is likely due to the fact the annual reports are not evaluations per se and therefore of little use to non-governmental stakeholders. In other words, they are interested in whether or not a program(s) worked for them and, if not, how it will be changed to meet their needs (interview with Ontario official).

To this end, the reports offer little in understanding what difference they made in the lives of persons with disabilities (interview with Alberta official). This is underscored by the structure of the LMAPDs. For instance, they focus on job training, preparation, and placement, and not on ongoing attention to their employment needs (e.g., up-grades or replacement of hearing aids or communication devices) in order to keep them in the labour force. This is complicated by the fact programs tend to focus on those with mild disabilities, given that governments receive the same credit for placing persons with disabilities whether they are mildly, moderately, or severely disabled. In other words, there is no incentive for more challenging placements – further contributing to the irrelevance of the annual reports (interview with New Brunswick official).

Nevertheless, even when the community tries to use the reports to gauge what is working and what is not, the lack of a consistent reporting template across jurisdictions, as well as the 'thinness' of reporting, leads community researchers to conclude that it is 'difficult to make any comparisons or general conclusions as to measures that are working effectively' (Crawford 2004, vii). This is readily seen in relation to the LMAPD annual reports, with Alberta's annual reports, for instance, regularly six to seven pages long while Nova Scotia's average forty pages (see Canada-Alberta and Canada-Nova Scotia LMAPD annual reports 2003–4 to 2007–8). The interpretation outlined in the preceding few paragraphs was reinforced by federal officials who noted non-governmental stakeholders were much more cognizant of 'shifts in the wind' related to the Opportunities Fund. This is not surprising, given their *direct* funding interests in the Opportunities Fund.

There is therefore a significant gap between the expressed intention of the EAPD and LMAPD to value stakeholder participation, and to use it to assess the effectiveness and efficiency of these initiatives, and the creation of planning and reporting mechanisms that encourage it. It is indeed here that the process is the most deceiving, albeit less from an accountability perspective than a social learning one. We are sceptical that the indicators and program metrics to be reported on, in the context of these agreements, can ever do much to hold governments to account. The linkage from the outcomes on a set of indicators, to a judgment on the capacity of a given government to affect those outcomes, to effective political mobilizations to sanction or reward particular government actions is a difficult one to coax into being at the best of times and probably next to impossible when it involves a small program affecting one aspect of policies for a relatively marginalized group. We are therefore not scandalized when provinces decide not to invest in expensive data-generating exercises whose only purpose seems to be to please federal bureaucrats with a weak appreciation of the division of powers, and to instead do the bare minimum set out in the agreements.

We are, however, disappointed when this neglect is not paired with alternative efforts to enrich consultation and participation in policy evaluation and development in the area, which, after all, was part of the announced goals of the LMAPD. In a sense, this is the clearest indication that the overriding concern with public reporting in these agreements is really still the federal-provincial relationship.

Some Normative Conclusions

From the above, it is tempting to make conclusions about tensions between federalism and democracy in this realm. One could argue that provincial resistance has protected federalism by largely neutralizing the central government's attempts to be involved in an area of provincial jurisdiction, and indeed pushing back the forms of conditionality found in the VRDP that did not square with the federal ideas of non-hierarchy and non-subordination. In the process, though, lines of accountability grew blurred, and citizens were denied the transparency necessary both for informed participation and for holding governments to account.

While this argument is partially persuasive, we hesitate to make it our own. Part of it has to do with the fact that federalism itself does not emerge so well from the process. While the provinces have managed to protect their jurisdiction, this has come at the price of ongoing bickering over small sums of money – bickering that stands in the way of more productive forms of managing the complex mix of independence and interdependence that policymaking in a federation entails. In our interviews with provincial officials, we noted both their interest in telling 'old war stories' of conflicts with the federal government, but also their impatience with such petty politicking. In almost all cases, they were waiting for the central government to get serious in bringing forward a more encompassing package of reforms to the disability sector that could allow for more creative ways to contend with disability policy and the division of powers. And, in fairness to the central government, it is likewise true that a meaningful reinvention and reinvestment in disability policy seems off the policy radar in most provinces unless federal dollars are involved. In other words, we see a logjam in accountability, where the protection of provincial jurisdiction prevents forms of learning and citizen participation. However, we wonder how much this logjam is determined by fundamental tensions between these values, and how much it is a reflection of the lack of reformist energy and new financial resources in the sector (for a fuller discussion, see Graefe and Levesque 2010). The relative immobility of the governments in areas where they can act alone, with the exception of some use of the federal tax / transfer system around the turn of the century, reinforces our scepticism.

One means to test the weight of these determinants would be to experiment with institutions that untangled the accountability and social learning aspects of reporting so that one does not block the other, such as Jenson's (2004) suggestion of creating 'meeting places' for the ongoing review of evidence and social policy assumptions (see also Graefe 2008; Saint Martin 2004). Presumably, if this led in the short term to substantially better performance, learning, and innovation, we could conclude that the current form of intergovernmental relations is the culprit.

Another way to break the logjam would be to follow Cameron and Simeon (2002) in proposing the creation of standing committees on intergovernmental relations in the Canadian legislatures to review and debate the provincial reports. If this turned accountability away from central government surveillance and towards meaningful debate on provincial choices and outcomes within provincial institutions, it could provide far more meaningful channels of citizen participation and oversight without greatly changing the dynamic of federal-provincial jurisdictional squabbles. Yet we also question the efficacy of this idea. No one needs another layer of bureaucracy with little tangible results, that is, of little benefit to program users. After all, that is what non-governmental stakeholders are seeking, and it is hard to see how this avenue would rectify this situation.

There is yet a third possibility for breaking up this logjam between accountability and learning and that is to take a more direct route to the disability community. As it stands, all efforts have been channelled through provincial governments, with disability groups largely voicing their concerns from the sidelines. Learning and innovation has been stifled by being folded into the accountability process. The federal and provincial governments could encourage the creation of peak disability associations in the provinces (representing all disability groups within each province) through which funds could be directed for program innovation and delivery. It is this lack of provincial peak associations, that is, a unified voice, that officials we spoke with identified as a significant contributing factor (as well as funding) for the lack of provincial interest, resulting in few programmatic changes. In essence, a competitive climate would be created to stimulate programmatic innovation – long the main goal as identified by non-governmental stakeholders. At the same time, peak association oversight might compel the governments to honour accountability commitments in something more than the narrowest sense possible. This option of going directly to the affected groups is not a foreign idea (e.g., funding of language minority groups in the 1970s and 1980s), yet we recognize the need for further work on this front to tease out its inner workings and political saleability, especially given the current political climate and other social policy agreements. Indeed, the authors of this chapter are not agreed on whether the support of provincial peak associations should be a unilateral effort by the federal government or a joint federal-provincial undertaking.

A perverse benefit of the current government's lack of social policy purpose is that it has put intergovernmental social policy discussions on hold. While this is regrettable in terms of creating policies responding to social needs, it does allow for two things. First, it enables a reassessment of the new accountability mechanisms, and the possibility of crafting alternative ones. Second, it enables social policy actors to elaborate a reform agenda and to mobilize a supporting coalition that is not as bound up in short-term calculations of federal-provincial negotiations. In the case of disability policy, we might hope it could lead to ideas about disentangling accountability and learning, on the one hand, and to building the political will to more fully realize the ambition of full participation, on the other.

NOTE

1 Aspects of the information and arguments presented here were previously presented in Graefe and Levesque (2006, 2010). We thank SSHRC for financial support in conducting this research.

REFERENCES

Alberta. 2004–9. *Canada-Alberta Labour Market Agreement for Persons with Disabilities Report*. Annual Reports. Edmonton: Human Resources and Employment.
Cameron, David, and Richard Simeon. 2002. 'Intergovernmental Relations in Canada: The Emergence of Collaborative Federalism.' *Publius* 32 (2): 49–71.
Canada. 1997. 'Multilateral Framework on Employability Assistance for People with Disabilities.' Wayback Machine. http://web.archive.org/web/20080603192856/http://socialunion.gc.ca/pwd/multi_e.html.

- 2003a. 'Framework for Demonstration or Bilateral Evaluations.' Wayback Machine. http://web.archive.org/web/20100218010055/http://www.socialunion.gc.ca/pwd/framework-eval2003_e.html.
- 2003b. 'Multilateral Framework for Labour Market Agreements for Persons with Disabilities.' Human Resources and Skills Development Canada. http://www.hrsdc.gc.ca/eng/disability_issues/labour_market_agreements/framework.shtml.
Canada. Chambres des Communes. 1985. *Rapport du Comité parlementaire sur les droits à l'égalité: Égalité pour tous*. Ottawa: Imprimeur de la reine.
Canada. Commission Royale d'Enquête sur l'Égalité en Matière d'Emploi. 1984. *Rapport de la Commission royale sur l'égalité en matière d'emploi*. Ottawa: Approvisionnements et services Canada.
Canada. Human Resources and Skills Development. 2008. 'Advancing the Inclusion of People with Disabilities (2008).' http://www.hrsdc.gc.ca/eng/disability_issues/reports/fdr/2008/page07.shtml.
- 2010. *Evaluation of the Canada-Manitoba Labour Market Agreement for Persons with Disabilities: Final Report*. http://www.hrsdc.gc.ca/eng/publications_resources/evaluation/2010/sp_949_05_10e/sp_949_05_10_eng.pdf.
Canada. Human Resources and Social Development Canada. 2002. *Promising Practices in Employability Assistance for People with Disabilities (EAPD) Funded Programs and Services*. http://www.hrsdc.gc.ca/eng/cs/sp/sdc/evaluation/sp-ah196e/page01.shtml. Date of Access: June 16, 2010.
Canada. Human Resources Development Canada. 2002. '1999–2000, 2000–2001 Employability Assistance for People with Disabilities (EAPD) National Report.' Wayback Machine. http://web.archive.org/web/20071206004725/http://socialunion.gc.ca/pwd/EAPD2002/index_e.htm.
Canada. Treasury Board of Canada Secretariat. 2011. *Report on Plans and Priorities, 2011–2012*. http://www.tbs-sct.gc.ca/rpp/2011-2012/inst/csd/st-ts04-eng.asp.
Crawford, Cameron. 2004. *Improving the Odds: Employment, Disability and Public Programs in Canada*. North York, ON: L'institut Roeher.
Graefe, Peter. 2008. 'The Spending Power and Federal Social Policy Leadership: A Prospective View.' *IRPP Policy Matters* 9 (3): 53–106.
Graefe, Peter, and Mario Levesque. 2006. 'La nouvelle gouvernance fédérale et les politiques sociales au Canada: Leçons des ententes en matière de l'intégration en emploi des personnes ayant des handicaps.' *Lien social et politiques* 56:75–88.
- 2010. 'Accountability and Funding as Impediments to Social Policy Innovation: Lessons from the Labour Market Agreements for People with Disabilities.' *Canadian Public Policy* 36 (1): 45–62.

Jenson, Jane. 2004. *Canada's New Social Risks: Directions for a New Social Architecture*. Research Report F | 43. Ottawa: Canadian Policy Research Networks.

Ministres Responsables des Services Sociaux. 1998. 'In Unison: A Canadian Approach to Disability Issues.' http://www.ccdonline.ca/en/socialpolicy/poverty-citizenship/income-security-reform/in-unison.

Nova Scotia. 2004–7. *Canada–Nova Scotia Labour Market Agreement for Persons with Disabilities Annual Reports*. Halifax: Community Services.

Prince, Michael. 2002. 'Designing Disability Policy in Canada: The Nature and Impact of Federalism on Policy Development.' In *Federalism, Democracy and Disability Policy in Canada*, edited by Alan Puttee, 29–77. Montreal and Kingston: McGill-Queen's University Press.

Saint-Martin, Denis. 2004. *Coordinating Interdependence: Governance and Social Policy Redesign in Britain, the European Union and Canada*. Research Report F41. Ottawa: Canadian Policy Research Networks.

7 Multi-Level Governance, Infrastructure, and the Transformation of Accountability Regimes in Canada

LUC TURGEON AND JOSH HJARTARSON

Urban affairs have been back on the federal policy agenda for almost a decade now (Andrew, Graham, Phillips 2002). This renewed interest in the plight of cities, more than twenty-five years after the abolition of the federal Ministry of Urban Affairs, has been driven largely by Canada's extraordinary infrastructure deficit. In 2007, a report commissioned by the Federation of Canadian Municipalities (FCM) estimated the municipal infrastructure deficit to be in the range of $123 billion for existing infrastructure (Mirza 2007, 17). According to the federal government, 'modern, efficient and reliable infrastructure is essential to the country's prosperity today and for the long-term' (Infrastructure Canada 2007, 6).

As a result of the growing recognition of the importance of upgrading Canada's infrastructure, the federal government has played an increasingly visible and important role in this policy sector, first following the adoption by Paul Martin's Liberal government of a New Deal for Cities and Communities, and more recently through the Conservative government's Building Canada Plan (BCP). The latter pledged investments of $33 billion between 2007 and 2014, which would leverage up to $60 billion in additional provincial and municipal investment. As in new investment in the social policy sector, much of this investment has also been accompanied by adjustments to accountability mechanisms and new forms of collaboration, the main objectives of which are said to be the efficient and transparent use of public dollars.

The political and policy context in which such investments are being made is significantly different from the one that prevailed during previous periods of infrastructure development. First, years of neglect by the federal government have tarnished its image and limited its capacity to impose priorities and conditions on provinces and municipalities.

Second, Canadian municipalities, who for a long time were disorganized and had limited political clout in intergovernmental relations, have become better organized under the umbrella of the FCM (Cameron 2002). Finally, the urban reform coalition that emerged throughout Canada supported municipal autonomy and the call for more funding and therefore enhanced the legitimacy of the FCM and municipal leaders' demands (Turgeon 2009).

The objectives of this chapter are twofold. First, it explores whether this new context has had a significant impact on the types of accountability mechanisms put in place in the infrastructure sector. Second, it examines the extent to which recent accountability regimes in the infrastructure sector have promoted *policy effectiveness and learning, intergovernmental cooperation* (including a key role for municipalities), and *citizen empowerment.*

The chapter is divided in four sections. The first discusses accountability in the context of federal-provincial-municipal relations. The second presents an overview of the types of accountability mechanisms that have been adopted in past intergovernmental infrastructure agreements. And the last two sections explore two recent infrastructure programs with different accountability regimes: the Gas Tax Fund and the Building Canada Plan.

Accountability and Federal-Provincial-Municipal Relations

According to the Canadian constitution, municipal institutions are the jurisdictional responsibility of provinces. However, both levels of government have responsibility for infrastructure. The federal government has control over public infrastructure on federal lands, and public infrastructure located offshore or for broadband and telecommunication infrastructure such as telecommunication transmission towers and satellites (see Girard and Mortimer 2005). As argued by Berdahl (2006, 27), 'The federal government is prohibited from interfering with the structure and operation of municipal institutions, but it faces no such constitutional restraint when it comes to urban issues such as housing, public transportation, infrastructure or the arts.' As such, 'federal engagement in urban affairs is unavoidable, a fact of political life.'

While both levels of government have played an important role in the development of infrastructure, ultimately the key policy entrepreneurs in that policy area have been municipalities, as they are responsible for water, sewage, public transit, and land use planning. However, as argued by Andrew and Morrison (2002, 242–3), the history of the twentieth century is one of municipal efforts to get other levels of government to pay for municipal services, and especially for expensive infrastructure, reflecting the limited fiscal capacity of municipalities.

Depending on the era, such efforts have produced varying degrees of success. This patchwork of success, combined with constitutional disputes between the federal government and the provinces over the legitimacy of federal intervention in this area of jurisdiction, has resulted in the adoption of a number of different accountability mechanisms over the years. In some cases, different mechanisms have cohabitated within the same agreement among the federal, provincial, and municipal governments.

As presented in the first chapter of this book, the first model of accountability draws on the principal-agent perspective, which entails a delegation of authority from an individual or an institution in which it was originally vested (i.e., the principal) to one or more agents. Two approaches to accountability can be derived from this perspective. The first one is electoral accountability, according to which government actors are the agents of citizens that can be sanctioned for their (poor) performance through elections. Direct electoral accountability is complicated in the infrastructure sector by the limited fiscal capacity of the municipalities, which has often made the involvement of upper-levels of government necessary. As such, a second approach, which might be described as imposed accountability, occurs when one order of government acts as an agent of another and is held accountable by the principal through sanctions. Considering that municipalities have been viewed in Canada as 'creatures of the provinces,' this has tended to be the favoured approach to provincial–municipal relations.

However, as stressed in the introduction to this volume, this model does not take into consideration the complexity of accountability mechanisms in federations, especially in relation to federal-provincial-municipal relations. The principal-agent model is based on a hierarchical view of the relationship between levels of government, which is problematic, considering that federalism is based on the notions of shared rule and self-rule. As such, it does not take into consideration the reciprocal notion of accountability, as not only agents, but also principals are required to fulfil certain obligations. More relevant when thinking of accountability in a federal state is the concept of 'intra-state accountability' associated with the work of Scott Mainwaring (2003). This perspective first rejects the necessarily hierarchical nature of the principal-agent approach, making the case that such a perspective neglects some 'formalized relationships of oversight and potential sanctioning' (15). Intra-state accountability refers to forms of accountability between autonomous actors or agencies of the state (the executive or the judiciary) or levels of government (federal or provincial). Because of the autonomous nature of these agencies or levels of government, the hierarchical nature of the principal-agent metaphor is inadequate to understand accountability mechanisms between these different actors. These mechanisms are often the object of negotiations rather than being imposed by one actor. This is why we label this form of accountability as 'reciprocal accountability.'

'Societal accountability' is the final form of accountability. It refers to the actions of citizens, associations, movements, or the media that mobilize to fulfil watchdog functions. It is a non-electoral mechanism that enlarges the number of actors involved in the exercise of control. A number of commentators have dismissed such mechanisms as nothing less than weak or toothless, as they have not been accompanied by legal sanctions. Nevertheless, we follow Smulovitz and Peruzzotti in arguing that while they mostly entail symbolic rather than legal sanctions, these mechanisms nevertheless can have the potential to threaten public officials with the imposition of *reputational or electoral consequences* (Smulovitz and Peruzzotti 2003, 310–11). However, there is no doubt that such mechanisms of accountability are more diffuse and weaker than those associated with a principal-agent perspective. This is the type of mechanism, as argued in the introduction of this book, that is said to have emerged in the social policy sector in the post-SUFA period.

In this chapter, we explore whether recent intergovernmental agreements regarding infrastructure have included forms of (a) 'reciprocal accountability' in which cities play a key role in negotiating the terms of those agreements, and (b) 'societal accountability' similar to those adopted in the social policy sector. In order to make the case that such a transition has occurred, we must first explore the accountability mechanisms that existed in the past.

Infrastructure Agreements in Canada from the Great Depression to the Canada Infrastructure Works Program

Throughout the twentieth century, the federal government adopted a number of programs specifically dedicated to the development of urban infrastructure. This assistance has taken the form of loans, unconditional transfers of funds to qualified applicants (grants), or, alternatively, conditional payments (contributions) (Office of the Auditor General

Table 7.1 Overview of infrastructure programs

Period	Federal program	Form of federal financial assistance
1938–49	Municipal Improvement Assistance Act	Maximum $30 million in loans, of which approximately $7 million was paid out
1958–68	Municipal Winter Works Incentive	$267 million provided to municipalities in payments for 50% of direct payroll costs
1961–74	Sewer Treatment Program	$979 million in loans and $131 million in grants
1963–6	Municipal Development and Loan Act	About $397 million in loans
1973–9	Neighbourhood Improvement Program	$100 million in loans and $200 million in grants
1975–8	Municipal Infrastructure Program	Over $1 billion in loans and $395 million in grants
1979–84	Community Services Contributions Programs	$400 million in grants
1982–6	Employment Creation Grants and Contributions Program	$205 million in grants and contributions
1994–9	Canada Infrastructure Works Program	$2 billion in federal contributions, matched by $4 billion from province and local governments (Phase 1); $425 million

Source: Office of the Auditor General (1996)

1996). In most cases, the objective of these programs was job creation. Table 7.1 presents an overview of the different infrastructure programs that were adopted throughout the twentieth century, excluding regional economic programs or programs that may have contributed to the improvement of infrastructure.

Most of the programs adopted before the 1980s by the federal government took the form of loans and unconditional transfer of funds, based on the principle that the voters in cities would hold their municipal leaders accountable for how they spend the money. As such, it was very much based on a principal-agent approach to accountability. At the same time, it was also a reflection of the federal government's cautious approach to occupying a policy sector that many provinces viewed as their sole responsibility.

However, from the second half of the 1970s, provinces increasingly asserted their power over municipalities and insisted that any accord include them. The Quebec government even adopted an act that explicitly stated that 'no municipal body or school body may, without the prior authorization of the Government, enter into any agreement with another government in Canada or one of its departments or government agencies, or with a federal public agency.'[1] As a result of the growing assertiveness of provincial governments, the direct relationship between the federal government and municipalities largely came to an end in the 1970s. However, as provincial spending on infrastructure started to decline around the same time, provincial governments were unable and / or unwilling to oppose further federal intervention in this policy sector. As a result, infrastructure agreements were shared-cost programs much like those in place in the social policy sector, albeit with a third player, municipalities. As such, the lines of accountability became increasingly blurred.

The most important of these federal-provincial-municipal agreements was adopted in the early 1990s after more than a decade of lobbying of the Federation of Canadian Municipalities. The Canada Infrastructure Works introduced in 1994 was a temporary shared-cost program with the objectives of assisting in the maintenance and development of infrastructure and the creation of employment. The federal government entered into a separate agreement with each province. The programs thus varied slightly from one province to another.[2] Under these agreements, the federal government contributed up to one-third of eligible project costs, and the provincial and local governments and other partners contributed to the remainder. In most cases, the municipalities identified their priorities for infrastructure program funding on the basis of local requirements and submitted projects for provincial review (Office of the Auditor General 1999, 7). Provinces would then forward the projects selected to the federal government for review and approval. In accordance with the different provincial agreements, a joint federal-provincial management committee was created in each province to carry out the responsibilities of the federal and provincial governments, although in four provinces (Alberta, New Brunswick, Nova Scotia, and Ontario) municipal governments were also represented on these committees (Morrison 1996, 84).

Canada Infrastructure Works was a contribution program, which means that the federal government would pay only if performance conditions and program requirements were met. When a project was approved by a specific province's management committee, the local order of government was then responsible for contracting out the work involved, as well as for covering the full cost of the project (Morrison 1996, 84). The municipality would then be reimbursed by the province itself for two-thirds of the total cost, after which the federal government would reimburse the province one-half. The municipalities were responsible, as the agents of the upper levels of government, for ensuring that all contract, labour, and safety regulations were respected and upheld (84–5). In some ways, the program combined two forms of accountability: reciprocal accountability between the federal and provincial order of government, and imposed accountability between municipalities and their respective provincial government.

The program was said to have contributed to harmonious federal-provincial relations in the infrastructure sector. It seemed to have been flexible enough to allow provincial governments to invest in their respective priorities, as reflected in important provincial variations in where money was allocated (Morrison 1996, 89). However, while generally satisfied with the program after years of declining investment in infrastructure, the municipalities complained through the FCM and the local provincial umbrella organizations about the lack of inclusion of municipal representatives on management committees in most provinces (Andrew and Morrison 1995, 118).

Despite the relative success of the program, the auditor general found that it was essentially 'running on trust,' with little accountability (Office of the Auditor General 1999, 5). It especially denounced what it viewed as the limited oversight of local projects by federal agencies: 'Most of the federal and provincial project files we examined lacked persuasive evidence to support the claims of project applicants relating to selection criteria. Although some files for large and complex projects contained more detailed analyses, most applications were prepared in qualitative and often vague terms, with no information, other than certificates by projects applicants, to back up claims that criteria were being met. In most cases, federal officials endorsed provincial assessments without ensuring that provincial officials had received and analyzed the appropriate information or requiring direct supporting information themselves' (Office of the Auditor General 1999, 12).

As a result, the auditor general proposed that 'in future programs of this type, the government should ensure that project selection criteria are clearly defined, and that persuasive information and analyses are available and have been assessed to support recommendations for project approval' (Office of the Auditor General 1999, 14).[3] In short, the auditor general argued that the 'reciprocal accountability' framework, between the federal and provincial governments, which left significant leeway to the provinces, was inadequate to ensure that federal money was properly used. As shown in the next section, much like in other policy sectors, the solution to this problem would increasingly be a greater emphasis on public reporting, what we have previously called 'societal accountability.'

As noted in the introduction, the federal government's approach to asserting social policy leadership shifted in the mid-1990s. The shift took several forms, one of which was the implementation of results-based accountability across the federal departments and across funding relationships with third parties (including provinces and municipalities). The adoption of this approach to accountability in the 1990s was devised to allow citizens to better assess program outcomes against objectives. As shown in the next section, a similar approach was also adopted in the infrastructure arena.

The New Deal for Cities and Communities and the Gas Tax Fund

The federal government signalled a dramatic new approach to the municipal sector in 2002, when Prime Minister Paul Martin addressed the Federation of Canadian Municipalities conference. The prime minister's speech was official recognition that cities simply could not address their crumbling infrastructure deficit (estimated at $60 billion) without significant new investment from the federal government. Cities and communities were to get a 'New Deal.'

The deal included two important long-term, stable, and predictable funding packages. The first was a municipal rebate on the Goods and Services Tax, announced in Budget 2004, worth about $7 billion over ten years. In addition to a very welcome cash infusion, there was implicit symbolism in the decision. Provinces are exempt from paying federal taxes because they are recognized in the constitution as an order of government. Until the 2004 announcement, cities had to pay this tax.[4]

The New Deal also included a portion of federal revenue from the gas tax. Budget 2005 allocated $5 billion over five years to municipalities through the Gas Tax Fund (GTF). The funding was to be earmarked for environmentally sustainable infrastructure projects.

The New Deal also contained the promise of a new approach to priority setting, accountability, and reporting. Reflecting trends elsewhere in government, reporting incorporated a results-based approach typical of non-hierarchical *and* society-centred accountability. The intergovernmental agreements that dispersed the GTF typically included commitments on behalf of the signatories to 'report regularly to

Canadians on the outcomes achieved with gas tax funds using agreed upon performance measures' (Infrastructure Canada 2005b).

The approach to accountability and priority setting was symbolic of the 'third component' of the New Deal, which included a commitment to 'partnership' with municipalities. The federal government at the time 'felt it very important that the municipalities be at the national table' and full participants in 'the national conversation' (Campion-Smith 2010). The creation of a new Department of Infrastructure and Communities was intended to foster direct links between the federal government and municipalities. These results-based accountability mechanisms were to address concerns, such as those voiced by the auditor general, and enable the federal government to hold provincial and local governments accountable for how they use federal dollars. As noted, however, they were intended to also facilitate societal accountability, whereby citizens could judge the performance of government on the basis of results achieved.

An Evaluation of the Gas Tax Fund

For municipalities, the Goods and Services Tax (GST) rebate and the GTF constituted a welcome infusion of funds. Both have been extended by the Conservative government and made permanent. Both were products of broad recognition at all levels of government that municipal infrastructure was in disrepair and that municipalities had insufficient resources. The accumulation of large federal surpluses and improving fiscal situations at the provincial level, as well as concerted public relations campaigns of the municipal sector, generated sufficient pressure on the higher orders of government to begin addressing this gap.

The GST rebate is a direct and unconditional transfer to municipalities that can be spent according to priorities of the municipalities. It is extremely flexible: municipalities are directly accountable to municipal taxpayers, and there is no separate reporting requirement. Since this is a rebate of a federal tax, municipalities viewed it as a 'righting of a historical wrong' and were not too forthcoming with overt praise.

The GTF provides municipalities with long-term, predictable funding for municipal infrastructure. It has been well received by the municipal sector, which had long complained that one-off and short-term federal and provincial investments in infrastructure thwarted its capacity to plan capital investments adequately. In total, the fund commits $13 billion in federal funding to Canadian municipalities between 2005 and 2014.

The funds are administered through federal-provincial agreements between the federal government and each provincial government. Municipal associations are also partners to the agreement in the case of Ontario and British Columbia. Toronto has a direct bilateral agreement with Ottawa. The fund is earmarked for environmentally sustainable infrastructure projects across six broad categories: public transit, drinking water, wastewater infrastructure, community energy systems, solid waste management, and local roads and bridges. The federal government requires that communities develop an Integrated Community Sustainability Plan (ICSP) in order to outline long-term plans for environmental sustainability. In that plan, municipalities must demonstrate that they have 'engaged residents in determining a long-term vision for the municipality' (Infrastructure Canada 2005a).

The fund provides monies upfront to municipalities for specific projects, with provinces and municipalities subsequently providing accountability reports. The provinces, or the municipal association in certain provinces, must submit an annual allocation and expenditure report as well as an audit report, prepared by the provincial auditor or an independent auditor, which provides an opinion as to whether the financial information contained in the annual allocation and expenditure report is accurate. Finally, provinces or municipal associations such as the Association of Municipalities of Ontario (AMO) agreed to prepare and make public by 2009 an outcomes report on the investments made with the GTF and the degree to which they contributed to cleaner air, cleaner water, and greenhouse gas reduction. For example, the Association of Municipalities of Ontario's (AMO) outcomes report is a synopsis of reported outcomes throughout Ontario and contains details on some 1,600 projects.

It is worth emphasizing that the GTF is a transfer to the provincial governments. Federal governments had previously and unabashedly used their spending powers to invade provincial jurisdiction through direct transfers to individuals and organizations (Courchene 2004). However, as a result of provincial push back and jealousy over the municipal sector, it was ultimately up to each provincial government to negotiate with its municipal stakeholders how the money was to be used and how projects would be selected. Some provincial governments chose to maintain a hierarchical, principal-agent approach. Others, such as Ontario and British Columbia (to a lesser extent) withdrew from decision-making and administration of the fund.

Quebec is viewed by the municipal sector as a worse-case scenario, taking a more paternalistic approach to administration and project selection, with revenue from the fund administered by the Société de financement des infrastructures locales du Québec (SOFIL). In its agreement with the province, the federal government agreed to transfer all funds directly to the agency 'to assist in the implementation of infrastructure projects involving drinking water, wastewater, local road networks and public transit, and infrastructure projects with urban or regional economic impacts' (Infrastructure Canada 2005b). SOFIL would also be responsible for reporting outcomes to the federal government and to the public through an annual report. Only two members of SOFIL's seven-member board of directors are from municipalities.

Despite the fact that SOFIL was authorized to have up to five employees, its board chose not to employ anyone. Demonstrating the extent of provincial control over these funds, SOFIL instead entered into agreements with the Ministry of Municipal Affairs, Regions and Land Occupancy (MAMROT), the Ministry of Transport, the Ministry of Finance, and Controller of Finance so that employees of these departments provide SOFIL administrative support necessary to accomplish its mission (Société de financement des infrastructures locales, 2007). Moreover, contrary to the case of other federal-provincial agreements, the Canada-Quebec one does not stipulate that ICSPs must be developed.

Ontario is considered a very positive example by the municipal sector. The Ontario government agreed to enable Ontario municipalities, through the AMO, and Toronto to work directly with the federal government to determine the best way to use federal gas tax revenues. Under the Gas Tax arrangement, municipalities were essentially free to define their priorities within the federal categories. Except for the Ontario government's role in administering the funds to unincorporated areas, the provincial government has played no role in the allocation formula for the funds, the disbursement of funds to municipalities, reporting, audit, or evaluation provisions, or any adjudication of disputes between the federal government and the other parties to this agreement. The provincial government's hands-off approach to the GTF was consistent with its general tendency to view the sector as a partner, as evidenced by a provincial-municipal memorandum of understanding that obliges the provincial government to consult the sector on legislative and regulatory changes that could affect municipal interests (AMO and the Province of Ontario 2008).

While the accountability regimes associated with the GTF have contributed to intergovernmental harmony and cooperation, it is less clear whether they have fostered policy effectiveness and citizen engagement – the two other evaluative criteria identified in the introduction to this volume.

In terms of policy effectiveness, it is clear that the GTF has contributed to necessary investment in infrastructure that has had positive outcomes on the environment. For example, in 2009, the AMO estimated that improvements to water-related infrastructure (to which the GTF contributed) reduced the amount of water-main breaks by over 47 per cent between 2005 and 2008 (AMO 2009, 3). However, it is clear that in almost all provinces, most of the fund has been used to upgrade local roads and bridges. For example, between 2005 and 2008 in Saskatchewan, 66 per cent of the province's share of the GTF had been allocated to that category (Saskatchewan 2009, 10). Similarly, in 2009 in Ontario, 65 per cent of the GTF was used to upgrade local roads and bridges (AMO 2010, 10). The overwhelming focus on roads and bridges has been decried at times by activists and citizens as inconsistent with the stated environmental objectives.

In terms of reporting, an internal audit of the program by Infrastructure Canada (INFC) has found that the management control framework in place and the management practices that have been put in place are 'satisfactory to ensure compliance, program effectiveness and financial integrity' (INFC 2009a). At the same time, it reported that almost all provinces had a different reporting system, which meant 'a manual process of national consolidation that is cumbersome, time-consuming, vulnerable and sensitive to error.' A national summative evaluation also stated that while there had been many initiatives to develop the Performance Measurement Framework that were put in place to help provinces with their 2009 outcomes report, 'collecting relevant data remains a challenge that will require continued efforts' (INFC 2009b).

With regards to citizen engagement, a number of factors contributed to limit the capacity of citizens to influence local policymakers' decisions and hold them accountable for their policy choices. While the GTF became effective in 2005–6, ICSPs did not have to be completed until 2010. As such, municipalities could fund projects for that period without public participation or clear sustainability plan. In Ontario, a municipality does not need to prepare an ICSP if an Official Plan is already in place (AMO 2009).[5] As argued by Laurie Miller (2010, 45), 'Because the province is not involved in the funding program, Official Plans are not reviewed in the context of the goals and objectives of the Gas Tax Program.'

The Building Canada Fund

The election of a Conservative federal government in 2007 resulted in enhancements to federal investment in municipal infrastructure announced in the New Deal. New investment in infrastructure was a key component of the Conservative vision for boosting Canada's competiveness, as outlined in the 2006 Advantage Canada economic plan. In its 2007 budget, the Conservative government announced $33 billion in infrastructure investment under the Building Canada Plan (BCP) over seven years. The announcement included $17.6 billion in base funding for municipalities, comprising a Goods and Services Tax rebate and $11.8 billion through the Gas Tax Fund.

Federal investment in infrastructure was again increased by $10.3 billion in the 2009 federal budget as part of the broader federal economic stimulus response to the financial crisis and the economic downturn. Specifically, the budget included a new $4 billion Infrastructure Stimulus Fund in support of provincial, territorial, and municipal rehabilitation, retrofit, and maintenance projects.

When the BCP was announced, the response from provincial and municipal officials was muted. There was broad recognition that the 'rules of the game' negotiated under the New Deal were subject to change and possibly up for renegotiation. Enhanced accountability had been a key component of the new federal government's election platform. Further, the new federal government identified five new national priorities, some of which were at odds with provincial and municipal capital plans that were crafted under the auspices of the New Deal.

Fearful that the agreements negotiated with the previous federal government would be torn up, provincial governments declared that the new federal government should work with them to ensure that all project selection would be conducted jointly and that the process would respect provincial priorities. The extent to which these provincial priorities were also municipal priorities varied greatly across the country.

Provincial governments lobbied hard for provincial administration of federal funds and adherence to the accountability mechanisms already negotiated. For good measure, the provinces also took the opportunity to restate their old case for deference to provincial accountability requirements. In a letter sent in advance of the 2007 federal budget, the Council of the Federation requested that all future transfers be unconditional block transfers. The council also argued that the federal government should apply the recommendations of the Treasury Board's own Blue Ribbon Panel report *From Red Tape to Clear Results*, which suggested that it is redundant for the federal government to impose accountability obligations in addition to provincial standards in future transfers. Note that most of the provinces had adopted a results-based, public reporting approach to accountability that, to a large degree, mirrored the federal approach. Federal deference to provincial mechanisms was a longstanding municipal preference too, seen as the lesser of two evils. The greater evil was, of course, that the new federal government would identify new and different priorities and impose new and more rigorous reporting and audit requirements.

Over 2007–8, the federal and provincial governments signed new Infrastructure Framework Agreements. The new agreements established the terms and conditions guiding joint federal-provincial infrastructure investments under the seven-year BCP. The agreements set out cost-sharing frameworks, which afforded the federal government a great deal of discretion in determining policy and expenditure decisions. The agreements also contained the details of federal allocation of funds and provincial and municipal financial contributions. The federal government communicated to the provinces that it would like two-thirds of federal funding in the Building Canada Fund to go towards five national priorities: the national highway system, drinking water, wastewater, public transit, and green energy. While the categories were sufficiently broad to ensure some overlap with provincial priorities, many provincial and municipal priorities would not be eligible for funding.

The agreements were hammered out behind closed doors and without, in most instances, municipal or public input. Ontario was the only province to include municipal representatives in federal-provincial discussions on the BCP. Outside of Ontario, throughout the process of negotiating the flow of BCP funding, meetings were not trilateral. If the municipal sector had any input into the discussions, it was through advance consultation with or lobbying of their provincial counterparts.

The federal government under Paul Martin was more inclined when it struck the New Deal to advocate on municipalities' behalf. However, the Conservative government was eager to adhere to the principles of 'open federalism,' which include respecting areas of provincial jurisdiction. The open federalism mantra is silent on municipalities and therefore implicitly acknowledged that municipalities were the creatures of the provinces (Young 2006).[6]

On this note, the Framework Agreements also typically established Infrastructure Framework Committees – joint federal-provincial committees of officials to oversee the progress of the Building Canada Plan. Further, joint secretariats comprising federal-provincial officials were created to evaluate applications under the application-based programs. There was no municipal role envisioned for either.

With respect to reporting, the agreements typically included high-level statements on principles and the need to ensure accountability to each party's legislature and the public. Specific reporting requirements were to be hammered out in a separate addendum within a year of signing the agreement. By then, the federal government had signalled that it would retain the results-based reporting approach to accountability negotiated for the New Deal agreements. Results of cost-shared investments were to be reported back to the federal government and made publicly available so that Canadians would be aware of implementation and outcomes.

The specifics across each federal-provincial / territorial infrastructure agreement negotiated during the period varied by program objectives and by province. However, the typical accountability arrangements include receipt of federal and provincial funds for the agreed portion of project costs once the municipalities 'report back' on outcomes.

Reporting back usually means describing the specific uses of the funds and explaining how the projected benefits of the project have been or are being achieved. The results are typically measured against a variety of interim and outcome categories. Interim categories include (Infrastructure 2008, 42):

- Expeditious negotiation and completion of agreements and projects
- Collaborative support of other government departments, provinces, territories, and key partners
- Resources levered from partners
- Effective program management and oversight of agreements (e.g., risk management, monitoring and reporting, e-management)

Outcome categories include:

- Safe, reliable transportation
- Sustainable economic development
- Sustainable use and quality of water, and efficient wastewater treatment
- Safe and efficient borders
- Improved innovation and delivery of public services via connectivity
- Efficient and sustainable energy systems

- Improved capacity for integrated community sustainability planning
- New collaborative mechanisms

These results are normally collected by the federal and provincial governments and are made public on the Internet.

However, while most of the programs were to be cost-shared federal-provincial-municipal, decision-making and project selection would be federal-provincial. Federal officials indicated applications would be based on merit, which meant project readiness, eligibility, and adherence to accountability mechanisms as prescribed. Many critics have argued, however, that the program provided plenty of scope for the federal government to fund pet projects despite federal pronouncements to the contrary.[7] Allocation of stimulus funding has therefore led to allegations of pork-barrelling.

In reality, the federal government had considerable incentive to cooperate with provinces. Since the announcement of the enhanced funding, federal officials have been relying heavily on the provincial governments to select projects, deliver the money, and exercise oversight. Rolling out the funding was going to be a daunting task. For the programs under the Infrastructure Stimulus Fund, Ontario alone received over 2,700 applications from municipalities with total project costs of over $6 billion.

From the perspective of the municipalities, these programs were problematic from a planning point of view. First, because the funding was one-off and had expiration dates, they distorted municipal capital investment already approved and brokered among stakeholders and constituents. For example, the City of Guelph had to nearly rewrite its approved five-year capital plan. Few municipalities, however, could pass on temptation to leverage federal and provincial dollars, even if this meant forgoing local priority projects.

Municipal associations did not protest. There was no appetite for openly taking on the federal and provincial governments. Municipalities were fairly confident that they could not count on the public in a battle over project selection. Further, as noted previously, since the infrastructure deficit was sufficiently large and municipal needs vast, most municipalities felt that they could make good use of the funds anyway.

The implementation of results-based and public reporting had minimal effect on the relationship with the provincial and federal governments. For example, even though 'collaborative support of other government departments, provinces, territories and key partners' was a new and explicit interim benchmark to be reported on to the public, municipalities had, in fact, little leverage in ensuring locally defined infrastructure needs were met.

Like the New Deal and the Gas Tax Fund, the Building Canada Plan and the associated accountability regimes spurred, in the words of the FCM, 'a new spirit of intergovernmental partnership' (FCM 2010). Despite the fact that municipalities faced challenges in directing funds to match local priorities and away from federal and provincial partisan and pet projects, they were grateful for the additional funding.

There is some evidence to suggest that the BCP was a step forward in policy effectiveness, the second evaluative criterion identified in the introductory chapter. The Parliamentary Budget Office reported in 2010 that the recipients of the Infrastructure Stimulus Fund generally believed that the funding improved the 'general welfare' and 'environmental quality' in their communities (Parliamentary Budget Office 2010) – a conclusion generally support by the FCM (FCM 2010). Both these sentiments might be classic demonstration that 'beggars can't be choosers' in the face of a massive infrastructure deficit. As one official interviewed for this study suggested, there is clearly a desire among municipal officials not to rock the boat, especially in the run-up to 2014, when the BCP expires.

With respect to citizen engagement, the third evaluative criterion, it may be too early to tell. As noted in the introduction, results-based public reporting is intended to enlarge the number of actors involved in the exercise of control. According to one official in a municipal association, the adoption of public reporting does not appear to have affected the level of citizen engagement in the sector (interview, Anonymous, 18 July 2011). The primary locus of citizen engagement remains at the municipal level in the planning phase. For example, municipal officials cannot count on broader support as additional leverage in their negotiations with the federal and provincial officials as a result of a broader reporting mechanism. And there appear to be few electoral consequences for funding improperly allocated.[8]

Conclusion

We have argued in this chapter that the emergence of new forms of accountability postulated by social policy scholars now extend into the infrastructure sector. The provisions within the New Deal and the

Building Canada Plan are essentially consistent with trends in social policy whereby the 'vocabulary' of accountability now centres on 'reporting and having provinces submit reports on where money is spent, and on mutually agreed upon performance standards.' Emphasis has been on reporting results and 'performance-based management,' intended also to facilitate societal accountability. We have also demonstrated that classical mechanisms of 'reciprocal accountability' have in certain provinces and in some accords (especially the GTF) contributed to a greater partnership role for municipalities.

We have also examined the extent to which recent accountability regimes in the infrastructure sector have promoted *intergovernmental cooperation*, *policy effectiveness*, and *citizen empowerment*. In general, the system seems to have been welcomed by provincial authorities as well as municipalities. Again, the GTF is particularly well regarded. The current accountability regimes have also proved to be flexible enough to respect different provincial preferences in the degree and type of participation of municipal actors, ranging from Quebec's more centralizing approach to Ontario's decentralized one.

However, when it comes to the last two criteria, we are definitely more tentative in our evaluation – a reflection in part of the fact that some audits of the infrastructure programs have been available only recently. It is evident that the programs have gone some distance in addressing the infrastructure deficit in a relatively short period of time. Moreover, audits have generally confirmed that general safeguards against abuse are in place and functional. Overall, the frameworks have not contributed to significant citizen empowerment. Decisions about 'who funds what' and 'what gets built' remain more dependent on intergovernmental bargaining than citizen input.

NOTES

1 An Act respecting the ministère du Conseil exécutif, R.S.Q., c. M-30, 3.11.
2 For a good overview of provincial variations in the implementation of the program, see Andrew and Morrison (1995).
3 Note, however, that the auditor general's prescription was at odds with provincial and municipal conceptions of the federal role. The provinces and the municipalities have been steadfast in the assertion that the federal government should retreat from defining specific project guidelines and imposing burdensome information requirements, since it is too far removed to

understand local needs. Of course, this perspective was often trumped by the need for federal funds.

4 A third program, first adopted by the Chrétien government and then further formalized under the government of Paul Martin, the Green Municipal Fund, had shown the potential for the development of new intergovernmental mechanisms in Canada. The fund devolved responsibility for federal investment in infrastructure projects and feasibility studies to contain urban sprawl and reduce greenhouse gas emissions to the FCM. A board composed of members of the FCM, individuals representing different ministries of the federal government, and civil society actors was charged with accepting or rejecting demands by municipalities. In exchange, the FCM had to submit an annual report three months after the fiscal year to the ministers responsible, based on information derived from a results-based management framework; prepare an annual statement of plans and objectives prior to the end of each fiscal year; and conduct third-party financial audits and regular program reviews. The provinces are largely absent from this program. While this program survived the arrival of a new Conservative government, provinces would largely re-establish their predominance in this policy sector.

5 An Official Plan is a document that presents the land-use policy directions of a municipality, shaping as such growth and development.

6 Municipalities get scant mention in any of the Conservative policy papers and pronouncements. When municipalities are mentioned, it is in conjunction with provincial and territorial authorities.

7 According to the Liberal Party of Canada, in a review of the first billion dollars, specific announcements made under the Building Canada Fund in 1997 and 2008 demonstrated that 78% were in Conservative-held ridings. See Liberal Party (2009).

8 In fact, as demonstrated in the allocations of the G8 Infrastructure Fund, politicians can be rewarded for skirting rules in order to bring funding to local projects. See Office of the Auditor General (2011).

REFERENCES

Andrew, Caroline, Katherine Graham, and Susan Phillips, eds. 2002. *Urban Affairs: Back on the Policy Agenda*. Montreal and Kingston: McGill-Queen's University Press.

Andrew, Caroline, and Jeff Morrison. 1995. 'Canada Infrastructure Works: Between "Picks and Shovels" and the Information Highway.' In *How*

Ottawa Spends, 1995–96: Mid-Life Crises, edited by Susan Phillips, 107–35. Ottawa: Carleton University Press.

– 2002. 'Infrastructure.' In *Urban Policy Issues: Canadian Perspectives.* 2nd ed., edited by Edmund P. Fowler and David Siegel, 237–52. Don Mills, ON: Oxford University Press.

Association of Municipalities of Ontario. 2009. *Gas Tax Fund and Transit Fund Outcomes Report.* http://www.gastaxatwork.ca/news/outcomesfull.pdf.

– 2010. *The Most Stable and Predictable Source of Municipal Infrastructure Funding: 2009 Annual Expenditure Report (Part 1).* http://www.amo.on.ca/AM/Template.cfm?Section=AMO_s_Annual_Reporting&Template=/CM/ContentDisplay.cfm&ContentID=159169.

Association of Municipalities of Ontario and the Province of Ontario. 2008. 'First Joint Annual MOU Statement.' http://www.amo.on.ca/AM/Template.cfm?Section=Home&TEMPLATE=/CM/ContentDisplay.cfm&CONTENTID=152053.

Berdahl, Loleen. 2006. 'The Federal Urban Role and Federal–Municipal Relations.' In *Municipal-Federal-Provincial Relations in Canada,* edited by Robert Young and Christian Leuprecht, 25–43. Kingston: Institute of Intergovernmental Relations.

Cameron, Ken. 2002. 'Some Puppets! Some Shoestrings! The Changing Intergovernmental Context.' In *Urban Affairs: Back on the Policy Agenda,* edited by Caroline Andrew, Katherine Graham, and Susan Phillips, 303–8. Montreal and Kingston: McGill-Queen's University Press.

Campion-Smith, Bruce. 2010. 'Canadian Cities Mark "New Deal" Milestone.' *Toronto Star,* 23 May. http://www.thestar.com/news/canada/article/813550.

Courchene, T.J. 2004. 'Hourglass Federalism: How the Feds Got the Provinces to Run Out of Money in a Decade of Liberal Budgets.' *Policy Options/Options Politiques* (Apr.): 12–17. http://www.irpp.org/po/archive/apr04/courchene.pdf.

Federation of Canadian Municipalities. 2010. *Securing Our Foundations: A Plan to Continue Building Canada.* http://www.ptsc-online.ca/blogs/criticalinfrastructureprotection/addressingcanadasinfrastructuredeficit.

Girard, Michel, and Michael Mortimer. 2005. 'The Regulatory and Standards Landscape of Canada's Public Infrastructure.' Paper prepared by the Canadian Standards Association for Infrastructure Canada. www.csa.ca/climatechange/.../pdf/Regulatory_Stds_Landscape.pdf.

Infrastructure Canada. 2005a. *Gas Tax Fund Agreement: Canada–Ontario–Association of Municipalities of Ontario–City of Toronto.* http://www.infrastructure.gc.ca/prog/agreements-ententes/gtf-fte/on-eng.html.

– 2005b. *Gas Tax Fund Agreement: Canada-Quebec.* http://www.infrastructure. gc.ca/prog/agreements-ententes/gtf-fte/qc-eng.html.
– 2007. *Building Canada: Modern Infrastructure for a Strong Canada.* http:// publications.gc.ca/collections/collection_2008/ic/Iu154-4-2007E.pdf.
– 2009a. *Audit of the Management Control Framework for the Gas Tax Fund.* http://www.infrastructure.gc.ca/pd-dp/ia-vi/gtf-fte-eng.html.
– 2009b. *National Summative Evaluation of the Gas Tax Fund and Public Transit Fund.* http://www.infrastructure.gc.ca/alt-format/pdf/nse-esn-eng.pdf.
Liberal Party. 2009. '78 Per Cent of Building Canada Fund Announcements Made in Conservative Ridings.' 9 February. http://www.liberal.ca/ newsroom/news-release/78-per-cent-of-building-canada-fund-announcements-made-in-conservative-ridings/.
Mainwaring, Scott. 2003. 'Introduction: Democratic Accountability in Latin America.' In *Democratic Accountability in Latin America*, edited by Scott Mainwaring and Christopher Welna, 3–33. Oxford: Oxford University Press.
Miller, Laurie Yeatman. 2010. 'Allocating the Gas Tax in Frontenac County: A Decision for Sustainability.' MA thesis, Royal Roads University.
Mirza, Saeed. 2007. *Danger Ahead: The Coming Collapse of Canada's Municipal Infrastructure.* Ottawa: Federation of Canadian Municipalities.
Morrison, Jeff. 1996. 'Multidimensional Federalism: A Revision of the Two-Tier Federal Structure as Seen through the Canada Works Infrastructure Program.' MA thesis, University of Ottawa.
Office of the Auditor General. 1996. *Report: Chapter 26 – Canada Infrastructure Program; Lessons Learned.* Ottawa: Office of the Auditor General.
– 1999. *Report: Chapter 17 – Canada Infrastructure Works Program; Phase II and Follow-up of Phase I Audit.* Ottawa: Office of the Auditor General.
– 2011. '2011 Spring Report of the Auditor General of Canada.' Chapter 2. http://www.oag-bvg.gc.ca/internet/English/parl_oag_201104_02_e_ 35221.html.
Parliamentary Budget Office. 2010. *Infrastructure Stimulus Fund – Survey of Recipients.* http://www.parl.gc.ca/PBO-DPB/documents/ISF_Survey_ Findings.pdf.
Saskatchewan. New Deal Secretariat. Saskatchewan Municipal Affairs. 2009. *Outcomes Report on the Federal Gas Tax & Public Transit Funds.* http://www. municipal.gov.sk.ca/FGT/Outcomes-Report
Smulovitz, Catalina, and Enrique Peruzzotti. 2003. 'Societal and Horizontal Controls: Two Cases of a Fruitful Relationship.' In *Democratic Accountability in Latin America*, edited by Scott Mainwaring and Christopher Welna, 309–32. Oxford: Oxford University Press.

Société de financement des infrastructures locales. 2007. 'Conseil d'adminis-
    tration.' http://www.sofil.gouv.qc.ca/conseil/index.asp.
Turgeon, Luc. 2009. 'Cities within the Canadian Intergovernmental System.'
    In *Contemporary Canadian Federalism: Foundations, Traditions, Institutions*,
    edited by Alain-G. Gagnon, 358–78. Toronto: University of Toronto Press.
Treasury Board Secretary. 2006. *From Red Tape to Clear Results: The Report of the
    Independent Blue Ribbon Panel on Grant and Contribution Programs*. Ottawa:
    Treasury Board of Canada Secretariat.
– 2008. 'Section II: Analysis of Program Activities by Strategic Outcome.'
    In *2008–2009 Reports on Plans and Priorities – Infrastructure Canada*.
    http://www.tbs-sct.gc.ca/rpp/2008-2009/inst/inf/inf02-eng.asp.
Young, Robert. 2006. 'Open Federalism and Canadian Municipalities.' In *Open
    Federalism: Interpretations, Significance*, edited by Keith G. Banting, Roger
    Gibbins, Peter M. Leslie, Alain Noel, Richard Simeon, and Robert Young,
    7–24. Kingston: Institute of Intergovernmental Relations.

PART THREE

Alternative Accountabilities:
Comparative and Normative Examples

8 Convergence through Benchmarking and Policy Learning: The Impact of the Open Method of Coordination on Social Policy within the European Union

DANIEL V. PREECE

The process through which European integration has evolved redefines the relationship between the member states and the European Union (EU).[1] To a large degree, the deepening of integration has resulted in an institutional arrangement that is neither solely intergovernmental nor clearly supranational. Within policy areas like social policy, the scope of policy sharing between jurisdictions resembles the relationship between the central and the sub-central governments in a federal system. In this way, the coordination of social policies is defined largely by the dual principles of social sovereignty and subsidiarity, and the member states largely resist any efforts to directly shift competency up to the EU. Even with the adoption of the Employment Chapter within the Treaty Framework in 1997 and the development of the European Employment Strategy (EES) – which explicitly endorsed the belief that some form of coordination of social policies was a necessary precondition to deepening economic integration – the responsibility of social policies remains national. Reflecting this sentiment, the open method of coordination (OMC) was developed as the means through which the principles of de-commodification and social solidarity could be promoted within the EU, while still allowing for national differences in implementation.

This chapter examines the development and implementation of the OMC in both employment and social exclusion to demonstrate the impact of this policy mechanism on the harmonization of welfare reforms throughout the EU. First, the chapter surveys the development of the OMC and shows how the initial proposals reflected the social democratic project of entrenching the idea of Social Europe within the treaty architecture. Second, the chapter examines the influence of the OMC on national social policy reforms, by outlining how competing actors in the

Republic of Ireland drew upon European developments to influence government reforms over both employment and social inclusion policies. Finally, the chapter analyses how the efforts in the mid- to late-2000s to create a greater linkage between economic and social policy at the EU level shifted the orientation of welfare reforms within the OMC towards neoliberalism and brought these debates in line with the overall mode of governance in the EU.

Because of the different national traditions of socioeconomic governance practised by the member states, it is generally believed that it is not possible to shift the competency over welfare policies to the EU through formal integration and binding legislation. Following the initial work by Gøsta Esping-Andersen (1990), it is generally accepted that there are at least three to five separate types of welfare regimes within Europe. For example, Peter Abrahamson (1999), Mark Kleinman (2002), and Stephen Liebfried (1993) begin their analysis with Esping-Andersen's typology, but add a fourth category, the Mediterranean model, that takes into account the highly polarized and family-centred welfare traditions in Southern European states, such as Spain, Italy, Portugal, and Greece. As well, the Eastern enlargement of the EU in 2004 and 2007 has prompted discussion of the 'post-Soviet' welfare tradition and the implications that this will have on attempts to further coordinate social policies between the member states (Aidukaite 2004; Babajanian 2008; and Wagener 2002). As a result of this variety of welfare traditions, the terrain of social policy in the EU is defined largely as a collection of European social *models* – and not a singular *model* – and the member states have consistently resisted transferring authority over social policy to the EU level and adopting binding regulations within the Treaty framework (Kleinman 2002: 82–109; Preece 2009, 43–63; and Wincott 2003).

Because of the diversity of welfare regimes throughout Europe, the process of harmonizing both welfare regimes and social policies within the EU is particularly relevant for federal systems like Canada and understanding how governance operates across a system of overlapping jurisdictions. To a large degree, the operation of social policy within the EU reflects a form of nascent federalism; while the various levels of government are understood to exist within a strict segregation of responsibilities and jurisdictions, both levels also need to coordinate their public policies in a manner that harmonizes their behaviour and encourages collaborative action. In other words, the EU – much like Canada – is a mixed regime, where different actors within the system hold 'different policy styles and decision-making philosophies,' yet still collaborate to develop mutually beneficial outcomes (O'Neill 1996, 108). Within such a system, decisions made by any actor are not performed in isolation but are informed and redefined by the interests and actions of the opposing actors. Furthermore, this also means that there are multiple loci of authority with the system, so that neither the EU nor the member states are able to act as lead actor or principal and set goals for the other level of government to implement. As noted by Héritier and Lehmkuhl (2011, 134), this implies that the application of new forms of governance, such as the OMC, represents a 'second-best solution' for the European Commission: while it 'would have preferred the community method, … it anticipate[d] the opposition of member states to propose legislation in matters previously confined to domestic competence' and settled on a 'softer' form of cooperation and governance. Of particular significance to this volume and its examination of public reporting as a form of intergovernmental accountability in Canada, the OMC similarly aims to facilitate accountability directly to citizens through public reporting. Echoing some of the Canadian discourse examined in other chapters of this volume, public reporting, as a key aspect of the OMC, is expected to facilitate coordination by highlighting best practices and shaming laggard states.

Examining the operation of the OMC, and the degree to which it has been used by the Commission to coordinate social policy in a multi-level political system, sheds new light on the Canadian experience and offers the opportunity to refine Canadian practices. Even though the Commission does not have jurisdiction over social policy in the EU, much like the federal government in Canada, the deepening of integration since the mid-1990s now means that national governments are no longer able to determine their social policies in isolation, and the need for effective intergovernmental cooperation is becoming increasingly important.

With a number of areas of economic governance subject to Europeanized regulation, such as trade, competition, and monetary policies, the European Council decided to move towards a greater linkage of 'national economic, employment, and social policy reforms' with the adoption of the Employment Chapter in the Treaty of Amsterdam (Heidenreich and Zeitlin 2009, 1). Following these amendments, the treaty now commits the EU to 'contribute to a high level of employment by encouraging co-operation between Member States and by supporting and, if necessary, complementing their actions' without limiting the actions of supranational organizations beyond stating that 'the competencies of the Member States shall be respected' (Art. 127). As such, both the extent and the limits of the EU in the provision of social policies within the member states are nebulous. Still, by mandating that social policies are a matter of joint concern, these amendments create a demand for cooperation between the different levels of governance (Scharpf 1999, 158–9). As such, this change acted as a wedge that enabled the Commission to demand the enhanced harmonization of social policies, especially in the areas of employment policy and social inclusion / exclusion, without explicitly shifting competency. Toward this end, the OMC was developed as the means through which the principles of de-commodification and social solidarity could be promoted within the EU, while still allowing for national difference in implementation.

Nevertheless, the ability of the OMC to achieve these dual goals of both coordinating social policy reforms among the member states and establishing a policy regime that effectually promotes de-commodification and social solidarity throughout the EU is problematic. As a form of soft law, the OMC facilitates only weak levels of accountability, both at the horizontal level between the EU and the member states and at the vertical level between a government and its citizens. To begin with, the European Commission lacks legitimacy within the policy process to act proscriptively regarding the direction of social policy reforms, which means that it is unable to enact compliance from the member states. At the same time, the emphasis of the OMC as a mechanism of policy learning and development of best practices recasts the operation of social policy within the EU as primarily a technical and an administrative matter to be determined by experts. Even though the principal form of accountability is meant to be public reporting, in which non-compliant member states are 'named and shamed,' the ability of citizens to sanction laggards and to participate within the policy process is minimal. Moreover, as the OMC gradually evolved to become even more technocratic, the question of social policy became effectively 'de-politicalized' as a matter 'to be resolved by the application of rational knowledge and professional expertise in relation to objective and apparently neutral criteria' and not something that should be subjected to democratic input and control (Rose and Miller 1992, 197). In this way, the ability of citizens to ensure that the operation of social policy is in accordance with societal demands and expectations of enhancing de-commodification and social solidarity was circumscribed. While the OMC has influenced policy choices within the member states, the way in which the policy environment has evolved at the EU level has also shifted the overall orientation of welfare reforms throughout the EU away from social democratic ideals and towards more neoliberal objectives.

Constructing a 'Decentralized Approach' to Policy Learning

The contemporary trend toward the development of Social Europe and use of the OMC to coordinate social policies within the EU may be traced to the policy initiatives proposed in the 1993 *White Paper on Growth, Competitiveness, and Employment*. In light of the formation of the European Economic and Monetary Union, the Delors presidency of the Commission published this document in an attempt to shape the policy debate at the European level and ensure that social issues were included in the treaty framework (Preece 2009, 48–51). In particular, the Commission argued that job creation had to be seen as a necessary component of the European market in order for the EU to remain competitive within the global economy and acted in an 'entrepreneurial' manner to create a coalition of member states to support a European approach to employment policy (Rhodes 2005, 291). In order to foster support for regionalization, Delors chose to temper his earlier emphasis on the broader concepts of Social Europe and the European Model of Society to an almost exclusive concentration on employment, as the question of job creation was seen to be less contentious than other areas of social policy (Wincott 2003, 293–5). Toward this end, the Delors white paper advocated the integration of employment policies into the broader structures of economic governance at the European level.

During the Essen European Council held in 1994, the member states addressed the suggestions posed by the Delors white paper. While the Commission's proposals sought to construct a consensus between competing interests throughout Europe, strong opposition from several member states essentially halted the initiatives (Rhodes 2005, 291). Rather than establishing employment policy as an active policy domain for the EU, or even as an area of shared competence, the agreement reached at Essen only reinforced the principle of intergovernmentalism by reasserting employment policy as an exclusively national competence. The idea of coordination barely survived; member states were asked to take the general recommendations of the European Council into consideration as they developed their national employment policies, and they were expected to provide an annual report on their progress, but these were understood as voluntary conditions that did not limit the autonomy of the member states (Tidow 2003, 81–3).

As the non-binding Essen Strategy had virtually no impact on social and economic governance within Europe, the Commission – in conjunction with a broad coalition of social forces – still sought to construct a more formalized policy framework. Drawing together groups such as the Group of European Socialists, the European Trade Union Congress, and left-leaning governments, the Commission facilitated negotiations between member states at both the Madrid European Council in December 1995 and the Dublin European Council in December 1996 to develop a more institutionalized approach. At the same time, a coalition of member states, led by Sweden, Finland, and the Netherlands, turned to the EU as a means to strengthen their domestic welfare regimes in response to increasing global competition (Gray 2004, 67). Believing that the socioeconomic changes accompanying increased globalization severely restricted the ability of any nation state to pursue an autonomous policy regime, these states sought to work through the EU to enhance the relative power of social democratic ideals within the global political economy (Bieler 2002). Throughout 1996, the Commission brokered a compromise between the member states on the regionalization of social policy, which resulted in the adoption of the EES and the inclusion of the Employment Chapter within the Amsterdam Treaty. To a large degree, the institutionalization that occurred with the Amsterdam amendments can be traced to the Luxembourg European Council six months earlier, where a 'happy coincidence' of factors came together to ease its acceptance: 'a political shift in member-states to the left, the determination of the Luxembourg Presidency, in conjunction with the Commission pushing it, and the declining economic environment in the EU' (author's interview).[2] At the Luxembourg European Council in November 1997, the member states agreed to coordinate national employment policies through the process of policy deliberation that has become known as the OMC.

In order to enable coordination in absence of formal integration, the OMC was introduced as a 'new' mode of governance within the EES that allows for national variation while still implying 'that solutions are to be developed in a European framework, drawing upon experiences and knowledge of other EU member states and their representatives, or of European institutions such as the Commission' (Walters and Haahr 2005, 131). Moreover, the OMC is largely assumed to be an objective process that 'relies on the systematic comparison of national policies, with "best practices" identified to facilitate "benchmarking," whereby national policies are periodically measured to see how close they come to matching the success of the most successful member state' (Stubb, Wallace, and Peterson 2003, 143). In this way, Commission officials promote this process as 'harmonization through policy learning' and as 'the pragmatic development of solutions' (author's interview). Indeed, a number of commentators have heralded the OMC as a new form of governance that replaces ideology for 'the real experience and policies of the member-states, [so] even trade unions are beginning to look to "best practices" as a pragmatic and professional solution' (Deppe, Felder, and Tidow 2003, 192), as if trade unions represent some benchmark of political intractability. While the OMC has been adopted in a number of policy areas, the process is most formalized for the coordination of employment policy.

Within the context of employment policy, the OMC consists of four stages. First, the European Council uses qualified majority voting to adopt the Employment Guidelines proposed by the Commission, which provide the overarching guiding principles for the EES. In the first five years of the strategy, 1997–2002, the process was performed yearly; however, the timeframe for the policy process shifted to every three years after the review of the EES in 2003. In addition, the Employment Guidelines consisted of approximately twenty objectives organized around the four pillars of the EES until 2002: employability, entrepreneurship, adaptability, and equal opportunities. After the review in 2003, the guidelines were changed into ten 'results-oriented' priorities clustered around three primary objectives: full employment, quality and productivity at work, and strengthening social cohesion and inclusion. In the second stage of the OMC, the Commission and the European Council develop the joint employment report, which assesses the employment environment throughout Europe and the progress each member state has made to achieve the broad objectives of the EES. Initially prepared by the Commission, the report may be amended by the Employment, Social Affairs, Health, and Consumer Affairs Council before it is endorsed and forwarded to the European Council for approval. On the basis of the assessment made in the joint employment report, the Commission then issues specific policy recommendations to the member states. As the third stage of the process, the member states then prepare National Action Plans (NAP) in response to the recommendations, in which they detail the policies they will be adopting to achieve the objectives of the strategy.

Finally, during the fourth stage of the OMC process, the NAPs are peer-reviewed within the Employment Committee (EMCO) – a forum that European officials generally describe as 'technical and technocratic' (author's interview) – in which the discussions are limited to the identification of 'best practices' in labour market policies and the development of indicators to assist benchmarking. The EMCO was set up in

2000 under the auspices of Article 130 of the treaty establishing the European Community, and it is designed to 'promote coordination between Member States on employment and labour market policies' and 'to monitor the employment situation and employment policies in the Member States and the Community' (Art. 130). Consisting of two representatives from every member state and two members from the Directorate General (DG) Employment and Social Affairs, one European official notes the 'EMCO is populated by the highest civil servants' from national ministries of labour and suggests its 'information and policy sharing role is quite fruitful in influencing and redefining policy' (author's interview). Indeed, another Irish official noted that during these initial meetings the member states compared and contrasted different types of employment policies in an attempt to determine the 'best practice' for reaching the broad objectives and that the EMCO often acted as the 'catalyst for processing and supporting the European Council in its decisions' regarding employment policy, and the early debates often encompassed broader questions surrounding the content of the employment guidelines (author's interview).

Drawing upon the successful use of the OMC in the development of the EES, the European Council moved to adopt the OMC as the principal mechanism to achieve its goal of making the EU 'the most competitive and dynamic knowledge-based economy in the world, capable of sustainable economic growth with more and better jobs and greater social cohesion' by 2010 during the 2000 European Council Meeting in Lisbon (European Council 2000, 2). As detailed by the European Council in the Lisbon Strategy, the OMC was framed as a 'fully decentralized approach' that consists of four principal components:

1 fixing guidelines for the Union combined with specific timetables for achieving the goals which they set in the short, medium and long terms;
2 establishing, where appropriate, quantitative and qualitative indicators and benchmarks against the best in the world and tailored to the needs of different Member States and sectors as a means of comparing best practice;
3 translating these European guidelines into national and regional policies by setting specific targets and adopting measures, taking into account national and regional differences;
4 periodic monitoring, evaluation and peer review organized as mutual learning processes. (European Council 2000, 12)

In addition, the member states also made a decision at that European Council to reorient the direction of European social policy. Prior to that decision, regional coordination was focused primarily on employment, but there was an unspoken assumption throughout Europe that it might also encompass other policy areas – as demonstrated by the initiatives such as the Social Charter. However, at Lisbon the member states formally severed the more entrenched tradition of employment policy from other social issues. Drawing upon the successful use of the OMC in the development of the EES – as well as recognizing that the existence of the EES limits future discussion over social policy to employment issues only – a coalition of interests, led by the Commission, sought to develop a parallel program for social exclusion.

The member states of the EU began to embrace a European approach to combating social exclusion in 2000 when they adopted the OMC process in this policy area at the Nice European Council. Similar to the EES, the Commission sets out four objectives to shape, define, and coordinate member state policies combating social exclusion: 'to facilitate participation in employment and access by all to the resources, rights, goods and services; to prevent the risks of exclusion; to help the most vulnerable; and, to mobilize all relevant bodies' (European Council 2002). In response, each member state is then responsible for submitting a National Action Plan on Inclusion (NAP / incl) that outlines the policies it has undertaken to achieve the guidelines and reduce poverty within its respective populations. Finally, the Commission reviews the NAPs / incl to coordinate policies among the member states through identifying best practices and recommending which policies member states should pursue in the future to best achieve the Inclusion Guidelines. While the member states have accepted this process for social exclusion, the authority for the Commission to act as a regional coordinator is even more tenuous than in employment policy; unlike the limited provisions regarding employment policy within the treaties, there is no parallel language regarding social exclusion, and it is based solely upon a broad statement within the Treaty of Nice directing the Community to support and complement the member states in 'combating social exclusion' (Art. 137). In other words, even within the designation of 'soft law,' the regional coordination of poverty reduction is even 'softer.' Nevertheless, this process has been accepted in practice and social inclusion and anti-poverty policies have emerged as key activities of the DG Employment, Social Affairs and Equal Opportunities, despite having no clear mandate to do so within the treaties.

As the OMC does not create a set of binding conditions on the member states, the influence of this policy mechanism on the types of reforms implemented by national governments is a matter of substantial debate. In particular, the emphasis of the OMC on 'soft law' makes it hard to determine the direct impact this mechanism has on policy learning and the degree to which European coordination influences national reforms and debates (Heidenreich 2009, 10–11). On the one hand, proponents of the OMC maintain that it is a much more effective form of governance within the EU context – and in social policy in particular – than hard regulation, as the actors that bear the cost of implementation have a direct impact in the formation of the objectives, thereby ensuring that achievable targets and reforms are adopted (Héritier 2001, 18–20). On the other hand, the non-binding nature of the OMC means that, ultimately, the objectives articulated through this process 'must avoid all challenges to the *acquis* of the internal market and monetary union'; as the OMC does not establish similar sanctions or enforcement mechanisms, its impact on the member states will always be limited (Scharpf 2002, 655). Nevertheless, as Jonathan Zeitlin (2009, 216) points out, even though the OMC has not led to substantive policy change, it has led to 'other types of impact, including not only procedural changes in governance and policy-making processes, but also cognitive and discursive shifts, along with changes in issue salience and political agendas.'

The Impact of the OMC on Domestic Welfare Reforms

Employment policies and welfare regimes are jealously protected by the member states of the EU, which tend to actively resist the development of regional power that might overrule the existing orientation of their welfare regime and force them to adopt undesirable policies. As a result of the pressure from social democrats operating transnationally in the mid-1990s, the authority for the Commission to coordinate employment policies between the member states was agreed to within the Amsterdam Treaty. However, because of the interaction of competing social forces operating at the European level, this intention to develop a strong coordination of employment policy that would work in conjunction with harmonized monetary policy and the Broad Economic Guidelines was tempered to merely a matter of joint concern. Still, even this minor policy change redefined the social policy environment in the EU and influenced how the member states now approach labour market and poverty reduction strategies.

Granted, determining a direct causal link between developments at the EU level and policy reforms implemented by the member states is problematic. As member states participate directly in formulating the objectives and evaluating their progress, the relationship is clearly not unidirectional; member states have both 'learned to "upload" their own priorities' into the policy discussions at the EU level and 'have also exercised considerable selectively (both consciously and unconsciously) in "downloading"' (Zeitlin 2005, 454–5). Nevertheless, some degree of influence through the use of the OMC can be identified on the policy process within the member states, both through the 'creative appropriation' of European concepts by domestic actors and through the broader influence of 'discursive diffusion' (Zeitlin 2009, 229–31). In this way, the Republic of Ireland provides a very illustrative example of the influence of the OMC on both the national policy debate and the new strategies that national actors undertake to promote their desired policy reforms.

With the unemployment rate in the Republic of Ireland peaking at 17.5 per cent during the economic crisis of the 1980s, the goal of stimulating employment growth became a key feature of the government's plan for economic recovery, even though the mechanisms for doing so were initially left unexamined. Focusing government policy on merely attracting foreign direct investment to stimulate growth, it was assumed that this investment would necessitate a subsequent growth in jobs. However, one of the most distinguishing features of the early years of the Irish boom was that it was marked largely by jobless growth; the unemployment rate was still at 10.3 per cent in the late 1990s, and Ireland did not experience much job creation until after 1997, when the Irish government began shifting towards more supply-side employment measures.

To a large degree, the shift in policy was influenced directly by the adoption of the EES in 1997. Even though a group of civil servants within the Department of Enterprise, Trade, and Employment were advocating 'for a more robust inter-linkage between the manpower service and the welfare system' as a key component of the Irish approach to the labour market before the EES was adopted, the political elite in Ireland did not initially support this policy shift (author's interview). However, by pointing to the international commitment made by the Irish government in the adoption of the EES, and the subsequent requirements it imposed to take a more active role in the labour market, proponents of more supply-side measures were then fairly successful in institutionalizing their desired policy reforms. For these officials, the creation of the Improving Employability pillar of the EES and the adoption of the active and preventative measures guideline 'was the catalyst for change. It was that which enabled [these officials] to say to our minister, "You guys have all signed up to this." And that happened fairly quickly, because we had to develop a national action plan for employment, and we had to demonstrate that we were going to meet this commitment' (author's interview). In other words, Irish civil servants engaged in 'creative appropriation' and utilized the EES 'to legitimate and push through contested reforms' (Zeitlin 2009, 231). Despite the 'soft law' nature of the EES, its focus on activation increased the relative importance of more supply-side labour market strategies centred on skill development, retraining, and job placement in Irish policy debates (McCormick 2003, 20; Murphy 2002, 109–10), which directly facilitated the rapid reduction in unemployment Ireland experienced from 1997 to 2007.

As well, Ireland also demonstrates how the adoption of the OMC in the area of social exclusion has shifted the debate over poverty reduction within the member states. Throughout the entire growth period of the 1990s, the earnings dispersion within Ireland rapidly expanded; while per capita Gross Domestic Product (GDP) had grown by over 40 per cent during this time, over 1 per cent of the total income in Ireland shifted away from the bottom 30 per cent of the population during the same period. As a result of this redistribution, Ireland emerged as the most unequal state within Europe, and better than only the United States in the entire Organization for Economic Co-operation and Development, by the turn of the century (O'Hearn 2003, 47). Increasingly, these concerns surrounding socioeconomic equity and poverty reduction are being addressed to a greater degree within Ireland, in response to the increased profile these issues have received at the European level through the adoption of the OMC process for social exclusion.

Following the increase of relative poverty and income inequality that accompanied the high levels of economic growth in the 1990s (Kirby 2002, 55–60), groups critical of the development strategy endorsed by social partnership became more visible within Irish society. By drawing upon European developments, different groups in Ireland have sought to augment their relative position within national debates over welfare reform and expand the scope of active labour market and social inclusion policies. Through 'cognitive diffusion,' the debate at the EU level over social exclusion slowly penetrated into national policy circles to 'act as a switchboard for "path breaking" learning' and prompted a reconfiguration of the Irish approach to poverty (Visser 2009, 50). In this way, one Irish official maintains that this emerging debate in Europe had an 'overarching impact' within the national discourse by promoting the notion 'that the economic and the social should be integrated in the sense that economic development and change, and employment, depended on a high level of social inclusion … and that equally, the promotion of social inclusion depended on a dynamic growing economy' (author's interview). As such, the use of OMC within the area of poverty reduction has reshaped the socioeconomic debate within Ireland, introducing concepts such as social exclusion that expanded and redefined the national debate over relative poverty (Ryan 2000, 66–7). By creating a 'new' policy area, the European debate over social exclusion further legitimized the critiques being raised regarding the polarizing effect of the rapid development, as non-governmental actors were also able to reference the commitments made by the Irish government at the EU level. In an attempt to engage with these concerns, the practice of social partnership was extended to include civil society organizations focusing on poverty reduction and social exclusion.

However, the extent to which the increased regional coordination of social policies will actually lead to the development of the most effective and viable welfare reforms throughout the EU is highly debatable. While the process is supposed to enable member states to discover the most effective approach to social policy through sharing best practices and policy learning at the regional level, in practice the range of policies deemed acceptable are being restricted at the outset. Reflecting the overarching mode of regulation that is increasingly defining European integration, the regional coordination of social policies is premised on the belief that paid employment is the sole mechanism for achieving social integration and cohesion (Walters 2000, 128–30). Through assertions like 'the best safeguard against social exclusion is a job' (European Council 2000), this discourse effectively frames the debate over the desired objective of welfare reforms as focused solely on job creation. As demonstrated in the following section, the dominance of this discourse with debates over social policy in the EU has had a substantive influence in shaping the 'best practices' that become dominant through the OMC process.

Policy Convergence through Benchmarking and Best Practices

The assumed pragmatism that is promoted by the OMC and benchmarking fundamentally reflects a particular power dynamic. As noted by William Walters and Jens Henrik Haahr (2005, 119), 'The world of partnership frameworks, benchmarking, league tables, best practice standards, and performance contracts is one that subtly constrains and shapes us, enjoining us to exercise our freedoms and liberties in particular ways, and towards particular ends.' In effect, the act of benchmarking – and, by extension, the entire OMC process – creates the illusion of agency; while the rejection of the traditional Community method suggests the adoption of a decentralized policy model that allows for national variation, benchmarking still enables a gradual policy convergence. Moreover, the convergence is occurring in a way that neutralizes political discourse and allows for the promotion of particular world views under the guise of 'ideologically neutral' best practices. Rather than engaging in a debate over which socioeconomic model is most appropriate for all member states, the OMC allows competing social forces to effectively sidestep this debate by proclaiming its focus on 'a "new" problem-solving logic based on deliberation and "policy learning"' (Rhodes 2005, 292). Thus, the capacity for democratic accountability within the process becomes further restricted as the space for public input and influence shrinks in favour of technocratic governance. Granted, there are still mechanisms for public input and consultation, but 'the involvement of civil society is only weakly institutionalized [and] ... is not sufficient to correct possible negative externalities caused by new modes of functional governance' like the OMC (Héritier and Lehmkuhl 2011, 139–40). While the member states still have a choice in the type of policies that they follow, key changes at the regional level have redefined the policy environment throughout the EU, which limits the range of viable and / or acceptable choices. With the direction of social policy increasingly being held subordinate to the principles of economic efficiency and flexibility, these structural constraints further reinforce the neoliberal model of governance throughout Europe.

A key implication of this change can be seen in how the dynamic role of the EMCO in facilitating communication between the member states and the Commission – as well as its ability to develop innovative approaches to social policy – was severely curtailed after the five-year review. Rather than being focused on thematic discussions over the core ideals of the EES, one European official complains the debates have become more 'technical and technocratic [and] led the committee to become more process oriented than content' oriented (author's interview). Observing that it 'has been an objective of the UK to weaken the community approach to employment,' another European official suggests this pressure led to the debate within the EMCO being both limited to the implementation of the policies and constrained to a debate over best practices and benchmarking (author's interview). Similarly, one German official protests that 'the analysis [in the EMCO] is too shallow and should be deeper ... [There is a] discussion of best practices, but the overview is not given enough time' (author's interview). As well, one Irish official notes that 'the EMCO is a forum for changing the [employment] guidelines officially, but its role is really very marginal and incrementalist. To the extent that there has been any significant shifts, they have been initiated by the Commission, rather than by the EMCO' (author's interview). To a large degree, this limited role is reflected in the changing composition of the committee; as the EES has evolved, member states have begun to send representatives of decreasing rank to participate in the process. By sending lower level bureaucrats, the discussions within the EMCO become effectively limited to the most efficient means of implementing the objectives formulated by the European Council.

Nevertheless, this shift has not led to any increase in horizontal legitimacy and accountability within the process, as the EU has not gained any further competency over social policy. Most notably, the application of the OMC does not strengthen the scope of principle-agent accountability between the European Commission and the member states, so there is no institutional demand to foster deeper cooperation between the actors. In this way, the application of the OMC represents a 'second-best solution' for intergovernmental policy cooperation and reflects a compromise solution in the face of 'member-states' reluctance to yield legislative competences to the European level' (Héritier and Lehmkuhl 2011, 134–5). The inability to shift competency over social policy up to the EU level meant that actors who sought to increase the level of influence that could be exercised by the EU within the intergovernmental policy process needed to align this policy process with a policy area or process in which the central government could exercise more control. Whereas a central government in a federal system like Canada would be able to exercise this control through the use of spending power, this option does not exist within the EU. Instead, these actors exercised ideational power by aligning the operation of social policy with the emerging discourse on competiveness that was increasingly defining economic governance within the EU.

Gradually, the reference point used to gauge the relative competitiveness of the European economies has shifted to emphasize flexibility, productivity, entrepreneurialism, and employability since the mid-1990s.

By applying these discourses to the operation of social policy, participants within the policy process began to adopt the belief that only the market can provide a viable solution to job creation and poverty reduction (Preece 2009, 67–75). As a direct result of limiting the range of acceptable solutions, 'all of the national plans focused on work as a solution to poverty' as an end in itself, without recognizing 'the possibility that [this emphasis] may actually worsen job quality and intensify the well-known problem of the benefits trap' (Gray 2004, 71–2). In this way, the use of the OMC mechanism to facilitate social policy coordination leads to a groupthink environment, which insulates the policy process from social demands and expectations, and circumvents the ability of citizens to exercise accountability within the decision-making process. Despite the assertion by the Commission that the best practice for social inclusion should be policies that are 'supportive and developmental and not punitive' (European Commission 2002, 35), the question of job quality within this process is addressed largely only superficially by focusing on various forms of employment benefits or wage subsidies. Similarly, these discourses are beginning to promote social policies that attempt to subordinate concerns of de-commodification and social solidarity 'to the demands of labour market flexibility and employability and to the demands of structural or systemic competitiveness' (Jessop 2003, 39). By embedding the debate over socioeconomic governance within both the 'cultural pattern' of neoliberalism (van der Pijl, 1989, 31) and the 'ethos of contractualism' (Walters and Haahr 2005, 121–4), the language and idiom practised by the OMC process is reshaping the policy debate throughout the EU in a way that neutralizes political discourse and allows for the promotion of particular world views under the guise of ideologically neutral 'best practices.'

The operation of social policy within the EU member states became further constrained in 2005, when the 2005 Spring European Council formally adopted a 'streamlined' reporting and monitoring procedure to 're-launch the Lisbon Strategy' and coordinate activities to enhance the competitiveness of the EU. In this manner, the European Council (2005, 11) decided to shift towards developing a set of 'integrated guidelines' consisting of two elements: broad economic policy guidelines (BEPGs) and employment guidelines (EGs). As a general instrument for coordinating economic policies, the BEPGs should continue to embrace the whole range of macroeconomic and microeconomic policies, as well as employment policy insofar as this interacts with those policies; the BEPGs will ensure general economic consistency between the three strands of the strategy.

In effect, these integrated guidelines reoriented the coordination of employment policy within the EU so that it is formally 'subordinated to the objective of price stability and, therefore, concentrated on supply-side measures such as lifelong learning and labour market deregulation' (Bieler 2006, 179). The effort to coordinate employment policy at the EU level became reinterpreted through the neoliberal discourse on competitiveness; 'European employment policy was made to fit the existing integration project … [and] became one of the pillars of supply-side-oriented neoliberal restructuring' (Tidow 2003, 78). Even though this deepened the level of intergovernmental cooperation over welfare reforms within the EU, it did so at the expense of democratic accountability over the policy process.

This effect became even further reinforced with the adoption of both the Treaty of Lisbon in 2009 and the so-called Agenda 2020 for Growth and Employment in 2010. Within both of these documents, the OMC is largely absent; the Treaty of Lisbon makes no explicit reference, and the only reference within the Agenda 2020 Strategy is to call upon the member states to 'transform the open method of coordination on social exclusion and social protection into a platform for cooperation, peer-review and exchange of good practice' (European Commission 2010, 18). Moreover, within both documents, there is a consistent attempt to bring the OMC mechanisms more closely in line with the operation of the broad economic guidelines in a manner that may 'harden' the practice of OMC within the EU. In particular, the Agenda 2020 Strategy 'will be established institutionally in a small set of integrated "Europe 2020" guidelines (integrating employment and broad economic policy guidelines)' that will further entrench the discussions surrounding Social Europe within the existing neoliberal discourse governing the EU (European Commission 2010, 26). In a systematic manner, the promise of the OMC as a 'fully decentralized approach' to determine the best practices in social policy is being subverted to promote a specific policy orientation while still being presented as an ideologically neutral process.

NOTES

1 This research was supported by the Social Sciences and Humanities Research Council grant no. 752-2001-1190.
2 Interviews were conducted in person with representatives from the major stakeholders in the formation of social policy within the EU, Ireland, and Germany in 2003–4. Interview participants were guaranteed confidentiality

and, as such, the material gleaned from the interviews has been incorporated in the text without attribution unless the interviewee has explicitly
granted consent to be quoted.

REFERENCES

Abrahamson, Peter. 1999. 'The Welfare Modeling Business.' *Social Policy &*
Administration 33 (4): 394–415.

Aidukaite, Jolanta. 2004. *The Emergence of the Post-Socialist Welfare State – The*
Case of the Baltic States: Estonia, Latvia and Lithuania. Södertörn Doctoral
Dissertations, University College of South Stockholm: Södertörns
Högskola.

Babajanian, Babken V. 2008. 'Social Welfare in Post-Soviet Armenia: From
Socialist to Liberal and Informal?' *Post-Soviet Affairs* 24 (4): 383–404.

Bieler, Andreas. 2002. 'Austria's and Sweden's Accession to the European
Union: A Comparative Neo-Gramscian Analysis.' In *New Regionalisms in the*
Global Political Economy, edited by Shaun Breslin, Christopher W. Hughes,
Nicola Philips, and Ben Rosamond, 150–62. New York: Routledge.

– 2006. *The Struggle for a Social Europe: Trade Unions and EMU in Times of Global*
Restructuring. New York: Manchester University Press.

Deppe, Frank, Michael Felder, and Stefan Tidow. 2003. 'Structuring the State:
The Case of European Employment Policy.' In *Linking EU and National*
Governance, edited by Beate Kohler-Koch, 175–200. Toronto: Oxford
University Press.

Esping-Andersen, Gøsta. 1990. *The Three Worlds of Welfare Capitalism.*
Princeton: Princeton University Press.

European Commission. 2002. *European Social Fund 2000–2006.* Brussels:
European Commission.

– 2010. *Europe 2020: A Strategy for Smart, Sustainable and Inclusive Growth.*
Brussels: European Commission.

European Council. 2000. *Presidency Conclusions of the Lisbon European Council,*
March 23–24, 2000. (DOC/00/8). Brussels: European Council.

– 2002. *Fight against Poverty and Social Exclusion: Common Objectives for the*
Second Round of National Action Plans. (14164/1/02 REV 1 SOC 508).
Brussels: European Council.

– 2005. *Presidency Conclusions of the Brussels European Council*, March 22–23,
2005. (7619/05). Brussels: European Council.

Gray, Anne. 2004. *Unsocial Europe: Social Protection or Flexploitation?* Ann
Arbor: Pluto.

Heidenreich, Martin. 2009. 'The Open Method of Coordination: A Pathway to the Gradual Transformation of National Employment and Welfare Regimes?' In *Changing European and Employment Welfare Regimes: The Influence of the Open Method of Coordination on National Reforms*, edited by Martin Heidenriech and Jonathan Zeitlin, 10–36. London: Routledge.

Heidenreich, Martin, and Jonathan Zeitlin. 2009. 'Introduction.' In *Changing European and Employment Welfare Regimes: The Influence of the Open Method of Coordination on National Reforms*, edited by Martin Heidenriech and Jonathan Zeitlin, 1–9. London: Routledge.

Héritier, Adrienne. 2001. 'New Modes of Governance in Europe: Policy-Making without Legislating?' MPI Collective Goods Preprint No. 2001/14. http://papers.ssrn.com/sol3/papers.cfm?abstract_id=299431.

Héritier, Adrienne, and Dirk Lehmkuhl. 2011. 'New Modes of Governance and Democratic Accountability.' *Government and Opposition* 46 (1): 126–44.

Jessop, Bob. 2003. 'Changes in Welfare Regimes and the Search for Flexibility and Employability.' In *The Political Economy of European Employment: European Integration and the Transnationalization of the (Un)employment Question*, edited by Henk Overbeek, 29–50. London: Routledge.

Kirby, Peadar. 2002. *The Celtic Tiger in Distress: Growth and Inequality in Ireland*. New York: Palgrave.

Kleinman, Mark. 2002. *A European Welfare State? European Union Social Policy in Context*. New York: Palgrave.

Liebfried, Stephen. 1993. 'Towards a European Welfare State?' In *New Perspectives on the Welfare State in Europe*, edited by Catherine Jones, 120–43. London: Routledge.

McCormick, Brian. 2003. *The Performance of the Irish Labour Market in an EU Context: 1/2003 FAS Labour Market Update*. Dublin: FAS.

Murphy, Candy B. 2002. 'Assessment of the Policy-Making Process.' In *Impact Evaluation of the European Employment Strategy in Ireland*, edited by Philip J. O'Connell, 103–21. Dublin: Department of Enterprise, Trade and Employment and ESRI.

O'Hearn, Denis. 2003. 'Macroeconomic Policy in the Celtic Tiger: A Critical Reassessment.' In *The End of Irish History?: Critical Reflections on the Celtic Tiger*, edited by Colin Coulter and Steve Coleman, 34–55. Manchester: Manchester University Press.

O'Neill, Michael. 1996. *The Politics of European Integration: A Reader*. New York: Routledge.

Preece, Daniel V. 2009. *Dismantling Social Europe: The Political Economy of Social Policy in the European Union*. Boulder: FirstForumPress / Lynne Rienner Publishers.

Rhodes, Martin. 2005. 'Employment Policy: Between Efficacy and Experimentation.' In *Policy Making in the European Union*, 5th ed., edited by Helen Wallace, William Wallace, and Mark A. Pollack, 278–304. New York: Oxford University Press.

Rose, Nikolas, and Peter Miller. 1992. 'Political Power beyond the State: Problematics of Government.' *British Journal of Sociology* 43 (2): 173–205.

Ryan, Liam. 2000. 'Strengthening Irish Identity through Openness.' In *Europe: The Irish Experience*, edited by Rory O'Donnell, 55–68. Dublin: The Institute of European Affairs.

Scharpf, Fritz W. 1999. *Governing in Europe: Effective and Democratic?* Toronto: Oxford University Press.

– 2002. 'The European Social Model: Coping with the Challenges of Diversity.' *Journal of Common Market Studies* 40 (4): 645–70.

Stubb, Alexander, Helen Wallace, and John Peterson. 2003. 'The Policy-Making Process.' In *The European Union: How Does It Work?*, edited by Elizabeth Bomberg and Alexander Stubb, 136–55. Toronto: Oxford University Press.

Tidow, Stefan. 2003. 'The Emergence of European Employment Policy as a Transnational Political Arena.' In *The Political Economy of European Employment: European Integration and the Transnationalization of the (Un)employment Question*, edited by Henk Overbeek, 77–98. London: Routledge.

van der Pijl, Kees. 1989. 'Ruling Classes, Hegemony, and the State System: Theoretical and Historical Considerations.' *International Journal of Political Economy* 19 (3): 7–35.

Visser, Jelle. 2009. 'Neither Convergence nor Frozen Paths: Bounded Learning, International Diffusion of Reforms, and the Open Method of Coordination.' In *Changing European and Employment Welfare Regimes: The Influence of the Open Method of Coordination on National Reforms*, edited by Martin Heidenriech and Jonathan Zeitlin, 37–60. London: Routledge.

Wagener, Hans-Jürgen. 2002. 'The Welfare States in Transition Economies and Accession to the EU.' *West European Politics* 25 (2): 152–74.

Walters, William. 2000. *Unemployment and Government: Genealogies of the Social*. New York: Cambridge University Press.

Walters, William, and Jens Henrik Haahr. 2005. *Governing Europe: Discourse, Governmentality and European Integration*. New York: Routledge.

Wincott, Daniel. 2003. 'The Idea of the European Social Model: Limits and Paradoxes of Europeanization.' In *The Politics of Europeanization*, edited by Kevin Featherstone and Claudio M. Radaelli, 279–302. Oxford: Oxford University Press.

Zeitlin, Jonathan. 2005. 'The Open Method of Co-ordination in Action: Theoretical Promise, Empirical Realities, Reform Strategy.' In *The Open Method of*

Co-ordination in Action: The European Employment and Social Inclusion Strategies, edited by Jonathan Zeitlin and Philippe Pochet, with Lars Magnusson, 447–503. Brussels: PIE – Peter Lang.

– 2009. 'The Open Method of Coordination and Reform of National Social and Employment Policies: Influences, Mechanisms, Effects.' In *Changing European and Employment Welfare Regimes: The Influence of the Open Method of Coordination on National Reforms*, edited by Martin Heidenriech and Jonathan Zeitlin, 214–45. London: Routledge.

9 Global Governance and Canadian Federalism: Reconciling External Accountability Obligations through Internal Accountability Practices

GRACE SKOGSTAD

Global and regional governance subjects Canadian governments – federal and provincial – not only to internal accountability norms but also to external accountability obligations.[1] External accountability obligations, arising from Canada's membership in international organizations, require Canadian governments to account to others affected by their actions, most obviously their peer members in international organizations. In the case of the World Trade Organization (WTO) and the North American Free Trade Agreement (NAFTA), external accountability obligations are legally binding; failure to conform to them carries the threat of punitive trade sanctions. More broadly, Canada's international reputation as a reliable member of regional and global governing institutions would be seriously compromised if Canadian governments failed to honour Canada's treaty and membership commitments. External accountability obligations, nonetheless, rest in uneasy coexistence with norms of internal accountability that require Canadian governments to account for their actions to the Canadian public in order to maintain the latter's confidence and support.

The coexistence of external accountability obligations alongside internal accountability norms raises important challenges for federal systems, like Canada. The challenge is most manifest when one order of government has sole legal authority to sign and ratify international treaties that entail external accountability obligations – and this authority includes obligations that can trespass into subnational governments' areas of jurisdiction. How can the federal principle of non-interference of one order of government in the affairs of the other order be respected when external accountability obligations do not themselves respect the federal principle? How have Canadian governments met this challenge?

Have external accountability obligations to third parties affected inter-governmental relations in Canada by de facto altering the jurisdictional authority of governments? Have they induced conflict across govern-ments, or, alternatively, cooperation? And how do external account-ability requirements affect the internal accountability of Canadian governments to Canadian citizens? Are Canadian governments less – or, counter to what we might expect, more – internally accountable as a result of Canada's incorporation into institutions of regional and global governance?

This chapter addresses and provides answers to these questions. In answer to the first set of questions, it argues that external accountability obligations stemming from Canada's membership in institutions of global and regional economic governance have indeed affected inter-governmental relations. They are turning what is de jure a federal area of jurisdiction into a de facto one of shared federal-provincial / territo-rial responsibility as norms of horizontal accountability operate across federal and provincial governments. Further, while intergovernmental tensions are never absent, the two orders of government do work to-gether in undertaking and meeting external obligations to third parties who are joint members of NAFTA and the WTO.

The most important explanation for why external accountability obligations have engendered horizontal coordination and horizontal accountability norms in Canadian intergovernmental relations lies with Canada's constitution. While it empowers the Government of Canada with the sole authority to make decisions regarding the country's mem-bership in regional and global trade agreements / institutions (that is, both the authority to negotiate and ratify these agreements), the constitu-tion also limits the Government of Canada's authority to implement the treaties that such membership entails. The Government of Canada can implement treaty matters that lie within its jurisdiction, but provinces have legal authority to implement provisions of international treaties that fall within their jurisdiction. Overcoming this constitutional restric-tion has led to the emergence of norms and procedures of horizontal accountability across federal and provincial / territorial governments.

In answer to the second set of questions of whether there is a trade-off between external and internal accountability norms, the answer pro-vided here is more ambivalent and revolves in large part around how one defines internal accountability. Internal accountability, as measured by a traditional notion of executives being subject to popular control via elected representatives, is not altogether absent, but it is weak. Neither national nor provincial legislators have much capacity to hold their executives / governments to account when it comes to decisions to encumber external accountability obligations. However, if we measure internal accountability in terms of private sector stakeholders' ability to hold executive decision-makers to account, then internal accountability is more robust. Governments work hard to ensure that they render an account of their actions to those with a direct economic stake in regional and global governance obligations. This situation of weak popular control via elected legislatures but stronger popular control via stakeholder accountability is problematic to critics of Canada's entry into international economic organizations, but it is less of a concern for the majority of Canadians who broadly support internationalism. Canadians appraise the accountability of Canadian governments largely in fiduciary accountability terms: that is, in terms of the outputs (of economic performance) that result from Canada's membership in regional and global institutions of economic governance.

This chapter organizes its inquiry into the relationship between Canadian federalism and external accountability. Part 1 discusses the plural and contested meanings of accountability in four parts. It distinguishes between four logics of accountability: (1) a fiduciary logic of accountability as effective performance and independence from political control; (2) a popular control logic of executives to legislatures (representative accountability); (3) a popular control logic of executives to societal stakeholders (functionalist accountability); and (4) an intergovernmental logic of horizontal accountability of different orders of government to one another. Part 2 discusses norms and practices of horizontal accountability across the two orders of government, traces their roots to Canada's constitution, and shows how these norms are shifting as Canada negotiates a Comprehensive Economic and Trade Agreement with the European Union. Part 3 examines internal accountability mechanisms – as manifest in the incorporation of societal groups (functionalist accountability) and legislatures into foreign trade policymaking (representative accountability). It argues that popular control norms of representative accountability are weak, while functionalist accountability mechanisms are much stronger, at least on the part of the Government of Canada. Part 4 concludes, discussing whether Canadian accountability practices strike an appropriate balance between giving decision-makers the flexibility they need to act decisively on the country's behalf and constraining their actions in order to respect federalism and democratic norms.

External and Internal Accountability Logics

Those who regulate and govern the behaviour of others do so conditional on the latter's acceptance of their right to do so (Bentham 1991). In liberal democracies, this perception of political legitimacy – the belief that those who make and / or enforce binding rules have the right to do so and their actions should thus be obeyed – is closely related to the belief that decision-makers can be held to account for their actions. Thus, and consistent with the definition of accountability provided in the introduction to this text, accountability is a relationship between an actor and others that is characterized by the former's obligation to explain and justify his or her conduct to the latter and to face consequences when it is found wanting (Bovens 2007, 107). Notwithstanding rough agreement on what accountability entails, it nonetheless is often a contested concept as disagreements arise within and across liberal democracies over to whom an account is to be rendered, for what, and by what means (107; Fisher 2004).

These disagreements about accountability manifest themselves in the distinction between external accountability and internal accountability. External accountability obligations are consistent with the notion of international surveillance that is introduced in the introduction to this text. External accountability arises when countries join intergovernmental institutions of global and regional economic governance and agree to abide by their terms of membership. One of these terms of membership is an agreement to limit the exercise of national sovereignty in return for anticipated gains that result from other members also curbing their domestic decision-making authority. International organizations tie their country members' hands by requiring they take into account the impact of their decisions on other countries that are also members of the international organization. For a medium-sized country like Canada that is heavily dependent upon export markets for its prosperity, membership in regional and global institutions of economic governing is a means to require our fellow members – who are also our major trading competitors and partners – to be accountable to us for their actions. Requiring fellow members of international organizations to set aside their domestic electoral incentives to advance the interests of domestic constituents (protectionism, in trade policy parlance) is expected to yield benefits (in economic growth, for example) that will, in turn, increase public support for domestic politicians.

Given their raison d'être, global and regional governing institutions thus rely almost exclusively for their legitimacy on a *fiduciary* logic of independent delegated authority. It conceives accountability as being rendered when decision-makers in international institutions effectively perform the functions assigned them – by being independent of and beyond the direct control of those (member countries) who have delegated them authority (Majone 2001). A fiduciary notion of accountability places decision-makers beyond the reach of politicians and political calculations.

Fiduciary notions of public accountability – as rendered by politically independent authorities – are not absent from liberal democracies, including Canada.[2] However, they coexist with, and usually take second place to, a *popular control logic* of political authority that conceives accountability as popular representation and popular control and dominates the discussion of accountability elsewhere in this text, including in the introduction. On the popular control logic, it is 'the people' (as voters) who vest decision-makers (elected governments) with their authority and who have the right to demand accountability of decision-makers by requiring them to provide a narrative account of their actions. If this requirement for decision-makers to justify and explain behaviour is to be effective, then citizens also need access to information, and decision-makers must behave in a transparent way. The logic of popular control also means that accountability necessarily extends to the ability of 'the public' to reward good behaviour and to punish poor performance.[3]

Still, as any observer of domestic politics knows, debates rage about the range of matters for which decision-makers can reasonably be expected to be held to account, the appropriate sanctions when their behaviour is found wanting, and even to whom they should be accountable. On this last matter, is it the public writ large to whom accountability is owed, or is it those most directly affected by their actions? In representative democracies, accountability as popular control is owed by executives / decision-makers to elected legislatures. Yet evolving governing practices in Canada and elsewhere indicate that representative accountability increasingly coexists with – and sometimes is even supplanted by – another conception of popular control. It is a *functionalist logic* of accountability by which governments owe accountability to those with a direct (economic) stake in their decisions, and, further, this accountability is assured by consulting closely with and incorporating societal actors directly into decision-making processes.[4]

In addition to these 'vertical' conceptualizations of accountability (of the agent to the principal), systems in which political authority is divided across units or orders of government give rise to yet another conception of accountability. It is *horizontal accountability*: that is, the requirement for state political actors who are in a relationship of independence with one another – rather than a hierarchical one of delegated authority – to account for their behaviour to one another (O'Donnell 1998, 17–19; Schedler 1999, 24–5). As the introduction to this text observes, horizontal relationships of accountability are more consistent with the logic of a federal system than are vertical accountability relationships. Horizontal accountability to other state actors can require not encroaching on their authority, but because courts usually enforce this aspect of horizontal accountability, it is not a good indicator of horizontal accountability norms. Better measures are the limits that state actors impose upon their own behaviour out of a recognition of their mutual interdependence, even within a system of independent legal authority. In multi-level governance systems (like federal systems), examples of such horizontal accountability measures are that state actors at one order do not act without consulting one another; governments at one order accommodate the views of governments at the other order, even when these views are not part of the majority; and governments provide 'escape routes' that enable other governments to accommodate local popular concerns.[5]

The next section of this chapter examines norms and practices of horizontal accountability that have lessened, although not eliminated, intergovernmental tensions around encumbering external accountability obligations stemming from membership in regional and global governing institutions. It explains their constitutional origins and documents their evolution over time.

Canadian Federalism and Horizontal Accountability Norms

The norms and practices of horizontal accountability that prevail with respect to Canadian governments entering into external accountability obligations have their roots in Canada's constitution. It gives the Government of Canada alone the legal authority to engage in international relations. The Government of Canada has the exclusive right to represent Canadians in international institutions. Provincial governments can acquire that right only as a result of an invitation from the Government of Canada.[6] The Government of Canada also has sole legal authority to *sign* and *ratify*[7] international treaties, including those that could cause a diminution in not only its own legal powers but also those of provincial governments. However, ratified treaties must be turned into domestic law in order to be implemented, and judicial review has divided jurisdiction over their implementation. The 1937 judicial ruling in *Attorney General for Canada v. Attorney General for Ontario* decreed that the federal government's right to negotiate and ratify international treaties does not extend to implementing provisions of international agreements whose subject matter falls within provincial jurisdiction.[8] That is, only provincial legislatures can implement provisions of international treaties that fall within provincial jurisdiction.

This legal constraint to its authority to implement international treaties does not obviate the Government of Canada from its obligations to enforce treaties. NAFTA obligates the Canadian government to take 'all necessary measures' to give effect to the provisions of the agreement; the WTO requires it to take all 'reasonable measures.' When it comes to initiating trade complaints against countries that Canada believes have breached their external accountability commitments to us, again provincial governments lack legal authority. Although private firms can initiate disputes under NAFTA's Chapter 11 on Investment, provincial governments cannot. Among governments, only the Government of Canada can initiate dispute settlement procedures and name Canada's members to NAFTA panels. It also has the exclusive right to initiate a formal WTO complaint. Simply put, Canada's constitution thus creates a situation of legal and political interdependence of the two orders of government; neither order of government can realize its trade policy objectives without the cooperation and collaboration of the other.

If it is important, as it is, for Canada to be able to capture the benefits of regional and global governing institutions, then how can it enter into external accountability obligations without inciting intergovernmental tensions with the provinces / territories? The solution embraced by Canadian governments is horizontal accountability practices and norms that entail extensive consultation with the provinces with the objective of obtaining their agreement on the terms of any international commercial treaty. These consultative practices were fully evident during the negotiation of the 1989 free trade agreement with the United States, the 1994 NAFTA with the United States and Mexico, and the 1995 World Trade Organization agreements (de Boer 2002; Hale 2004; Hocking 2004; Kukucha 2004, 2008; Skogstad 2008). Ottawa obtained provinces' agreement for these treaties and the external accountability obligations that went with them. It did not attempt to bind provinces to international treaties that affected provincial jurisdiction without first obtaining their consent. The Government of Canada also successfully negotiated the exclusion of matters from international agreements – for example, provincial procurement policies – on which provincial consensus and consent were not forthcoming.

The negotiation of NAFTA's environmental and labour side agreements (the North American Agreement on Environmental Co-operation and the North American Agreement on Labour Co-operation) established a larger role for provinces. Because the two agreements had greater impact on provincial jurisdiction than they did on federal, provinces were 'completely involved in the drafting of the Canadian proposals' and had access to all the Mexican and American position papers on these two agreements.' They were also invited to the final stages of the negotiations in Washington in August 1993 (Kukucha 2004, 31). Further, in recognition of the fact that these agreements fell largely within provincial jurisdiction, the Government of Canada initially bound only itself under these agreements. It would become responsible for any provincial breach of the enforcement rules of these agreements only when a sufficient number of provinces agreed to be bound by their terms.

Horizontal accountability norms of provincial input and consent to external accountability obligations also operate in resolving trade disputes. The two orders of government work closely to avoid disputes with trading partners and to settle trading tensions in advance of formal complaints. When such disputes escalate to formal complaints, the interaction across federal and provincial officials is continuous. Provinces also participate as members of the Canadian delegation in international meetings and forums to resolve trade disputes that are of interest to them (Dymond and Dawson 2002, 8).[9] Significantly, provinces are consulted not only when implementing the terms of international treaties requires provincial cooperation but also when it does not; that is, when federal policies alone are disputed as violations of external accountability obligations (Skogstad 2008).

These consultative horizontal accountability norms have not satisfied all provinces; some argue that respect for the federal principle requires more. The Parti Québécois has long argued that provinces should not only be a part of the Canadian negotiating team, but also be at the negotiating table and able to intervene directly on issues of importance to a local industry. Both British Columbia and Quebec have argued that trade agreements that affect provincial jurisdiction should require the formal approval of provincial legislatures (British Columbia 2000; Quebec 2002). At the national level, Bloc Québécois members of Parliament introduced private member's bills on three occasions to require the Government of Canada to consult provincial governments before negotiating or concluding a treaty in an area under provincial legislative authority or that affects provincial legislative authority. These bills, including Bill C-260, introduced in November 2004 in the Thirty-Eighth Parliament, appeared to be motivated primarily by the desire to protect provincial, i.e., Quebec, rights in the areas of education and culture. In somewhat more ambiguous language, Canada's premiers, through the Council of the Federation (2005), collectively proposed that provinces be given 'a significant and clear role in the development of Canada's international position on areas within provincial and territorial responsibility.'

Liberal governments in Ottawa rebuffed requests for provinces to have a formal role in the negotiation and ratification of international treaties. They pointed out that provinces already have significant participation in international treaties, with the federal government consulting them when treaties affect areas of provincial jurisdiction. Since current mechanisms to ensure provincial participation were working well, they argued there was no need to formalize them.

Since it took office in January 2006, the Harper Conservative government has taken a different strategy to the role of provinces in international institutions and negotiations. Prime Minister Harper departed from his Liberal predecessors by inviting the province of Quebec to represent itself at UNESCO (Canada, Office of the Prime Minister 2006). The Harper government has also deviated substantially from Liberal predecessors in the role it is allowing provincial governments to play in negotiations for a Comprehensive Economic and Trade Agreement (CETA) with the European Union. Such an agreement has been strongly promoted by the Canadian business community.[10] It is also one zealously advocated by Quebec Premier Jean Charest.[11]

Initially reluctant to undertake trade negotiations with Canada – in part because an earlier 2005 attempt had failed – the EU agreed to formal negotiations in May 2009. Among the EU's highest priorities are obtaining the right for European companies to bid for provincial and municipal government procurement contracts for goods and services. Elimination or harmonization of regulatory barriers to trade is another EU priority; several provincial and municipal governments give preference to local / provincial residents and companies in procurement contracts. There are also disparities across provinces in regulatory standards and they create interprovincial barriers to trade in goods and services for both Canadian and non-Canadian companies and individuals. Among the goals that provincial governments are seeking is improved EU-Canada market labour mobility via mutual recognition or harmonization of professional accreditation standards. Unlike with earlier trade negotiations and agreements, then, a host of the subjects at the fore of the EU-Canada negotiations fall full-square in provincial matters of jurisdiction.

Before agreeing to negotiations, the European Union wanted assurance that provinces were committed to the process and would implement any concluded agreement (Benzie 2008; Taber and Séguin 2009). As chair of the Council of the Federation, Quebec Premier Jean Charest obtained the support of the provinces for a trade deal with the EU.[12] The one exception was Newfoundland and Labrador, whose premier, Danny Williams, was sceptical that the province's interests would be advanced by a negotiation in which the EU was seeking to maintain its ban on seal products and its high seafood tariffs.

The fact that provincial matters are so integral to CETA has given provinces an unprecedented role in trade negotiations. Canada's chief trade negotiator, Steve Verheul, described that 'unique' involvement to the House of Commons Standing Committee on International Trade on 15 June 2010: 'This [provincial] involvement includes participating in negotiating rooms on issues under their jurisdiction. We have had between 40 and 60 provincial and territorial representatives at each of the negotiating rounds, and we have been meeting them frequently … We also meet with them on the eve of every round [of negotiations] as well as at the close of each day of negotiations.'[13] Whether CETA negotiations will succeed is not yet clear.[14] If they do – and Canadian provinces are responsible in part for that success – they will signal an important shift in intergovernmental norms of horizontal accountability, conferring on provinces a status of virtually equal partners with the Government of Canada in international trade negotiations. The result will be to transform what is legally a matter of exclusive federal authority into one of de facto shared jurisdiction. If the CETA negotiations fail, and provinces' role in the negotiations is deemed to be one reason why, the Government of Canada may well reconsider the merits of inviting provinces to the table when it negotiates international trade agreements.

Whatever the outcome of the CETA negotiations, there is evidence that the practice of horizontal accountability in international trade policy negotiations has had salutary effects on intergovernmental relations.

In March 2011, the province of Newfoundland and Labrador announced that it would shift from being an 'observer' at the negotiating table to henceforth take 'a more active role in negotiations.' Among the reasons for its altered stance, said the responsible Newfoundland and Labrador minister, was the respectful manner in which the province had been treated by Canada's chief negotiator throughout the negotiating process (Government of Newfoundland and Labrador 2011). Other provincial trade officials have also praised the manner by which federal negotiators have included provincial trade officials in the CETA negotiations.[15]

Norms and Practices of Internal Accountability via Popular Control

Respect for popular control norms of internal accountability require Canadian governments to account to Canadians for the initial decision to submit to regional and global governing via an international commercial treaty, and subsequently for their conduct under this treaty / governing institution. In terms of representative accountability – that is, of executives to legislators – Canada's constitution does *not require* such accountability when it comes to the negotiation and ratification of international agreements. These powers are prerogative rights of the Crown, vested in the Cabinet and prime minister. There is no requirement for Parliament to give its prior approval to treaties, although its agreement must be sought for any changes to domestic law that are needed to implement treaty provisions.

The scope for elected representatives to be accountable to Canadians for commercial trade agreements and the external accountability obligations they incur is quite uneven across the two orders of government. At the national level, parliamentary standing committees responsible for international trade have provided an opportunity for groups representing economic and social interests to present their views on Canada's trade policies.[16] These committees also serve as a forum for trade negotiators to brief parliamentarians on the progress of trade negotiations and to address their questions. Still, there are real questions about their adequacy. For example, the first briefing of the House of Commons Standing Committee on International Trade on Canada-EU trade negotiations occurred only after three formal rounds of negotiations.

Provincially elected representatives have even less of an institutionalized role in trade policy, and hence less opportunity to be accountable to their constituents for it (Kukucha 2008, 94–7). Some provinces (the NDP in BC and Ontario) have had legislative committees study and hold hearings on trade and investment agreements, but most provinces have not. Quebec is an important exception to all provinces – and indeed, to the Government of Canada – in its respect for representative accountability. Since the passage of Bill 56 in 2002, the Quebec National Assembly (NA) is required to ratify a federal treaty that affects the province's jurisdiction.

Opposition parties' proposals to strengthen the role of the Canadian Parliament in international treaty negotiations and ratification have not borne fruit. A private member's bill introduced by a Bloc Québécois MP in the Thirty-Eighth Parliament, which would have required the House of Commons to give its prior approval to ratification of an 'important' treaty, was dismissed by the majority Liberal government. It rejected the rationale of the sponsoring MP – that international treaties have a discernible impact on Canadians' lives, but because they are 'negotiated in secret,' a formal ratification role for Parliament is needed both 'to ensure real transparency' in treaty-making and to make it 'more democratic' (Roy 2005). The Liberal government stated this description did not reflect the 'reality' of ample opportunities for consultation of non-state interests in Canadian treaty-making.

Indeed, as measured by criteria of functional accountability, the government of Canada scores much higher in its processes for encumbering Canada with external accountability obligations to trading partners. It struck consultative committees (known as sectoral advisory groups on international trade, or SAGITs) that included representatives from industry / sectoral interests during the negotiations on free trade agreements in North America and the Uruguay Round of the General Agreement on Tariffs and Trade (GATT) (1986–93). These were expanded by the Department of Foreign Affairs and International Trade (DFAIT) into multi-stakeholder consultations and information briefings during negotiations on the aborted Free Trade Area of the Americas (Hocking 2004, 18), and the latter were supplemented by a dedicated multimedia Internet site and parliamentary hearings (16). During the EU-Canada negotiations on CETA, Canadian negotiators consulted a private sector group they assembled, as well as civil society, included by an online questionnaire in fall 2009.[17] They also held at least one briefing of civil society on the state of negotiations.[18]

This informational and consultative strategy on mobilized publics has earned both praise and criticism. On the one hand, it has been lauded for its 'transparency' (Kukucha 2004); the Canadian government's formal and informal mechanisms for consultation, education, and information dissemination, described as 'exemplary' (Dymond and Dawson 2002, 15). On the other hand, there are worries that these accountability practices emphasize 'process over content,' and many of the civil society groups that participate lack 'legitimate representative authority' (15). While recognizing that governments have little option but to consult broadly in order to provide legitimacy for their policies, Hocking (2004, 26) suggests that doing so creates a strong likelihood for 'a clash of expectations regarding what can be realistically achieved.' Whereas business and trade officials share the goal of trade liberalization, NGOs often do not and attempt to use multi-stakeholder processes to redefine the political agenda away from trade liberalization to embrace other goals.

Organized groups with an interest in Canadian trade policy / international economic governance do find fault with existing consultative and informational mechanisms. This criticism is perhaps not surprising from groups like the Council of Canadians or the newly formed Trade Justice Network, opposed in principle as they are to international treaties and institutions whose mandate is to liberalize trade and financial flows. But so do others who seek these treaties and institutions; federal and provincial governments' communications on the current CETA negotiations have been described as inadequate by the business community.[19]

However inadequate, the Canadian government's consultations and briefings of civil society nonetheless have exceeded those of most provinces, at least when it comes to formal consultations and briefings. Provincial consultations with civil society groups have been described as 'ad hoc,' 'limited to specific sectoral disputes and international negotiations,' and 'politicized' (Kukucha 2004, 125). That situation may be changing, with provinces having acquired a role more equal to that of the federal government in the CETA negotiations. For example, the Government of Ontario's Ministry of Economic Development and Trade (2010) has sought input (via a questionnaire) from the business community to help it identify specific barriers and opportunities that could be used to shape the province's negotiating strategy for CETA.

Conclusion

This chapter has examined norms and practices of accountability surrounding Canadian government decisions to encumber external accountability obligations to third parties by signing international treaties and joining international organizations. It has argued that a major priority of Canadian federal governments, who have exclusive legal authority to sign and ratify international treaties but not to implement provisions therein that fall within provincial jurisdiction, has been to create an ex ante consensus for its trade policies. These consensus-building initiatives are consistent with norms of horizontal accountability across the two orders of government and that respect the federal principle of non-interference by one order of government in the jurisdiction of the other order. Perceived requisites of consensus-building with civil society have also given rise to what are here called relationships of functional accountability with stakeholders, especially those in the economic and financial sectors directly affected by international commercial treaties and organizations.

Are Canadians well served by these accountability relationships? First, do they enable Canadian governments to act decisively and effectively to advance the Canadian political community's collective interests vis-à-vis external parties and countries? And do accountability relationships provide legitimacy to Canadian governments' decisions to encumber external accountability obligations – and in so doing, limit internal control over our affairs? Measures of the efficacy of accountability relationships are (1) whether they generate domestic consensus rather than conflict; (2) whether they result in outcomes that can be honoured to third parties; and (3) whether they produce optimal outcomes for Canadians. The perceived legitimacy of accountability relationships is tapped by measures 1 and 2.

Although conflict is never absent from the negotiation of international trade agreements, federalism-induced norms of horizontal accountability and fiduciary accountability norms to 'stakeholders' do have the salutary effect of mitigating domestic tensions around external accountability decisions. Having been given an appreciable role in Canadian external trade policy, provinces have reduced leverage, and, indeed, incentives to engage in the politics of 'blame avoidance' – to shift blame to the federal government for any diminution of popular control that accrues from membership in regional and global economic governing institutions. This blame game has been largely avoided in Canada when it comes to external trade policy. Moreover, Canadian provinces are adhering to provisions in international trade agreements and decisions of international regulatory bodies that affect their legislative authority (de Boer 2002). Accountability to private actors, through their consultation on and involvement in domestic decision-making regarding international treaties / institutions has also worked to minimize, although not to eliminate entirely, domestic tensions around global and regional governance.

At the same time, critics suggest these domestic accountability relationships result in sub-optimal outcomes for Canadians as a whole.

Those who believe a liberal trade policy and membership in liberal international institutions are optimal outcomes for Canada are inclined to lament the constraints of horizontal accountability norms. Too often, in their view, these norms enable provinces to protect local economic sectors to the detriment of the well-being of the Canadian economy as a whole. This worry has grown with provinces' augmented role in the negotiation of the Canada–European Union Comprehensive Economic and Trade Agreement. International trade lawyer Lawrence Herman (2010) argues that by having not only federal but also provincial and territorial negotiators at the actual negotiating table, 'Canada is risking trade negotiations with the Europeans by presenting a team that emphasizes, rather than diminishes, internal difference and divided interests.' Even while Ottawa cannot 'dictate terms to the provinces' or 'create consensus where it does not exist' (Brown 1991, 122), extending horizontal accountability norms beyond consulting provinces and securing their agreement to bringing them directly into negotiations is a suboptimal move.

From a different perspective, and as noted earlier, those opposed to liberal trade agreements fault the legitimacy of existing accountability norms and practices. Coalitions like the Council of Canadians and the Trade Justice Network deplore not only the substance of agreements to liberalize trade and investment but also the inadequacy of opportunities for the public to engage in debates around these agreements.[20] Strengthened representative accountability norms and practices would help to overcome this criticism.

For their part, most Canadians appear to grant governments considerable scope to act as fiduciaries on our behalf when it comes to Canada entering into regional and global governing institutions that entail external obligations to other countries. Canadian governments have long championed the virtues of multilateralism or internationalism – cooperation among countries for the purpose of mutual benefit (Keating 2002; Nossal 1997). Governments' support for internationalism has been grounded in the reality of the country's status as a 'middle power' and not a 'great power.' And the Canadian public appears largely to agree on the values of internationalism, particularly when it comes to the pursuit of economic benefits (Munton and Keating 2001; Wolfe and Mendelsohn 2004). Analysts suggest that support for internationalism creates 'a permissive consensus' whereby Canadians defer to governments when it comes to negotiating international trade agreements (Mendelsohn, Wolfe, and Parkin 2001). This deference is rooted in the view that such trade agreements provide real economic benefits to individual Canadians and the Canadian economy as a whole (Wolfe and Mendelsohn).[21]

Accountability practices around external trade agreements and membership in international economic organizations have evolved in Canada and are continuing to evolve. Norms of intergovernmental horizontal accountability and functional accountability are strong. Much weaker are practices of representative accountability – of executives to elected representatives of the public. Strengthening representative accountability norms by augmenting the role of elected legislatures would likely increase the conflict around Canadian trade policy, but it would also have the desirable effect of publicizing the highly significant decision of Canadian governments to encumber external accountability obligations to other countries.

NOTES

1 The discussion of external accountability has been informed by Keohane (2003).
2 For example, Canada's judicial system rests on a fiduciary logic. So do a host of boards and agencies at federal and provincial orders that are delegated responsibility for such tasks as food inspection, the implementation of human rights legislation, and the regulation of dangerous substances. These bodies' possession of specialist expertise and their independence from political intervention are seen to be requisite to these bodies' accountability – as manifest in effective performance – to the Canadian public.
3 Although there are controls to the discretionary behaviour of fiduciaries, they are not popular control mechanisms. Rather, they are possession of expertise and professional credentials, requirements to give reasons and make transparent the bases for their decisions, and judicial review of these decisions (Dyrberg 2002, 83; Harlow 2002, chap. 6; Majone 1994, 2, 22–3).
4 What is here called *functionalist accountability* is referred to by Bovens (2007, 112) as social accountability to capture civil society forums as a whole. The term *functionalist* is preferred, because state actors are more inclined to perceive themselves as owing accountability to societal actors who perform an important economic – or, more rarely, social – function. Hartley and Skogstad (2005) provide a discussion of the different logics of democracy that provides the basis for the distinction here between representative and functionalist popular control logics.

5 These indicators are informed by Heritier's (1999, 2003) analysis of horizontal accountability norms within the European Union's Council of Ministers.

6 A good example is the decision of the Harper Conservative government to invite the province of Quebec to represent itself at UNESCO (Canada Office of the Prime Minister 2006).

7 Ratification of treaties entails a formal process of confirming agreement to be bound by a treaty. In Canada, the executive – the Cabinet – has the authority to commit Canada to be bound by an international treaty. It does so by preparing an Order in Council that authorizes the minister of foreign affairs to sign an Instrument of Ratification. This instrument means that Canada is bound by the treaty as soon as it comes into force.

8 Some constitutional experts argue that the Supreme Court of Canada would sanction federal intrusions into provincial areas of jurisdiction in order to implement international treaties, as consistent with federal legal authority with respect to 'peace, order, and good government' (*R. v. Crown Zellerbach*, 1984) or 'the general regulation of trade' (*General Motors v. City National Leasing*, 1989). The Government of Canada has not yet explicitly tested this rendering of the constitution.

9 While provincial officials are often present at international consultations to resolve trade disputes, the norm is for provincial representatives to intervene only when asked to do so by the (federal) head of the Canadian delegation.

10 See statement of Roy MacLaren (2008), as co-chairman of the Canada-Europe Roundtable for Business.

11 Séguin (2008) reports, 'For the past two years, [Quebec Premier] Mr Charest has been pursuing a free trade agreement with Europe, working aggressively to eliminate resistance expressed by other provinces and territories.' See also Benzie (2008).

12 See Council of the Federation (2009) for the declaration of the support of the provinces (excluding Newfoundland and Labrador) for the negotiation of an EU-Canada agreement.

13 House of Commons. Standing Committee on International Trade. 15 June 2010.

14 At the time of writing (spring 2012), negotiations were scheduled to conclude by the end of the year.

15 This statement is based on information communicated to the author in a series of telephone interviews conducted in late 2010 and early 2011 with officials from several Canadian provinces who are representing their governments in the CETA talks.

16 This practice has been observed for the Canada-U.S. free trade agreement, NAFTA, the Uruguay and Doha Rounds of GATT/WTO, the inconclusive Free Trade Area of the Americas, and the Canada-EU Comprehensive Free Trade Agreement.

17 This information was acquired from an online document at the website of DFAIT, Government of Canada: http://www.international.gc.ca/cip-pic. Accessed in June 2010, the document, entitled 'Summary of Responses to Canada-EU eDiscussion,' has subsequently been removed from the website and is no longer available online.

18 See testimony of Steve Verheul, Canada's chief negotiator, to the House of Commons Standing Committee on International Trade, 15 June 2010.

19 See Todgham Cherniak (2010). An alternate view is provided by the Canada-Europe Roundtable for Business, which states that Ottawa has offered the business community an unprecedented level of consultations and direct participation in the negotiations. See O'Neil (2009).

20 See Council of Canadians (2010) lamenting the inadequacy of government briefings and public input.

21 Wolfe and Mendelsohn (2004, 277) report that almost 50 per cent of Canadians believe that international institutions are not sufficiently demo-cratic, but they also do not expect 'to be actively involved themselves in decision making at the international level.'

REFERENCES

Benzie, Sean Gordon Robert. 2008. 'Brothers in Arms; McGuinty and Charest Throw Down Gauntlet in Battle with Ottawa.' *Toronto Star*, 3 June.

Bentham, David. 1991. *The Legitimation of Power.* London: Macmillan.

Bovens, Mark. 2007. 'New Forms of Accountability and EU-Governance.' *Comparative European Politics* 5:104–30.

British Columbia. Ministry of Employment and Investment. 2000. 'International Trade Policy.' Accessed 27 Apr. 2000, http://www.ei.gov.bc.ca/Trade&Export/FTAA-WTO/provincial.htm.

Brown, D.M. 1991. 'The Evolving Role of the Provinces in Canadian Trade Policy.' In *Canadian Federalism: Meeting Global Economic Challenges*, edited by Douglas M. Brown and Murray G. Smith, 81–128. Kingston, ON: Institute of Intergovernmental Affairs, Queen's University.

Canada. Office of the Prime Minister. 2006. 'Prime Minister Harper and Premier Charest Sign Historic Agreement Establishing a Formal Role for Québec in UNESCO.' 5 May. http://pm.gc.ca/eng/media.asp?category=2&id=1152.

Council of Canadians. 2010 'Letter to the Minister of International Trade Re: CETA.' 23 February. http://www.canadians.org/trade/issues/EU/letter-van-loan-0210.html.

Council of the Federation. 2005. 'Council of the Federation Seeks Views of Federal Party Leaders.' 19 Dec. http://www.councilofthefederation.ca/newsroom/seekviews_dec19_05.html.

– 2009. 'Statement of the Council of the Federation – Support for the Negotiation of a New and Comprehensive Economic Agreement with the European Union.' 2 February. http://www.councilofthefederation.ca/pdfs/Statement-EU-20Feb09.pdf.

de Boer, S. 2002. 'Canadian Provinces, US States and North American Integration: Bench Warmers or Key Players?' *Choices* 8 (4): 2–22.

Dymond, W.A., and L.R. Dawson. 2002. *The Consultation Process and Trade Policy Creation: Political Necessity or Bureaucratic Rent-Seeking*. Ottawa: Centre for Trade Policy and Law, Carleton University.

Dyrberg, Peter. 2002. 'Accountability and Legitimacy: What Is the Contribution of Transparency?' In *Accountability and Legitimacy in the European Union*, edited by Anthony Arnull and Daniel Wincott, 81–96.Oxford: Oxford University Press.

Fisher, Elizabeth. 2004. 'The European Union in the Age of Accountability.' *Oxford Journal of Legal Studies* 24 (3): 495–515.

Government of Newfoundland and Labrador. 2011. 'Provincial Government to Participate in Canada–European Union Trade Negotiations.' 17 March. News release. http://www.releases.gov.nl.ca/releases/2011/intrd/0317n02.htm.

Hale, G.E. 2004. 'Canadian Federalism and the Challenge of North American Integration.' *Canadian Public Administration* 47 (4): 497–522.

Hartley, Sarah, and Grace Skogstad. 2005. 'Regulating Genetically Modified Crops and Foods in Canada and the United Kingdom: Democratizing Risk Regulation.' *Canadian Public Administration* 48 (3): 305–27.

Harlow, Carol. 2002. *Accountability in the European Union*. Oxford: Oxford University Press and Academy of European Law.

Héritier, Adrienne. 1999. 'Elements of Democratic Legitimation in Europe: An Alternative Perspective.' *Journal of European Public Policy* 6:269–82.

– 2003. 'Composite Democracy in Europe: The Role of Transparency and Access to Information.' *Journal of European Public Policy* 10 (5): 814–33.

Herman, Lawrence. 2010. 'Buy American: We Need Only One Voice at the Table: This Latest Trade Experience Taught Us That Internal Bickering Doesn't Make a Deal.' *Globe and Mail*, 9 February.

Hocking, Brian. 2004. 'Changing the Terms of Trade Policy Making: From the "Club" to the "Multistakeholder" Model.' *World Trade Review* 3:3–26.

Keating, Tom. 2002. *Canada and the World Order: The Multilateralist Tradition in Canadian Foreign Policy*. 2nd ed. Toronto: Oxford University Press.

Keohane, Robert O. 2003. 'Global Governance and Democratic Accountability.' In *Taming Globalization: Frontiers of Governance*, edited by David Held and Mathias Koenig-Archibugi, 130–59. Cambridge: Polity.

Kukucha, Christopher J. 2004. 'The Role of Provinces in Canadian Foreign Trade Policy: Multi-Level Governance and Sub-National Interests in the Twenty-first Century.' *Policy and Society* 23 (3): 113–34.

– 2008. *The Provinces and Canadian Foreign Trade Policy*. Vancouver: UBC Press.

MacLaren, Roy. 2008. 'Free Trade Comment: Why a Canada-EU Deal Matters.' *Globe and Mail*, 15 October.

Majone, Giandomenico. 1994. *Independence vs. Accountability? Non-Majoritarian Institutions and Democratic Governance in Europe*. EUI Working Paper SPS No. 94/3. Florence: European University Institute.

– 2001. 'Two Logics of Delegation: Agency and Fiduciary Relations in EU Governance.' *European Union Politics* 2:103–21.

Mendelsohn, Matthew, Robert Wolfe, and Andrew Parkin. 2001. 'Globalization, Trade Policy, and the Permissive Consensus in Canada.' Working Paper. Kingston, ON: School of Policy Studies, Queen's University. http://www.queensu.ca/sps/publications/workingpapers/27.pdf.

Munton, Don, and Tom Keating. 2001. 'Internationalism and the Canadian Public.' *Canadian Journal of Political Science* 34 (3): 517–49.

Nossal, Kim. 1997. *The Politics of Canadian Foreign Policy*. 3rd ed. Scarborough, ON: Prentice Hall.

O'Donnell, Guillermo A. 1998. 'Horizontal Accountability in New Democracies.' *Journal of Democracy* 93 (3): 112–26.

O'Neil, Peter. 2009. 'Objections Won't Scuttle Trade: EU; N.L. Premier Danny William Opposes Deal, but Officials Say There's Enough Canadian Support.' *Edmonton Journal*, 24 February.

Ontario Ministry of Economic Development and Trade. 2010. 'Ontario Seeks Your Views on the Canada-EU Comprehensive Economic and Trade Agreement Negotiations.' http://www.ontariocanada.com/ontcan/1medt/en/about_eu_en.jsp.

Roy, J.-Y. 2005. 'Private Members' Business: Hansard.' House of Commons, 18 May. Access at: http://www.parl.gc.ca/38/1/parlbus/chambus/house/debates/101_2005–05–18/han101_1800-e.htm.

Schedler, Andreas. 1999. 'Conceptualizing Accountability.' In *Power and Accountability in New Democracies*, edited by Andreas Schedler, Larry Diamond, and Marc F. Plattner, 13–28. Boulder, CO: Lynne Rienner.

Séguin, Rhéal. 2008. 'Sarkozy's Visit to Cement New Ties with Quebec; Province Courting EU with Free-Trade Agreement as French President Gets Set for Unprecedented Speech at Legislature Next Month.' *Globe and Mail*, 20 Sept.

Skogstad, Grace. 2008. 'Canadian Federalism, International Trade, and Regional Market Integration in an Age of Complex Sovereignty.' In *Canadian Federalism: Performance, Effectiveness, and Legitimacy*, edited by Herman Bakvis and Grace Skogstad, 223–45. Toronto: Oxford University Press.

Taber, Jane, and Rhéal Séguin. 2009. 'Harper Talks Free Trade with European Union; Quebec Takes Seat at Table Saying Provinces Want to Influence Deal, but Nfld. Opposes EU Discussions Due to Seal-Product Ban.' *Globe and Mail*, 7 May.

Todgham Cherniak, Cyndee. 2010. 'Canada–European Union CETA Negotiations: What We Have Is a Failure to Communicate.' Trade Lawyers Blog. 24 January. http://www.tradelawyersblog.com/blog/article/canada-european-union-ceta-negotiations-what-we-have-is-a-failure-to-communicate.

Wolfe, Robert, and Matthew Mendelsohn. 2004. 'Embedded Liberalism in the Global Era.' *International Journal* 59 (4): 261–80.

10 The No Child Left Behind Act and Educational Accountability in the United States[1]

PAUL MANNA

Since the 1960s in the United States, developments in education policy have altered relationships between federal, state, and local overseers of the nation's elementary and secondary schools. This chapter examines those relationships, focusing in particular on the No Child Left Behind Act (NCLB), the most ambitious federal effort to hold schools accountable for academic performance. Passed by the United States Congress in December 2001 and signed into law on 8 January 2002 by President George W. Bush, NCLB was the latest reauthorization of the Elementary and Secondary Education Act of 1965 (ESEA), the federal government's primary law addressing American schools.[2] Since 2001, the country's experience with NCLB has revealed how federal efforts to promote educational accountability are fundamentally limited by the intergovernmental actors that craft, interpret, and implement education policy in the United States. Examining NCLB's performance requires one to consider federal actions, but equally important has been behaviour in state and local venues.

Even as state education officials and local decision-makers took their procedural cues from NCLB, a federal law, their own policy choices imputed specific meaning to the law's core concepts such as educational equity, excellence, and accountability. As such, NCLB did not amount to a federal takeover of the nation's system of elementary and secondary education. Rather, although NCLB demanded greater quality in American schools, its accountability framework afforded state governments with much leeway to define the substantive meaning of quality. Further, as with all federal education laws, NCLB relied heavily on states and local school districts to make the law's provisions work. As a result, NCLB really led to the creation of fifty different systems of educational accountability, one for each state, along with local adaptations, rather than one coherent federal system that many people wrongfully believe now exists in the United States.

The four sections in this chapter analyse some of NCLB's key goals, mechanisms, and results to illustrate how educational accountability and intergovernmental policy implementation operated in the United States after 2001. The chapter also reflects on NCLB alongside policy changes in Canada that have influenced the politics and practice of intergovernmental accountability. The first section briefly describes the landscape upon which American education policy is made and implemented. The second summarizes the principal accountability mechanisms of NCLB, which connected governments across federal, state, and local levels. The third considers some of NCLB's effects on policy conflict, policy development, and policy legitimacy. The final section concludes.

Overall, the chapter shows that despite producing some positive impacts that are worth recognizing, given the highly fragmented nature of educational governance and administration in the United States, NCLB fell short of achieving its primary goal of promoting accountability for educational results. Two particular lessons emerge that speak to Canada's experiences and its own accountability reforms that have unfolded since the mid-1990s. NCLB reveals how central governments can be challenged to impose more uniform accountability expectations when policies are multidimensional and serve numerous diverse communities. It also shows how transparency is only one of several elements required of leaders who aim to craft systems that promote greater public involvement in holding governments to account.

Institutions and Finance

A popular saying in the United States maintains that elementary and secondary (K–12) education is a national concern, a state responsibility, and a local function.[3] That portrayal foreshadows why the country has struggled to design and implement a coherent system of educational accountability. Befitting of the diversity of people and cultures that inhabit the United States, a view of education from 30,000 feet reveals a largely decentralized and highly variable system. Consider two important measures of this system-wide variation: the institutions responsible for designing and implementing education policy and the division of labour for funding education across levels of government.

The American intergovernmental system contains institutions at all levels that influence the design and implementation of education policy.

When considering accountability for educational results, three points about these institutions are worth elaborating. First, consider local factors. As in Canada, implementation of education policy in the United States occurs in diverse local settings including large urban centres, upper-class and working-class suburbs, small quiet towns, and isolated rural communities. Those locales educate children with myriad ethnic, linguistic, and socioeconomic backgrounds ranging from the most to least economically advantaged.

In contrast to its Canadian neighbours, though, the United States maintains many more local institutions to govern and implement education policy. Such differences exist even when one accounts for the overall population differences between the two countries. The United States maintains almost 14,000 local school districts – each, typically, with its own governing board and education bureaucracies – and nearly 100,000 public schools. Such a fragmented administrative environment creates significant challenges for any accountability regime aiming to standardize practice or measurement of progress across the country.

Second, until the early 1990s, the federal government had been a minor player in the promotion of educational accountability. Before then, federal policies or major federal court decisions in education tended to focus on one or two activities, and sometimes both. Federal actions promoted greater access to educational opportunities for previously disenfranchised or marginalized groups, especially students of racial, ethnic, or linguistic minorities and students with disabilities. Also, the federal government redistributed financial resources to assist communities with large numbers of economically disadvantaged children (Cross 2004; Kaestle and Smith 1982). Those activities still persist and remain major centres of federal attention. But the idea that federal officials would promulgate laws, regulations, or decisions designed to hold schools accountable for academic performance began to emerge seriously only with the ESEA reauthorization of 1994, called the Improving America's Schools Act (IASA), which NCLB extended in 2001 (Jennings 1998; Manna 2006). The main reasons for that historically light federal footprint on accountability matters were the country's tradition of state and local control of education and the fact that the U.S. Constitution does not mention education explicitly.

Third, and finally, is the crucial role of state governments, which have become increasingly important since the 1970s. Several forces have promoted a surge of state interest and involvement in education, including shifts in economic conditions that led governors and state legislators – prompted by the business community – to become more interested in educational quality; state court decisions and subsequent legislative enactments that gave states more power over school funding vis-à-vis local communities; and finally, the rise of the educational standards movement (Evans, Murray, and Schwab 1997; Murphy 1990; Vinovskis 2008). The last development, which began in earnest during the 1980s and accelerated during the 1990s after a major summit of governors and President George H.W. Bush in 1989, helped establish the idea that schools would enjoy greater success if they assisted students in meeting challenging standards in key academic subjects. From the state standards movement emerged several governors who eventually exercised substantial power on the national stage, helping to propel the standards movement forward.

One reason why states wield tremendous power in education is the pivot point they inhabit in the American intergovernmental system. Education receives explicit and often detailed attention in state constitutions, which empowers state officials to craft laws establishing systems governing teaching and learning in local communities. The 14,000 school districts mentioned earlier, although governed by locally elected boards, are essentially administrative agents of the states that can be created, dissolved, or merged by state-level decisions. At the same time, states are crucial conduits for major federal policies that are designed to affect educational opportunities and practices in schools (Epstein 2004). For most federal education policies, administrators in the U.S. Department of Education rarely deal directly with local districts or schools. Instead, federal officials rely upon the states, who themselves rely on school district personnel to administer federal initiatives in local communities. Those links between federal, state, and local institutions create challenging administrative realities that have implications for how accountability policies unfold in practice.

Further complicating the picture is that many state education department employees administer federal programs while other different state department staff focus on state-developed programs and initiatives (General Accounting Office 1994). Often these federal and state programs operate on parallel but rarely intersecting tracks, sometimes called 'program silos,' that create fragmented regulatory and administrative environments (Hill 2000). Those dual roles of state agencies can complicate the efforts of staff or elected officials in governors' offices, legislatures, and state boards of education as they attempt to oversee the daily workings of state education departments. It also can challenge local school district officials, who must manage relationships with states while adhering to federal and state requirements that state agency officials interpret and enforce.

Examining the sources of revenue for K–12 education reveals additional insights about the relationships between federal, state, and local governments.[4] Overall revenue patterns across the last four decades suggest two main conclusions that are relevant for discussions of accountability. First, as a percentage of all K–12 education revenues, federal contributions have remained quite steady, typically hovering between 7 and 10 per cent. Second, of the remaining 90 per cent or so, revenues from state sources now exceed those from local communities – a trend that emerged in the mid-1990s. During the 2008–9 school year, the most recent for which data are available, states contributed 49 per cent and local governments 41 per cent of the funds that finance American schools, while the remaining 10 per cent came from the federal government. This division of financial labour contrasts with Canada's arrangement, where provincial governments wield near absolute authority over the finance of public education.[5]

Breaking down the patterns of revenue by states shows an additional layer of diversity. State and local contributions can vary widely. Within individual states, additional data from 2008–9 show that state contributions range from a high of 86 per cent in Vermont to a low of 28 per cent in Illinois. The vast majority of states shoulder between 35 and 65 per cent of the funding burden. There is also variation in the amount of federal money flowing into each state. Although all states receive federal education funds, federal contributions as a percentage of all revenues for K–12 education vary from 4 per cent in New Jersey and Connecticut to 16 per cent in Mississippi, Louisiana, and South Dakota. A main factor driving these differences is state-level poverty rates, which large federal education programs rely upon heavily to determine state allocations.

The No Child Left Behind Act

Over time, federal, state, and local governments have produced numerous 'educational accountability' policies in the United States. Sometimes, local school districts have promulgated such policies to hold their own schools accountable; in other cases, state governments have enacted laws to hold districts and schools accountable; and several federal policies have emerged to hold states and local districts accountable. In general, the vast majority of intergovernmental policies promoting accountability have prioritized adherence to bureaucratic rules and typically have been part of auditing requirements associated with the receipt of government grants.

In fact, for most of their histories, state education agencies and the U.S. Department of Education, which opened in 1980, have existed primarily as large grant-making machines dispensing federal and state dollars and then monitoring how and where the money was spent.[6] Until relatively recently, little if any of that monitoring involved holding recipients accountable for whether substantive educational outcomes – such as higher student achievement or improved high school graduation rates – had resulted. In instances where substantive – rather than simply process-oriented – performance was measured, typically the accountability system attached limited consequences for results. High or low performance rarely would trigger rewards or tough interventions, especially when the distribution of federal education aid to states and local districts was involved. So although these systems were oriented around 'command and control,' as Graefe, Simmons, and White describe in their accountability framework in the opening chapter, enforcement of grant program requirements often was weak and rarely triggered the recapturing of funds.

The passage of NCLB, which extended the accountability elements of its predecessor law, the IASA, nevertheless represented a new venture in educational accountability for federal policymakers. Although not altering the balance of financial power discussed earlier (the federal contribution still amounts to pennies on the dollar), NCLB was the first major federal attempt to foster accountability in education for both process requirements and the production of substantive outcomes. Some authors have dubbed it a federal takeover, representing a fundamental shift away from traditions of state and local control of American schools (McGuinn 2005). Subsequent sections of this chapter will challenge that interpretation, but before discussing NCLB's implementation and impacts, the rest of this section describes the law's key elements and anticipated outcomes.

Overall, NCLB was indeed a massive statute that influenced educational policy and practices across the country. In all, the law contained more than four dozen individual program authorizations, the vast majority being quite small, that touched on several different dimensions of American education. Most crucial were the law's accountability and funding provisions contained in Title I. Since the ESEA's original passage in 1965, Title I has been the principal vehicle by which the federal government has distributed funds to eliminate educational inequity.[7] Formulas in Title I direct federal dollars to states and then school districts (states have no control over district allocations of Title I funds), using poverty rate and population as the key variables to distribute money. Still, given the need to develop broad legislative coalitions of support, Title I dollars typically flow to over 90 per cent of American school districts. Changes in NCLB attempted to increase targeting of funds to the nation's most impoverished communities, but to some degree Title I dollars still benefit nearly all corners of the country (Manna 2008).

As a condition of receiving Title I funds, NCLB directed states to develop educational accountability systems involving three main activities: student testing, measurement of adequate yearly progress (AYP) for individual schools, and the implementation of consequences for schools that failed to make AYP each year.[8] Let's consider these three elements in turn. First, regarding testing, NCLB required states to develop rigorous content and performance standards in reading and math for Grades 3 through 8 and for at least one of Grades 10 through 12, and then to assess students each year using exams aligned with those standards.[9] In other words, states were charged with defining what students should know and be able to do in those subjects and grade levels (content standards) and then determining how well students needed to know the material to reach proficiency (performance standards). These standards could vary from state to state and still be consistent with NCLB's requirements.

Using those test results, the law also required states to develop a school-level reporting system to guarantee that achievement gaps between advantaged and disadvantaged students were closing. Most crucial was that the percentage of students achieving at proficient levels or better needed to be reported by student subgroups. That requirement was intended to prevent overall school averages from hiding the fact that some groups were falling behind. The subgroups were defined by race, ethnicity, whether the students had a disability or were still learning English, and whether they were in poverty. The law set an eventual deadline that by the end of the 2013–14 school year, students in all subgroups would be proficient in reading and math.

Second, NCLB required states to establish a system for judging schools, based primarily on student test scores, known as AYP. Although one could imagine several possible arrangements to hold schools accountable for academic performance, the AYP system of NCLB was rather specific. Leading up to the 2013–14 goal of universal proficiency in reading and math, states were required to set intermediate achievement goals. Each year, schools had to have a specified percentage of students in each subgroup make proficient scores or better. For example, a state might have required that 55 per cent of students across subgroups be proficient in reading and math by the end of 2007–8. (Other states might have different intermediate targets.) In subsequent years, that percentage would have to increase, although not necessarily in equal increments, so that by 2013–14 the goal of universal reading and math proficiency – 100 per cent of students across all subgroups – was achieved. If any of a school's subgroups failed to have the required percentage of students scoring at proficient levels or better on either reading or math, then the school failed to make AYP.[10]

The judgments rendered by the AYP metric were based on an all-or-nothing approach. In other words, a very diverse school could have all but one of its subgroups with sufficient percentages of students proficient, and the school would nevertheless miss AYP. That school would be classified the same as another diverse school that missed AYP as the result of poor performance among several subgroups. In short, the law made no distinctions between schools that missed AYP by a lot and those that came up just short.

Third, NCLB required a series of consequences for schools receiving Title I dollars that consistently failed to make AYP. Although the law mandated that states rate all schools for AYP, only schools receiving funding from NCLB's Title I program – the law's primary funding stream that was briefly discussed earlier – were subject to its escalating cascade of consequences. Thus, unlike changes in Canada during the 1990s, which downplayed government-to-government reporting and attempted to engage citizens more directly in holding governments to account, NCLB's reporting requirements provided some of both approaches. Any interested citizen could access accountability reports for any school, which were generated by state governments and distributed by the state education agency and local school districts. In Title I schools, those reports guided state and local interventions in schools that failed to make AYP. School-level reporting thus created the potential for public naming and shaming as well as prompting additional required measures in schools that received federal aid.

Title I schools missing AYP for two consecutive years became schools 'in need of improvement,' which was sometimes referred to as being 'in improvement status' or just simply 'in improvement.' (In colloquial discussions, people often used the moniker *failing*, although federal officials resisted that term.) Those schools were required to allow their students to transfer to another public school that was making AYP – a policy known as NCLB school choice. Schools in improvement for another year were required to continue providing NCLB school choice, but also to offer after-school tutoring or other assistance, known as supplemental educational services. Typically, those services were provided by the school district itself or by for-profit and non-profit organizations that the state had approved.

Title I schools that continued to miss AYP were subject to organizational changes. Those entering a third year of improvement status needed to adopt at least one corrective action, while continuing to offer NCLB school choice and supplemental educational services. Potential corrective actions included making staff changes, decreasing some of the school's management authority over its operations, introducing outside consultants to help the school improve, extending the school day or year, altering the curriculum, or reorganizing some aspect of the school's operations. Finally, schools that continued in improvement status for a fourth year were required to continue implementing the prior consequences, while also planning for more major restructuring and then, if still in improvement, were required to implement that restructuring plan during their fifth consecutive year in improvement. Restructuring measures outlined in the law were essentially more aggressive forms of the corrective actions just described, as well as an open-ended option, which some reform advocates criticized as a loophole (Mead 2007) that allowed other state or locally designed approaches under the umbrella of restructuring.

Canadian readers accustomed to provincial sovereignty over education will likely find NCLB's requirements an astounding exercise of federal power, especially given that states and local governments provide the vast majority of funds for education in the United States. Even though, by constitutional design, state governments and not the federal government are the main stewards of American elementary and secondary education, the federal requirements in NCLB are constitutionally permissible. The primary reason is that when states voluntarily accept federal funds under NCLB they are bound to follow its requirements.

The federal courts have consistently upheld that proposition, and as a result, federal policymakers have used their spending power to force state action in several areas, not just education.[11]

Accountability in Theory and Practice

Despite NCLB's accountability demands, rather than fundamentally unifying the nation's intergovernmental system, the law essentially underscored and made more salient the pre-existing division of labour. As a condition for receiving federal funds under NCLB, the federal government imposed upon states and local school districts a series of procedural requirements for annual testing, school evaluations based on the AYP system, and the implementation of consequences for schools in improvement. But, among other things, states retained the power to define academic expectations in reading and math and to produce the tests that would determine whether students were proficient in these subjects. Further, states and local school districts possessed much discretion in implementing NCLB's consequences for schools that missed AYP. In fact, federal education officials expected that state education agencies and local school districts would work with their schools to do so.

Such patterns of interaction meant that intergovernmental agreements and understandings governing NCLB's implementation tended to be worked out along two lines of communication – an approach that had governed prior versions of the ESEA as well. A federal–state line of communication led to the development of fifty different state accountability plans, which the states developed and federal education officials vetted to determine whether they met NCLB's requirements. Even after plans were approved, states could request changes, which federal education department officials would evaluate. A state-local line of communication also facilitated implementation of those state accountability plans in local schools and districts. Echoing an earlier, more general point, these government-to-government relationships illustrate how states inhabit an important pivot point in the intergovernmental system. State institutions and policy were crucial for NCLB's implementation because they bridged the gap between federal mandates and local implementation.

In terms of the accountability typology that Graefe, Simmons, and White offer in this volume's introduction, a sort of 'command-and-control' approach is apparent, given that federal laws and regulations created a framework that states needed to follow as they developed their accountability plans and held schools accountable. The amount of leeway that states had to negotiate the particulars of their plans also suggests a sort of process characteristic of the 'incentive-compatible instruments' approach that the editors also outline. Still, NCLB does depart from both of these accountability types in two ways. For one thing, the courts' role was quite small. Regarding the development of state accountability plans, specifically, enforcement (or non-enforcement) from the federal education department was much more consequential. Also, the performance elements that often characterize incentive-compatible instruments did not exist with NCLB. For example, states, school districts, or schools that made large academic gains did not earn exemptions from reporting or other NCLB requirements, as sometimes occurs when overseers reward high-performers by lessening their administrative burdens.

Overall, NCLB followed prior versions of the ESEA in establishing bureaucratic process requirements while letting states define substantive goals (e.g., definition of content and performance standards). Key reasons for that arrangement were the lack of capacity in the federal education department to do much more and, most important, the nation's tradition of state and local control of education. That strong tradition had rebuked prior federal efforts that might have moved toward the establishment of national standards (Jennings 1998; Ravitch 1995). NCLB's resulting design had important implications for how the law's implementation would play out in the nation's intergovernmental system. The rest of this section offers illustrative examples to address three of the law's impacts: the nature of intergovernmental conflict that NCLB prompted, the opportunities the law provided for policy learning, and the extent to which the law fostered legitimate results that were consistent with the nation's broader democratic aspirations.[12]

Policy Conflict

Given the assumptions of NCLB's primary authors and advocates, it was unsurprising that the law produced intergovernmental conflict. A main criticism of earlier federal education initiatives was that the federal government tended to offer money to states and localities without demanding substantive results in return. NCLB broke with the past by increasing pressure on states and local school districts to design accountability systems and enforce specific consequences if schools missed state-determined standards. Although NCLB's predecessor law, the

IASA, did require states to establish content and performance standards and implement testing in at least three grades, it did not contain federally defined consequences for poorly performing schools. Rather, it left states to define those remedies. Thus, the consequences for failing to make AYP were a new addition with NCLB, as were the increased number of tests required. At least three dimensions of conflict emerged.

First, NCLB's prescriptive approach to accountability, based on annual testing and the AYP system, clashed with many states' own accountability systems that existed before NCLB became law. In prior years, state governments had developed a diverse array of systems to hold schools accountable for results. Some of those systems were a response to the less prescriptive IASA, others were not. Predictably, given the diverse institutional and cultural terrain on which K–12 education operates, there was tremendous variation in the quality and comprehensiveness of these state systems prior to NCLB. Further, states with quite different systems often produced similar results. Therefore, there was no clear consensus or research base to show that educational accountability as NCLB defined it – in particular the law's annual testing requirements and AYP system of school ratings and possible consequences – was necessarily the best way to improve school performance. As drafts of NCLB moved through the legislative process in 2001, for example, state critics argued against proposals for annual testing by noting that some of the highest-performing states in the country did not test students each year and possessed other systems based on different accountability models (Manna 2006).

Despite disagreements about whether NCLB's approach was best, all states agreed to accept funding under the law and therefore were obligated to construct accountability systems consistent with its mandates. But that requirement still allowed states to maintain their own separate systems to evaluate schools. State leaders in Florida, for example, were quite vocal in defending their approach, which rated schools on a sliding scale using the sort of A to F system that often appears on student report cards. Florida's system allowed state officials to note finer gradations in the progress of individual schools, rather than the all-or-nothing approach that the AYP system required. NCLB's defenders responded by noting that one flaw in systems such as Florida's was that they ignored the performance of student subgroups, which federal lawmakers perceived as a threat to equity. Florida officials defended their plan by arguing that it rewarded schools for making strides among its lowest quartile of achievers, many of whom would overlap with the disadvantaged subgroups defined in NCLB (Matus 2006).

The existence of federal and state accountability systems, which judged schools by different criteria, often fostered local confusion and sometimes anger. In some instances, schools learned that they received high marks from their state, which sometimes came with honours and cash awards for teachers. Not long thereafter the same schools would learn that they had missed AYP, entered improvement status, and were required to begin implementing NCLB's remedies for schools in improvement (Winerip 2003b). Because NCLB's accountability system did not always replace state systems, such results were possible and challenged local officials, community members, and parents to understand how to evaluate school performance, given the different conclusions that each accountability system reached.

Second, local situations fostered additional conflicts with NCLB's requirements, especially its remedies for schools that were in improvement. Local school districts were often unable to faithfully fulfil their obligations when states experienced delays in scoring student tests and rating schools for AYP. An ideal implementation situation was for schools to learn well in advance of the coming school year if they had made AYP. That would give school districts time to alert parents of their access to NCLB school choice or supplemental educational services. It would also enable schools to plan for corrective action or restructuring. But states were slow to notify local districts of school AYP rankings (Hess and Finn 2007). Some schools would learn of their status only after the school year had begun, making swift, accurate, and faithful implementation of the law difficult, even in communities that otherwise embraced NCLB's assumptions and requirements.

Another set of local challenges prompting conflict centred on the diverse conditions in local school districts, which complicated efforts to implement the law's accountability requirements. In urban communities, for example, frequently so many schools would miss AYP that it was physically impossible to accommodate all students who might be eligible to transfer under the NCLB choice provisions (Hess and Finn 2007; Winerip 2003a). In contrast, highly remote rural school districts also had difficulty implementing the law's remedies, but for different reasons. It was hard to offer NCLB choice when the closest school might be several hours away and alternative school providers had little incentive to start new schools in these communities. Some rural communities also failed to attract supplemental educational services providers to their locales, or they were unsuccessful in forging university or non-profit partnerships (a common strategy in urban or suburban settings) to help assist schools that had entered corrective action and restructuring (Government Accountability Office 2005).

Third, in addition to clashing with state and local policies and conditions, NCLB sometimes created conflicts as state and local officials implemented it alongside other federal programs. One example involved teachers attempting to serve students who were not competent in English, known as English-language learners (Government Accountability Office 2006). For these students, NCLB's internal tensions fostered implementation problems across the intergovernmental system.

Recall that Title I of NCLB included requirements for testing and AYP, but among its many other titles, the law also addressed the needs of English-language learners. In trying to facilitate state and local implementation of NCLB's AYP provisions and to serve this student subgroup, the federal government allowed states to administer tests to English-language learners in their native language for up to two years. States that chose this route essentially created incentives for local schools to prepare these students for state tests in their native languages, thus further delaying their ability to master English.

The strategy of offering native-language tests conflicted with the ambitions of other English-language learner provisions in NCLB. Another major section of the law provided funding and programs to serve these students. That section encouraged states and localities to help these students develop competency in English as quickly as possible, but native-language testing, which encouraged native-language instruction, undermined it. Interestingly, then, in trying to smooth conflict by offering states the option for native-language testing, federal policy choices heightened internal tensions within NCLB itself while simultaneously stoking conflicts between local educators who served English-language learners (Zehr 2006). Allowing these students to take tests in their native languages may have helped schools make AYP, but it also sowed frustrations among teachers in subsequent grades who expected these students to be more comfortable using English.

Policy Development

Just as NCLB stoked intergovernmental conflict, it also produced new state and local policies to meet the law's mandates. That broad outcome was predictable, given the nature of educational governance in the United States and federal officials' need to rely upon state and local governments to implement federal initiatives. In other work, I describe that process as 'borrowing strength,' whereby actors at one level of government can attempt to advance their priorities by leveraging the justifications for action or capacities available at other levels (Manna 2006). When NCLB became law, the federal government had neither the budgetary power nor the administrative capability to initiate a system of performance-based accountability in American schools. Achieving their ambitions to promote educational accountability required federal policymakers to seek leverage from state and local capabilities. As the borrowing strength model predicts, effective leveraging can produce policy changes that advance federal goals. But poor assessments of state and local capabilities can generate wasteful or even counterproductive policy responses from these levels of government. In considering policy development, NCLB's track record showed some positive signs, but at least one powerfully negative one as well.

One promising trend, which NCLB's emphasis on standardized testing and AYP ratings helped to advance, was the increased school-level use of student achievement data to make instructional decisions (Hoff 2007; Kanstoroom and Osberg 2008; Marsh, Pane, and Hamilton 2006). Interestingly, as state-level testing in reading and math proliferated in response to NCLB's mandates, local school districts and schools discovered that data from those exams were often the least helpful in guiding their daily work. Because exams for school accountability typically occur in the spring, and results become available only at the school year's end or into the summer, schools cannot act upon the results until the fall. In response to those limits, schools and sometimes entire school districts increasingly began to administer their own assessments at more frequent intervals. Those assessments were designed to measure students' progress and to adapt instructional methods when needed, with the overall goal being that students would master classroom material and be better prepared for state exams. Thus, decisions about lesson planning and student learning became more directly tied to empirical evidence rather than intuition or, even worse, stereotypes about which students were most capable of learning.

Responding to NCLB's mandate to test and report scores for student subgroups produced additional positive policy changes in some local communities. Two notable areas were in how schools worked with teachers to educate English-language learners and students with disabilities. Given that the law incorporated test scores from these two subgroups into a school's AYP calculations, some schools made efforts to help traditional classroom teachers and teachers specially trained for these student populations to collaborate. In other words, some traditional English or math teachers were likely to have more regular interactions with special education teachers and teachers who were language specialists. Further, school districts directed increasing numbers of professional development dollars toward training these teachers to better address the unique challenges facing students with disabilities and students who were English-language learners (Cech 2009; National Center for Learning Disabilities 2007).

Certainly, adaptations in local policies on data use and teaching of student subgroups were not uniformly positive. As with all measurement tools that generate data, there are proper and improper ways to use them. Some local assessments were used simply to implement narrow strategies of 'teaching to the test,' which prepared students by drilling them on disconnected sets of facts or test-taking strategies (Rothstein, Jacobsen, and Wilder 2008). Additionally, in attempting to meet the accountability pressures that AYP requirements created, some schools dramatically curtailed the exposure of vulnerable student subgroups to other courses and programs in the curriculum. A narrow focus on preparation in English and math, at the expense of science, social studies, and creative electives sometimes dominated those students' schedules (Rothstein, Jacobsen, and Wilder 2008). Although NCLB also promoted such negative local responses, it is worth recognizing that some communities used the law to improve the use of data and meet the needs of student subgroups whose academic progress received less serious attention before NCLB's enactment (Chenoweth 2007).

Positive adjustments to local policies notwithstanding, NCLB produced one overwhelmingly negative development that undermined its core goals of promoting academic excellence and reducing achievement gaps between students. In practice, NCLB's focus on process requirements rather than substantive outcomes produced state policies that were often consistent with the law yet undermined educational quality. This problem stemmed from a fundamental design issue at the heart of NCLB that flowed from the traditional allocations of responsibility for education in the American intergovernmental system. The law's authors imposed upon states and localities a prescriptive way to measure school progress (the AYP system) while simultaneously following tradition by allowing states to set academic standards and define how students would demonstrate proficiency in reading and math. That division of labour involved in designing and implementing educational account-ability created an implicit trade-off, which many states resolved in ways that undercut expectations for academic rigour.

The trade-off went as follows. On one hand, setting ambitious reading and math standards would mean that schools would have difficulty making AYP, especially as the 2014 deadline for 100 per cent proficiency approached. As a result, more and more schools, even some that were reasonably good or even strong, based on reasonable judgments, would be required to devote time and money to carrying out the law's reme-dies for schools in improvement. Undertaking those efforts would waste resources in some schools that perhaps needed marginal changes, not major improvements, and it would complicate state and district efforts to meet the needs of truly troubled schools. On the other hand, states could avoid having hundreds of schools miss AYP by having less rigor-ous academic expectations, and thus making it easier for students to demonstrate proficiency. Of course, students would pay the ultimate price of such a decision.

Unfortunately, the evidence from NCLB's implementation strongly indicates that states decided against ambitious expectations, thus pro-viding students with less than rigorous academic experiences (Carey 2006; Government Accountability Office 2009). Helping schools address the short-term goal of making AYP tended to win out over the long-term goal of ensuring that students were prepared for their adult lives, includ-ing future training in college, employment, and the ability to participate in their communities as informed, active citizens. In one of his first major speeches on NCLB and its impacts, President Barack Obama's secretary of education, Arne Duncan, advanced this view in very direct terms. While also praising the law's ambitions and its attention to the needs of disadvantaged students, Duncan criticized the movement to lower expectations. 'The biggest problem with NCLB,' he argued, 'is that it doesn't encourage high learning standards. In fact, it inadver-tently encourages states to lower them. The net effect is that we are lying to children and parents by telling kids they are succeeding when, in fact, they are not. We have to tell the truth, and we have to raise the bar' (Duncan 2009).

Policy Legitimacy

When read carefully, Secretary Duncan's primary criticism of NCLB implied much more than a judgment about the quality of state policy. It implied that a core assumption of the law's authors – that state-defined tests and expectation levels could serve as the primary basis for judging schools under AYP – was essentially flawed. In practice, state tests struck many observers as invalid measures of school progress. People reached that judgment in part because of the lowered expectations that the secretary mentioned. But that conclusion surfaced, too, because some of the law's most vocal critics suggested that judging schools primarily on the basis of reading and math performance ignored the many other purposes for which American schools exist (Meier and Wood 2004; Rothstein, Jacobsen, and Wilder 2008). A more valid measure would have required higher expectations for reading and math, and additionally the incorporation of other measures of valued outcomes such as the ability of students to participate in their communities as informed citizens and productive workers.

As scholars of performance management have argued, accountability systems can achieve their objectives when they incorporate valid metrics that provide program overseers and implementers with useful information (Gormley and Weimer 1999; Moynihan 2008; Radin 2006). In the context of educational accountability, federal, state, and local education officials, in addition to parents and community members, must possess confidence in the measures used to evaluate schools. At the school level, principals and teachers must believe that the information the accountability system generated was accurate, fair, and likely to help them improve future school and student performance. Fundamentally, the middling or low expectations that NCLB allowed and the contradictory results that sometimes emerged from state accountability systems using different criteria hindered the law from fostering widespread confidence in the judgments it rendered. That was a major shortcoming. Systems of accountability need to inspire confidence if they are to become the basis for organizational improvement.

Other aspects of NCLB's implementation appeared to undermine principles of transparency and democratic openness, which hampered legitimacy in other ways. A primary source of these problems was in the intergovernmental negotiations between the federal education department and state officials, especially those in state education agencies who had major day-to-day responsibilities for implementing the law. As noted earlier, in fulfilling their process obligations under NCLB, states had to develop and present their accountability plans to the federal education department for approval. As in any intergovernmental grant program, those interactions generated discussions between federal and state officials about which elements of state plans were acceptable and which required changes. Major conversations focused on the methods by which states would implement the various requirements for AYP. Those discussions included how many students a subgroup needed for it to count in a school's AYP calculation; the way that states would incorporate scores of students who received testing accommodations due to a disability; and how states would evaluate student subgroup scores to determine whether a school had made AYP. Even after state plans were settled, subsequent discussions ensued when states proposed changes in what the federal education department had previously approved.

As conversations unfolded, the decision-making process in Washington made it difficult for outsiders to understand the basis for federal judgments. Federal officials would sometimes deny proposed changes to certain states, but then several months later accept similar requests from others (Erpenbach, Fast, and Potts 2003; Fast and Erpenbach 2004). These decisions were not consistently put in writing, making systematic outside assessments of federal acceptances and denials impossible to track. It also complicated the work of state agency officials who may have heard one message from the federal education department but then inferred something different when discussing matters with their colleagues in other states. Given that these dynamics were sometimes difficult for state officials to track, one can safely conclude that officials in local school districts and average citizens would have had a nearly impossible time doing the same.

Despite the validity problems and lack of transparency on process matters that plagued NCLB, the law did produce some results that were consistent with important democratic principles. The style of school-level reporting that NCLB mandated gave all Americans more information about school performance, especially the progress of student subgroups. No longer could schools rely upon their elite students to make overall school performances in reading and math seem acceptable when in reality their disadvantaged students struggled. As a result, NCLB increased attention to the needs of traditionally underserved students. Even Secretary Duncan, who otherwise criticized the law for encouraging states to lower expectations, credited it with forcing the nation to confront educational inequities unlike ever before (Duncan 2009). In some communities, that attention inspired and gave local reformers added credibility as they pushed for changes in schools that desperately needed them. In that way, NCLB provided them with valuable leverage to accomplish their local reform objectives, a form of borrowing strength (Hess and Finn 2007; Manna 2006).

Of course, the added attention did not mean that federal, state, or local policymakers always took steps to alleviate persistent inequities. People could properly credit NCLB for raising awareness while simultaneously criticize it for failing to improve the experiences of underserved student groups (Wiener 2006). Also, rigorous analyses of NCLB's AYP system based on subgroup reporting revealed statistical limitations in what those scores could accomplish, further questioning the system's effectiveness at judging schools (Kane and Staiger 2002; Kane, Staiger, and Geppert 2002). Those limitations are important to note because they undermined NCLB's ability to produce valid measurements to promote intergovernmental accountability. Even so, despite the technical limitations, the embrace of greater transparency that the law favoured did embody a democratic principle worth advancing.

Conclusion

Although NCLB made some valuable contributions and better highlighted the needs of disadvantaged students, in general it fell short of achieving its primary goal of promoting accountability for educational results. The constraints imposed by the American intergovernmental system, the tradition of state and local control of schools, and NCLB's policy levers combined to produce this outcome. As federal policymakers designed NCLB to accomplish grand and noble ambitions, they failed to consider deeply and realistically the incentive structures they were adopting and the implications for performance measurement and accountability that those structures would produce. In practice, the law generated results that undercut its ability to be a valid measurement instrument that would promote needed changes to help American students achieve at high levels.

Although many critics of NCLB reside across the political spectrum in the United States, the law's reauthorization, which was supposed to occur in 2007, remains undone nevertheless, as of 2012. Disagreements among members of Congress and the Obama administration about the proper lessons one should draw from NCLB's track record, combined with the nation's highly polarized political environment, have prevented a revision plan from emerging that federal legislators and the president would accept. This political deadlock at the federal level and persistent state anxiety, given that the law's 2013–4 deadline for 100 per cent proficiency fast approaching, have moved Secretary Duncan and President Obama to offer states waivers of certain NCLB provisions in exchange for states advancing initiatives consistent with the administration's priorities, especially the priorities announced in their Race to the Top initiative – a competitive federal grant program designed to enhance state educational reforms (Manna and Ryan 2011). The administration's waiver proposal has sparked both support for the relief it promised and outrage from others who believed the proposal, despite its promise for flexibility, simply meant adherence to a new set of federal requirements. Further, some members of Congress were especially exercised because in their view the conditions states were forced to accept to receive a waiver went too far and amounted to the executive branch usurping the legislature's lawmaking function (Klein and McNeil 2011).

In all, given the evolution of federal-provincial relationships in Canada since the mid-1990s, the case of NCLB suggests at least two broad lessons for Canadian scholars and policymakers who are interested in improving Canada's own approach to accountability in education and other areas. First, the NCLB case provides a useful cautionary tale about the ability of the central government to shape the development of accountability systems at subnational levels. One reason federal officials attempted to assert themselves with NCLB's prescriptive system of testing and AYP was federal frustration at the pace of educational improvement in the states. While NCLB helped them to address those frustrations, importantly, the law showed how difficult it can be to advance otherwise noble goals in such a large and diverse society. It is interesting to contrast that result with the trajectory of Canadian education policy that Jennifer Wallner discusses in her chapter 11 in this volume. In Canada, a system driven by provincial leadership, not federal oversight, appears to have produced a reasonably consistent set of practices and expectations across the provinces. In the United States, a major federal effort in the form of NCLB was unable to foster a similar level of consistency in expectations or dissemination of best practices across the fifty states. These contrasting experiences suggest that the presence of an assertive federal government may not be a precondition for the development of a 'national' system of educational accountability. Scholars and policymakers in other areas beyond education would be well served to consider whether that same notion also applies to their particular sector of interest.

Second, NCLB shows that transparency is a necessary but insufficient condition for enabling citizens to play a greater role in holding governments to account. In the United States, NCLB did help make more information available to citizens, but it sometimes confused rather than clarified matters. The presence of multiple systems of accountability – schools might look good on the basis of the state's own metrics but poor on the basis of NCLB's – was one problem. Also problematic was the blunt instrument of AYP, which labelled schools as making adequate progress or not, with no rating categories in between. Helping citizens to understand these intricacies requires much more than making results transparent. That lesson is important for Canada in light of reforms from the mid-1990s that valued and emphasized citizen oversight rather than government-to-government reporting to foster accountability. The myriad intergovernmental agreements that link Canada's federal government with its provinces, especially in the complex arena of social policy, have the potential to sow confusion unless transparency is accompanied by clear reporting of metrics that citizens can understand.

As the future unfolds, it will be interesting for American and Canadian observers to track the development of a new and still-developing effort in the United States, known as the Common Core State Standards Initiative. Led by the National Governors' Association and the Council of Chief State School Officers, the latter an organization representing the leaders of state education departments, in 2009 forty-eight states joined to develop common standards in key academic subjects. Additional state-level collaborations have followed to write student exams that will accompany the standards.[13] Supporters of the initiative hope that it will provide states with a consistent framework that they can adopt to better serve their students and communicate more uniform expectations across the country to citizens and public officials alike. Importantly, supporters also hope that such coordination will occur without the heavy hand of the federal government intervening in the process. Such a view parallels the optimism in Wallner's chapter regarding how the Council of Ministers of Education, Canada (CMEC) has contributed to the effective and generally consistent accountability regimes in the provinces.

Whether Common Core will replicate CMEC's successes and, in practice, actually spur coordination and common expectations remains to be seen. Already some states that were involved in the initial development of Common Core standards have since decided to stick with their own state-developed standards instead. Additionally, the Obama administration has strongly endorsed the work of Common Core and even linked state participation to its own Race to the Top initiative.[14] It is unclear how well this added federal interest will accelerate the policy development and implementation work of the Common Core states or, alternatively, whether it may poison the well of state enthusiasm. Either way, the unfolding of Common Core as well as future changes to NCLB, when the law finally is reauthorized, will nevertheless provide additional useful lessons for the people of Canada and the United States as they wrestle with intergovernmental accountability regimes in education and other policy areas.

NOTES

1 I owe many thanks to Linda A. White, Julie M. Simmons, Peter Graefe, Thomas Hueglin, and Jennifer Wallner for offering valuable feedback on this chapter.
2 Use of the term *federal government* in this chapter refers to the national government based in Washington DC and includes the president, Congress, Supreme Court, and the federal bureaucracy.
3 *K–12* refers to kindergarten through Grade 12. Students in the United States usually begin Kindergarten at age five and typically complete Grade 12 and graduate from high school by the time they are seventeen or eighteen years old.
4 The statistics discussed here are from the 2008–9 school year, as cited in the U.S. Department of Education's 'Digest of Education Statistics,' http://nces.ed.gov/programs/digest/.
5 See Wallner's chapter 11 in this volume for discussion of provincial power over education finance.
6 Before 1980, the main federal education programs were administered by the Department of Health, Education, and Welfare. A government reorganization separated the education function from the health and welfare function, producing the federal education department and the Department of Health and Human Services – both of which continue to operate today.
7 Title I, Part A, which provides funds to local school districts, is NCLB's primary funding stream. From fiscal year 2002 to 2008, federal appropriations for this part of the law increased from just over $US10 billion to just under $US15 billion.
8 Because space is limited, the ensuing discussion omits two other areas in which NCLB tried to promote accountability. First, individual school districts are also required to make AYP. This chapter focuses on AYP as it applies to individual schools. Second, NCLB also established requirements

that schools hire what the law defined as 'highly qualified teachers' in core subjects.

9 NCLB also required the administration of science tests in these grades. However, the law's accountability mechanism, to be discussed next, did not incorporate the use of these science test results.

10 A somewhat technical provision in the law, known as 'safe harbour,' allowed for some exceptions to this rule. See Hess and Petrilli (2006) for a brief summary of safe harbour.

11 See, for example, the U.S. Supreme Court decision in *South Dakota v. Dole* (1987), which upheld federal requirements that states raise their drinking ages to twenty-one years of age in order to receive certain federal highway funds.

12 Many studies have examined the performance of No Child Left Behind. Interested readers should consult the large corpus of work published by the Center on Education Policy (http://www.cep-dc.org) and the U.S. Government Accountability Office (http://www.gao.gov) for a useful start. See also Gamoran (2007), Hess and Finn (2007), Kahlenberg (2008), and Manna (2011).

13 Information on the initiative, and the standards it has developed, is available at http://www.corestandards.org. Alaska and Texas were the two states that did not participate.

14 State applications for Race to the Top grants were judged on a 500-point scale. States could earn 40 points toward their total if they had adopted the Common Core standards.

REFERENCES

Carey, Kevin. 2006. 'Hot Air: How States Inflate Their Educational Progress under NCLB.' Washington, DC: Education Sector.

Cech, Scott J. 2009. 'Weigh Proficiency, Assess Content.' *Education Week*, 8 January.

Chenoweth, Karin. 2007. *It's Being Done: Academic Success in Unexpected Schools*. Cambridge, MA: Harvard University Press.

Cross, Christopher T. 2004. *Political Education: National Policy Comes of Age*. New York: Teachers College Press.

Duncan, Arne. 2009. 'Reauthorization of ESEA: Why We Can't Wait.' 24 September. ED.gov. http://www.ed.gov/print/news/speeches/2009/09/09242009.html.

Epstein, Noel, ed. 2004. *Who's in Charge Here? The Tangled Web of School Governance and Policy*. Denver, CO: Education Commission of the States and the Brookings Institution.

Erpenbach, William J., Ellen Forte Fast, and Abigail Potts. 2003. 'Statewide Accountability under NCLB.' Washington, DC: Council of Chief State School Officers.

Evans, William N., Shelia E. Murray, and Robert M. Schwab. 1997. 'School-houses, Courthouses, and Statehouses after Serrano.' *Journal of Policy Analysis and Management* 16 (1): 10–31.

Fast, Ellen Forte, and William J. Erpenbach. 2004. 'Revisiting Statewide Educational Accountability under NCLB.' Washington, DC: Council of Chief State School Officers.

Gamoran, Adam, ed. 2007. *Standards-Based Reform and the Poverty Gap: Lessons for No Child Left Behind*. Washington, DC: Brookings Institution.

General Accounting Office. 1994. 'Education Finance: Extent of Federal Funding in State Education Agencies.' Washington, DC: General Accounting Office.

Gormley, William T., and David L. Weimer. 1999. *Organizational Report Cards*. Cambridge, MA: Harvard University Press.

Government Accountability Office. 2005. 'No Child Left Behind Act: Additional Assistance and Research on Effective Strategies Would Help Rural Districts.' Washington, DC: Government Accountability Office.

– 2006. 'No Child Left Behind Act: Assistance from Education Could Help States Better Measure Progress of Students with Limited English Proficiency.' Washington, DC: Government Accountability Office.

– 2009. 'No Child Left Behind Act: Enhancements in the Department of Education's Review Process Could Improve State Academic Assessments.' Washington, DC: Government Accountability Office.

Hess, Frederick M., and Chester E. Finn, Jr, eds. 2007. *No Remedy Left Behind: Lessons from a Half-Decade of NCLB*. Washington, DC: American Enterprise Institute.

Hess, Frederick M., and Michael J. Petrilli. 2006. *No Child Left Behind Primer*. New York: Peter Lang.

Hill, Paul T. 2000. 'The Federal Role in Education.' In *Brookings Papers on Education Policy*, edited by D. Ravitch, 11–40. Washington, DC: Brookings Institution.

Hoff, David J. 2007. 'A Hunger for Data.' *Education Week*, June 20.

Jennings, John F. 1998. *Why National Standards and Tests? Politics and the Quest for Better Schools*. Thousand Oaks, CA: Sage.

Kaestle, Carl F., and Marshall S. Smith. 1982. 'The Federal Role in Elementary and Secondary Education, 1940–1980.' Special issue, *Harvard Educational Review* 52:384–412.

Kahlenberg, Richard D., ed. 2008. *Improving on No Child Left Behind: Getting Education Reform Back on Track.* New York: Century Foundation.

Kane, Thomas J., and Douglas O. Staiger. 2002. 'Volatility in School Test Scores: Implications for Test-Based Accountability Systems.' In *Brookings Papers on Education Policy*, edited by D. Ravitch, 235–69. Washington, DC: Brookings Institution.

Kane, Thomas J., Douglas O. Staiger, and Jeffrey Geppert. 2002. 'Randomly Accountable.' *Education Next* 2 (1): 57–61.

Kanstoroom, Marci, and Eric C. Osberg. 2008. *A Byte at the Apple: Rethinking Education Data for the Post-NCLB Era.* Washington, DC: Thomas B. Fordham Institute.

Klein, Alyson, and Michele McNeil. 2011. 'Waiver Plan Generates Relief, Fret.' *Education Week.* 22 Aug.

Manna, Paul. 2006. *School's In: Federalism and the National Education Agenda.* Washington, DC: Georgetown University Press.

– 2008. 'Federal Aid to Elementary and Secondary Education: Premises, Effects, and Major Lessons Learned.' Washington, DC: Center on Education Policy.

– 2011. *Collision Course: Federal Education Policy Meets State and Local Realities.* Washington, DC: CQ Press.

Manna, Paul, and Laura L. Ryan. 2011. 'Competitive Grants and Educational Federalism: President Obama's Race to the Top Program in Theory and Practice.' *Publius* 41 (3): 522–46.

Marsh, Julie A., John F. Pane, and Laura S. Hamilton. 2006. *Making Sense of Data-Driven Decision Making in Education.* Santa Monica, CA: RAND.

Matus, Ron. 2006. 'Progress on FCAT Has Federal Caveat.' *St Petersburg Times,* 15 June.

McGuinn, Patrick. 2005. 'The National Schoolmarm: No Child Left Behind and the New Educational Federalism.' *Publius* 35 (1): 41–68.

Mead, Sara. 2007. 'Easy Way Out: "Restructured" Usually Means Little Has Changed.' *Education Next* (Winter): 52–6.

Meier, Deborah, and George Wood, eds. 2004. *Many Children Left Behind: How the No Child Left Behind Act Is Damaging Our Children and Our Schools.* Boston: Beacon.

Moynihan, Donald P. 2008. *The Dynamics of Performance Management: Constructing Information and Reform.* Washington, DC: Georgetown University Press.

Murphy, Joseph, ed. 1990. *The Educational Reform Movement of the 1980s: Perspectives and Cases*. Berkeley, CA: McCutchan Publishing.

National Center for Learning Disabilities. 2007. 'Rewards and Roadblocks: How Special Education Students Are Faring under No Child Left Behind.' New York: National Center for Learning Disabilities.

Radin, Beryl A. 2006. *Challenging the Performance Movement: Accountability, Complexity, and Democratic Values*. Washington, DC: Georgetown University Press.

Ravitch, Diane. 1995. *National Standards in American Education: A Citizen's Guide*. Washington, DC: Brookings Institution.

Rothstein, Richard, Rebecca Jacobsen, and Tamara Wilder. 2008. *Grading Education: Getting Accountability Right*. Washington, DC: Economic Policy Institute and Teachers College Press.

Vinovskis, Maris A. 2008. *From a Nation at Risk to No Child Left Behind: National Education Goals and the Creation of Federal Education Policy*. New York: Teachers College Press.

Wiener, Ross. 2006. 'Guess Who's Still Left Behind.' *Washington Post*, 2 January.

Winerip, Michael. 2003a. 'No Child Left Behind Law Leaves No Room for Some.' *New York Times*, 19 March.

– 2003b. 'A Star! A Failure! Or Caught between Unmeshed Yardsticks?' *New York Times*, 3 September.

Zehr, Mary Ann. 2006. 'No Child Effect on English-Learners Mulled.' *Education Week*, 1 March.

11 Internal Answerability and Intergovernmental Policy Learning: Accountability in Canadian Mandatory Education

JENNIFER WALLNER

Federalism, which allocates powers between national and subnational governments, complicates accountability in many ways, especially when financial transfers from one order of government to another are involved. Where two or more orders of government share responsibility, they can transfer blame to avoid answering for their actions. Jurisdictional uncertainty, where no order of government is formally responsible, can also translate into an accountability vacuum (Harrison 1996). The necessity of collaborative action among different orders of government further conflicts with the accountability provisions demanded by the principle of parliamentary sovereignty, as there is no clear hierarchy in the governance structure (M. Brown 1983). Finally, as other chapters in this volume detail, the unavoidable intergovernmental collaborations may generate perverse reporting incentives, incoherent reporting practices, and incomparable data, subsequently jeopardizing the availability of accurate information that is a necessary component of effective accountability.

The realization of accountability is most feasible when the principle of watertight federalism is preserved and exclusive responsibilities among the different orders of government prevail. The watertight principle resonates with the principle of parliamentary sovereignty as the legislature in question is the sole authority in a particular policy field. In conditions such as these, logic dictates that answerability is more easily achieved as state officials maintain obvious authority and it is evident to citizens who should answer for decisions, actions, and outcomes.

This chapter probes the accountability regime at work in Canadian mandatory education.[1] Unlike other sectors, mandatory education comes closest to replicating the principle of watertight federalism. Barring some limited exceptions, the provinces exercise exclusive authority over the field, with little intervention from the federal government (Wallner 2010). Where the federal government increasingly intruded in other areas of social policy throughout the post-war period (Banting 1987), mandatory education remained firmly under the purview of provincial officials. Cost-sharing agreements and block grants did not come to dominate the field, nor did national standards formulated by the federal government emerge.[2] And, unlike other sectors falling within the Social Union Framework Agreement (SUFA), the health-care accords, and the infrastructure agreements, mandatory education has not seen the emergence of intergovernmental arrangements that have established horizontal (government-to-government) commitments to accountability. Finally, in contrast to many other policy areas, the administration of mandatory education continues to reflect a remarkably traditional command-and-control configuration with the provincial governments enjoying extensive authority over school boards and education professionals.

Education has witnessed the onset of concerted efforts by politicians and public servants to improve the quality of information available to parents, teachers, administrators, and citizens more generally. Driven by the belief that economic competitiveness rests in citizens' skills, moreover, governments across Canada have committed to measuring and improving schooling outcomes. From greater specification of curriculum standards and increased pressures on teachers to improve, common features across all provinces have been the development of mandatory assessment programs and the institutionalization of new performance-reporting regimes, following the trend of creating accountability systems built on public reporting. Consequently, instruments for further accountability in education are increasingly intertwined with mechanisms oriented toward policy learning and evaluation.

Despite the watertight principle, intergovernmental interactions are not absent from the education sector. These interactions, moreover, carry certain implications for accountability at work within the individual provincial systems. Recognizing the inherent interdependencies of public schooling, provincial officials and education stakeholders fashioned formal and informal channels for information exchanges and coordination such that provincial education systems do not operate in isolation. Efforts at improving performance reporting, moreover, have spilled beyond provincial borders. Under the auspices of the Council of Ministers of Education, Canada (CMEC), the provinces have developed standardized indicators and instituted a pan-Canadian assessment program to ensure the production of interprovincially comparable data.

International assessments have also penetrated provincial education systems, providing feedback that reinforces the domestic efforts of performance reporting. Put together, these intergovernmental initiatives have culminated in the creation of a new pan-Canadian reporting regime in the education sector. While not being used for horizontal (or province-to-province) accountability, the information derived is put towards program improvements and vertical accountability within each of the provincial systems. This outcome in education thus indicates how federalism and intergovernmental activity can strengthen and complement steps being taken within each of the provinces if governments fashion clear and consistent public reporting practices that are systematically and effectively monitored to advance both learning and accountability in a policy sector.

This chapter revolves around four objectives. It opens with a description of the vertical accountability regimes in mandatory education. The second section considers the intergovernmental dimension and maps out the connections for interprovincial learning. The third section evaluates these regimes with an eye to determining the interactive effects of intergovernmental learning on internal vertical accountability. The chapter concludes by considering the unique features of education that may contribute to or detract from accountability. The analysis suggests that the accountability mechanisms within the provinces are strengthened by intergovernmental policy learning, while intergovernmental activity is facilitated by the hierarchical accountability arrangements and considerable state capacity relative to non-state actors that characterizes the sector.

Accountability in Mandatory Education

Across the provinces, the political executives have upheld the principles of parliamentary government and the accountability provisions it mandates. All provinces employ a common administrative model that revolves around strong central authority vested in the hands of an individual minister of education, who heads a department devoted almost exclusively to educational affairs.[3] Administrative powers are parcelled out to local school boards (or districts) made up of locally elected trustees advised by provincially appointed superintendents. School boards oversee the management of local schools staffed by professional educators. Interestingly, in an effort to strengthen citizen engagement, in the 1980s the provinces mandated the creation of individual school councils consisting of parents, teachers, staff, and local community representatives. Despite this tacit policy of decentralization, however, the bulk of formal authority remains firmly in the hands of the provincial ministries of education, with civil society largely in the background.

The clear pinnacle of the vertical accountability hierarchy is the minister of education, supported by his or her department. According to provincial legislation, ministries of education are required to produce annual reports that are tabled in the respective legislatures. While the details of the reports vary, they summarize the principal activities of the ministry, revisit the goals set by the political executive and their subsequent realization, and provide pertinent information on finance and performance including enrolment patterns, student-teacher ratios, and graduation rates. Ministries of education also release strategic action plans, newsletters, brochures, and reports to keep the public apprised of developments and raise awareness of looming deficiencies in the system.

As a separate administrative layer responsible for implementing central decisions, locally elected school boards could obfuscate lines of accountability. If, for example, local boards exercise significant fiscal and policy autonomy from provincial officials, public answerability may be confused. Indeed, the authoritative influence of school boards has waxed and waned over the years. Historically, school boards enjoyed considerable fiscal independence, as they were allowed to set property tax rates unconstrained by the provincial governments. This gave school boards the freedom to fund alternative programs separate from those mandated by the provinces. During the 1960s, the provinces also curbed their policy authority over school boards and allowed them to direct their own agenda to loosen central regulations and inspire local innovation. Larger boards reaped sizable benefits from these decisions, as they had the necessary capacity to capitalize on their new-found freedoms and pioneer novel programs. In some provinces, powerful boards came to almost rival the leadership of provincial officials exerting considerable influence over the broad policy agenda (Brown 1990).

Unfortunately, the benefits of local autonomy were not felt equally within each provincial system, and smaller boards with less fiscal capacity found themselves falling further behind. Faced with mounting declarations that standards in public schools were in decline and that there was a general lack of accountability in mandatory education, in the 1990s provincial decision-makers moved to regain control (Manzer 2003, 261). One *Globe and Mail* editorial observed, 'The trouble with school boards as they exist ... is that they are somewhat accountable in theory, but barely accountable in practice' (quoted in Fleming 1997). Administrative restructuring thus became a pervasive theme.

All provinces initiated district consolidations to reduce the number of school boards operating across the country from 800 in 1990 to the current number of 427 (Fleming 1997; Manzer 2003, 267). Efforts to centralize control and reinforce vertical accountability further materialized in the spread of full provincial funding as the financial model for the sector. Most ministries of education reclaimed school board taxation powers and started covering the full cost of education with funds drawn from the general tax base.[4] Under this new model, school boards can no longer deviate from provincial mandates, as they lack the necessary fiscal autonomy to pursue alternative programs. Like municipalities, school boards are also prohibited from running deficits and face the threat of provincial takeover if they fail to adhere to the central regulations. In this context, lines of accountability are transparent, as there is a consistent hierarchy at work where provincial officials can authoritatively coerce school boards, compel them to provide information (to both the ministry and the public at large) and to adhere to provincial standards, and impose sanctions for transgressions.

Professional educators could also compromise the vertical chain of accountability as their services are contracted by the education sector. Bovens (2005, 198) explains that 'the logic of contracts implies a horizontal relationship, because both parties are free (not) to enter into the contract.' The accountability problem that arises here centres on the issue of whether or not the contractor can effectively evaluate and oversee the work of the employee. In the context of professional service delivery, such as health or education, such services involve professional autonomy and knowledge that may not be spelled out easily in contracts with measurable performance indicators (Broadbent, Dietrich, and Laughlin 1996).

Teachers in Canada, however, exercise only limited professional autonomy from the provincial governments. The bulk of their influence is felt in terms of industrial relations through the unions that represent their interests at the bargaining table. While significant in regards to salary, benefits, and certain day-to-day conditions in the classroom, the impact of the unions in other aspects of the education sector are more circumscribed. The centralized command-and-control model maintained by the individual ministries of education curbs the substantive autonomy that teachers could exercise. Across all public schools, teachers are required to adhere to a provincial curriculum, use provincially approved texts, and maintain certification under provincially developed standards, rather than codes developed by independent professional associations.[5]

The spread of reforms under the moniker of New Public Management (NPM) has generated scholarly debate on the potential diminishment or transformation of governmental accountability (Trebilcock and Iacobucci 2003). Of particular concern is the NPM prescription for privatization of public services, which 'can run counter to popular control conceptions of accountability that hold elected decision-makers ultimately responsible for that task' (Skogstad and Wallner 2009, 11). Despite the infiltration of NPM-styled reforms, the traditional, publicly run configuration for schooling has remained largely intact. Privatization carried little weight with Canadian educators, with the result that elected decision-makers have retained their authority in the field.

The new trend that captured mandatory education is performance-based reporting. Similar to the revolution in health care documented by Patrick Fafard in chapter 2 in this volume, over the past twenty years, education officials have focused their efforts on establishing universal assessment programs and developing standardized reporting practices (Levin and Wiens 2003, 2). Mandatory assessments are administered at regular intervals, typically in Grades 3, 6, and 9. These programs are intended to measure the efficacy of the curriculum while providing the opportunity for officials to gauge the quality of teachers, administrators, and local boards in developing and implementing successful education plans.

Overall, the structure and configuration of the education sectors in each of the ten provinces is centred on vertical accountability relationships where principals and agents are clearly defined, in a classic Weberian fashion. Public accountability is exercised through ministerial responsibility, and all of the authoritative components are nested beneath this hierarchy. In theory, provincial officials exercise considerable influence over school boards and the education professionals who deliver public programs translating into a solid foundation for public accountability in mandatory education. Furthermore, while performance-based reporting has entered the education scene, the responsibility for monitoring results does not fall exclusively on parents or the broader public. To be sure, parental and public attentiveness encourages the effective monitoring and evaluation of educational outcomes. However, as documented below, the responsibility for measuring transgressions and applying sanctions remains firmly in the hands of the education ministries.

The Intergovernmental Dimension

The arrangements for internal vertical accountability within each of the provincial systems operate alongside a growing context of intergovernmental connectivity. Interprovincial activity in education has been a constant feature of the Canadian sector, despite the formal division of powers. Education inherently involves externalities that spill out over provincial borders and subsequently demand official attention. The guarantee of interprovincial mobility, moreover, means that Canadian children can transfer between provincial systems. If the systems are not somewhat coordinated, new students will face significant barriers in the advancement of that schooling that would compromise educational equality across the country. Similarly, education professionals may wish to move between provincial systems, and inconsistencies would impede labour mobility.

Furthermore, because the provinces are, to use Simeon and Nugent's parlance (2008, 41), responsible for the 'shared management of the federal system,' major disparities in educational investments and achievements would undermine equality across the federation. Finally, education is a vital component of a national endeavour, as formal schooling boosts economic development while simultaneously transmitting cultural ties. As Green, Preston, and Janmaat (2006, 3) point out, policymakers see education as 'a crucial incubator of traits of individual trust, tolerance, and civic participation which are said to underpin the relations of reciprocity in well-functioning participative communities.' For these reasons, provincial officials and education professionals have long engaged in activities that transcend provincial borders.

Early in Canada's history, provincial educators recognized the need for regular information exchanges and created the Dominion Education Association (DEA) in 1891, which later became the Canadian Education Association (CEA). According to its constitution, 'Any person interested in the work of Education shall be eligible for membership,' meaning that all components of the sector were actively involved in the association, from teachers and superintendents, to bureaucrats and politicians, and even parents and concerned citizens.

Important initiatives were advanced under the CEA oriented towards interprovincial policy learning. By the turn of the nineteenth century, the association was producing the student-transfer guide to inform provincial officials of course equivalents for students who move between provinces and institutionalized annual conferences to bring educators from across the country together. Despite these successes, by the 1960s, it was clear that the association's capacities as an intergovernmental forum were limited at best. The plurality of interests that participated compromised the ratification of coherent program agendas, and political leadership was impossible in the CEA, as it lacked a clear administrative structure amenable to elected leaders, meaning much was left in the hands of bureaucratic officials who could not commit their respective provinces to collaborative action. Therefore, in 1967, the provincial ministers created the Council of Ministers of Education, Canada (CMEC), as an interprovincial forum to strengthen information exchanges and mobilize formal cooperation in the sector.

Like other intergovernmental tables, proceedings are held in camera, with limited information made available to the public through press releases. Non-governmental actors are excluded from negotiations, although input from the policy community is supposed to be gathered at the provincial level and carried forward to the pan-Canadian arena. The CMEC Secretariat produces annual reports on its initiatives; however, there are no requirements for the individual provinces to table these reports in their respective legislatures and debate the relative merits of the accomplishments for the year. Each province reports individually to its respective citizenry on the various undertakings of the council, but this reporting is ad hoc and occurs at the discretion of the individual ministers.

Unlike other intergovernmental tables, the CMEC has not inculcated hierarchical or pan-Canadian accountability that would undermine the internal vertical accountability arrangements within the provinces. One province cannot dictate policy prescriptions to another, and the federal government is excluded from proceedings on K–12 education.[6] Activities are voluntary, and agreements are non-binding, thus unenforceable by the secretariat. Provinces are free to select which collaborations they wish to participate in, and projects can go forward without unanimous consent.

Collaborations have included a drive to install performance-based reporting, which emerged on the council's policy agenda as it took root in the individual provinces. For years, the provinces had been collecting and disseminating information on education according to their own standards and measures. This meant that comparing public education across the provinces was a challenge at best. In 1989, the CMEC and Statistics Canada entered into a partnership to establish the Canadian Education Statistics Council (CESC). Composed of the deputy ministers for education in the provinces and the chief statistician of Canada, the CESC has as its express purpose to 'improve the quality and comparability of Canadian education data and to provide information that can inform policy development in education' (CMEC, n.d.a).

The CMEC also pioneered a pan-Canadian assessment program to complement provincial initiatives. Originally known as the Student Achievement Indicators Program (SAIP), the assessment has been in operation since 1993. The program measures the achievements of Canadian students in reading, writing, mathematics, and science, and is administered to thirteen- and sixteen-year-olds from coast to coast. In 2003, the CMEC started work on a new assessment to reflect changes in provincial curriculum and integrate testing across the core subjects, rather than evaluating each one in isolation. These efforts culminated in the creation of the Pan-Canadian Assessment Program (PCAP), a new cyclical test of student achievement.

The CMEC also facilitates provincial participation in the OECD's Programme for International Student Assessment (PISA). The program assesses the performance of fifteen-year-olds in reading, mathematics, and science, over a three-year cycle. Through the efforts of the CMEC, the sample size allows provincial officials, education professionals, and citizens to see not only how well Canada as a whole performs relative to other countries, but also the achievements of the individual provinces themselves. The international assessment adds yet another instrument in the performance-reporting regime in Canadian education.

Evaluating Accountability in Mandatory Education

We can start at the base of the hierarchy with individual classroom teachers. Powerful sanctions are imposed on individual teachers who violate professional standards and behavioural codes of conduct. Provincial registrars set the standards for all teachers in the system, which can be administered by a central union, as is the case in Alberta with the Alberta Teachers' Association (ATA), or a semi-autonomous professional association like the British Columbia College of Teachers. School boards also check the behaviour of teachers, as evidenced by the Winnipeg Public School Board in Manitoba, which imposed disciplinary measures on two teachers for performing a mock lap dance during a high school rally caught on video. As a result of their behaviour, one teacher was forced to resign and the other did not have his contract renewed (Martin 2010).

Moving up the educational hierarchy, each school board is required to submit detailed financial statements to account for provincial funds subjected to a ministry audit. Deficits are not permitted, and boards that cannot balance their budgets risk the appointment of a provincial supervisor. The authority of the board is effectively suspended and is returned only once the fiscal situation is improved. Such vertical coercion has become a regular occurrence across the provinces as boards in Alberta, Ontario, and British Columbia have found themselves temporarily governed by provincial appointees. Ministry officials thus keep close tabs on the financial affairs of these administrative units.

Close checks, however, do not completely eliminate financial mismanagement. In 2010, a study conducted by the *Globe and Mail* revealed that rules in Ontario allowed retired teachers to supply-teach while still collecting their pensions. According to the study, a twenty-year-old policy meant to temporarily deal with teacher shortage has cost Ontario taxpayers millions of dollars as retired teachers have been allowed to 'double dip' through loop-holes and insufficient oversight of regulations (Alphonso and Hammer 2010). The response from officials was swift. The Ontario government immediately announced its intention to change the regulations, and a number of school boards planned to reconfigure the arrangements for supply teachers. This example indicates that when transgressions are uncovered, remedial actions are taken, translating into successful accountability for public funds.

School boards must also provide an annual education plan to the provincial government outlining key challenges and goals that the board intends to meet throughout the year. All members of the public can access these plans, and provincial officials review them to determine their feasibility and appropriateness relative to the objectives of the central government. Certain provinces have also taken steps to ensure that information is presented comprehensibly, rather than in educational jargon. Manitoba, for example, has developed 'parent-friendly materials … on outcomes and expectations so that parents and the public can have a clear sense of what is expected from students at various grade levels' (Levin and Wiens 2003, 662).

In principle, provincial officials monitor the progress being made by the school boards and annually assess the extent to which educational goals are being met. School boards in turn determine the extent to which individual schools and teachers are meeting performance objectives. However, in contrast to the explicit sanctions imposed for financial mismanagement, penalties, disciplinary, or corrective measures are less clear for performance shortfalls at both the board and school level. Underperforming schools and districts may become the focus of remedial efforts rather than punitive sanctions, which are neither as easily defined nor as consistently imposed, given that they need to be tailored to the particular cases at hand. Furthermore, in regards to individual teachers, unions work to actively defend the interest of their members and may protect teachers that are not producing successful results. Additional research is necessary to determine the role that unions play in holding teachers individually responsible for their performance.

This leads us to the peak of the educational hierarchy. Each ministry of education is compelled to produce annual reports that are tabled and debated in the provincial legislatures. These reports are a means to ensure popular control and maintain the legitimate authority of the government by making information available on the objectives and achievements of the ministry. Since the 1990s, the structure of these reports has shifted from a singular focus on inputs and processes to presenting clear goals and targets. In Ontario, for example, in addition to the traditional reports, the Ministry of Education also produces a Results-Based Plan to clarify core objectives, primary targets, and final results (Ontario, Ministry of Education 2009). Similarly, in British Columbia, 'the annual report has responded to the larger accountability agenda ... by using a framework based on the current goals and attributes of education as the vehicle for communication' (Hodgkinson 1995 19). And in Manitoba, the province produces an annual report on student achievement that draws from a variety of indicators aggregated at the provincial level, including marks in various subjects, grade retention, high school completion, and participation in post-secondary education (Levin and Wiens 2003, 662).

The efficacy of internal accountability in education is also apparent from the sanctions that have been imposed on provincial governments by the public. If the substantive policy agenda deviates from public expectations, political executives have faced considerable repercussions. In the 1990s, the British Columbia government was forced to back away from its preferred educational reforms because it failed to garner sufficient public support. More recently, the New Brunswick government faced a major outcry when the minister of education, Kelly Lamrock, announced his intention to eliminate the province's early French immersion programs in response to poor performance rates. In light of the reaction, the government decided instead to form the Commission on

Francophone Schools with a mandate to ameliorate the gaps between the anglophone and francophone systems (Commission on Francophone Schools 2009). The Ontario government was also forced to pull its proposed curriculum changes for sexual education in response to objections from Christian and Muslim groups in the province (Hammer and Howlett 2010). Provincial governments have even faced consequences if they formulate and execute policies in ways that contravene procedural norms, as reflected in the period of protracted conflict between the Ontario government and education professionals in the 1990s (Wallner 2008). Put together, this suggests that internal vertical accountability in terms of answering for actions is being maintained in the policy sector.

Despite the fact that all the provinces have implemented some type of assessment program, there are a number of pertinent differences in the execution of these assessments, with certain implications for accountability. Some provinces, such as British Columbia and Alberta, release results down to the board and even the individual school level. This means that parents can use the information when selecting a school for their children (when the province does not have boundary catchment rules), thereby putting schools in competition with one another on the basis of their achievements on provincial tests. Other provinces, like Manitoba and Nova Scotia, have resisted this competitive impulse in standardized assessments, releasing the data for only the province as a whole. When results are published as provincial averages, parents cannot determine which schools are generating higher achievements, and school and boards cannot use the results to compete with one another to attract pupils from neighbouring areas. Assessment results are instead used exclusively for the minister to gauge the performance of different boards and individual schools; public accountability comes into play only in regards to provincial performance as a whole over time, rather than at the level of the board or individual school.

Non-state actors, such as think tanks, have played an important role here, pushing particular agendas and providing information beyond what the provincial government may intend. The Fraser Institute has heavily promoted performance-based reporting, compiling data and releasing it to significant media attention. For more than a decade, the institute has encouraged the dissemination of assessment results to the lowest possible level by producing detailed report cards on school performance in Alberta, British Columbia, New Brunswick, Ontario, and

Quebec. Assembling publicly available student performance data, the institute suggests that the report cards are 'designed to help parents assess schools in their local district and across their province' (Easton 2005,10). Together with the media, the Fraser Institute and others like it have worked to elevate performance-reporting on the public's agenda.

Moving to the intergovernmental plane, pan-Canadian collaborations intended for policy learning have indirectly contributed to the internal accountability systems at work within the provinces. The student-transfer guide that was initiated by the CEA, maintained by the CMEC, provides indirect signposts to provincial curriculum developers of potential discrepancies between individual provinces. Decision-makers can then use this information to determine if remedial action is required to better align course content with counterparts in the rest of Canada.

The combined efforts of Statistics Canada and the CMEC have improved the production of interprovincially comparable data. Historically, researchers and other interested individuals had to painstakingly comb through individual provincial reports to determine provincial graduation rates, student-teacher ratios, per-pupil spending, and other pertinent indicators of investments and achievements in the policy sector. Today, such information is easily accessible and reliably compiled by the Canadian Education Statistics Council. Through its work, the CESC produces detailed reports on the state of provincial education outcomes that are now both temporally and spatially comparable, rationalizing the process and standardizing core reporting practices and techniques. Canadians can now determine such things as interprovincial variations in students' readiness to learn and literacy in core subject areas, while being able to consider interprovincial similarities and differences in features of the educational systems and cross-referencing those with demographic patterns and trends. These data have become an invaluable resource for provincial officials, education professionals, and others, including parents, interested in improving educational outcomes and holding those in charge of the systems responsible for their actions, further empowering both state officials and civil society through more detailed and effective reporting.

According to the CMEC, pan-Canadian and international tests are 'not intended to replace provincial and territorial assessments, but rather to complement them ... [J]urisdictions can validate the results of their own assessments against PCAP results as well as those of the Programme for International Student Assessment' (CMEC, n.d.b). A survey of the annual provincial reports reveals that most of the provinces provide the results from pan-Canadian and international testing when they are released. Ontario, for one, explicitly states that the province uses the results to assess the efficacy of its own assessment program and gauge the quality of its own curriculum, and makes adjustments accordingly (Education Quality and Accountability Office 2000). Because there are no mandatory requirements to include the data in provincial annual reports, results from pan-Canadian and international tests are not consistently reported in the same way at the provincial level.

Nevertheless, the CMEC Secretariat provides some standardization here. After each cycle of the domestic and international assessments, the secretariat produces detailed reports and analyses of the results, down to the individual provincial level. Strengths and weakness in performance outcomes are highlighted and explored, comparisons among the different systems are offered, and these reports become the basis for many provincial studies. The secretariat has thus helped to compensate for provincial inconsistencies in reporting practices.

Conclusion

Paul Pierson (2004, 114) has summarized the problems of establishing accountability. Outcomes are frequently difficult to measure. There are often long lags and complex causal chains connecting political actors to political outcomes. The complexity of the goals of politics and the loose and diffuse links between actions and outcomes render politics inherently ambiguous. Even if failures in politics are relatively apparent and the culpability of 'agents' can be established, efforts of principals to sanction those agents may be difficult. Many participants in politics (voters, members of interest groups) engage in activities only sporadically. Put together, these features of the political environment place serious limitations on holding public decision-makers responsible for their actions. The Canadian education arena sidesteps a number of these challenges in a variety of ways.

To start, the accountability regimes in each of the provinces are centred on maintaining clear vertical lines of responsibility that meet at the apex headed by the individual minister of education and the provincial executive as a collective. Starting at the base of the system with individual teachers and rising through the school boards and up to the ministry and government itself, the causal chains to connect actions to outcomes are relatively transparent and easily perceived by the public, which is extremely attentive to educational programs and results. Furthermore, through the efforts of the individual provinces and the CESC, the measurability of education outcomes is becoming increasingly standardized, and the goals of provincial decision-makers progressively clarified. This means that the potential for ambiguity in the sector is being reduced, subsequently increasing the capacity of principals (here both citizens and education officials) to make agents (school boards and education professionals) answer for their actions.

The execution and delivery of other social policy programs typically involves the engagement of powerful non-governmental agents that exercise considerable autonomy from provincial directives. The healthcare sector is illustrative. Ministers of health have noticeably less control over regional health authorities and medical professionals employed in the system. The ministers retain only formal responsibility for policy formulation, as the operational responsibilities have transferred to the heads of regional health boards. The consequences of this devolution have proven in some provinces to be catastrophic, as demonstrated by events in Newfoundland when Eastern Health, the largest health authority in the province, covered up mistakes in cancer testing and misreported the information to ministry officials, including the Minister of Health John Ottenheimer.

In education, no other component of the sector rivals the capacity of the provincial ministry. In every province, education is one of the largest line ministries and is staffed with former educators and policy experts who have detailed knowledge of the field. Consequently, while not absolute, the provincial ministries exercise considerable autonomy from the policy community in education. This is not to say that provincial administrations can do whatever they want in education, but rather that they have a marked ability to oversee and evaluate the activities of the various agents involved in delivering provincial programs.

Finally, much of the efficacy of accountability turns on the attentiveness of the accountee. Public reporting, comparable data, and performance measures are valuable only to the extent that they are observed and understood by vigilant citizens. Many scholars have expressed scepticism on the power of citizens as a force of accountability (Kershaw 2006, 200; Phillips 2003, 103); there are, however, some reasons for optimism in education. Education professionals are highly informed stakeholders with direct connections to provincial governments because they are public employees. They are important gatekeepers who are quick to point out when the government is not fulfilling its mandate. The CESC and think tanks like the Fraser Institute are producing standardized data that are readily available to any who wish to see it. Finally, as one former minister of education in Alberta put it, everyone watches and has an opinion of schools because 'Everyone went to school' (personal interview, 16 April 2005). Opinion polls consistently demonstrate that education is always a key concern for Canadians, and the sector receives extensive coverage in the media. Consequently, the idea of the vigilant citizen is not implausible in mandatory education.

Certain features of the sector also facilitate cooperative intergovernmental relations. First and foremost, the degree of complexity in intergovernmental relations is somewhat minimized in education. Internal administrative practices demonstrate strong consistency across the ten jurisdictions, meaning that coordinative discourse for policy construction occurs among individuals who maintain comparable positions, thus simplifying negotiations and deliberations (Schmidt 2008, 310). Second, non-governmental participants are excluded from the processes, and communication with stakeholders is isolated within each province. While compromising democratic deliberations, from an efficiency standpoint, the intergovernmental environment within which provincial officials operate is more standardized in education, potentially easing interactions among them.

Finally, trust among pertinent players is a fundamental concept of successful collaborations. In many areas of social policy, Ottawa's intrusions on the basis of 'federal statecraft' (Graefe 2008) have corroded the trust ties among government officials. Unfunded mandates, unilateral actions, and vertical (or horizontal) bullying are common realities at many intergovernmental tables. Furthermore, there are often strong incentives for the provinces to resist reporting procedures, diminishing the quality and quantity of available information. Dynamics like this do not appear in mandatory education. There is no hierarchical component in either the individual initiatives at the pan-Canadian table or in the organization itself. Particular provinces do not try to systematically dominate the agenda or impose preferred mandates on the others. Rather, as players in a nested game (Tsebelis 1990), the provinces build relationships with each other, regularize their interactions, and manage interdependence to produce cooperation. The dedicated secretariat of the CMEC also reduces transaction costs (providing an institutional history) and offers administrative assistance to the leaders of any intergovernmental project.

Overall, the message presented here is one of optimism. Accountability in mandatory education has not suffered as a result of intergovernmental activities; rather, the information being made publicly available has been enhanced through provincial collaboration. Improvements could be made, nevertheless. The CMEC could become a more open and transparent body by standardizing its annual reporting practices and having the provinces commit themselves to submitting these reports to their respective legislatures. Stakeholder engagement could be strengthened if the individual provinces institutionalized consultative techniques prior to the pan-Canadian meetings. Finally, while accountability for a majority of Canadians is functioning well, a number of groups are falling through the cracks. First Nations, minority language–students, and visible minorities consistently lag behind in educational outcomes, with little consequences for educational authorities. Such disparities compromise the equality of the system and signal that accountability in mandatory education is not yet a perfect regime.

NOTES

1 *Mandatory education* refers to K–12 or, in the case of Quebec, K–11.
2 This is a situation significantly different from that in other countries such as the United States, as documented by Paul Manna in chapter 12 in this volume.
3 Provinces vary in terms of the scope of the ministries. PEI and Saskatchewan merged K–12 and post-secondary education (PSE) under one roof; New Brunswick, Ontario, Alberta, and British Columbia maintain separate ministries for the two sectors; Nova Scotia nests education with cultural affairs, while Quebec's also includes sports; Manitoba's incorporates citizenship and youth; and, finally, in Newfoundland and Labrador, the ministry encompasses all stages of education from early childhood through PSE and adult education.
4 Manitoba and Saskatchewan were exceptions to this trend; however, both provinces increased central contributions to education, and Saskatchewan is in the process of introducing full provincial funding.

5 Canadian teachers are one of the most government-regulated professions. Unlike doctors, lawyers, accountants, and engineers, who have independent professional organizations, teachers work under a regime constructed almost entirely by government officials.
6 The federal government does participate in the CMEC negotiations when they pertain to PSE.

REFERENCES

Alphonso, Caroline, and Kate Hammer. 2010. 'Ontario Schools Crack Down on Retirees Who "Double-Dip" with Supply Jobs.' *Globe and Mail*, 25 April.

Banting, Keith. 1987. *The Welfare State and Canadian Federalism*. 2nd ed. Montreal and Kingston: McGill-Queen's University Press.

Bovens, Mark. 2005. 'Public Accountability.' In *The Oxford Handbook of Public Management*, edited by Ewan Ferlie, Laurence E. Lynn Jr, and Christopher Pollitt, 182–208. Oxford: Oxford University Press.

Broadbent, J., M. Dietrich, and R. Laughlin. 1996. 'The Politics of Blame Avoidance: Defensive Tactics in a Dutch Crime-Fighting Fiasco.' In *When Things Go Wrong: Organizational Failures and Breakdowns*, edited by H.K. Anheir, 123–47. Thousand Oaks, CA: Sage.

Brown, Daniel J. 1990. *Decentralization and School-Based Management*. Bristol, PA: Falmer.

Brown, M. Paul. 1983. 'Responsiveness versus Accountability in Collaborative Federalism: The Canadian Experience.' *Canadian Public Administration* 26 (4): 629–39.

Commission on Francophone Schools. 2009. *Education in Acadian New Brunswick: A Path to Cultural and Linguistic Self-Sufficiency*. http://www.gnb.ca/0000/publications/comm/CEF%20Report.pdf.

Council of Ministers of Education Canada. n.d.a. 'Education Data & Research.' http://www.cmec.ca/143/Programs-and-Initiatives/Education-Data--Research/Overview/index.html.

– n.d.b. 'Pan-Canadian Assessment Program (PCAP).' http://www.cmec.ca/240/Programs-and-Initiatives/Assessment/Pan-Canadian-Assessment-Program-(PCAP)/Overview/index.html.

Easton, Stephen T. 2005. 'Who Wants to Know What? School Performance in Canadian Provinces.' *Fraser Forum*. September. http://www.fraserinstitute.org/publicationdisplay.aspx?pageid=569&id=10617&ekfxmen_noscript=1&ekfxmensel=e0fa05764_34_2147483650.

Education Quality and Accountability Office. 2000. *School Achievement Indicators Program (SAIP) 1999 Science Assessment (13- and 16-Year-Old Students): Ontario Report*. Toronto: Education Quality and Accountability Office.

Fleming, Thomas. 1997. 'Provincial Initiatives to Restructure Canadian School Governance in the 1990s.' *Canadian Journal of Educational Administration and Policy* 11. http://www.umanitoba.ca/publications/cjeap/articles/fleming.html.

Graefe, Peter. 2008. 'The Spending Power and Federal Social Policy Leadership.' In *Defining the Federal Government's Role in Social Policy: The Spending Power and Other Instruments*, 54–106. Montreal: Institute for Research on Public Policy.

Green, Andy, John Preston, and Jan Germen Janmaat. 2006. *Education, Equality and Social Cohesion: A Comparative Analysis*. Houndmills, UK: Palgrave Macmillan.

Hammer, Kate, and Karen Howlett. 2010. 'Muslims, Christians Challenge Ontario's More Explicit Sex Ed.' *Globe and Mail*, 21 April.

Harrison, Kathryn. 1996. *Passing the Buck: Federalism and Canadian Environmental Policy*. Vancouver: University of British Columbia Press.

Hodgkinson, Douglas. 1995. 'Accountability in Education in British Columbia.' *Canadian Journal of Education* 20 (1): 18–26.

Kershaw, Paul. 2006. 'Weather-Vane Federalism: Reconsidering Federal Social Policy Leadership.' *Canadian Public Administration* 49 (2): 196–219.

Levin, Ben, and John Wiens. 2003. 'There Is Another Way: A Different Approach to Education Reform.' *Phi Delta Kappa International* 84 (9): 658–64.

Manzer, Ronald. 2003. *Educational Regimes and Anglo-American Democracy*. Toronto: University of Toronto Press.

Martin, Nick. 2010. 'Lap-Dancing Teachers Gone from Winnipeg High School.' *Winnipeg Free Press*, 19 April.

Ontario. Ministry of Education. 2009. *Results-Based Plan 2009/10*. http://www.edu.gov.on.ca/eng/about/annualreport/.

Phillips, Susan. 2003. 'SUFA and Citizen Engagement: Fake or Genuine Masterpiece?' In *Forging the Canadian Social Union: SUFA and Beyond*, edited by Sarah Fortin, Alain Noel, and France St-Hilaire, 93–154. Montreal: Institute for Research on Public Policy.

Pierson, Paul. 2004. *Politics in Time: History, Institutions and Social Analysis*. Princeton: Princeton University Press.

Schmidt, Vivien. 2008. 'Discursive Institutionalism: The Explanatory Power of Ideas and Discourse.' *Annual Review of Political Science* 11:303–26.

Simeon, Richard, and Amy Nugent. 2008. 'Parliamentary Canada and Inter-
governmental Canada: Exploring the Tensions.' In *Canadian Federalism:
Performance, Effectiveness, and Legitimacy*, edited by Herman Bakvis and
Grace Skogstad, 89–111. Don Mills, ON: Oxford University Press.

Skogstad, Grace, and Jennifer Wallner. 2012. 'Transnational Ideas, Federalism
and Public Accountability: Food Safety and Mandatory Education Policies
in Canada.' In *From New Public Management to New Political Governance*,
edited by Herman Bakvis and Mark Jarvis, 242–67. Montreal and Kingston:
McGill-Queen's University Press.

Trebilcock, Michael, and Edward Iacobucci. 2003. 'Privatization and Accountability.' *Harvard Law Review* 116:1422–53.

Tsebelis, George. 1990. *Nested Games: Rational Choice in Comparative Politics*.
Berkley: University of California Press.

Wallner, Jennifer. 2008. 'Legitimacy and Public Policy: Seeing beyond
Effectiveness, Efficiency, and Performance.' *Policy Studies Journal* 36 (3):
421–44.

– 2009. 'Beyond National Standards: Reconciling Tension between Federalism
and the Welfare State.' *Publius* 40 (4): 646–71.

12 Accountability Regimes for Federal Social Transfers: An Exercise in Deconstruction and Reconstruction[1]

BARBARA CAMERON

Transfers from the federal government to the provinces for social programs within provincial legislative jurisdiction played an important role in both the promotion and the erosion of social citizenship rights in Canada. The constructive use of the transfers was seen in the creation of a Canada-wide system of universal, publicly administered medical insurance (medicare) and national norms for social assistance under the Canada Assistance Plan. With the elite retreat from the Keynesian welfare state, the destructive possibilities were apparent in unilateral reductions by the federal government in the amounts transferred to provinces and the weakening or outright elimination of the conditions attached to the funds. As a consequence, social rights advocates in Canada outside of Quebec became increasingly concerned about accountability in the transfers. They continue to call not only for increases in funding for social transfers but also and very emphatically for the enforcement of existing federal conditions (in the Canada Health Act), the reinstatement of federal conditions that were eliminated (for social assistance in the Canada Assistance Plan), the introduction of new federal standards (for post-secondary education, housing, poverty), and the creation of new programs with enforceable standards (for child-care services). The alternatives proposed to federal social transfers – in the form of the social and economic union provisions of the Charlottetown Agreement, the Social Union Framework, interprovincial cooperation through the Council of the Federation, or devolution to the provinces – have not been seen by these advocates as initiatives to strengthen social rights.

The federal spending power and the social transfers that are based on it are problematic, not least because of the historic opposition to them by Quebec governments supported by social rights advocates in that province.[2] One can imagine alternatives, but these would involve either a major constitutional change that recognizes the multinational character of the country (the preferred option of the author of this chapter), or an unprecedented degree of cooperation of the provinces to create the mechanisms to hold themselves accountable for social rights.[3] As neither of these alternatives is likely in the foreseeable future, social rights advocates have to advance their demands to protect and expand social citizenship rights within the constraints of the existing federal division of powers. In recognition of this, the chapter has three objectives: to outline a framework for analysing (and constructing) accountability regimes for federal social transfers, to use this framework to identify the key elements of the three accountability regimes that have governed federal social transfers, and to apply this framework to the challenge of developing an alternative regime for federal social transfers that is consistent with Canada's constitutional order and with the advancement of social rights and that builds on the experience of the previous regimes of accountability.

A fundamental constitutional constraint is that Canada is a federal state with a Westminster system of government. This means that transfers of money from the central to subnational governments require an accountability regime that respects two fundamental constitutional principles: federalism and responsible government. The federal principle requires respect for the constitutional division of powers, which in Canada's case has evolved over time to give the federal government exclusive jurisdiction over unemployment insurance, shared jurisdiction with the provinces over pensions, and a shared responsibility with the provinces under section 36(1) of the Constitution Act, 1982, for '(a) promoting equal opportunities for the well-being of Canadians; (b) furthering economic development to reduce disparity in opportunities; and (c) providing essential public services of reasonable quality to all Canadians.' The provinces have exclusive legislative jurisdiction over social services, but both levels can spend on social benefits and services. Respect for the principle of responsible government requires that the executive branch be accountable to the elected legislature for spending money according to purposes approved by Parliament, even when the money is being spent by another level of government. Successive federal Liberal governments in Canada have attempted to design accountability regimes for federal social transfers that address, in different ways and to different extents, the constraints of these two fundamental constitutional principles.

This chapter identifies three accountability regimes that have governed federal social transfers to the provinces. Identifying these distinct regimes, however, is not sufficient for accomplishing the underlying objective of this chapter, which is to propose a framework for developing an alternative regime of accountability that addresses some of the problems with past regimes and accommodates the objectives of social rights organizations. For this purpose it is necessary to deconstruct an accountability regime into the relationships and main elements that constitute it. The chapter begins with an outline of a general model of accountability and the elements that are essential to an accountability relationship. Using this model, it is possible to identify the main accountability relationships that underpin Canadian social transfers. The chapter then examines the three regimes of accountability that have governed Canadian social transfers, highlighting the ways each addresses the balance between responsible government and federalism, configures the elements that constitute an accountability relationship, and succeeds or fails to address the central accountability challenges of federal social transfers. The final section of the chapter outlines an alternative regime of accountability that addresses some of the weaknesses and builds on some of the strengths in the regimes studied.

A General Model of Accountability

The question that underlies even the most basic relationship of accountability is who is accountable to whom and for what. The focus of this chapter is on complex, institutionalized accountability relationships that involve formalized procedures. Such an accountability relationship may be defined as a relationship between parties whereby one party is answerable to the other for the performance of commitments or obligations that are evaluated against criteria or standards known to the parties, and sanctions are applied for failure to meet the commitments. A regime of accountability as the term is used in this chapter involves one or more sets of formal accountability relationships.

In her study of internal contracts in the British National Health System, Anne Davies identifies four key features of an institutionalized accountability relationship (or what she describes as an accountability mechanism): 'setting standards against which to judge the account; obtaining the account; judging the account, and deciding what consequences, if any should follow from it' (Davies 2001, 81–2). These features are actually processes that she boils down to three activities: standard setting, monitoring (including obtaining and judging the account), and enforcement (89). This approach is closest to the classical understanding of accountability identified in the introduction to this volume, with the difference that Davies emphasizes the standard-setting process. An advantage of Davies's public law framework is its consistency with an established approach to accountability for social rights under intergovernmental agreements: the one used by United Nations treaty bodies to monitor country compliance with obligations under international human rights treaties, including those dealing with social rights such as the International Covenant on Economic, Social and Cultural Rights, the Convention on the Elimination of Discrimination against Women, and the Convention on the Rights of the Child.[4]

Slightly modified, Davies's framework may usefully be applied to the study of the accountability relationships inherent in Canadian intergovernmental social transfers. The processes identified by Davies presuppose an instrument that establishes the accountability relationship, such as the internal contract she studies, treaties, a piece of legislation, or an intergovernmental agreement. Other elements necessary to an accountability relationship are parties to the relationship, the obligations or commitments they undertake, standards or criteria against which the performance of the parties is evaluated, monitoring procedures, and sanctions. In the case of federal transfers, the funding mechanism for the transfer (cost-shared or block grant) also needs to be included as an element of an accountability regime. To summarize, using this approach to distinguish different accountability relationships involves identifying for each:

- The parties to the accountability relationship and the nature of the relationship (who is accountable to whom)
- The obligations undertaken as part of the relationship (what one party is accountable to the other for)
- The instrument that establishes the accountability relationship
- The standards or criteria by which performance in meeting the obligations is to be judged
- Standard-setting procedures
- Monitoring mechanisms
- Sanctions for non-performance and enforcement procedures
- Funding mechanism

This framework allows us to identify three distinct accountability relationships implicated in regimes of accountability for federal social transfers to the provinces. The first of these is the relationship of legislators to citizens for the fulfilment of commitments regarding social entitlements (the social rights relationship). The second is the relationship of the federal executive branch to the House of Commons for spending federal money according to purposes approved by Parliament (the responsible government relationship). The third is the relationship between the executive branches at the federal and provincial levels for the performance of obligations undertaken under the administrative arrangements for the transfer (the federal relationship). The regimes of accountability that have governed the federal social transfer have not clearly distinguished these three relationships of accountability. The result is a confusion of the lines of accountability and, most importantly, obstacles for Canadians attempting to hold governments accountable for promises made regarding social rights.

Three Regimes of Accountability

Three different accountability regimes have governed federal social transfers to the provinces at different times. These differ in terms of the balance established between the principles of responsible government and federalism, the priority given one or other of the three accountability relationships involved in federal social transfers, and the way that the elements identified above are configured. The first accountability regime I describe as the 'administrative regime' because the monitoring and enforcement is largely located with federal officials. It is typified by the cost-shared agreements of the post–Second World War era, including the Canada Assistance Plan. The second regime I call the 'political regime' of accountability to reflect the significant shift of the monitoring and enforcement of standards from officials to the political executive. This regime is exemplified by the Canada Health Act, which has been the model for many social rights advocates. The third regime is the public reporting regime of accountability characteristic of the child-care and health-care agreements concluded in the era of the Social Union Framework Agreement (SUFA).

Administrative Accountability Regime

The administrative regime of accountability is typical of the cost-shared, conditional grant programs of the Keynesian era and is found in legislation such as the Hospital Insurance and Diagnostic Services Act, 1957, and the Canada Assistance Plan, enacted in 1966. In this regime, the monitoring, reporting, and some of the enforcement activities are located substantially in the bureaucracies of the federal and provincial governments. The three accountability relationships identified above – legislators to citizens; executive branch to legislatures, and provincial and federal executive branches to each other – are configured according to the Westminster model, modified to accommodate Canada's federal structure.

The primary *instruments* of accountability are statutes enacted by federal and provincial legislatures and a bilateral intergovernmental agreement concluded between representatives of their executive branches. The federal legislation delegates authority to the federal minister to enter into an agreement with a province and specifies the mutual *obligations* of governments in the form of the terms and conditions of that agreement, including the requirement for, and some of the content of, a provincial statute. Through the bilateral agreement, the provincial government commits to enacting legislation that conforms to the criteria in the federal statute and to respect its reporting requirements, and the federal government commits to transferring money once the provincial legislation is in place according to the terms and conditions specified in the federal statute and the bilateral agreement.

Within this model, *standards* or conditions are set out in the federal statute, repeated in the intergovernmental agreement and again in the provincial statute. The social programs of the Keynesian era were influenced by the rights discourse of the time, including that found in the Universal Declaration of Human Rights, which provides in article 22 that 'everyone, as a member of society, has the right to social security and is entitled to realization, through national effort and international co-operation and in accordance with the organization and resources of each State, of the economic, social and cultural rights indispensable for his dignity and the free development of his personality' (United Nations General Assembly 1948). However, to the extent that rights were recognized in legislation of this period, they were not articulated clearly in the language of rights. Rather, they were expressed as terms of an intergovernmental agreement, along with other more administrative provisions, such as record-keeping requirements. Social rights were realized through conditions attached to the federal transfer, such as the Canada Assistance Plan's prohibition on making participation in work activity projects a condition of receipt of welfare or the requirement that provincial social welfare plans provide assistance based on need taking into account budgetary requirements. The *standard-setting* process included negotiations with the provinces, but it is the federal government that played the predominant role as a result of its financial clout. The federal Parliament was involved through enactment of dedicated statutes that set out the purposes of the transfers.

Within the administrative accountability regime, two types of *monitoring* were provided for: monitoring provincial compliance with the terms of the agreements, and monitoring the performance of the Cabinet by the House of Commons. Monitoring of the minister was provided for in the requirement that he or she report annually to Parliament on the operation of the agreements and on the payments made to the provinces. Monitoring of provincial compliance was done through a process whereby provincial programs to be cost-shared had to be approved by federal officials and listed in schedules to the bilateral agreement, which were updated regularly. In addition, federal officials audited provincial records and accounts. The enforcement mechanism related to provincial accountability was a certificate issued by the minister of health and welfare, based on the results of the auditing of provincial records, which would trigger the final payment by the minister of finance. Federal money was both a carrot and a stick, with the refusal to fund a program or transfer money the ultimate sanction. Yet it was federal officials, not Cabinet ministers, who were on the front line of monitoring and enforcement. Federal money was not so much withheld by ministers to punish non-complying provinces as transferred on the authority of these ministers to provinces once federal officials had determined that provincial programs and expenditures complied with standards contained in federal legislation. In the case of the Canada Assistance Plan, there was an additional enforcement mechanism in the form of the requirement that the provincial law provide for an appeals mechanism for individuals affected by the decisions of officials administering programs under the authority of the province. The penalty for the failure of an administrator to respect the provincial statute was a reversal of the decision in favour of the individual rights claimant.

The *funding mechanism* for programs operating within the administrative accountability regime was an open-ended cost-sharing grant, with the federal government contributing 50 per cent of whatever the province spent. The link between the amount of the federal transfer and provincial spending meant that a province had to document the amount spent on programs approved and listed in the schedules to the agreement. An audit of provincial records by federal officials was necessary before the minister of health and welfare recommended that the minister of finance release the funds. Cost-sharing can therefore be seen as a part of the accountability regime. There was a wrinkle in these funding arrangements introduced to accommodate the Quebec government's opposition to the exercise of the federal spending power in areas of provincial jurisdiction. In 1965, in anticipation of the coming into effect of the Canada Assistance Plan, the federal government offered provinces the choice of receiving the transfer in cash or tax points. The tax point offer included the safeguard of a cash top-up if the tax points resulted in less money than a province would have received under the cash formula. The Quebec government expected the tax point arrangement to make the transfer effectively unconditional, because once the tax points were transferred, there would be no way for the federal government to enforce the conditions. While offered to all provinces, only Quebec was expected to take advantage of it and only Quebec did (Vaillancourt 1994, 172).

The administrative accountability regime favoured the executive / legislative accountability relationship over the federal relationship, involving as it did an intrusive role for federal officials in monitoring provincial compliance. It was, however, the federal government's concern with the open-ended nature of the intergovernmental transfers and the requirement that it match provincial spending, more than provincial chafing under the accountability rules, that led to the demise of the regime for health care in 1977 and social assistance in 1995. Some of the conditions attached to the transfers did protect fundamental social rights, such as the obligation to provide assistance based on budgetary requirements. However, these were not clearly expressed in the language of rights but instead appeared as terms of the intergovernmental agreement, along with administrative arrangements.

The Political Accountability Regime

The Canada Health Act, 1984, is the example of the political regime of accountability, so named because it replaces the administrative monitoring of the previous model with monitoring and enforcement by the political executive. The effect is that disputes over provincial compliance with standards in federal legislation rapidly become politicized and result in highly public fights between the federal and provincial governments. On paper, the regime seems to correspond closely to that of the Westminster model, with the primary accountability relationship being of the federal executive to the House of Commons for the expenditure of public funds. The principle of responsible government, however, is undermined by the dependence of the monitoring and enforcement provisions on the political will of the federal minister.

The Canada Health Act does contain substantive *standards* in the form of five criteria – public administration, comprehensiveness, universality, portability, and accessibility – set out in federal legislation (Canada Health Act, 1985). The approach adopted by the federal government to the *standard-setting* process was, in the end, a unilateral one. This was the case in both the substantive (social rights) standards and the operational ones covering provincial reporting requirements. The federal government adopted this approach when achieving a provincial consensus appeared impossible, particularly after the announcement by the Quebec government that it would not sign another agreement (Johnson 1984). The criteria in the Canada Health Act do, however, reflect those set out but not expressed so clearly in earlier legislation and subject to debate and negotiation at that time.

The primary accountability in the Canada Health Act is of the federal executive to the federal Parliament for the expenditure of public funds. The main *instrument* of accountability is the federal statute. It is through the procedures of parliamentary responsibility that the accountability of elected representatives to the public for a social right is to be achieved. The *obligation* of the executive branch to Parliament is to report on the administration and operation of the act; the implicit obligation of elected representatives to the public is to ensure that the stated objectives of government policy as expressed in the act are met. These are 'to protect, promote and restore the physical and mental well-being of residents of Canada and to facilitate reasonable access to health services without financial or other barriers.' In the relationships of the minister to Parliament and of elected representatives to the public, the regime is similar to that of the administrative accountability regime.

There is no *instrument* establishing the mutual accountability relationship between the federal and provincial executives. Rather, the terms on which a province may qualify for federal funding are set out only in the federal statute. The requirement of a provincial law reflecting the federal conditions is achieved through the definition section, which defines a provincial health insurance plan as 'a plan or plans established by the law of the province to provide for insured health services' and then specifying in section 7 of the act the criteria that a provincial health insurance plan must meet. The provincial executive assumes specific *obligations*, not through an intergovernmental agreement but through the act of accepting the federal transfer. There is no specific obligation undertaken by a province to introduce a provincial law establishing a system of health insurance that meets the federal criteria. However, if such a system is in place, the province will qualify for federal funding. The implied obligation is then to maintain such a system in exchange for continued federal funding. The other obligation is to 'provide the Minister with such information, of a type prescribed by the regulations, as the Minister may reasonably require for the purposes of this Act' and to recognize the federal transfer in public documents and promotional material.

The main *monitoring mechanism* in the Canada Health Act is the annual report by the minister of health to Parliament, supported by a legislated requirement for provincial reporting as a condition of federal funding. Under the act, the minister of health is to make an annual report to both the House of Commons and the Senate 'respecting the administration and operation of this Act for that fiscal year, including all relevant information on the extent to which provincial health care insurance plans have satisfied the criteria, and the extent to which the provinces have satisfied the conditions, for payment under this Act' (Canada Health Act s. 23, 1985). The act delegates to the minister the authority to introduce regulations governing the information provinces are required to provide on the operation of their plans, but no other monitoring mechanism is envisaged. In practice, no minister of health has used his or her authority to issue those regulations, and certainly none has used the authority in the act to withhold funding if a province does not provide the information necessary for the minister to report adequately to Parliament.

The ultimate *sanction* for failure to meet the conditions in the act is the withholding of all or part of the federal transfer. In the absence of effective monitoring procedures, violations of the criteria often come to the minister through complaints of advocacy groups or through the media. The CHA spells out a procedure that the minister of health is to follow in situations where he or she believes that a province is not respecting the standards set out in the legislation. The minister is to consult with the offending province and, if the province fails to remedy the problem, the minister refers the matter to the Cabinet, which may exercise its discretionary power to withhold all or part of the federal transfer to the provinces. A provincial violation of the extra-billing provisions of the act triggers a different sanction procedure. The act makes it mandatory for the minister to withhold payment to a province for services that have been subject to extra billing and directs the minister to deduct from the transfer to the province an amount equal to that billed over the provincial fee schedule by physicians or dentists. While there has been some enforcement of the extra-billing provisions, the Cabinet has not used its discretionary power to punish provinces that do not respect the five criteria of the act.

The *funding mechanism* typical of the political accountability regime is the block grant. Indeed, the shift from cost-sharing to the block grant for health care was initially associated with a move away from conditionality. However, public opposition to the removal of conditions and, particularly, to the practice of extra billing by physicians led the federal government to reintroduce conditions through the Canada Health Act in 1984.

The strength of the political accountability regime lies in the articulation of substantive *standards* that, in the case of the Canada Health Act, amount to a promised guarantee of a universal right to medically necessary services, irrespective of an individual's province or territory of residence. The clear statement of substantive standards (described as 'criteria') in the legislation has been helpful to those proponents of universal access to health-care services as a right of Canadian social citizenship. The weaknesses of the regime lies in (1) the absence of effective monitoring procedures and the reluctance of the federal minister to make use of the provisions in the legislation regarding provincial reporting, and (2) the unwillingness of the federal Cabinet to precipitate public fights with provincial governments by invoking the enforcement mechanisms. In the end, accountability of the federal executive branch to the House of Commons and of the elected legislators to citizens is sacrificed to the goal of maintaining intergovernmental peace.

Public Reporting Accountability Regime

The public reporting regime was typified by the multilateral intergovernmental agreements covering health care and programs for children concluded in the era of the Social Union Framework Agreement between 1999 and the coming to office of the Conservative government of Stephen Harper in January 2006.[5] This regime departed significantly from the other two regimes in the balance between the principles of responsible government and federalism. While the administrative accountability regime conformed closely to the Westminster model of the executive–legislature relationship and the political accountability regime formally conformed to it, the public reporting regime all but abandoned it. For the most part, it bypassed legislatures in favour of accountability relationships between the federal and provincial executive branches and between the executive branch at both levels and the public. The public, however, was positioned more as a consumer of information than an active party to the accountability regime, having no effective institutional avenues of participation. The discussion below focuses on the child-care agreements concluded within the framework of the Social Union Framework Agreement, including the 2000 Early Childhood Development Agreement (ECD) and the 2003 Multilateral Framework on Early Learning and Child Care.

In the public reporting regime, the primary *instrument* establishing the accountability relationships was the multilateral framework agreement concluded among Cabinet representatives of the federal and provincial governments. As a consequence of the Supreme Court 1991 decision in the Canada Assistance Plan reference,[6] parties to the agreements treat them as political accords rather than mutually binding contracts. The statutory basis for the accountability regime is very weak (for more discussion, see Cameron 2007). There were no dedicated statutes setting out Parliament's purposes for the funding under the child-care agreements. Instead, the multilateral framework agreements focused on the mutual *obligations* of the governments to each other and, to a lesser extent, to their publics.

The multilateral framework agreements contained very weak articulations of *standards*. Instead, the language of shared visions, objectives, or principles was used. In the case of the Canada Social Transfer, the only substantive standard continues to be the prohibition on provinces imposing a residence requirement for eligibility for social assistance in the Federal-Provincial Fiscal Arrangements Act. The Early Childhood Development agreement did not contain any language that could be described as a standard, let alone a condition for a transfer. Instead, it listed two very general objectives (promoting early childhood development and helping families support their children within strong communities) and identified four also very general key areas for action. These are the promotion of healthy pregnancy, birth, and infancy; improving parenting and family supports; strengthening early childhood development, learning, and care; and strengthening community supports. The Multilateral Framework Agreement on Early Learning and Child Care was more specific in naming the area of investment as government regulated early learning and child-care programs for children under six, and identified the principles associated with effective approaches in such settings as accessible, affordable, quality, inclusive, and parental choice. The multilateral agreements also outlined the principles (*standards*) or criteria to be used to evaluate the progress of a government in meeting its commitments, which was to take the form of indicators developed through intergovernmental negotiations.

The *standard-setting* process involved intergovernmental negotiations between representatives of the executive branch (first administrative and then ministerial) at the federal and provincial levels of government. These negotiations were conducted, as intergovernmental negotiations generally are, in private, with the results being communicated to the public through the media at the conclusion of first ministers' meetings. Both the ECD and Multilateral Framework Agreement were concluded among all the first ministers, with the exception of the premier of the province of Quebec.

The mechanism for *monitoring* the performance of governments in meeting their obligations under the agreements was an annual report produced by the governments, organized around the agreed upon criteria or performance measures. There was generally a reference to third-party involvement in monitoring, but this was honoured more in the breach than the observance. The Early Childhood Development agreement committed governments to report annually on their investments and progress in the four key areas and to work together to develop a shared framework that was to include jointly agreed comparable indicators. It gave as an example of indicators the availability and growth of services in each of the areas. The Multilateral Framework Agreement was more direct about the reporting requirements. It committed governments to release baseline information by the end of November 2003 and to release the first annual report in November 2004. The agreement further specified the kind of descriptive and expenditure information that was to be provided. Both agreements committed governments to ensure that there were unspecified 'effective mechanisms' to allow Canadians to participate in reviewing outcomes.

The *enforcement mechanism* in the public reporting regime was public approval or disapproval of a government's performance based on the information provided in the annual report. Even though the multilateral agreements were occasioned by a federal promise of new funding, the withholding of federal funds as a sanction was explicitly ruled out. Both agreements contained the sentence 'The amount of federal funding provided to any jurisdiction will not depend on achieving a given level of performance.' Furthermore, funding was not tied in any way to meeting the reporting commitments. Ultimately, the *enforcement mechanism* was the ballot for both the performance and reporting commitments in the agreements.

The Social Union Framework Agreement provided for an *enforcement mechanism* in the form of a dispute avoidance and resolution procedure that was to replace or modify the role of the federal minister in determining violations of the agreement. The dispute resolution mechanism agreed upon for health care specified an elaborate procedure that was to be followed where violations of the Canada Health Act were alleged, but the final decision was still to rest with the Governor-in-Council at the federal level (Health Canada 2007, Annex C). Federal Liberal Health Minister Ujjal Dosanjh initiated proceedings under the mechanism around private diagnostic clinics in April 2005, but this approach to enforcement (or to the Social Union more generally) did not survive the defeat of the Liberal Party in the general election of January 2006 (Madore 2005).

As with the political accountability regime, the *funding mechanism* for the public reporting model was the block grant, first introduced for social transfers to health and post-secondary education in 1977. In the case of social assistance, the block grant replaced the open-ended shared cost grant after the 1995 federal budget. The government of Prime Minister Paul Martin made use of dedicated transfers, flowed through trusts such as the Medical Equipment Trust or specially named transfers such as the Child Care Transfer, as well as the umbrella Canada Health Transfer and the Canada Social Transfer. The accountability mechanisms were generally too weak to ensure that the funds went to the targeted programs (Anderson and Findlay 2007, 2010). Under the Canada Social Transfer, the allocation of money between social assistance (income support and welfare services), post-secondary education, child care, and other social services was not specified during the period the Liberals were in office.[7] In 2005, the federal Liberal government moved to a different instrument – bilateral intergovernmental child-care agreements – after failing to gain the support of the provinces to a multilateral framework agreement to govern a promised $5 billion federal transfer over five years. There were two types of bilateral agreements: agreements-in-principle and funding agreements. In the spring and fall of 2005, the federal government reached agreements-in-principle with all the provinces except Quebec, and the more detailed funding agreements were reached with three provinces: Ontario, Manitoba, and Quebec. Like the multilateral framework agreements, these agreements were not enshrined in dedicated statutes, allowing the newly elected Conservative prime minister to unilaterally cancel them immediately after the swearing in of his government. There is, however, some evidence that the governments made an effort to ensure the bilateral agreements were more binding than the earlier agreements under this regime. In contrast to the multilateral agreements, the bilateral agreements-in-principle and the funding agreements were signed by representatives of the two levels of government. The funding agreements were written in contract-like language, although with a clause recognizing that the agreement could be terminated by either party on one year's notice and the caveat that the funding depended on annual approval of the necessary appropriations by Parliament.

The bilateral agreements can be viewed as both an extension of the public reporting model and a departure from it. Like the multilateral framework agreements, they relied heavily on public reporting as a *monitoring mechanism*, although there was also provision for a dispute resolution mechanism covering disagreements related to finances but not standards. The language around *standards* was stronger, echoing in some ways the criteria of the Canada Health Act, with the principles of quality, universally inclusive, accessible, and developmental being identified and defined. The *standard-setting process* departed from the executive-to-executive process of the multilateral agreements in that the standards are a modified version of the principles announced in the successful 2004 Liberal election campaign.[8] The most significant departures, however, related to accountability *instruments*: the use of bilateral rather than multilateral agreements and the innovation of a provincial Action Plan.

The bilateral agreements-in-principle required that a province publish an Action Plan as a condition for moving to a funding agreement. This was not a requirement for Quebec, which signed only a funding agreement. Under the agreements-in-principle, the provinces agreed to release an Action Plan covering the five years of new federal money by a specific date. Alberta did not agree to a specific date but instead had inserted in its agreement-in-principle the sentence 'Alberta agrees to develop and release as part of its business planning cycle, a strategic plan on early learning and child care regarding the five years of new federal funding under this initiative.' There were slight variations in the wording of the Action Plan section of the bilateral agreements, but all involved identifying priorities for investment, targets, and baseline expenditures against which progress toward meeting the objectives of the agreement may be measured.

The political accountability regime tipped the balance within the Canadian constitutional order very much toward the federal principle.

It provided virtually no role for the elected legislature in holding the Cabinet accountable for the expenditure of public funds according to purposes approved by Parliament, as required by the principle of responsible government. To the extent that there was any accountability on social rights, it was between the executive branch and citizens through the annual public reports. Citizens, however, had no effective way to hold the executive branch accountable, either directly or through their elected members of Parliament.

Towards an Alternative Regime

From the perspective of advocates of social rights, the primary purpose of federal social transfers is to expand the social citizenship rights of members of Canadian society. This final section of the chapter draws on lessons of past regimes of accountability to outline an alternative regime consistent with that purpose. It does not attempt to design an ideal system of accountability, which is impossible within the existing Canadian constitutional order. The objective, however, is to address from a social rights perspective the main shortcomings of past regimes and to accommodate as much as possible the inescapable tensions within the Canadian political system. The hope is that the approach here will be of assistance to those social rights advocates committed to ensuring that federal social transfers continue and that effective accountability regimes are put in place to govern them.

Following the approach outlined in this chapter, the first task for anyone designing an alternative regime of accountability for federal social transfers is to be clear about the three distinct accountability relationships that underlie such a regime, each involving different sets of actors. The accountability relationships are of (1) elected legislators to citizens, (2) the federal executive branch to the House of Commons, and (3) the executive branches at the federal and provincial level to each other. Once these are identified, the elements that constitute an accountability relationship need to be considered in turn. As described at the beginning of the chapter, these are the obligations the parties have assumed, instrument(s) establishing the accountability relationship, standards by which performance of obligations is to be assessed, the standard-setting procedure, monitoring mechanisms, sanctions for nonperformance, enforcement procedures, and, where appropriate, the funding mechanism.

The obligations undertaken by the parties to the accountability relationship (the 'what' of an accountability relationship) differ in each of the accountability relationships. The members of the House of Commons are accountable for fulfilling commitments regarding social entitlements or social rights. The federal Cabinet is accountable to the House of Commons for spending money for purposes approved by Parliament (the responsible government principle). The executive branches at each level are accountable to each other for carrying out the terms of their agreement, which in the case of the federal government means providing the agreed-upon funds, and of the provincial governments, spending that money in the ways agreed upon and then reporting on that spending.

Disentangling the three accountability relationships is an important step to avoid some of the confusion in previous regimes but, from a social rights perspective, it is not sufficient. If the purpose of the transfer is understood to be the realization of social rights, then the relationship between the elected legislators and citizens should be recognized as the primary accountability relationship. For the purposes of the social transfer, the relationship between the federal Cabinet and the members of the House of Commons, and the one between the executive branches at the two levels should be seen as secondary or implementing relationships.

A distinction between primary and secondary accountability relationships permits a further distinction between substantive standards and implementing standards or criteria. The substantive standards relate to the primary purpose of the social transfer, which is the realization of social rights. The implementing criteria relate to the secondary accountability relationships, which are the relationships between the executive branch at the federal level and the House of Commons, and between the executive branches at the federal and provincial levels. The five criteria of the Canada Health Act provide an illustration of substantive standards. The reporting requirements of the federal minister to the House of Commons or of the provincial executive to the federal minister are examples of secondary or operational standards. These two types of standards need to be distinguished in legislation and intergovernmental agreements on social programs.

The distinction between substantive and operational or administrative standards is helpful in conceptualizing and locating standard-setting procedures. Intergovernmental forums are a suitable place to determine the standards each level of government is to respect in meeting their mutual obligations. But the fundamental social rights of Canadians should not be determined in negotiations between representatives of the executive branches of the two levels of government. The realization of social rights involves choices about the allocation of society's resources and the regulation of markets that are essentially political.

In a democratic society, debates about what priority is to be given to them belong in forums that permit dialogue between elected representatives and the people, including election campaigns, transparent public consultations, and legislatures. Given the shared responsibility for social rights under Canada's constitution, such debates can occur at the federal or provincial levels or both. The standard-setting procedures for the executive–legislature relationship are the established parliamentary procedures and conventions.

Under the proposed alternative accountability regime, the statute would be the primary instrument for establishing the accountability relationship between legislators and members of society, and between the executive branch and the legislature. At the federal level, these should be dedicated statutes setting out the purposes of the transfer and the accountability regime to govern them, rather than omnibus financial legislation such as the Federal-Provincial Fiscal Arrangements Act that provides little more than spending authorization. The purposes and substantive standards of the transfer should be articulated clearly, using the language of social rights and referencing where appropriate Canada's international human rights commitments.[9]

These should be explicitly linked to the federal Parliament and government's role in promoting a shared, countrywide social citizenship and to their commitment under section 36(1) of the Constitution Act, 1982, to promoting equal opportunities for well-being and providing essential public services to all Canadians. The procedures governing the accountability of the minister to the House of Commons should be clearly specified, with details provided on the kind of reporting required. The nature and scope of the authority delegated to the minister to negotiate agreements with the provinces should also be clearly delineated. Intergovernmental agreements would be used to establish the accountability relationship between the executive branches at the two levels of government, as necessary. However, any such agreements should be seen as implementing instruments concluded under authority delegated through the statutes, which is consistent with their status as administrative agreements.

The monitoring and enforcement of standards have been the most problematic elements of previous regimes of accountability. Between elections, which are the ultimate enforcement procedure, citizens are dependent on the legislature to hold the executive branch accountable. They are assisted in this task mainly by non-governmental organizations that monitor the activities of government, usually with very limited resources. The accountability of the federal executive to the House of Commons is governed by the procedures and conventions of Parliament and the often very general statutory delegations of power. Legislative oversight is very weak and could be strengthened by measures such as requiring that intergovernmental agreements be tabled in the House of Commons and automatically referred to a standing committee, which is the current practice regarding regulations – another type of executive instrument. The agreements should also be made publicly available on government websites, as is the case with intergovernmental agreements in Quebec and international treaties at the federal level. Reporting requirements of the minister to the House of Commons could be made more explicit and stricter in legislation. Additional support could be provided to the elected legislature by the creation of a representative advisory council, as recommended below.

It is, however, the monitoring and enforcement procedures involved in the relationship between the executive branches at the two levels of government that have been the most contested and present the greatest challenges. There are two aspects to this. The first is the accountability of the provincial executive for spending federal money according to the terms of the agreement, which effectively means according to purposes approved by Parliament, and reporting on that spending. The second is the accountability of the federal government to deliver on the funding promised to the provinces in exchange for their acceptance of the federal conditions.

The alternative regime would address the tension between federalism and responsible government inherent in the provincial expenditure of federal tax dollars by locating as much of the monitoring and enforcement activity as possible at the provincial level. An innovative approach borrowed from the 2005 bilateral agreements-in-principle around the $5 billion promised by the government of Paul Martin for child-care transfers might help achieve this goal. Instead of tying federal funding to the realization of the substantive objective of the funding, the bilateral agreements made the trigger for the flow of federal money the publication by the province of an Action Plan. This plan was to show how the province intended to use the federal funding to progress toward the realization of objectives. The idea was that the citizens of a province rather than the federal government would hold the province accountable for carrying out its own Action Plan. As discussed earlier, the weakness of the accountability regime in the agreements was that it relied too heavily on public reporting by the provincial executive to the public. Instead, stronger mechanisms for monitoring a province's record in fulfilling its Action Plan need to be created at a provincial level. These mechanisms should provide increased avenues for public engagement linked to and supportive of the legislature's role in holding the executive branch accountable.

An example of a stronger monitoring mechanism was set out in Bill C-303, the private member's bill directed at putting in place an accountability regime for federal social transfers for child-care services.[10] The bill called for an Advisory Council to consist of individuals who support the purposes of the legislation and who would be chosen by a process involving the appropriate House of Commons standing committee. The Advisory Council was to report directly to Parliament, and the minister would be required to mention any advice received from the Council in his report to Parliament. An Advisory Committee with similar reporting powers at the provincial level could monitor progress under the province's Action Plan. Another way that monitoring could be located at the provincial level would be to have the provincial auditor general report on the province's use of a federal social transfer. An appeals procedure for individuals with rights under a program funded by the transfer could serve as both a monitoring and enforcement mechanism, as was the case under the Canada Assistance Plan.

The federal spending power is a blunt enforcement mechanism and has recently not ensured provincial respect for the criteria in the Canada Health Act. Intergovernmental dispute-resolution mechanisms may be appropriate for addressing disputes between the executive branches of government related to federal-provincial implementing arrangements. They are not at all appropriate for enforcing respect for fundamental social rights, which are matters between citizens and legislators. The alternative accountability regime would reserve the sanction of withholding federal money for enforcing provincial reporting (as a necessary condition for the minister's accountability to the House of Commons) and ensuring effective monitoring mechanisms are in place provincially. With respect to substantive standards that express social rights, the emphasis here is on creating mechanisms that facilitate public engagement and encourage enforcement through political means with the province rather than the federal government being the focus of attention. The emphasis should be on political *sanctions* enforced through public debate, political mobilization, and elections.

The accountability of the federal executive to the provincial executive to deliver on the promised funding is more difficult to resolve. Here, there are two problems: unilateral federal changes in the course of an

intergovernmental agreement, and the reductions in the federal contribution at the termination of an agreement. The first problem was caused
by the 1990 Supreme Court of Canada decision in the reference case on
the Canada Assistance Plan. While the Court made general statements
about the political rather than legal enforceability of intergovernmental
agreements, the reasons it gave were more specific, referring to the
appearance of the funding formulae only in the federal legislation and
not in the funding agreement and other details of the arrangement. Governments appeared to be trying to address these criticisms in the 2005
bilateral child-care funding agreements, which were written in contract-
like language. The second problem, sustaining the federal funding commitment over the long term, is essentially a political one, requiring
public pressure on the federal government. The provinces could facilitate this by educating Canadians about the shared federal and provincial responsibility for social rights and the role that the social transfers
play in this. Instead, the provinces frequently imply that the federal
government has virtually no role in social programs and then complain
about the inadequacy of federal funding.

The tension between federalism and responsible government needs
to be kept in mind in choosing the funding mechanism for the transfer.
The federal government can legitimately require that a province report
on its expenditure of federal revenue because it must have this information for its accountability to the House of Commons. The province is
accountable to its own legislature for the expenditure of revenue raised
through provincial taxation. From a practical perspective, a provincial
legislature cannot be expected to adopt as its own the purposes of the
federal Parliament unless the federal government makes a very significant contribution of money. In those cases, a shared-cost grant might be
the appropriate funding mechanism. In cases where the federal contribution does not represent a large, ongoing contribution, then a block
grant is more appropriate. Although the cost-shared grants have been
associated with the stricter accountability regimes in the past, it is possible to design a regime of accountability consistent with the alternate
regime outlined here for a block transfer.

No accountability regime can end the challenge by Quebec governments to the legitimacy of the federal spending power, which is the
constitutional basis for federal social transfers. Responding to Quebec
concerns ultimately requires constitutional change that recognizes the
unique role of the Quebec National Assembly with respect to the presence of a majority French-speaking population in that province. In the
meantime, influential social rights advocates in English Canada have

learned to accept the special status of Quebec and worked with opposition members of the Canadian Parliament to include a specific Quebec exemption in bills calling for national strategies and national standards. A parallel version of the following paragraph from Bill C-303 appears in Bill C-545 (An Act to Eliminate Poverty in Canada), which received first reading in the House of Commons on 16 June 2010:[11] 'Recognizing the unique nature of the jurisdiction of the Government of Quebec with regard to the education and development of children in Quebec society, and notwithstanding any other provision of this Act, the Government of Quebec may choose to be exempted from the application of this Act and, notwithstanding any such decision, shall receive the full transfer payment that would otherwise be paid under section 5.'[12]

The Quebec exemption allowed Bloc Québécois MPs to join their Liberal and New Democratic colleagues in supporting the child-care and anti-poverty bills. The provision makes explicit and public the recognition of Quebec's special status that political elites have privately accepted in intergovernmental arrangements since the mid-1960s.[13] In the current political context, it offers a path out of an impasse.

The proposed accountability regime outlined in this chapter does not purport to solve all the accountability problems related to federal social transfers. However, it has a number of advantages over the ones that have governed social transfers in the past. It highlights three distinct accountability relationships that underlie federal social transfers and identifies as the primary accountability relationship that of legislators to citizens for the fulfilment of social rights. It provides a reasonable basis for defining and delimiting the federal role by situating it as the promotion of a common social citizenship and emphasizing the social rights content of appropriate federal standards. By locating monitoring at the provincial level, it holds out a greater possibility for an interested public to force governments to deliver on promised social rights. It would allow the conflicts of interest that underlie political struggles around intergovernmental social transfers to play out within a framework in which the democratic issues at stake and the choices being made would be more visible.

NOTES

1 Research for this chapter was supported by the Social Sciences and Humanities Research Council of Canada (Community-University Research Alliance Program). The analysis in the chapter emerged out of the author's

collaboration with the Child Care Advocacy Association of Canada around Bill C-303, Early Learning and Child Care Act, a private member's bill introduced by the New Democratic Party in the 39th Parliament, 1st session, and the 39th Parliament 2nd session, where it was debated at third reading. It was reintroduced in the 40th Parliament, 2nd session as Bill C-373.

2 For a comprehensive summary, see Quebec, Secrétariat aux Affaires intergouvernementales canadiennes (1998).

3 The author's views on the dilemmas of Canadian federalism are elaborated in other publications. See Cameron (2004, 2006, 2007, 2008, 2009).

4 For a basic overview of UN monitoring, see Day (2007) and Stark (2009).

5 The Social Union Framework Agreement, an intergovernmental agreement involving the federal government and the nine provinces in English-speaking Canada, was concluded in 1999, but the public reporting approach contained in it was reflected in the 1997 agreements around the National Children's Agenda by the now defunct federal-provincial-territorial Council on Social Policy Renewal. The SUFA approach was a response to the near loss by federalists of the 1995 Quebec Referendum on sovereignty and was designed to prove that Canadian federalism could work, despite the evidence of the spectacular failures of two major initiatives of constitutional reform in the late 1980s and early 1990s.

6 The Supreme Court maintained at paragraphs 46 and 47 that an agreement between governments does not have the same binding effect or mutuality as ordinary contracts by virtue of the principle of parliamentary sovereignty. Unlike the 'mutually binding reciprocal undertakings' of ordinary contracts, the 'parties were content to rely on the perceived political price for non-performance.'

7 The Conservative government introduced a notional allocation of the CST in the 2007 federal budget, but this is not binding on the provinces.

8 The Liberals campaigned on the QUAD principles of quality, universal, affordable, developmental child care services. *Universal* was modified to *universally inclusive* in intergovernmental meetings in the fall of 2004 and appeared in the bilateral agreements-in-principle in this form, with a definition of each reminiscent of the language of the *Canada Health Act*. However, the indicators in the public reporting section of the agreements related only to availability, affordability, and quality.

9 An example of this was Bill C-304, An Act to Ensure Adequate, Accessible and Affordable Housing for Canadians, which explicitly referenced the International Covenant on Economic, Social and Cultural Rights. This private member's bill would have required that the federal government

consult with provinces with a view to establishing 'a national housing strategy designed to respect, protect, promote and fulfil the right to adequate housing as guaranteed under international human rights treaties ratified by Canada.'

10 See note 1.

11 Bill C-545, An Act to Eliminate Poverty in Canada. The precise wording of article 4 of that bill is 'Recognizing the unique nature of the jurisdiction of the Government of Quebec with regard to poverty elimination in Quebec society, and notwithstanding any other provision of this Act, the Government of Quebec may choose to be exempted from the application of this Act and, notwithstanding any such decision, shall receive the full transfer payment that would otherwise be paid within its territory under this Act.'

12 See note 1.

13 The author of this chapter was involved in the consultations that led to this provision and supports the approach, although would prefer the wording 'Quebec National Assembly' to 'government of Quebec.' On elite accommodation in the mid-1960s, see Vaillancourt (1994).

REFERENCES

Andersen, Lynell, and Tammy Findlay. 2007. *Making the Connections: Using Public Reporting to Track Progress in Child Care Services in Canada*. Ottawa: Child Care Advocacy Association of Canada.

– 2010. 'Does Public Reporting Measure Up? Federalism, Accountability and Child-Care Policy in Canada.' *Canadian Public Administration* 53 (3): 417–38.

Bill C-303. *Early Learning and Child Care Act*. (39th Parliament, 1st session: 1st reading, 17 May 2006; 2nd reading, 22 November 2006; committee report, May 2006. 39th Parliament, 2nd session: 1st reading, 2nd reading, committee report, 16 October 2007; report stage, 21 November 2007, debate at third reading, 20 June 2008. 40th Parliament, 2nd session: Reintroduced as Bill C-373: 1st reading, 21 April 2009.)

Bill C-304. *An Act to Ensure Adequate, Accessible and Affordable Housing for Canadians*. (40th Parliament, 2nd session: 1st reading, 10 February 2009; 2nd reading and referral to committee, 30 September 2009. 40th Parliament, 3rd session: reinstated 3 March 2010; Report Stage, 24 March 2010; 3rd reading, 20 October 2010; recommittal to committee, 24 November 2010; committee report to the House of Commons, 21 March 2011.)

Bill C-545. *An Act to Eliminate Poverty in Canada*. (40th Parliament, 3rd session, 1st reading, 16 June 2010.)

Cameron, Barbara. 2004. 'The Social Union, Executive Power and Social Rights.' *Canadian Woman Studies* 13 (3/4): 49–56.
- 2006. 'Federalism and Social Reproduction.' In *Social Reproduction: Feminist Political Economy Challenges Neo-Liberalism*, edited by Kate Bezanson and Meg Luxton, 45–74. Montreal and Kingston: McGill-Queen's University Press.
- 2007. 'Accounting for Rights and Money in Canada's Social Union.' In *Poverty: Rights, Social Citizenship and Legal Activism*, edited by Susan Boyd et al., 162–80. Vancouver: University of British Columbia Press.
- 2008. 'Harper, Quebec and Canadian Federalism.' In *The Harper Record*, edited by Teresa Healy, 419–33. Ottawa: Canadian Centre for Policy Alternatives.
- 2009. 'Political Will, Child Care, and Canadian Federalism.' *Our Schools, Ourselves* (Spring): 129–45.
Canada Assistance Plan, R.S.C. 1985, c. 1.
Canada Health Act, R.S.C. 1985, c. C-6. s. 7–12.
Davies, A.C.L. 2001. *Accountability: A Public Law Analysis of Government by Contract*. Oxford: Oxford University Press.
Day, Shelagh. 2007. 'Minding the Gap: Human Rights Commitments and Compliance.' In *Poverty: Rights, Social Citizenship and Legal Activism*, edited by Susan Boyd et al., 201–20. Vancouver: University of British Columbia Press.
Federal-Provincial Fiscal Arrangements Act, R.S.C. 1985, c. F-8, s. 24.
Federal/Provincial/Territorial Ministers Responsible for Social Services. 2003. *Multilateral Framework for Early Learning and Child Care*. 13 March. http://www.scics.gc.ca/english/conferences.asp?x=1&a=viewdocument&id=1238.
First Ministers' Meeting. 2000. 'First Ministers' Meeting: Communiqué on Early Learning and Development [Early Learning and Development Agreement].' 11 September. http://www.scics.gc.ca/english/conferences.asp?x=1&a=viewdocument&id=1145.
A Framework to Improve the Social Union for Canadians [Social Union Framework Agreement]. 1999. An Agreement between the Government of Canada and the Governments of the Provinces and Territories (except Quebec), 4 February 1999. http://www.scics.gc.ca/english/conferences.asp?a=viewdocument&id=638.
Health Canada. 2007. *Canada Health Act Annual Report, 2006–2007*. http://www.hc-sc.gc.ca/hcs-sss/pubs/cha-lcs/2006-cha-lcs-ar-ra/index-eng.php.
Hospital Insurance and Diagnostic Services Act, 1957, 5–6 Elizabeth II, c. 28., s. 3. Canada Assistance Plan, R.S.C. 1985, c. 1.

Johnson, A.W. 1984. *Social Policy in Canada: The Past as It Conditions the Present.* Ottawa: Institute for Research on Public Policy.

Madore, Odette. 2005. *Private Diagnostic Imaging Clinics and the Canada Health Act.* PRB 05-02E. Ottawa: Library of Parliament.

Quebec. Secrétariat aux Affaires intergouvernementales canadiennes. 1998. 'Québec's Historical Position on the Federal Spending Power 1944–1998.' http://www.saic.gouv.qc.ca/publications/documents_inst_const/positionEng.pdf.

Stark, Barbara J. 2009. 'Economic, Social, and Cultural Rights.' In *Encyclopedia of Human Rights*, edited by David P. Forsythe. Oxford University Press.

Supreme Court of Canada. 1991. *Reference Re Canada Assistance Plan (B.C.),* [1991] 2 S.C.R. 52.

– 1998. *Reference re Secession of Quebec,* [1998] 2 S.C.R. 217.

United Nations. General Assembly. Convention on the Elimination of All Forms of Discrimination against Women. Adopted 18 December 1979; entered into force 3 September 1981. http://www2.ohchr.org/english/law/cedaw.htm.

– Convention on the Rights of the Child. Adopted 20 November 1989; entered into force 2 September 1990.

– International Covenant on Economic, Social and Cultural Rights. Adopted 16 December 1966; entered into force 3 January 1976. http://www2.ohchr.org/english/law/cescr.htm.

– *Universal Declaration of Human Rights*, adopted and proclaimed by General Assembly resolution 217 A (III) of 10 December 1948. http://www.ohchr.org/EN/UDHR/Pages/Language.aspx?LangID=eng.

Vaillancourt, Yves. 1994. 'Quebec and the Federal Government: The Struggle over Opting Out.' In *Canadian Society: Understanding and Surviving in the 1990s*, edited by Dan Glenday and Ann Duffy, 168–89. Toronto: McClelland and Stewart.

13 Panacea or Peril? Intergovernmental Accountability and the Auditor General

JULIE M. SIMMONS AND AMY NUGENT

Since the auditor general of Canada began performing 'value for money' audits (now called performance audits) in 1977, this officer of Parliament has come to play a visible and sometimes controversial role in politics. The expansion of the auditor general's role beyond traditional auditing activities to assessing whether government funds have been spent efficiently or economically is part of an international shift (Mulgan 2001). This expanded role has been characterized as transforming the Office of the Auditor General from 'financial watchdog' to 'budget player' (Good 2010, 473). Others have characterized the transformation as one that threatens the neutrality of the Office of the Auditor General, making it an advocate for private sector–inspired managerialist reform of government departments and agencies (Sutherland 1980, 1986). Still others have described the performance audit function of the Office of the Auditor General as 'simultaneously push(ing) both for greater managerial decentralization and more controls and regulations in the administration of government' (Saint-Martin 2004, 122). Underlying all of these statements is the assumption that the Office of the Auditor General has influence on public servants and elected representatives. The *Performance Audit Manual of the Office of the Auditor General* states that 'it is generally understood that audits more usefully examine the implementation rather than the development of policy, and that audits do not question the merits of the government's programs and policies.' Nevertheless, it also states that an 'AG can legitimately play a role in shaping the public policy debate' (Office of the Auditor General of Canada 2004, 15). Paul Thomas has gone so far as to state that, with its approximately six hundred employees and budget of over $80 million, the OAG now 'ends up setting the agenda of Parliament ... rather than taking direction from and responding to the concerns of parliamentarians' (2010, 118).

Given the influential role of the auditor general, this chapter explores the fit between the results-oriented nature of value-for-money audits, and the turn to reporting on results as a form of accountability in intergovernmental relations. How does the work of the auditor general mesh with principles of federalism and the practice of intergovernmental relations in Canada? Should and can the auditor general play a role in making intergovernmental reporting to the public more effective as a form of accountability or as a way of generating effective public policy? Is it more appropriate – either on constitutional grounds or in terms of policy effectiveness – or desirable for provincial auditors general to play an enhanced role?

This chapter answers these questions by first outlining the formal scope of the OAG and comparing the logic of performance measurement through value-for-money audits to that of public reporting as a form of intergovernmental accountability. It then uses some examples of previous reports of auditors general to demonstrate how challenges to the legitimacy of the auditor general's value-for-money mandate resonate even more strongly when both orders of government are involved. The seemingly narrow focus of the auditor general does indeed affect intergovernmental policy, albeit indirectly, and with unpredictable effects on the push-pull of centralization and decentralization within the federation. In light of this finding and given that the auditor general is an officer of the federal Parliament, rather than provincial governments, the chapter concludes by probing some of the practical and political implications of coordinating federal-provincial auditors general reports. It argues that a coordinated approach upholds the spirit of provincial autonomy and equal orders of government but is not without its own shortcomings. If an enhanced role for provincial auditors general in the evaluation of intergovernmental agreements is to be pursued as a way of buttressing accountability, governments must address unevenness in both the independence and resources of provincial auditors general. To be effective, this change would have to be accompanied by meaningful consultations among governments to reach mutually acceptable accountability and performance standards in intergovernmental agreements.

The Logic of Value-for-Money Audits vs Intergovernmental Accountability through Public Reporting

Much of this volume examines the shift away from accountability through provincial answerability to the federal government to accountability through provincial and federal reporting to the public. A second dimension of this trend is a shift away from reporting on inputs and outputs to focusing on outcomes. In other words, the focus of public reporting is not on how specific funds were spent, but rather on the results they achieved. Measuring results is a trend evident within individual governments as well. Performance measurement is a tool that is now applied within the federal public service both to programs, and to individuals.[1] Since 1995, all federal departments have been required to develop performance measures and to report their performance to Parliament, a practice that has received even more emphasis in light of OAG and public scrutiny of government practices around the Sponsorship Scandal of 2004. Provinces have also embraced performance measurement, albeit not all to the same extent (McArthur 2007). In many respects, the Office of the Auditor General reinforces this preoccupation with measurement through its performance audits. The Auditor General Act authorizes the auditor general to investigate broadly, 'call[ing] attention to anything that he considers to be of significance and of a nature that should be brought to the attention of the House of Commons.' In addition to reporting when accounts have not been faithfully and properly maintained (traditional attest audits), auditors general may highlight instances where:

- money has been expended other than for purposes for which it was appropriated by Parliament;
- money has been expended without due regard to economy or efficiency;
- satisfactory procedures have not been established to measure and report the effectiveness of programs, where such procedures could appropriately and reasonably be implemented (Government of Canada 1985a).

These latter two instances establish the authority of the auditor general to conduct performance audits.

Several of the chapters in this volume raise questions about the reliability of the figures put forward by governments, and the difficulty of third-party verification. The auditor general is one 'third party' agent of accountability who routinely condenses and evaluates information on behalf of Parliament and the public (Thomas 2003). As the position of auditor general – be it at the provincial or federal level – connotes neutrality, autonomy, and accuracy in investigating 'the numbers,' and the OAG now evaluates results through performance audits, there seems to be a potentially worthwhile intersection of the work of auditors general and accountability through public reporting in intergovernmental agreements.

However, the pathway that has led to public accounting for results in intergovernmental agreements and the pathway that has led to performance audits embody different logics. All federal political systems have two or more orders of government, with some elements of shared and self-rule. One key attribute of federal systems is that neither order of government is constitutionally subordinate to the other (Smith 2004; Watts 1999). But there are many different ways to practise federalism, inspired by different definitions of federalism. Even within a single federation there are competing interpretations of the appropriate practice of federalism, constitutional divisions of powers, and the appropriate institutions and process by which to facilitate coordination between two orders of government. Often at issue is whether the *spirit* of federalism is upheld: whether provincial autonomy is compromised, whether one government is subordinate to the other. Given this context, reporting on results to the public, rather than to the central government, is thought to be a less stringent form of conditionality in federal-provincial agreements and one that avoids a hierarchy of governments in Canada (Boismenu and Graefe 2004; Graefe 2008; Simmons 2009). Stated another way, reporting to the public maintains provincial autonomy and promotes two equal orders of government.

In contrast, the logic of performance measurement within the public service is about equipping the legislature with tools for greater control *over* the bureaucracy. In this sense, it reinforces a hierarchy where public servants are accountable to elected representatives. Further, performance measurement within the federal public service tends towards greater detail and specificity in pursuit of accurate measures and evaluations of programs. In fact, the culture of measuring, evaluating, and reporting is so pervasive in the federal public service that it runs counter to other government initiatives to empower public servants and move away from a rules-oriented culture. To the extent that public servants direct their time and resources to devising performance measurements out of fear of or in response to public critique by the auditor general, the OAG buttresses the risk-averse, rule-bound culture of the public service. It is not surprising that, despite its supposed neutrality, the OAG has been labelled part of the 'control lobby' (Roberts 1996).

Should these different logics preclude further exploration of the intersection of the auditor general's performance-auditing role and public reporting as a form of public reporting in intergovernmental agreements?

Some may say yes, on the grounds that there will always be a tension between the two. Others may say no, precisely because there is a tension between the two. Perhaps auditors general could play a role in 'truing' the numbers reported by governments, thus enhancing the utility of intergovernmental public reporting schemes both in terms of account-ability and generating best policy practices across jurisdictions. But be-fore pursuing this option further, it is worthwhile considering how the OAG has approached intergovernmental agreements and issues of ju-risdiction in the past and what these cases reveal about the likely impli-cations of further auditors general activity in intergovernmental relations.

Compliance with the Canada Health Act

Like the line between policy and administration, the line between policy objectives and implementation is more easily drawn in theory than in practice. In theory, policy is 'made' by elected representatives and then implemented by the public service. Yet most observers would agree that this distinction ignores the policy advisory roles of the public service (e.g., Kernaghan and Siegel 1999, 341). In theory, every policy has clear objectives, which are established before implementation of the policy. In practice, however, the policy process is much messier (e.g., Kingdon 1995). Stated objectives of policies sometimes look much different from those intended by politicians, and policy objectives can tacitly shift as a policy is put into practice and matures, and as politics change. However, the work of the auditor general starts from the assumption of the second dichotomy (i.e., a line between policy objectives and implementation), and the results of the OAG further obfuscate the first (that is, a line between policy and administration).

The auditor general is held in high public regard because she or he is considered neutral, independent, and objective. One only needs to look at the popular support for the auditor general's quest to audit the ex-penses of members of Parliament (MPs) and the unpopularity of MPs' resistance as a gauge of the confidence Canadians have in the OAG (Galloway 2010). Engaged in the bland and assumedly straightforward act of auditing, the auditor general is thought to be removed from poli-cymaking. When, however, in conducting an audit, the auditor general finds that the stated objectives of a policy have not been met, and the public service then makes policy changes in response to these findings, the auditor general is playing a role in policymaking. This role is concerning, inasmuch as the Office of the Auditor General maintains its legitimacy precisely because it is thought to be independent from politics and the policy process. Yet audits come with a built-in preference for more, rather than less, measuring, and no room for capturing the unstated or shifting objectives of policies. In turn, what is measured, believe many governments and policy actors, becomes the policy.

In Canada, legislation involving both orders of government is all the more likely to have both stated and unstated objectives, which change over time. Such legislation and / or intergovernmental agreements are the culmination of often long, drawn-out, and nuanced negotiations, with much of the wording carefully and sometimes painfully crafted to allow for multiple interpretations to appease the greatest number of players at the negotiating table. These interpretations can reflect different perspectives about the right mix of provincial autonomy and central government involvement. Moreover, success is not necessarily measured in terms of action taken, but actions not taken. Rightly or wrongly, getting to the agreement is sometimes the end in itself, and one of several moves in a back-and-forth chess game that plays out over years. Alternatively, legislation involving both orders of government and / or intergovernmental agreements can be the hurried outcomes of ultimatum-driven bargaining, with provincial governments acquiescing to federal government terms, in return for transfers of funding (Simmons 2012). Under such circumstances, government commitments (both federal and provincial) to follow through on all stated terms of an agreement can waiver (Simeon and Nugent 2012). This is especially the case when intergovernmental arrangements lack legal status.

Thus, when the OAG audits programs with intergovernmental dimensions, we should anticipate that the auditor general will find reasons to criticize the government's activities. The auditor general has carefully indicated that it is Parliament's role to question government choices about the use of the federal spending power. For example, the 2008 auditor general's report states, 'We recognize that decisions on whether and to what extent conditions are attached to transfers are policy decisions that often involve sensitive negotiations among federal, provincial, and territorial governments. We do not question these decisions' (Office of the Auditor General 2008, 1). However, following the scope defined by the Auditor General Act, the auditor general reasons that 'the federal government must demonstrate that it is monitoring provincial and territorial compliance with these conditions and that it is taking action in cases of non-compliance' (18).

The auditor general has chosen on many occasions to highlight the federal government's 'non-intrusive' approach to monitoring provincial compliance with the Canada Health Act (CHA). The five criteria established in the CHA relate to the Canada Health Transfer: irrespective of where one lives, a person in Canada is to have universal access to a portable, publicly administered, comprehensive health insurance plan. Provinces must establish such a plan to receive federal cash in the form of the Canada Health Transfer. They also cannot engage in extra billing. The CHA requires provinces and territories to provide the federal government with information it would reasonably require to evaluate compliance with the criteria (Government of Canada 1985b).[2] Kenneth M. Dye (auditor general 1981–91), Denis Desautels (1991–2001) and his successor, Sheila Fraser (2001–11), have all reported on the lax federal monitoring of provincial compliance with CHA conditions (Office of the Auditor General 1987, 1999, 2002). The most recent major instance was in 1999 when the auditor general investigated whether federal efforts to support and monitor health-care delivery 'reflect[ed] clear objectives, adequately report[ed] performance, and facilitate[ed] review and evaluation' (Office of the Auditor General 1999, 29.29). Not surprisingly, the report found that Health Canada had taken a 'passive stance' toward gathering provincial information. The information on provincial health-care insurance plans that provinces were voluntarily submitting to the federal government was deemed insufficient. For example, according to the auditor general, Health Canada lacked 'reliable information on waiting lists, the geographical location of services, hospital-bed-to-population ratios, the extent to which Canadians are bypassing the public system and using privately available resources, and the impacts' – information the auditor general deemed would help assess whether provinces were meeting the accessibility criterion of the CHA (17). In addition to criticizing the passive approach to information gathering, the auditor general criticized Health Canada's policy instrument choices, noting that the department's reliance on discussion, negotiation, and persuasion in lieu of financial penalties for non-compliance had not led to 'the speedy resolution of these issues' (16). Regarding Health Canada's annual reports to Parliament, the auditor general encouraged the department to rely less on description of the provincial health-care insurance schemes and more on evaluation, calling on Health Canada to 'clearly indicate the extent to which each provincial and territorial health care insurance plan has satisfied the Canada Health Act criteria and conditions, and, where it does not provide this information, clearly explain the reasons' (17–18).

One take on these observations of the auditor general is that they usefully and objectively highlight a lacuna in the written federal-provincial entente governing health care in Canada. Provinces and territories are not required to report to the federal government on how they spend federal health-care dollars (Canada Health and Social Transfer funds – now the Canada Health Transfer), yet Health Canada is responsible for monitoring provincial and federal compliance with the Canada Health Act. Another take on these observations of the auditor general is that they are oriented by the unrealistic assumption that more accurate measures of provincial health-care insurance plans were possible, and they do not take into account that the federal government's approach to implementation of the Canada Health Act might have changed in response to tectonic shifts in the political landscape. Recall that in 1999 the provinces were still reeling from dramatic federal cuts to transfers to the provinces for health care introduced in 1995.[3] As such, the federal government's moral authority to compel strict and detailed compliance with the CHA was at an all-time low (Adams 2001; Fierlbeck 2004; Lazar, St-Hilaire, and Tremblay 2004).[4] The federal government's passive approach to information gathering and reliance on discussion, negotiation, and persuasion in lieu of financial penalties for non-compliance in part reflected the dip in federal legitimacy and leverage in the health-care arena in the aftermath of the introduction of the Canada Health and Social Transfer. Recall also that following the sovereignty referendum in Quebec in 1995, the federal government had embarked upon a strategy of 'collaborative federalism' and sought to demonstrate to Quebeckers the benefits of remaining in a flexible federation, where constitutional change was unnecessary (Cameron and Simeon 2002; Lazar 1998).

For some, the auditor general's blindness to the broader political context and federal dynamics is a virtue. By using the lens of compliance to evaluate the appropriateness of government instruments, the purposes they have served, and their effectiveness, the auditor general can bypass politics, serving as a guardian of the citizenship entitlement of universal health care, including when it is uncomfortable for the federal government to enforce it. Even if this argument is appealing, it is important to recognize that the auditor general's supposedly apolitical search for accurate measures of results can infuse in public debates a centralist orientation to the federation. The 1999 report acknowledges, 'There are no regulations that require [provinces] to submit specific information to Health Canada' and that 'regulations setting out information requirements were never promulgated because provinces and territories were concerned that meeting these requirements would be time-consuming and costly' (16). The report nevertheless draws a blueprint for the kinds of information the auditor general feels Health Canada should be using to evaluate compliance, and hence the nature of the information provinces should be collecting.

This concern is apart from the question of jurisdictional authority. The auditor general's position as an officer of the central government precludes him or her from directly auditing provinces. However, by identifying the nature of data that, in the opinion of the auditor general, would be required for measuring compliance, and hence the nature of data provinces would need to collect, the *influence* of the auditor general potentially extends beyond the federal sphere. In this particular case, it is difficult to trace a link between the outcome of the report and subsequent federal-provincial negotiations over health care or federal uses of the spending power. In the case that follows, however, the auditor general's centralizing effect on the federation and role in influencing federal intergovernmental policy is more evident.

The TBS Policy on Transfer Payments

Each auditor general exercises discretion in navigating the leeway provided under the Auditor General Act. Denis Desautels's two chosen areas of focus, outlined in his first report, dealt quite directly with intergovernmental relations: accounting for results, and coordination between the federal government and provinces 'in order to effectively hold to account those operating in areas where jurisdictions overlap' (Office of the Auditor General 1991, 1.30). The 1999 report of the auditor general described accountability for federal spending as 'at risk in arrangements that involve others in governing who are not directly accountable to a minister and are not subject to parliamentary scrutiny' (1999, 23.16.8) and stated that 'whoever holds discretionary authority to spend federal taxpayer money or to execute federal authority must not be exempt from potential scrutiny by Parliament' (9). This report did not distinguish between 'collaborative agreements' involving the federal and provincial governments and those the federal government entered into with other third parties 'in the planning, design and achievement of federal objectives' (5). The auditor general further took the position that 'trust and good will' among partners 'are not enough,' and called upon the federal Treasury Board Secretariat (TBS) to develop a framework for such 'new governance arrangements' to promote consistency across agreements (30). The report enumerated just what such a framework should contain, including the following:

- Appropriate reporting to Parliament and the public on the extent to which the arrangement has achieved its federal public policy purpose; and
- Effective accountability mechanisms to ensure that adequate and appropriate evaluation and audit regimes are established (15).

It is clear from these recommendations that they were crafted with an eye to facilitate the conduct of performance audits by the auditor general. Gibbins, Berdahl and Harmsworth argued that, in making such recommendations from this vantage point, the auditor general was 'insufficiently sensitive to the federal spirit' (2000, 19). They rightly pointed out that provincial governments are constitutionally distinct from private and voluntary sector partners and concluded that 'the OAG cannot be seen as a neutral body *in a federal sense*' (emphasis in the original) (20). For the auditor general, accountability for how funds were spent did not transfer to provincial governments along with the funds themselves.

The auditor general's perspective influenced the direction of the federal government in the negotiation of subsequent collaborative arrangements for the better part of the next decade. Taking its cue from the auditor general's report, the Treasury Board Secretariat released its Policy on Transfer Payments in 2000. Like the auditor general's report, it did not distinguish between transfers to other orders of government and those to other recipients. It defined transfer payments as 'transfers of money, goods, services or assets made from an appropriation to individuals, organizations or other levels of government, without the federal government directly receiving goods or services in return' (Government of Canada 2000). The lengthy policy required all departments to ensure that 'a result-based management and accountability framework is prepared which provides for appropriate measuring and reporting of results, as related to the purpose of providing resources thorough transfers.' It also included an extensive list of requirements for contribution agreements.

In 2006–7 just under 10 per cent of payments to provinces were contributions. The lion's share of federal funding to provinces is not considered under contributions and comes via the Canada Health

Transfer, the Canada Social Transfer, and Equalization. Together with territorial financing, these four programs represented just under 84 per cent of federal cash transferred to provinces in 2006–7 (Office of the Auditor General 2008, 14). Nevertheless, it is significant to note the implications of the TBS policy on transfer payments treating all recipients alike, whether another government, private or voluntary sector organizations, or individuals. We note several impracticalities with this approach. The list of twenty-two basic provisions for contribution agreements in the 2000 policy included 'reporting requirements expected of the recipient' and the minister's right to conduct an audit of a contribution agreement and 'a requirement for the recipient to declare any amounts owing to the federal government under legislation or contribution agreements and the recognition that amounts due to the recipient may be set-off against amounts owing to the government' (Government of Canada 2000). In practice, the last of these is particularly difficult to apply to provinces. Such a calculation is logical and feasible in the case of an organization participating in one or two contributions agreements. However, provinces are, at any given time, signatories to an array of contribution agreements involving a multitude of different federal departments, making such calculations challenging. Consider, for example, the over one hundred federal / provincial agreements pertaining to labour-market training examined in Klassen and Wood's contribution to this volume in chapter 5.

Beyond such impracticalities, the requirement that contribution agreements include a minister's right to audit impelled federal departmental negotiators to formalize a hierarchal relationship between the federal government and the provinces. The 2000 Policy on Transfer Payments did single out provincial governments in one instance, noting that 'the scope of federal contribution audits' should give due consideration 'to prior audits undertaken by the province' (Government of Canada 2000). Regardless of whether the right to audit was exercised, it had to be present in all contribution agreements. In presenting the TBS requirements as 'non-negotiables' or pro forma at the intergovernmental table, federal public servants had considerable control over the starting point of negotiations with provinces, and the (limited) degree of provincial autonomy reflected in contribution agreements.

These contours for contribution agreements, shaped largely by the auditor general's orientation towards conducting performance audits and without regard to principles of federalism, were changed only in

2008 and as a result of the alignment of three key factors: a change in governing party in Ottawa, yet another auditor general's report, and push back from provinces. At the request of Prime Minister Jean Chrétien, in 2004 the OAG reported on the Sponsorship Scandal, which shed light on Liberal mismanagement of over a $100 million paid to communications companies for services with virtually no benefit to Canadians. Upon election in 2006 and as part of their new Federal Accountability Act, the Conservatives established a blue ribbon panel to review 'the administrative requirements individuals and organizations must meet in order to access government grant and contribution programs' (Government of Canada 2006). The panel consulted the provinces, given their reservations about the 2000 policy on transfer payments. Accordingly, the panel argued for an accountability regime that is 'tailored to the circumstances and capacities of the recipient.' In the case of provincial and territorial governments the panel asserted that, given that 'audit standards and capacities may well be as high as those of the federal government, it seems pointless and, indeed, redundant for the federal government to impose audit obligations in addition to those of the recipient government. There should be more appropriate ways to integrate and collaborate in meeting audit objectives to avoid duplication and unnecessary burden on these recipients' (Treasury Board of Canada Secretariat 2006, 9).

This perspective is reflected in the new 2008 Policy on Transfer Payments and the accompanying directive (Government of Canada 2008b). Unlike the previous 2000 policy, which treated provincial governments in the same manner as private organizations to whom the government transferred funds, the 2008 directive enumerates requirements for transfer payments to other orders of government that 'are designed to respect the unique nature of federalism and government-to-government relations, and the jurisdiction and responsibilities of each order of government' (Government of Canada 2008a). To that end, the directions for preparing terms and conditions for transfer payments to other orders of government are peppered with phrases like *as applicable* and *where relevant*. The mandatory components of terms and conditions are limited to:

- A description of the transfer payment program, including the purpose, objectives and how transfer payment will be used to further departmental and government objectives;

- Identification of eligible recipients;
- Identification of a formula, or other method that determines the amount of payments to recipients;
- Method for establishing payment frequency;
- A description of the monitoring and reporting mechanisms, and the measures required to ensure program objectives are being achieved and that funds are being spent as intended; and
- A description of how federal department will ensure that obligations set out in Part VII Official Languages Act will be taken into account (Government of Canada 2008a).

In theory, federal negotiators of intergovernmental agreements do not have the same automatic leverage in the name of performance management as they did under the old transfer payment policy. No longer should federal departments perceive the federal right to audit as mandatory. In fact, the directive for the new Policy on Transfer Payments states that transfer payments to other orders of government should demonstrate 'respect for the jurisdiction and responsibilities of each order of government' and 'for the accountability mechanisms of each order of government to citizens' (Government of Canada 2008a).

This example indicates how the objectivity associated with the work of the auditor general can privilege certain kinds of information and recommendations. While the auditor general is not to comment directly on policy, this case reveals how government policy is made not just through legislation passed in the House of Commons, but also through the work of departments. In this case, the comments of the auditor general in 1999 significantly influenced policy affecting both orders of government. While government in Ottawa (with input from the provinces) ultimately reoriented the TBS Policy on Transfer Payments in 2008, the effect of the auditor general on federal-provincial relations may still be felt for years to come. The newer policy affords a great deal of discretion to federal negotiators. However, because they operate in the risk-averse, performance-management culture of the federal public service, it remains to be seen whether federal negotiators will exercise the discretion afforded to them in the new policy or whether they will maintain the contours of familiar templates when negotiating future contribution agreements. Early evidence suggests a possible path-dependency effect in negotiations with the federal government. That is, despite the new Treasury Board Directive, provincial experience suggests that in intergovernmental negotiations, federal departments present performance measures and accountability frameworks as standard templates. Or at least these templates seem to remain the opening negotiating stance of the federal officials.

A Prospective Role for Federal and Provincial Auditors General in Canada?

In light of the above illustrations, is it useful to explore a role for both the federal and provincial auditors general in evaluating government compliance and the effectiveness of the generation of intergovernmental agreements that emphasize public reporting on results as a form of accountability? On the one hand, we might say no because, particularly with performance audits, the objectivity of the auditor general and the position's independence from the policymaking process are more presumed than real; and because auditing work does not take into account logistical or political constraints, or principles of federalism. These 'challenges,' as Paul Thomas (2010) calls them, would be all the more glaring and have even greater consequences in intergovernmental contexts where so much of policymaking is not legislated, and where principles of federalism and overlapping political constraints are always at play. The work of auditors general would become both more politicized and more influential when the public wielded these authoritative audit findings to compel governments to act. On the other hand, we might say yes, because, recognizing that the work of the auditor general presents *a* truth and not *the* truth, compliance and performance audits of intergovernmental agreements would cut through the logjams created by governments' competing views of federalism and overlapping political constraints. A third argument is that we should pursue coordination between the work of provincial auditors general and the auditor general of Canada because, regardless of the implications of the institutional self-interest of auditors and the constructed nature of their objectivity, in the absence of a coordinated approach, the federal Office of the Auditor General will continue to investigate federal policies with intergovernmental dimensions and to introduce possible unproductive impacts on intergovernmental relations in both policy effectiveness and democratic terms – either preventing agreement if a province rejects a given set of accountability arrangements, or leading to a reporting structure that muddies the accountability of a provincial legislature to its population. Indeed, even after the Treasury Board Secretariat created the 2000 Policy on Transfer Payments, in 2002 the Office of the Auditor General issued 'Placing the Public's Money beyond Parliament's Reach,' concluding that TBS had to be more rigorous to ensure adequate reporting, ministerial oversight, and auditing of collaborative arrangements, including several of the intergovernmental agreements addressed in this volume such as the National Child Benefit, Employability Assistance for People with Disabilities, the Health Transition Fund, and Infrastructure Canada (Office of the Auditor General 2002). In fact, this report identified the need for greater measures in two intergovernmental agreements where no federal money flowed to provinces: the Canada-wide Accord on Environmental Harmonization and the Canadian Industry Program for Energy Conservation.

Perhaps auditors general could constructively align their investigations to facilitate the 'best practices' discussion that is ostensibly one of the benefits of public reporting on results within the federation. Just as the auditor general examined Health Canada's compliance with reporting obligations under recent intergovernmental agreements, so too could provincial auditors general examine provincial compliance, reporting to their respective legislatures. In its 2008 review of Health Canada, the OAG examined reporting obligations found in the 2000 First Ministers' Health Communiqué, the 2003 First Ministers' Accord on Health Care Renewal, and the 2004 First Ministers' 10-Year Plan to Strengthen Health Care (Office of the Auditor General 2008). The OAG focused exclusively on Health Canada's compliance with reporting obligations, and the report explicitly states that the audit 'did not examine the role of provinces and territories in providing information on the health of the population and the delivery of their health care services.' However, the OAG did mention provincial activity – Saskatchewan's approach to reporting on Health Indicators – to highlight how Health Canada could improve its own. What might we have learned if the provincial auditors general had coordinated their efforts elaborating on provincial activity?

Several caveats are in order. First, such joint activity would inevitably have a policy-harmonizing influence, with the criteria for 'best' established under the performance audit (value for money) rubric. It may not be appropriate in policy areas where governments seek to maintain a diversity of approaches meant to respond to a diversity of constituencies within the federation. With 'best practices,' there is an assumption that those not engaged in them will follow suit. Second, not all provincial bureaucracies have the capacity to follow suit, even if their government so desires. Third, as the examples considered in this chapter demonstrate, performance audits cannot factor in political or cultural contexts.

There is a relatively recent example of auditors general working together that that fits this criteria of harmonization. In April 2010, the OAG and six provincial legislative audit offices created a report summarizing performance audits they concurrently conducted on the development and implementation of electronic health records in their respective jurisdictions. Representatives from the audit offices of each of the participating jurisdictions formed a committee and agreed to 'examine planning, implementation and public reporting of results,' but each audit office determined the specific parameters of its own audit and reported to its legislature (Office of the Auditor General 2010, 2). While each jurisdiction has its own privacy and security requirements, there has been a push to make electronic health records compatible across the country, and a third party, Canada Health Infoway Inc., has worked with the provinces to develop a technologic framework for 'sharing health information securely and appropriately across Canada' (4).

However, in instances where auditors general constructively align their investigations, who, across the jurisdictions, has the power to decide when to engage in such group audits? Should this be the prerogative of auditors general, or at the request of individual governments or first ministers collectively, or possibly civil society actors? A related question is that of varying mandates, and financial and human resources across the ten provincial auditor general offices. Provincial auditors general are an under-studied aspect of public administration, and we know very little about their collective histories, and potentially varying relationships to their respective legislatures. What is known suggests that we should not assume the same degree of independence and scope of audit across jurisdictions. For example, one 2004 study of the Newfoundland and Labrador Office of the Auditor General notes that the resources at the disposal of the office had remained virtually the same since 1983–4 and the government has been hostile to increasing the power of the auditor, demonstrating a 'culture of antipathy to legislative auditing' (Dunn 2004, 190). The Canadian Council of Legislative Auditors, comprising the provincial auditors general and the auditor general of Canada, serves as a forum exchanging information and experience about methodology and professional practice, and bringing about consistency across jurisdictions (Canadian Council of Legislative Auditors 2012). It is individual legislatures, however, that establish the scope of audits. Finally, while it might be tempting to turn to auditors general in the most sticky or conflictual of intergovernmental files, auditors general themselves may not seek out such audits. Generally speaking, auditors general with performance audit mandates do not deliberately seek to audit controversial issues exclusively, as their work requires the cooperation of ministers and departments (Thomas 2010). They also attempt to steer away from instances where the conclusions of their investigation will reflect badly on elected representatives, focusing instead on the activity (or lack thereof) of public servants. In policy areas where intergovernmental relations are particularly conflictual, ministers engaged in drawn-out, dense, tit-for-tat power plays with their jurisdictional opponents will also be unlikely to consent to audits. We should thus approach collective auditor general reporting with caution and limit our expectations of what it may actually accomplish.

NOTES

1 For a detailed account of initiatives since 2000, see Lindquist (2006).
2 The only other requirement is that provinces publicly acknowledge the federal contribution to health care.
3 For a clear depiction of the magnitude of these cuts, see Hobson and St-Helaire (2000).
4 In fact, provinces might well have benefitted from their auditors general conducting reverse performance audits assessing whether federal funding was adequate to address provincial health care and other social policy objectives.

REFERENCES

Adams, Duane. 2001. 'Canadian Federalism and the Development of National Goals and Objectives.' In *Federalism: Democracy and Health Policy in Canada*, edited by Duane Adams, 61–106. Montreal and Kingston: McGill-Queen's University Press.
Boismenu, Gerard, and Peter Graefe. 2004. 'The New Federal Tool Belt: Attempts to Rebuild Social Policy Leadership.' *Canadian Public Policy* 30 (1): 71–89.
Cameron, David, and Richard Simeon. 2002. 'Intergovernmental Relations in Canada: The Emergence of Collaborative Federalism.' *Publius* 32 (2): 49–72.
Canadian Council of Legislative Auditors (CCOLA). n.d. 'What Is CCOLA?' http://www.ccola.ca.
Dunn, Christopher. 2004. 'The Quest for Accountability in Newfoundland and Labrador.' *Canadian Public Administration* 47 (2): 184–206.

Fierlbeck, Katherine. 2004. 'Paying to Play? Government Financing and
    Health Care Agenda Setting.' In *The Fiscal Sustainability of Health Care in
    Canada*, edited by Gregory P. Marchildon, Tom McIntosh, and Pierre-Gerlier
    Forest, 340–65. Toronto: University of Toronto Press.
Galloway, Gloria. 2010. 'MPs Will Open Their Books to Auditor-General.'
    Globe and Mail, 15 June. http://www.theglobeandmail.com/news/politics/
    ottawa-notebook/mps-will-open-their-books-to-auditor-general/
    article1604736/.
Gibbins, Roger, Loleen Youngman Berdhal, and Katherine Harmsworth. 2000.
    Following the Cash: Exploring the Expanding Role of Canada's Auditor General.
    Calgary: Canada West Foundation.
Good, David A. 2010. 'Budgeting in Canada: Beyond Spenders and Guard-
    ians.' In *The Handbook of Canadian Public Administration*. 2nd ed., edited by
    Christopher Dunn, 463–81. Toronto: Oxford University Press.
Government of Canada. 1985a. *Auditor General Act* (R.S., 1985, c. A-17).
– 1985b. *Canada Health Act* (R.S., 1985, c. C-6).
– 2000. *Policy on Transfer Payments*. Ottawa: Treasury Board of Canada
    Secretariat.
– 2006. 'Federal Government Takes Next Step to Restore Accountability and
    to Ensure Effective and Efficient Program Delivery.' News release, 6 June.
– 2008a. *Directive on Transfer Payments*. Ottawa: Treasury Board of Canada
    Secretariat.
– 2008b. *Policy on Transfer Payments*. Ottawa: Treasury Board of Canada
    Secretariat.
Graefe, Peter. 2008. 'The Spending Power and Federal Social Policy Leader-
    ship: A Prospective View.' *Policy Matters* 9 (3): 53–106.
Hobson, Paul A.R., and France St-Helaire. 2000. 'The Evolution of Federal-
    Provincial Fiscal Arrangements: Putting Humpty Together Again.' In
    *Canada: The State of the Federation 1999/2000: Toward a New Mission Statement
    for Canadian Fiscal Federalism*, edited by Harvey Lazar, 159–88. Montreal and
    Kingston: McGill-Queen's University Press.
Kernaghan, Kenneth, and David Siegel. 1999. *Public Administration in Canada:
    A Text*. 4th ed. Scarborough, ON: Nelson.
Kingdon, John. 1995. *Agendas, Alternatives, and Public Policies*. 2nd ed. New
    York: Harper Collins.
Lazar, Harvey. 1998. 'Non-Constitutional Renewal: Toward a New Equilib-
    rium in the Federation.' In *Canada: The State of the Federation 1997; Non-
    Constitutional Renewal*, edited by Harvey Lazar, 3–35. Montreal and
    Kingston: McGill-Queen's University Press.
Lazar, Harvey, France St-Hilaire, and Jean-Francois Tremblay. 2004. 'Federal
    Health Care Funding: Toward a New Fiscal Pact.' In *Money, Politics and*

Health Care: Reconstructing the Federal-Provincial Partnership, edited by Harvey Lazar and France St-Hilaire, 189–248. Montreal and Kingston: Institute for Research on Public Policy and Institute of Intergovernmental Relations, School of Policy Studies, Queen's University.

Lindquist, Evert. 2006. 'How Ottawa Reviews Spending: Moving beyond Adhocracy?' In *How Ottawa Spends 2006–2007: In from the Cold; The Tory Rise and the Liberal Demise*, edited by G. Bruce Doern, 185–204. Montreal and Kingston: McGill-Queen's University Press.

McArthur, Doug. 2007. 'Policy Analysis in Provincial Governments in Canada: From PPBS to Network Management.' In *Policy Analysis in Canada*, edited by Laurent Dobuzinskis, Michael Howlett, and David Laycock, 238–64. Toronto: University of Toronto Press.

Mulgan, Richard. 2001. 'Auditors-General: Cuckoos in the Managerialist Nest?' *Australian Journal of Public Administration* 60 (2): 24–34.

Office of the Auditor General of Canada. 1987. *Report of the Auditor General of Canada*. http://www.oag-bvg.gc.ca/internet/English/parl_oag_198711_e_ 1163.html.

– 1991. *Report of the Auditor General of Canada*. http://www.oag-bvg.gc.ca/ internet/English/parl_oag_199111_e_1159.html.

– 1999. *Report of the Auditor General of Canada*. November.

– 2002. *Report of the Auditor General of Canada to the House of Commons*. Ottawa: Minister of Public Works and Government Services Canada, April.

– 2004. *Performance Audit Manual of the Office of the Auditor General*. Ottawa: Minister of Public Works and Government Services Canada.

– 2008. *Report of the Auditor General of Canada to the House of Commons*. Ottawa: Minister of Public Works and Government Services Canada, December.

– 2010. *Electronic Health Records in Canada: An Overview of Federal and Provincial Audit Reports*. Ottawa: Minister of Public Works and Government Services Canada, April.

Roberts, Alasdair. 1996. 'Worrying about Misconduct: The Control Lobby and the PS 2000 Reforms.' *Canadian Public Administration* 39 (4): 489–523.

Saint-Martin, Denis. 2004. 'Managerialist Advocate or "Control Freak"? The Janus-Faced Office of the Auditor General.' *Canadian Public Administration* 47 (2): 121–40.

Simeon, Richard, and Amy Nugent. 2012. 'Parliamentary Canada and Intergovernmental Canada: Exploring the Tensions.' In *Canadian Federalism: Performance, Effectiveness and Legitimacy*. 3rd ed., edited by Herman Bakvis and Grace Skogstad, 59–78. Toronto: Oxford University Press.

Simmons, Julie M. 2009. 'Federalism and Accountabilities in the Social Arena.' *Optimum Online* 39 (2). http://www.optimumonline.ca/article.phtml?e= mesokurj&id=334.

– 2012. 'Democratizing Executive Federalism: The Role of Non-Governmental Actors in Intergovernmental Agreements.' In *Canadian Federalism: Performance, Effectiveness and Legitimacy*. 3rd ed., edited by Herman Bakvis and Grace Skogstad, 320–39. Toronto: Oxford University Press.

Smith, Jennifer, 2004. *Federalism*. Vancouver: University of British Columbia Press.

Sutherland, Sharon. 1980. 'On the Audit Trail of the Auditor General.' *Canadian Public Administration* 39 (4): 489–523.

– 1986. 'The Politics of Audit.' *Canadian Public Administration* 29 (1): 118–48.

Thomas, Paul. 2003. 'The Past, Present and Future of Officers of Parliament.' *Canadian Public Administration* 46 (3): 287–314.

– 2010. 'Parliament and the Public Service.' In *The Handbook of Canadian Public Administration*. 2nd ed., edited by Christopher Dunn, 8–105. Toronto: Oxford University Press.

Treasury Board of Canada Secretariat. 2006. *From Red Tape to Clear Results: The Report of the Independent Blue Ribbon Panel on Grant and Contribution Programs*. Ottawa: Treasury Board of Canada Secretariat.

Watts, Ronald L. 1999. *Comparing Federal Systems*. 2nd ed. Montreal and Kingston: McGill-Queen's University Press.

PART FOUR

Conclusion

14 Conclusion: Whither Accountability?

PETER GRAEFE, JULIE M. SIMMONS,
AND LINDA A. WHITE

In this concluding chapter we return to some of the themes discussed in the introduction, summarize the findings of the cases, and offer suggestions for how to better enhance both accountability and policy learning across jurisdictions in the absence of conditions imposed by the federal government on provincial programs funded in part through the federal spending power. In doing so we draw on the lessons gleaned from contributors' reviews of Canadian cases, as well as comparative assessments of accountability relationships in two key cases from other federal or multi-level modes of governance: the United States in the area of education and the European Union in the area of social policy.

Our assessment of the public reporting regime of accountability in Canada is rather negative in its ability to promote productive and effective intergovernmental relations, as a tool for policy learning, and in its ability to be used by citizens to hold governments accountable. This public reporting regime may help federal officials who are looking for ways to assemble a pan-Canadian story out of disparate provincial initiatives, or it may be acceptable to provincial officials who need the federal money and appreciate the lack of attached standards, but it is hard to see accountability in these arrangements, let alone the achievement of cognate goals associated with accountability, such as robust citizen and stakeholder participation, or the effective sharing of best practices.

The current regime does not provide accountability, as traditionally conceived of in the literature, as enforceability; furthermore, the requirements of reporting are vulnerable to veto players; it can be used merely as a marketing tool; and there are no incentives on the provincial side to make reporting more robust. We thus urge governments to abandon it and to turn to institutions and processes aimed specifically at innovation and policy learning. Some of the examples included in this volume point to ways that such innovation and learning can be achieved, and we reflect more on those models in this concluding chapter.

Findings from the Case Studies

This project began as a quest to establish a blueprint of similarities and differences across policy areas and jurisdictions in the use of public reporting as a form of accountability in intergovernmental agreements. The collection of cases examined here reveals considerable variation across policy fields, across jurisdictions, and over time in the construction of requirements for accountability through public reporting. In the Canadian case of early childhood education and care (ECEC), intergovernmental agreements were first multilateral, then bilateral, and over time have narrowed the scope of policy discretion afforded to provinces with specific public reporting requirements. Increasingly onerous reporting requirements characterize the shift in the disability file from the Employability Assistance for Persons with Disabilities to Labour Market Agreements for Persons with Disabilities. Intergovernmental agreements regarding health care have moved in the opposite direction, with the earliest agreement outlining some sixty-seven indicators of government results, and later agreements scaling back the number of measures. Somewhat perplexingly, then, the health policy field is also marked by a discursive shift towards results-oriented 'wait-time guarantees' and away from mere 'benchmarks'.

Some reporting regimes include prospective activities, such as the submission of annual plans in the case of the Labour Market Agreements for Persons with Disabilities, while others focus exclusively on policy outputs and outcomes, as in the National Child Benefit Governance and Accountability Framework, or the Multilateral Agreement for Early Learning and Child Care. Some include obligations to report to the federal government and to the public (for example, Building Canada), others stress reporting to Canadians (federal / provincial / municipal arrangements regarding the 'gas tax'). One case (ECEC) involved a third-party institution sponsored by just one order of government to monitor compliance. In the case of health care, provincial and federal governments jointly established a third-party institution. Over time, however, this institution has had its mandate scaled back.

It is also striking that the agreements themselves vary in their transparency or public availability across jurisdictions and time. The earliest Labour Market Development agreements, which transferred thousands of employees from federal to provincial workforces, came just shy of a constitutional revision to the division of federal and provincial areas of jurisdiction, yet, as Klassen and Wood explain, the first generation of these agreements are extremely difficult to locate, let alone evaluate.

This portrait suggests that the agreements themselves and their evolution are characterized by considerable idiosyncrasies. However, regardless of the contours of the agreements and the specific nature of the reporting requirements, most of the examples considered in this volume tell similar stories about the lack of transparency in the collection of data, lack of answerability in providing clear reasons for actions, lack of compliance in monitoring and evaluating actions, and lack of enforcement capacity in having the ability (or the will) to impose sanctions for shortfalls in compliance. Transparency, answerability, compliance, and enforcement capacity are all central to a robust form of accountability and provide an alternative or supplement to traditional political or public accountability. Thus, public reporting is not working effectively as a form of accountability.

In some cases, governments are not living up to their commitments to report on particular outcome indicators. Recall the disappointing results of the Making the Connections project in tracking spending on child care and early childhood development programs that Tammy Findlay's chapter discusses, or Patrick Fafard's observation that 2004 was the last time governments met their commitment to report every two years on specific health indicators. Even in cases where there was a solid track record of meeting reporting requirements, as discussed in Julie M. Simmons's chapter on the National Child Benefit, there are considerable lags between the time governments collect data and when they are reported. Peter Graefe and Mario Levesque, among others, attribute these problems partly to the variability of means across governments to meet onerous reporting requirements. Some agreements, such as the Multilateral Framework Agreement on Child Care, even explicitly acknowledge this variability, with governments committing to reporting on specific output indicators 'where available.' This variability can be linked to the varying sizes of provincial public services, but also varying histories of established provincial performance-management regimes. This latter theme is highlighted in both Patrick Fafard's chapter on health care and in Julie M. Simmons and Amy Nugent's discussion of auditors general.

The contributors in this volume also report that the transparency required for robust accountability is also compromised by a familiar performance measurement scenario: indicators have a tendency to reflect what data *can* be collected, without necessarily telling an accurate, complete story about what governments *are*, in fact, achieving, and there are few intrinsic incentives – such as the profit motive as exists in the private sector – for governments to engage in robust performance measurement. Thus, Fenna (2010, 6) concludes that the public sector, unlike the private sector, 'has neither the same *imperative* nor the same *capacity* for benchmarking' (emphasis in original).

In the cases reviewed in this volume, there is evidence of indicators that are defined too broadly. Such is the case of municipal projects deemed successful if oriented toward 'sustainable economic development' reviewed in Joshua Hjartarson and Luc Turgeon's chapter. But when policy *goals* are broad, such as the National Child Benefit's commitment to reducing the depth of child poverty, specific indicators are difficult to envision. In general, governments construct accounts of policy outcomes based on easily generated quantitative data such as the number of citizens benefiting from a program, rather than more expensive and challenging data that are qualitative, such as quality of life, reported levels of satisfaction with a program or service, and so on.

A common consequence of inaccurate or incomplete indicators is goal displacement. Governments tend to orient their projects to perform well against the commonly established indicators, regardless of whether these indicators are appropriate (see Fenna 2010; Fafard this volume). Such dynamics are reported in Peter Graefe and Mario Levesque's chapter on labour market training for people with disabilities. Joshua Hjartarson and Luc Turgeon also uncover a variant of goal displacement whereby the 'one-off' and time-sensitive character of federal funding under the Building Canada initiative distorted municipal capital investment priorities already established through careful negotiation with relevant stakeholders.

Still another dynamic inhibiting transparency in public reporting – compliance with reporting requirements and answerability through public reporting – is the predictable tendency for governments to mix the auditing purposes of public reporting with the communications strategies of governments. In many of the cases examined, the temptation to use public reporting to tell a 'positive story' about policy developments of a specific government usurped the development of comparable data across provinces or between jurisdictions. Familiar strategies of reporting on objectives rather than outcomes, describing programs rather than evaluating them, and omitting baseline information required for measuring improvement all serve marketing purposes for government. Rather than exposing program flaws and government shortcomings, these strategies give programs and governments a glossy sheen. Sometimes – as in the case of the Association of Municipalities of Ontario's Outcomes report summarizing 1,600 projects – there is just too much aggregation of information. In other instances, such as the combined 2004–5 and 2005–6 federal reports on early learning and child care – partisan politics seem to be at play. Recall that this latter report made no mention of the terminated bilateral agreements on early learning and child care, thus obscuring a major shift in the commitment of the federal government to a national plan.

Still another reason for the glossiness of public reports is the specificity of goals of the federal-provincial initiatives. The broader the goals, the less likely are specific performance indicators; the less specific the performance indicators, the greater likelihood of marketing rather than an evaluative feel of a public report. Hence, in the case of the National Child Benefit, annual reports bury which provinces 'flow through' or 'claw back' the value of the Canada Child Tax Benefit.

These dynamics – variability in compliance resulting from varied resources and cultures; difficulty devising accurate, compelling indicators; goal displacement; the tendency to focus on 'good news' in public reporting – all compromise the effectiveness of public reporting as an accountability tool. It should be said that they are not specific to intergovernmental relations. However, another dynamic emerges from the cases examined in this volume that is specific to the intergovernmental milieu of Canada and further complicates matters: the legacy of old principal-agent relationships found in traditional federal-provincial conditional fiscal arrangements. Indeed, relations of answerability, compliance, and enforcement could be mobilized to overcome these problems of transparency, but the capacity of the Canadian intergovernmental system to make use of these elements is constrained by the contested legitimacy of such hierarchical practices.

In the introduction to this volume we argue that control is possible only when it is perceived as legitimate by both the principals and the agents. In the case of public reporting as a form of accountability, legitimacy requires that governments acknowledge their role as agents and the public's role as the principals. The language of all of the agreements examined here explicitly acknowledges this relationship. We anticipated that, in practice, however, there would be evidence that some provincial actors perceived the federal government to be the de facto principal, and thus provincial governments would be reluctant to allow for monitoring and evaluation of procedures and outcomes or transparency.

The Canadian cases presented here indicate that at the very least, government actors – both federal and provincial – have not taken basic measures to enhance the workability of public reporting as a form of accountability *to the public*. We interpret this lack of action as evidence that intergovernmental agreements are oriented to societal accountability, but governments are unwilling to fulfil that commitment. Commitment to report to the public, rather than to each other, is the common ground reached through federal / provincial negotiations where the negotiators have competing perceptions of the right balance of provincial autonomy and federal oversight and, perhaps not explicitly, disparate adherence to visions of Canada as a community of ten communities or one single community. Precisely because these perceptions and visions, and perhaps a preference to avoid conflict, are at the base of intergovernmental experimentation with public reporting, governments are not equally willing *in practice* to report on indicators in a timely manner, to clearly track policy and investment changes from a baseline onward; to participate in third-party monitoring, to include municipalities in their negotiations and so on.

In other words, public reporting, by creating a principal-agent relationship between the public and both orders of government, enabled the federal and provincial governments to elide disagreements over the extent of hierarchy in federal-provincial relations. However, this simply displaced the disagreement to the area of reporting, so that reporting itself could not be used to support federal superiority. In the process, reporting became a charade, preventing the public, the supposed principals, from meaningful control over their agents. Even the decision whether to share a common reporting template across jurisdictions – something that seems relatively logical when societal accountability is the objective – is laden by different views of the nature of the federation. Governments end up debating whether a common template will adequately capture the diversity of provincial government programs thought to be a reflection of different provincial communities.

In the intergovernmental environment, commitments to public reporting connote non-hierarchical negotiations among equals about the mechanisms of accountability, or what Hjartarson and Turgeon define as 'reciprocal accountability.' Yet Hjartarson and Turgeon remind us that reciprocal accountability involves the agents and the principals in these negotiations. In the cases examined here, the public – as agents – are not part of the negotiations. The public has a profound lack of understanding of the principal-agent relationship, with the vast majority of Canadians, as principals, unaware that the federal and provincial governments, as agents, have committed to reporting to them. Our cases shed some light on whether Canadians indeed want this specific role as principals. In the case of early learning and child care, surveyed clients indicated a distrust in public reporting; in the disability file, clients were found to be more interested in whether a specific program worked for them personally rather than assessing how their provincial government measured up to others in the broad range of interventions covered by the LMAPDs. In health care, the suite of Labour Market Training agreements, and the National Child Benefit, the complexity of the programs and services and the web of relations between the two orders of government in delivering these programs and services are seen to hinder the use of public reports by parliamentarians, provincial legislators, the media, and organized interest and advocacy groups, much less the general public.

Our conclusion here is not that Canadians are apathetic or disinterested in intergovernmental accountability and policymaking, but that they are not fond of acting as the principals in intergovernmental public reporting arrangements. This is clear if we look at the Advisory Panel on Fiscal Imbalance, established by the Council of the Federation (Canada's premiers), which in 2005 commissioned Canadian Policy Research Networks to facilitate a Citizens' Dialogue on Sharing Public Funds for a Better Canada. The Dialogue found that citizens had an appetite for developing policy, but for leaving accountability to a federal oversight role that is far more hierarchical than accepted within the culture of contemporary federal-provincial negotiations. As part of the panel, ninety-three randomly selected Canadians participated in day-long regional dialogue sessions in the cities of Halifax, Montreal, Toronto, Edmonton, and Vancouver. Of those participants, twenty-one then participated in a national session. The participants' advice to decision-makers was to 'create a national vision and define the same acceptable standards for all Canadians' and include all levels of government, citizens, and stakeholders in defining the vision and standards (Watling, Nolté, and MacKinnon 2006, v). Participants expressed a decided preference (over 80 per cent) for direct federal spending in areas of provincial jurisdiction and for conditional transfers from the federal government to the provinces over unconditional transfers (under 40 per cent) or a tax point transfer (under 20 per cent) (22).[1] Participants called upon decision-makers to be guided by a series of values, which included 'enhancing accountability between government and to citizens' (v). Given their limited trust in federal and provincial governments, participants turned to conditional transfers, because 'at least that way the two orders of government could hold each other to account' (Maxwell, MacKinnon, and Watling 2007, 36). These recommendations indicate a preference among participants for a predominately Canada-wide sharing community, rather than a provincial sharing community, and for intergovernmental accountability through conditional grants, rather than societal accountability through public reporting.

Jennifer Wallner's chapter reminds us that when principals are apathetic, disinterested, or disengaged, there will be less incentive for agents to answer and explain their actions. With public reporting in the intergovernmental agreements examined in this volume, the designated principals – citizens – are unaware of their role. As a result, despite the role of citizens, in theory, to control agents by highlighting policy differences across provinces, and bring about policy change by voting retrospectively, the absence of knowledgeable principals results in very weak capacity to enforce or sanction.

It is difficult to draw conclusions about the impact of public reporting on policy effectiveness, in part because what constitutes effective policy is contingent on the policy preferences of the evaluator. Nevertheless, our contributors have variously reasoned that measuring effectiveness is difficult when signatories to agreements are not compliant with commitments to report; more directive agreements with required foci for investments will have greater influence on policies developed by participating governments; and agreements in policy areas where there is a shared embrace of a single national system will have greater influence on the policies of participating governments than those in policy areas where there is not.

With respect to whether public reporting has facilitated learning across participating governments, some cases in this collection indicate that traditional modes of intergovernmental information exchange in 'real time' still dominate the learning process. We conclude that the presence of a reporting or evaluation culture (evidenced here in the fields of health care and public education) does not affect whether public reporting facilitates learning or convergence in provincial policy outcomes. Instead, we argue that a commitment to compare oneself to others is key. Patrick Fafard's analysis of health care suggests that because governments vary in their commitment to systematically compare themselves to others, the potential of public reporting to facilitate learning is not realized. The importance of the shared commitment is again illustrated in Jennifer Wallner's chapter examining public education. In this policy field, in the absence of push-pull of federal/provincial dynamics, performance management functions quite well in facilitating policy learning across provinces.

Alternative Accountability Models

This negative assessment of the Canadian public reporting regime raises the question of alternatives, or how might things be done differently. We include comparative and alternative accountability models in this volume so as to examine what other federations do to grapple with the thorny problem of achieving coordination and policy learning across orders of government. We find first a negative example in the United States with No Child Left Behind. As Paul Manna's chapter documents, rather than establishing a federal accountability regime to raise education standards in the United States, NCLB established fifty different accountability regimes, as states were given the authority to establish their own accountability measures. One lesson we can draw from the U.S. education case is that, as in Canada, it is difficult to impose national standards on state governments. As in Canada, 'sticks' do not prove effective, especially when the amount of funds at stake is a small portion of overall education budgets. Instead, we are intrigued by U.S. federal government efforts to dangle 'carrots' in front of state officials by offering significant additional federal funds if states agree to sign on to national education standards under the federal Race to the Top Fund (Lewin 2010).

The use of 'carrots' is more visible in the case of the Open Method of Coordination in the European Union with regard to social policymaking. In the EU case, strong state governments resist coercive measures to ensure compliance with an EU vision. Instead, as Daniel Preece's chapter outlines, in acknowledgment of the dual principles of state sovereignty and subsidiarity on the one hand, and the need for coordination on the other, the EU developed the OMC mechanism to ensure harmonization, without explicitly shifting competency from the country level. As Preece's chapter outlines, the OMC experiment has in fact encouraged harmonization in thinking on social policy across EU states, but towards more liberal economic views and has, in fact, narrowed the range of policy choices in states that may wish to take more robust action against poverty. As the use of the OMC now stretches beyond a decade, the literature on its use remains sceptical of its capacity to create a European model, both as the result of a process that comes up short in known prerequisites for social learning and national political processes that add friction and static to the expected relationships between reporting, learning, and political accountability (e.g., see Kröger 2009). This scepticism arises in part by setting a very high bar ('European Social Model'), because most studies recognize that all the planning, consultation, reporting, and peer review is not without effect in shaping how member states identify problems and frame solutions, or how social learning processes are organized (e.g., Bruno, Jacquot, and Mandin 2006; Edquist 2006; Mabbett 2007).

This 'single mindset' thinking is one danger in attempts to coordinate action and harmonize practices across jurisdictions in the name of standard-setting. It can sometimes mean a movement away from the federal principle. As Grace Skogstad's chapter points out, Canada faces similar pressures as countries do in the EU in the era of globalization and international rule-making. Her chapter explores the conundrum that Canadian federal officials face in negotiating international treaties and participating in international organizations that demand compliance with rules set internationally, but lacking in the domestic authority to implement those international rules in Canada in a whole host of policy areas. Skogstad's chapter tackles two aspects of this accountability conundrum at the domestic level on two levels: the need to respect federalism and the need to respect democratic norms of popular approval of international rule-making. Following Grace Skogstad's attention to the potential of national and provincial legislative institutions to be sites of popular authority and democratic accountability in the area of international rule-making, both Barbara Cameron's chapter and Julie M. Simmons and Amy Nugent's chapter explore provincial legislatures as sites of accountability. It is to those alternative models of domestic accountability that we now turn.

A Way Forward for Canada

As the federal and provincial governments look to 2014 as the year to implement a new federal / provincial / territorial health agreement and as we rethink the broader envelope of provincial programs supported in part by the federal spending power, the question of how to ensure accountability in future agreements is worth some reflection. Even if the federal government executes an end-run around negotiations, such as its unilateral announcement of future health transfers at the 2011 meeting of the ministers of finance, any future attempt to tie federal money to provincial action will require revisiting accountability. As the intro-duction suggests, what makes for a 'good' accountability framework is related to the preferences and strategies of the actors. The tension between accountability, which assumes a hierarchical principal-agent relationship, and the claims of Canadian provinces to a semi-sovereign status can lead to a variety of prescriptions, depending on understandings of acceptable levels of hierarchy in the federation.

In this context, we recognize that we cannot propose an alternative that would represent the view of all of the contributors to this volume. Nevertheless, the accounts of the different policy fields assembled in this volume, along with reflections on processes in other multi-level systems and on alternative accountability models, have generated the following 'blue sky' thinking about an alternative way of ensuring accountability within the intergovernmental fields touched by the fed-eral spending power. This thinking is 'blue sky' in the sense that we understand that we are setting out a vision that is at odds in some respects with the interests of certain intergovernmental actors, but which could provide an option that provinces and citizens might rally to as a preferable alternative to the status quo. In that sense, we do not feel that it is simply 'pie-in-the-sky,' in that it provides one means of ensuring some basic accountability in a manner that does not impede cognate goals of policy learning and citizen participation. In most ways, the elements we propose are not new suggestions, but together they propose a different way of doing accountability that could either guide a new approach or stand as an alternative model when judging other templates for intergovernmental accountability.

We counsel first that governments take accountability seriously but think about doing it differently. It is worth remembering how notional accountability has been in the agreements of concern here. Provinces are compelled to produce reports, but the only effective sanction remains at the ballot box, which makes the link between performance and conse-quences largely fictional in light of current realities in Canadian electoral democracy. Yet if money is transferred or spent without Parliament being able to discern whether it was spent on the intended purpose, the concept of responsible government starts to break down. Simmons and Nugent note that several auditor generals of Canada have frequently raised this concern. Similarly, when accountability processes lack the transparency to let citizens know whether their representatives have fulfilled their promises on social programs, electoral accountability is in turn weakened.

There is no magic recipe to ensure accountability in these agreements, since the federal values of non-subordination and non-hierarchy cannot be easily squared with the hierarchy built into the concept of accountability. This circle likewise cannot be squared in the realm of Canadian practice, as the strength of the provinces and the reduced legitimacy of the federal government makes a return to the hierarchies built into conditional programs – such as the Canada Assistance Plan model that Barbara Cameron's chapter discusses, or the participants in the Citizens' Dialogue on Sharing Public Funds for a Better Canada seemed to prefer – unlikely. Certainly, as we look forward to the renegotiation of the health and social transfers and the equalization program, particularly with a Conservative majority government in power federally, it is hard to foresee a forceful return of conditional grants in the near term. Even the Liberal federal governments of the late 1990s and early 2000s were unwilling to invest the political capital or make the substantial and long-term financial commitments to impose conditionality on new transfers to provinces. In this context, and given the sophistication of the provincial public accounts, we feel it is worth pursuing Cameron's idea of placing accountability, especially in terms of monitoring and enforcement, firmly at the provincial level. This alternative accountability structure, as Cameron's chapter emphasizes, would require strengthening provincial legislative institutions around intergovernmental agreements, for instance, in ensuring a stronger statutory basis for new agreements, and in creating provincial legislative committees to examine new agreements and monitor any reports produced under them. For reasons outlined by Simmons and Nugent – the narrow criteria according to which provincial and federal auditors general evaluate government programs – we think the legislative committee route will yield more useful results.

A second aspect of our proposal is to reduce the need for such accountability mechanisms in the first place by limiting the degree of policy overlap (see also Mendelsohn, Hjartarson, and Pearce 2010). For some, this will evince a touching nostalgia for the 'watertight compartments' of a century ago but prove completely unworkable in a modern era full of policy interdependencies between governments. In this view, the interpenetration of policy responsibilities, even on the basis of the 1867 Constitution Act, requires the development of new collaborative mechanisms to manage the tangle of federal-provincial relationships (see also D. Cameron and Simeon 2002). However, it is worth asking whether an equally plausible strategy for dealing with interdependence is to try to reduce the amount of it to be managed. It may not be necessary to engage in more ambitious processes of uploading and downloading responsibility. Our intention is not to repeat the non-constitutional renewal of the federation, as the era following the 1995 Quebec referendum and the introduction of the Canada Health and Social Transfer is sometimes called (Lazar 1998). Still, one can imagine ways in many areas where responsibilities could be handled more neatly, and in a manner where the interdependencies to be managed would also be more limited. In these cases, asymmetrical arrangements could sand down Quebec's rougher objections about constitutional jurisdiction. Popular examples are the division of post-secondary responsibilities to limit the federal role to funding research, leaving student aid to the provinces, or the idea of passing responsibility for pharmacare to the federal government, as the premiers proposed in 2004.[2]

This second aspect raises a more general point. While accountability is important, it is not the only value or end to be sought, and it may be beneficial not only to reduce the number of places where it is needed (our point above), but also to reduce our expectations of what it can accomplish and to be more aware of how it may hinder the achievement of other goals. This is not a terribly original point in the broader sense. The obsession with accountability that flowed from the HRDC 'scandal' over grant and contribution agreements through the subsequent federal accountability legislation has been criticized for rendering the public sector excessively risk averse (Langford 2004; Zussman 2010). And since the 'production' of accountability is not costless, time and resources get devoted to accountability rather than other potentially more valuable public sector outputs. If creativity and responsible risk-taking at the line ministry level are important, then perhaps the forms and extent of accountability need to be relaxed.

On this note, it is perverse that the intergovernmental agreements treated in this volume regularly trumpeted the importance of innovation and learning through sharing information and best practices and public reporting of results, yet tried to get these results through accountability processes. While, on one side, the message to line departments is to participate in an open dialogue with other governments and stakeholders on best practices, on the other side are all the incentives to shirk, based on how such information could be used in a hierarchical accountability relationship. Rather than encouraging line ministries to experiment, innovate, and share advances, making public reporting a form of accountability encourages forms of game-playing that make innovation largely invisible to the public and other governments.

As such, as governments begin the renegotiation of Canada's large intergovernmental transfer programs, some thought has to be given to the sorts of outcomes that are sought, and to the institutions that may allow for their at least partial realization. Seeing innovation and learning as goals that are at least as important as accountability requires developing institutions and processes aimed specifically at these outcomes, rather than linking them to accountability, as the Open Method of Coordination does in the EU context. While we are not so naive as to believe that such goals stand outside of federal-provincial jockeying over jurisdiction and hierarchy, they do not require hierarchy by definition in the same manner as accountability.

Alan Fenna, in a 2010 occasional paper for the Forum of the Federations, dismisses both the problematic hierarchical accountability requirements of old and the idea of independent monitoring by a third party, which he claims is limited by the fact that governments have no ownership over the exercise and thus may dismiss the findings (14). He proposes instead collegial monitoring and benchmarking, with the federal government playing a facilitiative but not monitoring role.

One idea rooted in collegial benchmarking is to create ongoing 'learning tables,' perhaps under the auspices of the Council of the Federation. In some ways, this is reminiscent of the Ministerial Council on Social Policy Renewal of the mid-1990s, except that the point of institutionalizing provincial exchange is not to define a negotiating position with respect to the federal government, nor to create a body to enforce interprovincialist 'national standards,' but rather to ensure ongoing discussion and disclosure between governments regarding their policy initiatives and evaluations. However it is structured in terms of membership, the point of the institutional design is to make it a place of learning and exchange, not of intergovernmental posturing. A federal government that used its centrality to serve a clearinghouse function and to link discussion to international expertise could play a crucial role, while a federal government that arrogated leadership or that closed off learning through old hierarchical reflexes would make a strong case for a purely interprovincial forum. Some aspects of the creation of the National Child Benefit, as described by Simmons in her chapter, could orient this kind of institution building. Some reference to aspects of the Open Method of Coordination might play a similar role if the body remained purely interprovincial, as the presence of the federal government could change any dynamic of 'peer review' and benchmarking into a more hierarchical one.

In conjunction with these internal learning mechanisms, there may also be a point to developing 'conversation spaces' in order to engage a wider range of expertise, experience, and perspective. This idea is similar to Jane Jenson's (2004) call for 'meeting places' for the ongoing review and discussion of evidence and social policy assumptions. The Canadian Council on Social Development (2004) likewise put forward the idea of creating a Canada-wide stakeholders organization to measure investments and results, share innovations, and encourage citizen involvement in setting priorities. This was picked up by the Canadian Centre for Policy Alternatives (2005, 26) in its 2005 alternative federal budget, in its call for a 'Social Council' that would 'measure outcomes, share innovation, and foster citizen involvement on social issues.' In all cases, the idea is to promote a broader societal understanding of social policy challenges and solutions, both to inform and shape ideas of what good policy might be ahead of intergovernmental negotiations, and to spur forms of policy learning outside of intergovernmental power relations, and the manner in which these relations interfere with such processes.

The Council of Ministers of Education (CMEC) provides one model of a voluntary, non-coercive 'benchmarking club' that allows for the sharing of best practices across provinces (Parkin 2011). It may be a sui generic case, however, in that all of the provinces have developed similar criteria for evaluating their education systems, and each provincial ministry has a great deal of centralized authority over data collection, which facilitates the sharing of common data. Even so, it relies on data developed by independent monitoring agencies such as the OECD and the Canadian Education Statistics Council to generate international and pan-Canadian assessments of student performance. Furthermore, the provincial governments rely on statistical information collected by Statistics Canada. Thus, even the non-hierarchical, learning-driven CMEC relies on both independent monitoring agents and federal data for its activities. It would seem that these two elements would be necessary, even in a collegial benchmarking exercise. Ironically, the federal government's capacity to generate data has been affected by the cancellation of the mandatory long form census and the curtailing of other data collection by the federal government.

The foregoing chapters of the book and our blue sky thinking bring us full circle to the institutionalism of the introduction. Institutions need to be robustly designed in order to channel the goals of participants to the ends that are sought. Trying to enforce accountability through public reporting in a context where any strong notion of accountability to the federal government will be resisted by provinces, predictably leads to minimalist compliance, forms of gaming, and intergovernmental axe grinding. To attempt to do so on the basis of intergovernmental agreements that were sometimes little more than press releases and had an extremely weak statutory basis was to simply compound the problem. Trying to use this form of public reporting to also spur policy learning, on the one hand, and broader stakeholder involvement, on the other, likewise is inviting poor results. Instead, intergovernmental negotiations that had a clearer view of the values to be achieved in agreements, including policy learning, and that worked to develop institutions that might directly reach those values in light of the federal nature of the political community might produce a more valuable legacy than the fumbling attempts at accountability of the Social Union era.

We are currently in an intergovernmental lull on the social policy side. There is not much reformist energy in the federal government, either as the result of a succession of risk-averse minority governments, or of a ruling Conservative Party that has not had social policy on its agenda, beyond highly targeted and gimmicky tax credits. At the same time, observers have been preparing for the renewal of equalization and the Health Accord in 2014 as the next big window on the agenda. The Conservative federal government's attempt to unilaterally define health transfers somewhat closes that window, but it would be surprising if the provinces did not take steps to pry it open anew, as such unilateral action presents provinces with a challenge to their status as well as their budgeting. In addition, the social risks identified in the early 2000s discussions around social architecture, such as poverty, low-wage work, lack of care for young children and dependent seniors, and the limited upward mobility of new Canadians will not be cancelled for lack of federal interest and will demand some policy activity from both orders of government. This lull before the storm provides a space for thinking about how we might construct intergovernmental agreements differently, both in terms of accountability and in terms of how important it is to emphasize values other than accountability.

NOTES

1 Conditional transfers were defined as the method by which 'the federal government ... transfer[s] funds to provinces / territories with specific

targeted conditions to enable them to provide reasonably comparable (similar but not identical) services under certain rules and aimed at certain results' (Watling, Nolté, and MacKinnon 2006, 4).
2 See also Mendelsohn, Hjartarson, and Pearce (2010, 22–9) for a list of areas where disentanglement could prove fruitful.

REFERENCES

Bruno, Isabelle, Sophie Jacquot, and Lou Mandin. 2006. 'Europeanization through Its Instrumentation: Benchmarking, Mainstreaming and the Open Method of Coordination ... Toolbox or Pandora's Box?' *Journal of European Public Policy* 13 (4): 519–36.

Cameron, David, and Richard Simeon. 2002. 'Intergovernmental Relations in Canada: The Emergence of Collaborative Federalism.' *Publius* 32 (2): 49–71.

Canadian Centre for Policy Alternatives. 2005. *Alternative Federal Budget 2005: It's Time.* Ottawa: CCPA.

Canadian Council on Social Development. 2004. 'What Kind of Canada? A Call for a National Debate on the Canada Social Transfer.' http://www.ccsd.ca/pr/2004/social_transfer/st.htm.

Edquist, Kristin. 2006. 'EU Social-Policy Governance: Advocating Activism or Servicing States.' *Journal of European Public Policy* 13 (4): 500–18.

Fenna, Alan. 2010. 'Benchmarking in Federal Systems.' Occasional Paper No. 6. Ottawa: Forum of Federations.

Jenson, Jane. 2004. *Canada's New Social Risks: Directions for a New Social Architecture.* CPRN Research Report F43. Ottawa: Canadian Policy Research Networks.

Kröger, Sandra. 2009. 'The Open Method of Coordination: Underconceptualisation, Overdetermination, De-politicisation and Beyond.' Special issue, *European Integration Online Papers (EIoP)* 13 (1). http://eiop.or.at/eiop/texte/2009-005a.htm.

Langford, John. 2004. 'Acting on Values: An Ethical Dead End for Public Servants.' *Canadian Public Administration* 47 (4): 429–50.

Lazar, Harvey, ed. 1998. *Canada: The State of the Federation 1997; Non-Constitutional Renewal.* Montreal and Kingston: McGill-Queen's University Press.

Lewin, Tamar. 2010. 'Many States Adopt National Standards for Their Schools.' *New York Times*, 21 July. http://www.nytimes.com/2010/07/21/education/21standards.html.

Mabbett, Deborah. 2007. 'Learning by Numbers? The Use of Indicators in the Co-ordination of Social Inclusion Policies in Europe.' *Journal of European Public Policy* 14 (1): 78–95.

Maxwell, Judith, Mary Pat MacKinnon, and Judy Watling. 2007. *Taking Fiscal Federalism to the People.* CPRN Research Report. Ottawa: CPRN.

Mendelsohn, Matthew, Joshua Hjartarson, and James Pearce. 2010. *Saving Dollars and Making Sense.* Toronto: Mowat Centre for Policy Innovation.

Parkin, Andrew. 2011. *Case Study: Education.* Presentation on the Council of Ministers of Education. *Benchmarking and Canadian Federalism Workshop.* Co-sponsored by the Forum of the Federations and Mowat Centre for Policy Innovation, 13 May 2011, Toronto.

Watling, Judy, Judith Nolté, and Mary Pat MacKinnon. 2006. *Strengthening the Federation: Citizens' Dialogue on Sharing Public Funds for a Better Canada.* CPRN Research Report P08. Ottawa: Canadian Policy Research Networks.

Zussman, David. 2010. 'The Precarious State of the Federal Public Service.' In *How Ottawa Spends 2010–2011: Recession, Realignment and the New Deficit Era,* edited by G. Bruce Doern and Christopher Stoney, 219–42. Montreal and Kingston: McGill-Queen's University Press: 219–42.

Contributors

Barbara Cameron is an associate professor, School of Social Sciences, Atkinson College, York University.

Patrick Fafard is an associate professor, Graduate School of Public and International Affairs, University of Ottawa.

Tammy Findlay is an assistant professor of political and Canadian studies, Mount Saint Vincent University, Halifax.

Peter Graefe is an associate professor, Department of Political Science, McMaster University.

Josh Hjartarson is the policy director, Mowat Centre for Policy Innovation, School of Public Policy and Governance, University of Toronto.

Thomas R. Klassen is an associate professor, Department of Political Science and School of Public Policy and Administration, York University.

Mario Levesque is an assistant professor, Department of Politics and International Relations, Mount Allison University.

Paul Manna is an associate professor, Department of Government, College of William and Mary.

Amy Nugent is a former PhD candidate, Department of Political Science, University of Toronto, and has worked in intergovernmental relations for the Alberta, Quebec, and Ontario governments.

Daniel V. Preece is a Social Science and Humanities Research Council postdoctoral fellow, Department of Political Science, Carleton University.

Julie M. Simmons is an assistant professor, Department of Political Science, University of Guelph.

Grace Skogstad is a professor of political science, Department of Political Science, University of Toronto.

Luc Turgeon is an assistant professor, School of Political Studies, University of Ottawa.

Jennifer Wallner is an assistant professor, School of Political Studies, University of Ottawa.

Linda A. White is an associate professor of political science, and affiliate with the School of Public Policy and Governance, University of Toronto.

Donna E. Wood is a postdoctoral fellow, Department of Political Science, University of Victoria.

Index

**The Institute of Public Administration of Canada Series
in Public Management and Governance**